Taste of Home
365 Days of COOKIES

TASTE OF HOME BOOKS • RDA ENTHUSIAST BRANDS, LLC • MILWAUKEE, WI

Taste of Home

© 2017 RDA Enthusiast Brands, LLC, 1610 N. 2nd St., Suite 102, Milwaukee WI 53212. All rights reserved.
Taste of Home is a registered trademark of RDA Enthusiast Brands, LLC.

EDITORIAL

Editor-in-Chief: Catherine Cassidy
Vice President, Content Operations: Kerri Balliet
Creative Director: Howard Greenberg

Managing Editor, Print & Digital Books: Mark Hagen
Associate Creative Director: Edwin Robles Jr.

Editor: Christine Rukavena
Associate Editor: Julie Kuczynski
Art Director: Maggie Conners
Layout Designers: Catherine Fletcher, Nancy Novak
Editorial Services Manager: Dena Ahlers
Editorial Production Coordinator: Jill Banks
Copy Chief: Deb Warlaumont Mulvey
Copy Editors: Dulcie Shoener (senior), Ronald Kovach,
Chris McLaughlin, Ellie Piper
Editorial Services Administrator: Marie Brannon

Content Director: Julie Blume Benedict
Food Editors: Gina Nistico; James Schend; Peggy Woodward, RDN
Recipe Editors: Sue Ryon (lead), Irene Yeh

Culinary Director: Sarah Thompson
Test Cooks: Nicholas Iverson (lead), Matthew Hass
Food Stylists: Kathryn Conrad (lead), Lauren Knoelke,
Shannon Roum
Prep Cooks: Bethany Van Jacobson (lead), Aria C. Thornton
Culinary Team Assistant: Maria Petrella

Photography Director: Stephanie Marchese
Photographers: Dan Roberts, Jim Wieland
Photographer/Set Stylist: Grace Natoli Sheldon
Set Stylists: Melissa Franco (lead), Stacey Genaw, Dee Dee Schaefer
Set Stylist Assistant: Stephanie Chojnacki

Business Architect, Publishing Technologies: Amanda Harmatys
Business Analyst, Publishing Technologies: Kate Unger
Junior Business Analyst, Publishing Technologies: Shannon Stroud

Editorial Business Manager: Kristy Martin
Editorial Business Associate: Andrea Meiers

BUSINESS

Publisher: Donna Lindskog
Business Development Director, Taste of Home Live: Laurel Osman
Strategic Partnerships Manager, Taste of Home Live:
Jamie Piette Andrzejewski

TRUSTED MEDIA BRANDS, INC.

President & Chief Executive Officer: Bonnie Kintzer
Chief Financial Officer: Dean Durbin
Chief Marketing Officer: C. Alec Casey
Chief Revenue Officer: Richard Sutton
Chief Digital Officer: Vince Errico
Senior Vice President, Global HR & Communications:
Phyllis E. Gebhardt, SPHR; SHRM-SCP
General Counsel: Mark Sirota
Vice President, Product Marketing: Brian Kennedy
Vice President, Consumer Acquisition: Heather Plant
Vice President, Operations: Michael Garzone
Vice President, Consumer Marketing Planning: Jim Woods
Vice President, Digital Product & Technology: Nick Contardo
Vice President, Digital Content & Audience Development: Kari Hodes
Vice President, Financial Planning & Analysis: William Houston

International Standard Book Number: 978-1-62145-822-7
Library of Congress Control Number: 2017935181

Pictured on front cover (clockwise from left): Watermelon Slice Cookies, page 198; No-Bake Cereal Cookie Bars, page 311; Owl Cookies, page 377; Gingerbread Babies, page 369; Day of the Dead Cookies, page 360; No-Bake Minty Oreo Blossoms, page 420; Oatmeal Rollout Cookies, page 61; Peanut Butter Oatmeal-Chip Cookies, page 313; Frosty Polar Bears, page 73
Pictured on back cover (clockwise from left): Jumbo Brownie Cookies, page 401; Santa Claus Cookies, page 429; Thick Sugar Cookies, page 270; Trail Mix Cookie Cups, page 296; Glittering Cutout Cookies, page 285; How to Make Spritz, page 407; Halloween Peanut Butter Cookie Pops, page 346
Pictured on spine: Grandma's Star Cookies, page 301
Pictured on title page: Chocolate-Covered Cherry Cookies, page 16
Illustrations: Manon_Labe/shutterstock

For other *Taste of Home* books and products, visit us at **tasteofhome.com.**

Printed in China.
13 5 7 9 10 8 6 4 2

STACKED SNOWMAN COOKIES, PAGE 393

GET SOCIAL WITH US!

 LIKE US
facebook.com/
tasteofhome

 PIN US
pinterest.com/
taste_of_home

 FOLLOW US
@tasteofhome

TWEET US
twitter.com/
tasteofhome

To find a recipe
tasteofhome.com

To submit a recipe
tasteofhome.com/submit

To find out about other
Taste of Home products
shoptasteofhome.com

OCTOBER 31
NATIONAL CARAMEL APPLE DAY

CONTENTS

365 DAYS OF COOKIES

When it comes to smile-fetching sweets, you can't go wrong with cookies! From soft and chewy to crisp and crunchy, the buttery confections are a hit in every home. Now you can fill your cookie jar and satisfy your sweet tooth all year long, with *Taste of Home 365 Days of Cookies!*

ORANGE SUGAR COOKIES, PAGE 118

SANTA CLAUS COOKIES, PAGE 429

FROSTED HAZELNUT COOKIES, PAGE 155

APRIL 22
NATIONAL JELLY BEAN DAY

JELLY BEAN COOKIES, PAGE 151

ELF COOKIES, PAGE 404

TAKE A LOOK INSIDE, and you'll find after-school snacks, classroom treats and cookies perfect for bake sales and potlucks held throughout the year. Need a bite with your morning coffee? Turn to **page 74 for Pecan Goody Cups**. Looking for an easy dessert? Consider the **Folded Hazelnut Cookies on page 155.** Want to bring little ones into the kitchen for some baking fun? Check out the truly adorable **Beary Cute Cookies on page 255.**

Everyone is a cookie lover during Christmas! That's why you'll find an entire **bonus chapter** of seasonal bites to choose from. Fill your platter with any of the 40 Christmas cookies starting on page 388. From cute **elf-shaped treats on page 404** to **no-bake Santa delights on page 429,** this extra chapter promises to make your holiday merry and bright.

In addition, you'll find cookies for bridal and baby showers, backyard barbecues, Halloween and all of those other special occasions when a sweet treat fits the bill. You'll even find cookies celebrating holidays such as **National Potato Chip Day (March 14), Jelly Bean Day (April 22) and National French Toast Day (November 28).** Baking a batch of cookies has never been so much fun.

Photos of every recipe, prep and bake time info and hints, tips and reader reviews make *Taste of Home 365 Days of Cookies* the only cookbook you'll need when it comes to filling the cookie jar. Winter, spring, summer or fall, you'll find the perfect cookie for them all. Turn the page and bake up some smiles today!

Short & Sweet

SHORT ON TIME?
Look for this icon when from-scratch baking just doesn't fit your schedule. These short and sweet recipes come together easily with convenience items and/or no-bake directions.

COOKIE-BAKING BASICS

Our Test Kitchen experts share their top tips for cookie-baking success. Follow these guidelines to **bake up the best batches every time.**

HOW TO MIX

- Use softened butter if the recipe calls for it. You can soften it in the microwave; just make sure it doesn't melt.

- Add ingredients in the order given.

- Turn off the mixer and scrape batter down the sides of the bowl occasionally.

- If a recipe instructs to add wet and dry ingredients alternately, make sure you do so. Avoid overmixing the dough. If the dough is handled too much, it will be tough.

HOW TO START

- Use heavy-gauge dull aluminum baking sheets with low sides. If your pan is dark, the cookies may get over-browned.

- Lightly spraying baking sheets with cooking spray is a great way to avoid sticking. Lining sheets with parchment works, as well.

HOW TO BAKE

- Preheat the oven while you prepare the dough.

- Make cookies the same size and thickness and they'll bake evenly.

- For good heat circulation, place cookies 2-3 in. apart on the baking sheet, and leave at least 2 in. around the edges of the sheet.

- If using two baking sheets at a time, switch their positions halfway through the baking time.

- If using two oven racks, stagger the pans.

- Use a kitchen timer and check for doneness at the minimum time suggested in the recipe. Check every 1-2 minutes thereafter until the cookies meet the recommended doneness described in the recipe.

HOW TO COOL

- Unless otherwise directed, let cookies cool for 1 minute on the baking sheet before removing to a wire rack.

- Cool baking sheets completely between batches or cookies will spread.

- If cookies crumble when they are removed from the baking sheet, let them cool an extra minute or two.

- If cookies are hard and break when you remove them from the cookie sheets, they've cooled on the pans for too long. Return the baking sheet to the oven to warm the cookies slightly, then remove from the baking sheets.

- Always let cookies cool completely before frosting, decorating or storing.

HOW TO MEASURE

Liquid Ingredients
Place the measuring cup on a flat surface and view at eye level for a standard liquid measure (some measuring cups allow for viewing from above). For easier pouring and cleanup, spray the measuring cup with cooking spray before adding sticky ingredients such as molasses, corn syrup or honey.

Sour Cream
Spoon sour cream or yogurt into a dry measuring cup, allowing the mixture to mound a little. Level the top by sweeping a straight-edged spatula or knife across the rim of the cup.

Shortening
Press shortening into a dry measuring cup with a spatula until it is solidly packed, then level the top.

Stick Butter, Margarine or Shortening
The wrappers for these products come with markings for tablespoons, ¼ cup, ⅓ cup and ½ cup. Use a knife to cut the desired amount.

Dry Ingredients
Level any ingredient measured in a dry measuring cup by sweeping a straight-edged spatula or knife across the top.

Dry, Powdery or Fine-Textured Ingredients
Spoon dry ingredients, such as flour, sugar or cornmeal, into a dry measuring cup over a canister or waxed paper. Allow ingredient to overflow the cup, then level the top.

Brown Sugar
Because of the moist texture of brown sugar, recipes usually call for it to be packed into a measuring cup for an accurate measurement. Press or pack brown sugar into a cup using your fingers or the back of a spoon, then level the top. When tipped out of the cup, the brown sugar should hold its shape.

Using Measuring Spoons
Measure dry ingredients, such as flour, sugar or spices, by heaping them into the spoon, then leveling the top. Pour liquid ingredients into a measuring spoon over a custard cup or small bowl to catch spills.

STORING COOKIES & BARS

Cookies tend to change texture after storing. Here are some tips to keep these morsels at peak freshness.

- Store soft and crisp cookies in separate airtight containers. If stored together, the moisture from the soft cookies will soften the crisp cookies. Flavors can also blend during storage, so don't store strong-flavored cookies with delicate-flavored treats.

- Arrange cookies in a container with waxed paper between layers.

- Store cookies in a cool, dry place. Cookies with a cream cheese frosting should be covered and stored in the refrigerator.

- If your crisp cookies became soft during storage, crisp them back up by heating in a 300° oven for 5 minutes.

- Cover a pan of cookie bars with foil—or put the pan in a large resealable plastic bag. If the cookie bars are made with perishable ingredients, such as cream cheese or eggs, store covered in the refrigerator. Once cut, store bars in an airtight container in the refrigerator.

- For longer storage, freeze cookies for up to 3 months.

- Wrap unfrosted cookies in plastic wrap, stack in an airtight container, seal and freeze.

- Thaw frozen wrapped cookies at room temperature before frosting and serving.

PECAN SANDIES, PAGE 49

NO-BAKE CHOCOLATE MINT TREATS, PAGE 100
ITALIAN HONEY BALL COOKIES, PAGE 45

JANUARY 17
DAY OF ITALIAN CUISINES

PROBLEM-SOLVING POINTERS

COOKIES SPREAD TOO MUCH

- Set cookie dough on a cool baking sheet.

- Replace part of the butter in the recipe with shortening.

- If using margarine, check label and make sure it contains 80% vegetable oil.

COOKIES DON'T SPREAD ENOUGH

- Use all butter instead of shortening or margarine.

- Add 1-2 tablespoons of liquid such as milk or water.

- Let dough stand at room temperature before baking.

COOKIES ARE TOUGH

- The dough was overhandled or overmixed; use a light touch when mixing.

- Too much flour was worked into the dough.

- Add 1-2 tablespoons more shortening, butter or sugar than the recipe calls for.

COOKIES ARE TOO BROWN

- Check the oven temperature with an oven thermometer.

- Use heavy-gauge dull aluminum baking sheets.

- Dark baking sheets will cause the cookies to brown prematurely. Plan baking time accordingly, shortening time slightly if using darker pans.

COOKIES ARE TOO PALE

- Check the oven temperature with an oven thermometer.

- Use heavy-gauge dull aluminum baking sheets. Insulated baking sheets cause cookies to be pale in color.

- Use butter, not shortening or margarine.

COOKIE BARS BAKE UNEVENLY

- Spread dough/batter evenly in pan.

- Check to make sure oven rack is level.

COOKIE BARS ARE OVERBAKED

- Use pan size called for in recipe; too large a pan will cause bars to be thin and dry out.

- Check the oven temperature with an oven thermometer.

- Check for doneness 5 minutes sooner than the recommended baking time.

COZY BITES

It's time to get comfy! Grab a blanket and cuddle up with a piping hot cup of tea and any of the cookies you'll find here. Featuring cinnamon, ginger, molasses and other heartwarming ingredients, these sweet treats promise to chase away Jack Frost. Cookies with cranberries, nuts and chocolate will cheer up any home, and snacks with a hint of citrus will truly brighten up the day. See how easy homemade comfort can be. Bake up a batch of these cookies and get cozy today.

LOOK FOR THE SPECIAL DAYS IN THIS CHAPTER:

Need a reason to celebrate? Check out these fun, delicious holidays—then beat the winter doldrums by baking up a batch of smiles today.

FEBRUARY 5
WORLD NUTELLA DAY

FROSTED CRANBERRY DROP COOKIES

I started making these treats after tasting a batch my friend whipped up. I immediately requested the recipe and have been baking them by the dozens ever since.
—SHIRLEY KIDD NEW LONDON, MN

PREP: 25 MIN. • **BAKE:** 15 MIN./BATCH
MAKES: ABOUT 5 DOZEN

- ½ cup butter, softened
- 1 cup sugar
- ¾ cup packed brown sugar
- ¼ cup milk
- 1 large egg
- 2 tablespoons orange juice
- 3 cups all-purpose flour
- 1 teaspoon baking powder
- ½ teaspoon salt
- ¼ teaspoon baking soda
- 2½ cups chopped fresh or frozen cranberries
- 1 cup chopped walnuts

FROSTING
- ⅓ cup butter
- 2 cups confectioners' sugar
- 1½ teaspoons vanilla extract
- 2 to 4 tablespoons hot water

1. In a bowl, cream butter and sugars. Add milk, egg and orange juice; mix well. Combine the flour, baking powder, salt and baking soda; add to the creamed mixture and mix well. Stir in chopped cranberries and nuts.

2. Drop by tablespoonfuls 2 in. apart onto greased baking sheets. Bake at 350° for 12-15 minutes or until golden brown. Cool on wire racks.

3. For frosting, heat the butter in a saucepan over low heat until golden brown, about 5 minutes. Cool for 2 minutes; transfer to a small bowl. Add sugar and vanilla. Beat in water, 1 tablespoon at a time, until frosting reaches desired consistency. Frost the cookies.

CHOCOLATE-GLAZED DOUGHNUT COOKIES

My little nieces love to help decorate these doughnut-shaped cookies. They top them with sprinkles, chopped pecans or even crushed candies.

—JOLIE STINSON MARION, IN

PREP: 35 MIN. + CHILLING
BAKE: 15 MIN./BATCH + STANDING
MAKES: 1½ DOZEN

- 1½ **cups butter, softened**
- 1 **cup sugar**
- 1 **teaspoon vanilla extract**
- 3½ **cups all-purpose flour**
- 1 **teaspoon ground cinnamon**
- ¼ **teaspoon salt**

GLAZE

- ½ **cup butter, cubed**
- ¼ **cup half-and-half cream**
- 1 **tablespoon light corn syrup**
- 2 **teaspoons vanilla extract**
- 4 **ounces bittersweet chocolate, chopped**
- 2 **cups confectioners' sugar**
  Sprinkles and chopped nuts, optional

1. In a large bowl, cream butter and sugar until light and fluffy. Beat in vanilla. In another bowl, whisk flour, cinnamon and salt; gradually beat into creamed mixture.
2. Divide dough in half. Shape each into a disk; wrap in plastic. Refrigerate for 30 minutes or until firm enough to roll.
3. Preheat oven to 350°. On a lightly floured surface, roll each portion of dough to ½-in. thickness. Cut with a floured 3-in. doughnut-shaped cookie cutter. Place 1 in. apart on ungreased baking sheets.
4. Bake 12-14 minutes or until edges begin to brown. Cool on pans 2 minutes. Remove to wire racks to cool completely.
5. For glaze, in a small saucepan, melt butter over medium heat. Stir in cream, corn syrup and vanilla. Reduce heat to low. Add chocolate; whisk until blended. Transfer to a large bowl. Gradually beat in confectioners' sugar until smooth. Dip tops of cookies into glaze. Decorate as desired with sprinkles and chopped nuts. Let stand 30 minutes or until set.

FREEZE OPTION *Place wrapped disks in resealable plastic freezer bag; freeze. To use, thaw disks in refrigerator until soft enough to roll. Prepare, bake and decorate cookies as directed.*

DOUBLE CHOCOLATE BISCOTTI

Refrigerated cookie dough gives you a head start on making biscotti from scratch. For true chocolate lovers, substitute chocolate chips for the vanilla.

—TASTE OF HOME TEST KITCHEN

Short & Sweet

START TO FINISH: 30 MIN.
MAKES: ABOUT 2 DOZEN

- 1 **tube (18 ounces) refrigerated chocolate chip cookie dough**
- ½ **cup vanilla or white chips**
- ½ **cup coarsely chopped macadamia nuts**

1. In a large bowl, combine the dough, chips and macadamia nuts; knead until well combined. Divide dough in half.
2. On greased baking sheets, shape each piece into a 13x2½-in. log. Bake at 375° for 12-14 minutes or until golden brown.
3. Remove from oven; cut diagonally with a serrated knife into 1-in. slices, separating each piece about ¼ in. after cutting. Bake 5-6 minutes longer or until firm. Cool for 2 minutes before removing to wire racks.

CHOCOLATE-COVERED CHERRY COOKIES

I always make these cookies for family gatherings, and they never last long. They might require a little extra effort, but they're so well worth it!

—**MARIE KINYON** MASON, MI

PREP: 30 MIN. • **BAKE:** 10 MIN./BATCH
MAKES: 4 DOZEN

- ½   **cup butter**
- 1   **cup sugar**
- 1   **large egg**
- 1½   **teaspoons vanilla extract**
- 1½   **cups all-purpose flour**
- ½   **cup baking cocoa**
- ¼   **teaspoon salt**
- ¼   **teaspoon baking powder**
- ¼   **teaspoon baking soda**
- 48   **maraschino cherries, blotted dry**

FROSTING
- 1   **cup (6 ounces) semisweet chocolate chips**
- ½   **cup sweetened condensed milk**
- 1   **to 3 teaspoons maraschino cherry juice**

1. In a bowl, cream together butter and sugar until fluffy; beat in egg and vanilla. Combine the dry ingredients; gradually add to creamed mixture (batter will be very firm). Shape into 48 balls, about 1 in. round, and place on ungreased baking sheets. Push one cherry halfway into each ball.

2. For frosting, melt chocolate chips in milk in a small saucepan over low heat, stirring constantly. Remove from the heat; add cherry juice and stir until smooth. Spoon 1 teaspoon of frosting over each cherry (the frosting will spread over cookie during baking).

3. Bake at 350° for 10-12 minutes. Cool on wire racks.

JANUARY 3
NATIONAL CHOCOLATE-COVERED CHERRY DAY

ICEBOX HONEY COOKIES

My grandma always had a batch of these cookies in the cookie jar and another roll in the refrigerator ready to slice and bake. Their honey and lemon flavor is delicious!

—**KRISTI GLEASON** FLOWER MOUND, TX

PREP: 20 MIN. + CHILLING
BAKE: 15 MIN./BATCH • **MAKES:** 8 DOZEN

- 1½ cups shortening
- 2 cups packed brown sugar
- 2 large eggs
- ½ cup honey
- 1 teaspoon lemon extract
- 4½ cups all-purpose flour
- 2 teaspoons baking soda
- 2 teaspoons baking powder
- 1 teaspoon salt
- 1 teaspoon ground cinnamon

1. In a large bowl, cream shortening and brown sugar until light and fluffy. Add eggs, one at a time, beating well after each addition. Beat in honey and extract. Combine the remaining ingredients; gradually add to creamed mixture and mix well.

2. Shape into two 12-in. rolls; wrap each roll in plastic. Refrigerate for 2 hours or until firm.

3. Preheat oven to 325°. Unwrap and cut into ¼-in. slices. Place 1 in. apart on ungreased baking sheets. Bake for 12-14 minutes or until golden brown. Remove to wire racks to cool.

ORANGE MARMALADE LINZER TARTS

These little cutout tarts are almost too pretty to eat! The golden sandwich cookies dusted with confectioners' sugar reveal a colorful, citrusy center of orange marmalade.

—**TRISHA KRUSE** EAGLE, ID

PREP: 25 MIN. + CHILLING
BAKE: 10 MIN./BATCH • **MAKES:** 2½ DOZEN

- 1½ **cups all-purpose flour, divided**
- 1 **cup chopped almonds, toasted**
- ½ **teaspoon baking powder**
- ¼ **teaspoon salt**
- ½ **cup unsalted butter, softened**
- ⅔ **cup sugar**
- 4 **large egg yolks**
- ½ **teaspoon almond extract**
- ½ **teaspoon grated lemon peel**
- ¾ **cup orange marmalade**
- 2 **teaspoons confectioners' sugar**

1. In a food processor, combine ½ cup flour and almonds; cover and pulse until almonds are finely ground. Add baking powder, salt and remaining flour; cover and process just until combined.

2. In a small bowl, cream butter and sugar until light and fluffy. Beat in egg yolks, extract and lemon peel. Gradually add almond mixture to creamed mixture and mix well.

3. Divide dough in half. Shape each into a ball, then flatten into a disk. Wrap in plastic and refrigerate 1 hour.

4. Preheat oven to 350°. On a floured surface, roll out one portion of dough to ⅛-in. thickness. Cut with a floured 2-in. round cookie cutter. Using a floured 1-in. round cookie cutter, cut out the centers of half the cookies. Place solid and cutout cookies 1 in. apart on greased baking sheets.

5. Bake 6-8 minutes or until edges are lightly browned. Cool 5 minutes before removing to wire racks to cool completely. Repeat with remaining dough.

6. Spread 1 teaspoon marmalade on bottoms of solid cookies. Sprinkle cutout cookies with confectioners' sugar; place on top of marmalade. Store in an airtight container.

CRANBERRY WALNUT BISCOTTI

A chocolate drizzle lends a little sweetness to biscotti loaded with chopped walnuts and dried cranberries.

—JOAN DUCKWORTH LEE'S SUMMIT, MO

PREP: 25 MIN. • **BAKE:** 40 MIN. + COOLING
MAKES: ABOUT 1½ DOZEN

- 2 **cups all-purpose flour**
- ¾ **cup sugar**
- 1 **teaspoon baking powder**
- ⅛ **teaspoon salt**
- 3 **large eggs**
- 1½ **teaspoons vanilla extract**
- 1 **cup chopped walnuts, toasted**
- 1 **cup dried cranberries, chopped**
- ½ **cup milk chocolate chips**
- 1 **teaspoon shortening**

1. Preheat oven to 350°. In a large bowl, combine the flour, sugar, baking powder and salt. In a small bowl, whisk eggs and vanilla; add to dry ingredients just until moistened. Fold in walnuts and dried cranberries (dough will be sticky).
2. Divide dough in half. On a greased baking sheet, with lightly floured hands, shape each dough half into a 10x2½-in. rectangle. Bake 20-25 minutes or until golden brown.
3. Carefully remove to wire racks; cool 10 minutes. Transfer to a cutting board; cut diagonally with a serrated knife into 1-in. slices. Place cut side down on ungreased baking sheets. Bake biscotti 8-10 minutes on each side or until lightly browned. Remove to wire racks to cool completely.
4. In a microwave, melt chocolate chips and shortening; stir until smooth. Drizzle over biscotti. Let stand until set. Store in an airtight container.

CHERRY WALNUT BISCOTTI
Substitute chopped dried cherries for the cranberries.

DIPPED GINGERSNAPS

I get a great deal of satisfaction making and sharing time-tested treats like these soft, chewy cookies. Dipping them in white chocolate makes great gingersnaps even more special.

—LAURA KIMBALL WEST JORDAN, UT

PREP: 20 MIN.
BAKE: 10 MIN./BATCH + COOLING
MAKES: ABOUT 14½ DOZEN

- 2 **cups sugar**
- 1½ **cups canola oil**
- 2 **large eggs**
- ½ **cup molasses**
- 4 **cups all-purpose flour**
- 4 **teaspoons baking soda**
- 3 **teaspoons ground ginger**
- 2 **teaspoons ground cinnamon**
- 1 **teaspoon salt**
    Additional sugar
- 2 **packages (10 to 12 ounces each) white baking chips**
- ¼ **cup shortening**

1. In a large bowl, combine sugar and oil. Beat in eggs. Stir in molasses. Combine the flour, baking soda, ginger, cinnamon and salt; gradually add to creamed mixture and mix well.

2. Shape into ¾-in. balls and roll in sugar. Place 2 in. apart on ungreased baking sheets. Bake at 350° for 10-12 minutes or until cookie springs back when touched lightly. Remove to wire racks to cool.

3. In a microwave, melt chips and shortening; stir until smooth. Dip cookies halfway into the melted chips; allow excess to drip off. Place on waxed paper; let stand until set.

★ ★ ★ ★ ★ **READER REVIEW**

"These are always a favorite and requested often! I melt the chips in a mini slow cooker and it works beautifully."

ZEGUNISM TASTEOFHOME.COM

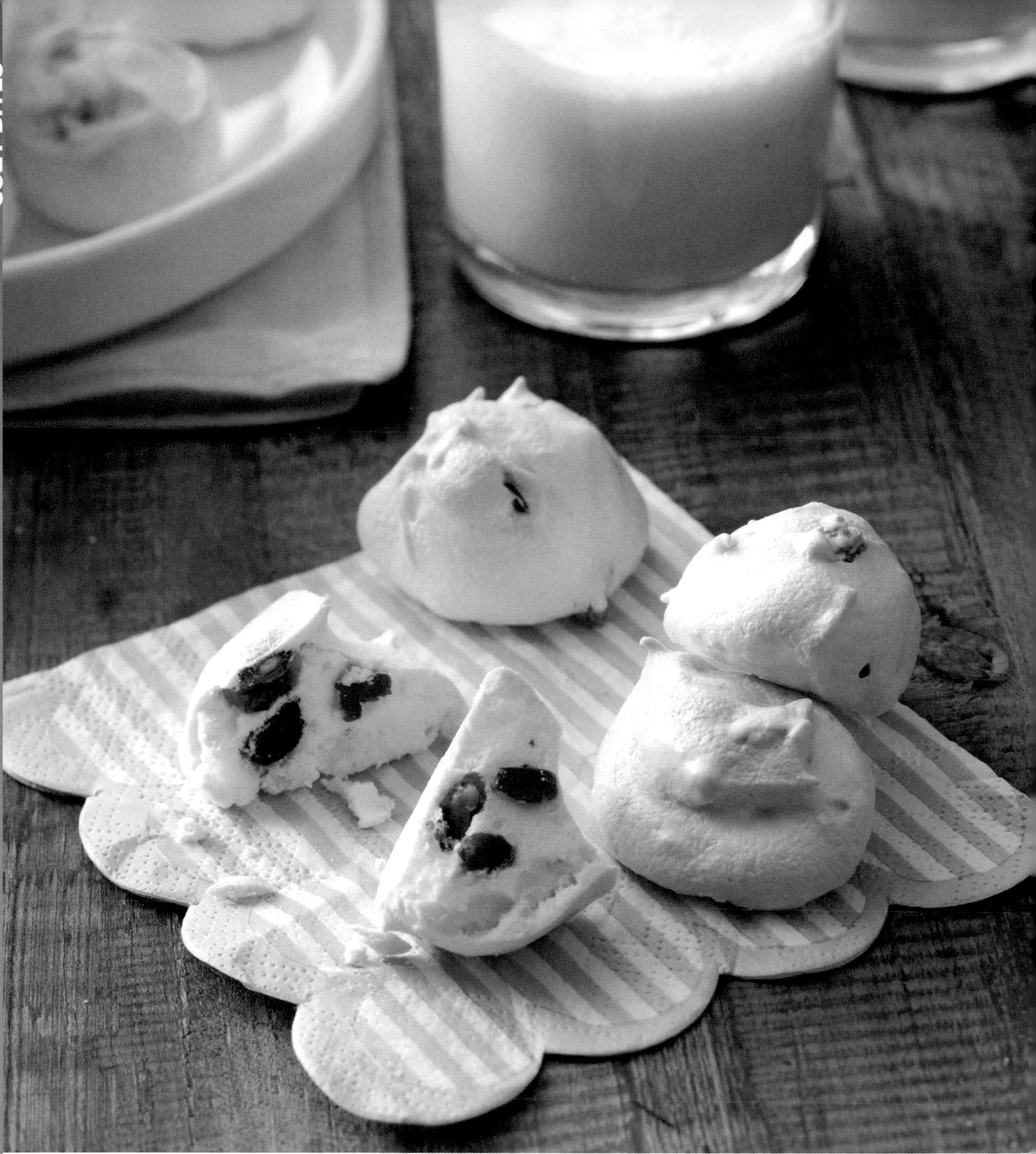

CHERRY KISSES

Is it any wonder these morsels disappear as fast as I can whip them up? The pillowy meringues filled with dates, cherries and walnuts simply melt in your mouth.
—JO ANN BLOMQUEST FREEPORT, IL

PREP: 10 MIN. • **BAKE:** 20 MIN./BATCH
MAKES: 6 DOZEN

- 4 **large egg whites**
- 1¼ **cups sugar**
- ⅓ **cup chopped walnuts**
- ⅓ **cup chopped pitted dates**
- ⅓ **cup chopped candied cherries**

1. Place egg whites in a large bowl; let stand at room temperature for 30 minutes. Beat on medium speed until soft peaks form. Gradually beat in sugar, 1 tablespoon at a time, on high until stiff glossy peaks form and the sugar is dissolved. Fold in the walnuts, dates and cherries.

2. Drop by teaspoonfuls 2 in. apart onto lightly greased baking sheets. Bake at 300° for 20-30 minutes or until firm to the touch. Cool for 1 minute before removing to a wire rack. Store in an airtight container.

APRICOT-FILLED SANDWICH COOKIES

I bake these delightful cookies every year for the holidays, and when I share a tray of my homemade treats with the faculty at school, they're always the first to disappear. I've even had requests to make them for a few wedding receptions.
—DEB LYON BANGOR, PA

PREP: 40 MIN.
BAKE: 10 MIN./BATCH +COOLING
MAKES: 4 DOZEN

- 1 **cup butter, softened**
- 1 **cup sugar**
- 2 **large eggs**
- 3 **cups all-purpose flour**
- ⅔ **cup finely chopped walnuts**

FILLING
- 2 **cups dried apricots**
- ¾ **cup water**
- ¼ **cup sugar**
- ½ **teaspoon ground cinnamon**

TOPPING
- ½ **cup semisweet chocolate chips**
- ½ **teaspoon shortening**
- 4 **teaspoons confectioners' sugar**

1. Preheat oven to 350°. In a large bowl, cream butter and sugar until light and fluffy. Beat in eggs. Combine flour and walnuts; gradually add to creamed mixture and mix well.

2. Shape into 1½-in.-thick logs. Cut into ¼-in. slices. Place 2 in. apart on ungreased baking sheets.

3. Bake 10-12 minutes or until bottoms begin to brown. Cool completely on pans on wire racks.

4. Meanwhile, in a large saucepan, combine apricots and water. Bring to a boil. Cook and stir 10 minutes or until apricots are tender. Drain and cool to room temperature.

5. In a blender or food processor, combine sugar, cinnamon and apricots. Cover and process until smooth. Spread over bottoms of half of the cookies; top with remaining cookies.

6. For topping, melt chocolate chips and shortening; stir until smooth. Drizzle over cookies. Sprinkle with confectioners' sugar.

JANUARY 9
NATIONAL APRICOT DAY

LEMON TEA COOKIES

My mother got this recipe for rich butter cookies from a French friend in the 1950s, and it's been popular in our family ever since. Mom always made them in winter, and now my sister and I do the same.

—PHYLLIS DIETZ WESTLAND, MI

PREP: 25 MIN. + CHILLING
BAKE: 10 MIN./BATCH
MAKES: ABOUT 4½ DOZEN

- ¾ cup butter, softened
- ½ cup sugar
- 1 large egg yolk
- ½ teaspoon vanilla extract
- 2 cups all-purpose flour
- ¼ cup finely chopped walnuts

FILLING

- 3 tablespoons butter, softened
- 4½ teaspoons lemon juice
- ¾ teaspoon grated orange peel
- 1½ cups confectioners' sugar
- 2 drops yellow food coloring, optional

1. In a large bowl, cream butter and sugar until light and fluffy. Beat in the egg yolk and vanilla. Gradually add the flour and mix well.

2. Shape into two 14-in. rolls; reshape each roll into a 14x1⅛x1⅛-in. block. Wrap each block in plastic. Refrigerate overnight.

3. Unwrap and cut into ¼-in. slices. Place 2 in. apart on ungreased baking sheets. Sprinkle half of the cookies with nuts, gently pressing into dough.

4. Bake at 400° for 8-10 minutes or until golden brown around the edges. Remove to wire racks to cool.

5. In a small bowl, cream the butter, lemon juice and orange peel until fluffy. Gradually add confectioners' sugar until smooth. Tint yellow if desired. Spread about 1 teaspoon on bottoms of the plain cookies; place nut-topped cookies over the filling.

CHEWY BROWNIE COOKIES

Bite into one of these chocolaty cookies, and you'll discover they're like chewy brownies inside. Yum!

—JONIE ADAMS ALBION, MI

PREP: 10 MIN. • **BAKE:** 10 MIN./BATCH
MAKES: 3 DOZEN

- ⅔ cup shortening
- 1½ cups packed brown sugar
- 2 large eggs
- 1 tablespoon water
- 3 teaspoons vanilla extract
- 1½ cups all-purpose flour
- ⅓ cup baking cocoa
- ½ teaspoon salt
- ¼ teaspoon baking soda
- 2 cups (12 ounces) semisweet chocolate chips
- ½ cup chopped walnuts or pecans, optional

1. In a large bowl, cream shortening and sugar until light and fluffy. Beat in the eggs, water and vanilla. Combine the flour, cocoa, salt and baking soda; gradually add to creamed mixture and beat just until blended. Stir in chocolate chips and, if desired, nuts.

2. Drop by rounded teaspoonfuls 2 in. apart on ungreased baking sheets. Bake at 375° for 7-9 minutes; do not overbake. Cool for 2 minutes before removing to wire racks to cool.

TOFFEE-CHIP SUGAR COOKIES

After you taste these chewy cookies, you won't believe they call for only two ingredients! Keep the ingredients on hand so you can make them upon request.
—*TASTE OF HOME* TEST KITCHEN

Short & Sweet

START TO FINISH: 20 MIN.
MAKES: ABOUT 2½ DOZEN

- 1 tube (18 ounces) refrigerated sugar cookie dough
- 4 Heath candy bars (1.4 ounces each), finely chopped

1. Slice cookie dough into ¼-in. slices. Place 2 in. apart on lightly greased baking sheets. Sprinkle each with 2 teaspoons chopped candy bars.
2. Bake at 350° for 7-9 minutes or until edges are lightly browned. Remove to wire racks to cool.

SUREFIRE SUGAR COOKIES *Slice and bake sugar cookies according to package directions; cool. Melt 1½ cups semisweet chocolate chips with 4½ teaspoons shortening; stir until smooth. Dip cookies halfway in melted chocolate. Place on waxed paper; immediately sprinkle with colored sprinkles, chopped nuts or flaked coconut. Let stand until set.*

PECAN-TOPPED SUGAR COOKIES
Beat one 8-ounce can almond paste with 3 ounces softened cream cheese; stir in ¼ cup flaked coconut. Cut cookie dough into ½-in. slices; divide each slice into four portions. Place on baking sheets as directed. Top each with ½ teaspoon almond mixture and 1 pecan half. Bake 10-12 minutes; cool.

FROM THE COOKIE JAR

For a fun presentation, here's an easy way to add sparkle to sugar cookies: As they come out of the oven, brush lightly with corn syrup and sprinkle with your favorite flavor of gelatin right from the box.

DUTCH TREATS

I was born and raised in Holland, where we used almond paste often in our baking. I created this recipe to capture the comforting flavors of home.
—AVA REXRODE BLUE GRASS, VA

PREP: 30 MIN. + CHILLING
BAKE: 25 MIN./BATCH + COOLING
MAKES: ABOUT 10 DOZEN

- 1 cup butter, softened
- 6 ounces cream cheese, softened
- 2 cups all-purpose flour
- **FILLING**
- 3 large eggs
- 1 cup sugar
- 1 can (8 ounces) almond paste, cut into cubes
- Sliced almonds

1. In a large bowl, cream butter and cream cheese until light and fluffy. Gradually add the flour. Cover and refrigerate for 1 hour or until easy to handle.
2. Roll into 1-in. balls. Press dough onto the bottom and up the sides of ungreased miniature muffin cups; set aside.
3. For filling, in a small bowl, beat eggs until foamy. Add sugar until blended. Beat in the almond paste. Spoon a rounded teaspoonful into each cup; top each with three almond slices.
4. Bake at 325° for 25-30 minutes or until lightly browned and filling is set. Cool for 10 minutes before removing to wire racks.

CHOCOLATE-DIPPED STRAWBERRY MERINGUE ROSES

Eat these kid-friendly treats as is, or crush them into a bowl of strawberries and whipped cream. Readers of my blog went nuts when I posted that idea!
—**AMY TONG** ANAHEIM, CA

PREP: 25 MIN. • **BAKE:** 40 MIN. + COOLING
MAKES: 3½ DOZEN

- 3 **large egg whites**
- ¼ **cup sugar**
- ¼ **cup freeze-dried strawberries**
- 1 **package (3 ounces) strawberry gelatin**
- ½ **teaspoon vanilla extract, optional**
- 1 **cup 60% cacao bittersweet chocolate baking chips, melted**

1. Place egg whites in a large bowl; let stand at room temperature 30 minutes. Preheat oven to 225°.

2. Place sugar and strawberries in a food processor; process until powdery. Add gelatin; pulse to blend.

3. Beat egg whites on medium speed until foamy, adding vanilla if desired. Gradually add the gelatin mixture, 1 tablespoon at a time, beating on high after each addition until sugar is dissolved. Continue beating until stiff glossy peaks form.

4. Cut a small hole in the tip of a pastry bag or in a corner of a food-safe plastic bag; insert a #1M star decorating tip. Transfer meringue to bag. Pipe 2-in. roses 1½ in. apart onto parchment paper-lined baking sheets.

5. Bake 40-45 minutes or until set and dry. Turn off oven (do not open oven door); leave meringues in the oven for 1½ hours. Remove from oven; cool completely on baking sheets.

6. Remove meringues from paper. Dip bottoms in melted chocolate; allow excess to drip off. Place on waxed paper; let stand until set, about 45 minutes. Store in an airtight container at room temperature.

JANUARY 10
NATIONAL BITTERSWEET CHOCOLATE DAY

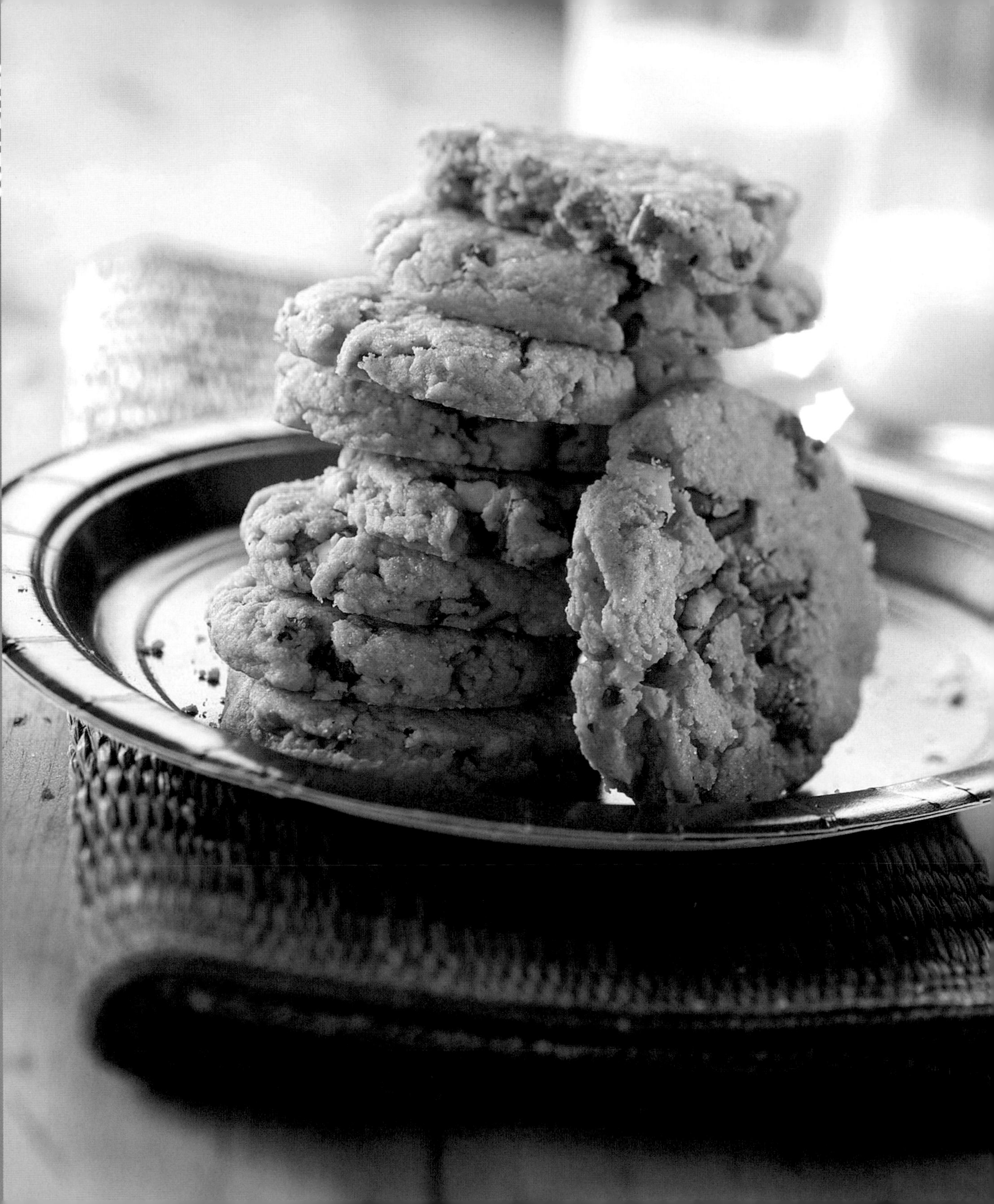

PECAN BUTTERSCOTCH COOKIES

I return to this recipe often because it produces the quickest, tastiest cookies I've ever made. Change the pudding flavor or type of nuts for a twist.
—**TRISHA KRUSE** EAGLE, ID

Short & Sweet

START TO FINISH: 25 MIN.
MAKES: ABOUT 1½ DOZEN

- 1 cup complete buttermilk pancake mix
- 1 package (3.4 ounces) instant butterscotch pudding mix
- ⅓ cup butter, melted
- 1 large egg
- ½ cup chopped pecans, toasted

1. In a large bowl, beat the pancake mix, dry pudding mix, butter and egg until blended. Stir in pecans.

2. Roll into 1½-in. balls. Place 2 in. apart on greased baking sheets. Flatten with the bottom of a glass. Bake at 350° for 8-10 minutes or until edges begin to brown. Remove to wire racks to cool.

NOTE *You may substitute biscuit/baking mix for the complete buttermilk pancake mix.*

RED VELVET WHOOPIE PIES

Everyone gets a kick out of this fun take on the trendy cake. Take a shortcut and use packaged cream cheese frosting for the filling.
—**JUDI DEXHEIMER** STURGEON BAY, WI

PREP: 40 MIN. • **BAKE:** 10 MIN./BATCH + COOLING
MAKES: 2 DOZEN

- ¾ cup butter, softened
- 1 cup sugar
- 2 large eggs
- ½ cup sour cream
- 1 tablespoon red food coloring
- 1½ teaspoons white vinegar
- 1 teaspoon clear vanilla extract
- 2¼ cups all-purpose flour
- ¼ cup baking cocoa
- 2 teaspoons baking powder
- ½ teaspoon salt
- ¼ teaspoon baking soda
- 2 ounces semisweet chocolate, melted and cooled

FILLING
- 1 package (8 ounces) cream cheese, softened
- ½ cup butter, softened
- 2½ cups confectioners' sugar
- 2 teaspoons clear vanilla extract

TOPPINGS
- White baking chips, melted
- Finely chopped pecans

1. Preheat oven to 375°. In a large bowl, cream butter and sugar until light and fluffy. Beat in eggs, sour cream, food coloring, vinegar and vanilla. In another bowl, whisk flour, cocoa, baking powder, salt and baking soda; gradually beat into creamed mixture. Stir in the cooled melted chocolate.

2. Drop dough by tablespoonfuls 2 in. apart onto parchment paper-lined baking sheets. Bake 8-10 minutes or until edges are set. Cool on pans 2 minutes. Remove to wire racks to cool completely.

3. For filling, in a large bowl, beat cream cheese and butter until fluffy. Beat in confectioners' sugar and vanilla until smooth. Spread filling on bottom of half of the cookies; cover with remaining cookies.

4. Drizzle with melted baking chips; sprinkle with pecans. Refrigerate until serving.

FREEZE OPTION *Freeze cookies in freezer containers. To use, thaw cookies in covered containers. Fill and decorate as directed.*

GINGERSNAP CREAM COOKIE CUPS

These little tassies are big on classic gingersnap flavor. The soft cookie cups are topped with velvety cream cheese filling.
—REBEKAH RADEWAHN WAUWATOSA, WI

PREP: 35 MIN. • **BAKE:** 10 MIN./BATCH
MAKES: 2½ DOZEN

- 1½ cups all-purpose flour
- ½ cup whole wheat flour
- ⅓ cup sugar
- 1½ teaspoons ground ginger
- 1 teaspoon baking soda
- 1 teaspoon ground cinnamon
- ½ teaspoon salt
- 1 large egg
- ¼ cup canola oil
- ¼ cup unsweetened applesauce
- ¼ cup molasses

FILLING

- 4 ounces reduced-fat cream cheese
- ½ cup confectioners' sugar
- ¾ teaspoon vanilla extract
- ½ cup heavy whipping cream, whipped

1. In a large bowl, combine the flours, sugar, ginger, baking soda, cinnamon and salt. In another bowl, combine the egg, oil, applesauce and molasses; add to dry ingredients. Stir until dough forms a ball. Roll into 1-in. balls. Press onto the bottoms and up the sides of miniature muffin cups greased with cooking spray.

2. Bake at 350° for 10-12 minutes or until golden brown. Cool for 5 minutes before removing from pans to wire racks to cool completely.

3. For filling, in a small bowl, beat the cream cheese, confectioners' sugar and vanilla until smooth; fold in whipped cream. Spoon 2 teaspoons into each cup.

SALTED BUTTERSCOTCH & PECAN NO-BAKES

When I was deciding what type of cookie to make for an exchange, I decided to make something with coconut, pudding mix and salted caramel. I like to drizzle caramel over the tops of the cookies before serving, too.

—STACEY RITZ SUDBURY, ON

....

PREP: 25 MIN. + CHILLING
MAKES: 4 DOZEN

- 1¾ cups pecans, toasted
- 1½ teaspoons kosher salt
- 1 can (14 ounces) sweetened condensed milk
- 1½ cups unsweetened finely shredded coconut
- 1 package (3.4 ounces) instant butterscotch pudding mix
- ½ cup sugar
- 48 pecan halves, toasted

1. Place 1¾ cups pecans and salt in a food processor; pulse until pecans are finely ground. Transfer to a large bowl. Stir in milk, coconut and pudding mix until blended. Refrigerate, covered, 30 minutes or until mixture is firm enough to roll.

2. Shape mixture into forty-eight 1-in. balls; roll in sugar. Top each with a pecan half, flattening slightly. Store in airtight containers in the refrigerator.

NOTES *To toast the nuts, spread in a 15x10x1-in. baking pan. Bake at 350° for 5-10 minutes or until lightly browned, stirring occasionally. Find unsweetened coconut in the baking or health food section of the grocery store.*

★ ★ ★ ★ ★ **5 STAR TIP**

Don't want to turn on the oven to toast nuts? Spread the nuts in a dry nonstick skillet and heat over low heat until lightly browned, stirring occasionally.

LEMON & ROSEMARY BUTTER COOKIES

Refreshing lemon and aromatic rosemary make these butter cookies stand out. I use them as hostess gifts or to punch up cookie trays for potlucks.
—**ELIZABETH HOKANSON** ARBORG, MB

PREP: 20 MIN. • **BAKE:** 15 MIN.
MAKES: ABOUT 2 DOZEN

- 1¼ cups sugar, divided
- 4 teaspoons grated lemon peel, divided
- 1 cup butter, softened
- 2 large egg yolks
- ¾ teaspoon dried rosemary, crushed
- 2½ cups all-purpose flour
- 1 teaspoon baking soda
- ¼ teaspoon salt

1. Preheat oven to 350°. In a small bowl, combine ¼ cup sugar and 1 teaspoon lemon peel. In a large bowl, beat butter and remaining sugar until light and fluffy. Beat in egg yolks, rosemary and remaining lemon peel. In another bowl, whisk flour, baking soda and salt; gradually beat into creamed mixture.

2. Shape dough into 1¼-in. balls; roll in sugar mixture. Place 2 in. apart on parchment paper-lined baking sheets. Flatten to ¼-in. thickness with the bottom of a glass. Sprinkle tops of cookies with remaining sugar mixture. Bake 12-15 minutes or until edges are golden brown. Cool on pans 2 minutes. Remove to wire racks to cool.

FREEZE OPTION *Freeze shaped balls of dough on baking sheets until firm. Transfer to resealable plastic freezer bags; return to freezer. Prepare and bake cookies as directed.*

DOUBLE CHOCOLATE LINZER TART COOKIES

I am asked to make these for baby showers, bridal showers, church socials, tea parties—you name it!

—**KIM VAN DUNK** CALDWELL, NJ

PREP: 30 MIN. + CHILLING
BAKE: 10 MIN./BATCH + COOLING
MAKES: ABOUT 2 DOZEN

- ¾ cup butter, softened
- 1 cup sugar
- 2 large eggs
- ½ teaspoon vanilla extract
- 2⅓ cups all-purpose flour
- ⅓ cup baking cocoa
- 3 teaspoons baking powder
- ½ teaspoon salt
- 8 ounces bittersweet chocolate, melted
- ½ cup seedless raspberry jam

1. In a large bowl, cream butter and sugar until light and fluffy. Beat in eggs and vanilla. In another bowl, whisk flour, cocoa, baking powder and salt; gradually beat into creamed mixture. Divide dough in half. Shape each into a disk; wrap in plastic. Refrigerate 2 hours or until firm enough to roll.

2. Preheat oven to 350°. On a lightly floured surface, roll each portion of dough to ⅛-in. thickness. Cut with a floured 2½-in. round cookie cutter. Using a floured 1-in. round cookie cutter, cut out the centers of half of the cookies. Place solid and window cookies 1 in. apart on ungreased baking sheets.

3. Bake 6-8 minutes or until set. Remove cookies from pans to wire racks to cool completely.

4. Spread ½ teaspoon melted chocolate on bottoms of solid cookies; refrigerate until firm. Spread ½ teaspoon jam on top of chocolate; top with window cookies. Drizzle with remaining chocolate; let stand until set.

FREEZE OPTION *Transfer wrapped disks to a resealable plastic freezer bag; freeze. To use, thaw dough in refrigerator until soft enough to roll. Proceed as directed.*

BROWNIE ALPINE BISCOTTI

Brownie mix makes these crunchy biscotti cookies easy to stir up, and a white chocolate and almond topping adds a special touch.

—**JEANIE WILLIAMS** MINNETONKA, MN

PREP: 25 MIN.
BAKE: 40 MIN. + COOLING
MAKES: 2½ DOZEN

Short & Sweet

- 1 package fudge brownie mix (13x9-inch size)
- ¾ cup ground almonds
- ½ cup all-purpose flour
- ¾ teaspoon baking powder
- 1 large egg plus 3 large egg whites
- 1 teaspoon almond extract
- ¼ cup sliced almonds, optional
- 3 ounces white baking chocolate, optional

1. In a large bowl, combine the brownie mix, ground almonds, flour and baking powder. In a small bowl, whisk egg, egg whites and extract. Add to the brownie mixture; stir until combined.

2. Divide dough into thirds. On a greased baking sheet, shape each portion into a 7x3½-in. rectangle. Bake at 350° for 24 minutes. Remove from the oven; cool on baking sheet for 5 minutes.

3. Transfer to a cutting board; cut diagonally with a serrated knife into ¾-in. slices. Place cut side down on greased baking sheets. Bake for 12-14 minutes longer or until firm.

4. Cool on wire racks. If desired, sprinkle with sliced almonds and drizzle with chocolate. Let stand until chocolate is completely set. Store in an airtight container.

MOLASSES COOKIES WITH A KICK

One of my mother's favorites, this cookie relies on a combination of spices that I have used for a long time. I get requests from her to make them year-round!

—**TAMARA RAU** MEDINA, ND

PREP: 40 MIN. + CHILLING
BAKE: 10 MIN./BATCH • **MAKES:** 8 DOZEN

- ¾ **cup butter, softened**
- ½ **cup sugar**
- ½ **cup packed brown sugar**
- ¼ **cup molasses**
- 1 **large egg**
- 1½ **teaspoons minced fresh gingerroot**
- 2¼ **cups all-purpose flour**
- 1 **teaspoon ground cinnamon**
- ¾ **teaspoon baking soda**
- ½ **teaspoon ground cloves**
- ¼ **to ½ teaspoon cayenne pepper**
- ¼ **teaspoon salt**
- ¼ **teaspoon ground nutmeg**
- ⅛ **teaspoon each ground white pepper, cardamom and coriander**
- ¾ **cup turbinado (washed raw) sugar**

1. In a large bowl, cream butter and sugars until light and fluffy. Beat in the molasses, egg and ginger. Combine the flour, cinnamon, baking soda, cloves, cayenne, salt, nutmeg, white pepper, cardamom and coriander; gradually add to creamed mixture and mix well. Cover and refrigerate for 1½ hours or until easy to handle.

2. Roll into ½-in. balls; roll in turbinado sugar. Place 3 in. apart on lightly greased baking sheets.

3. Bake at 350° for 8-10 minutes or until set. Cool for 2 minutes before removing from pans to wire racks. Store in an airtight container.

JANUARY 16
HOT AND SPICY FOOD DAY

CRANBERRY PISTACHIO BISCOTTI

Studded with dried cranberries and crunchy pistachios, this delicious biscotti goes well with tea or coffee.

—DIANE GRUBER SIOUX CITY, IA

PREP: 25 MIN. • **BAKE:** 30 MIN.
MAKES: ABOUT 2½ DOZEN

- ¾ cup sugar
- ¼ cup canola oil
- 2 large eggs
- 2 teaspoons vanilla extract
- 1 teaspoon almond extract
- 1¾ cups all-purpose flour
- 1 teaspoon baking powder
- ¼ teaspoon salt
- ⅔ cup chopped pistachios
- ½ cup dried cranberries

1. In a small bowl, beat the sugar and oil until blended. Beat in eggs, then extracts. Combine the flour, baking powder and salt; gradually add to sugar mixture and mix well (dough will be stiff). Stir in pistachios and cranberries.

2. Divide dough in half. With floured hands, shape each half into a 12x2-in. rectangle on a parchment paper-lined baking sheet. Bake at 350° for 18-22 minutes or until set.

3. Place pan on wire rack. When cool enough to handle, transfer to a cutting board; cut diagonally with a serrated knife into ¾-in. slices. Place cut side down on ungreased baking sheets. Bake for 12-14 minutes or until firm. Remove to wire racks to cool. Store biscotti in an airtight container.

★ ★ ★ ★ ★ **5 STAR TIP**

Store biscotti in airtight containers. If decorated with a coating, stack them between sheets of waxed or parchment paper. Biscotti also freeze well, but it's best to decorate, dip or drizzle them after removing them from the freezer.

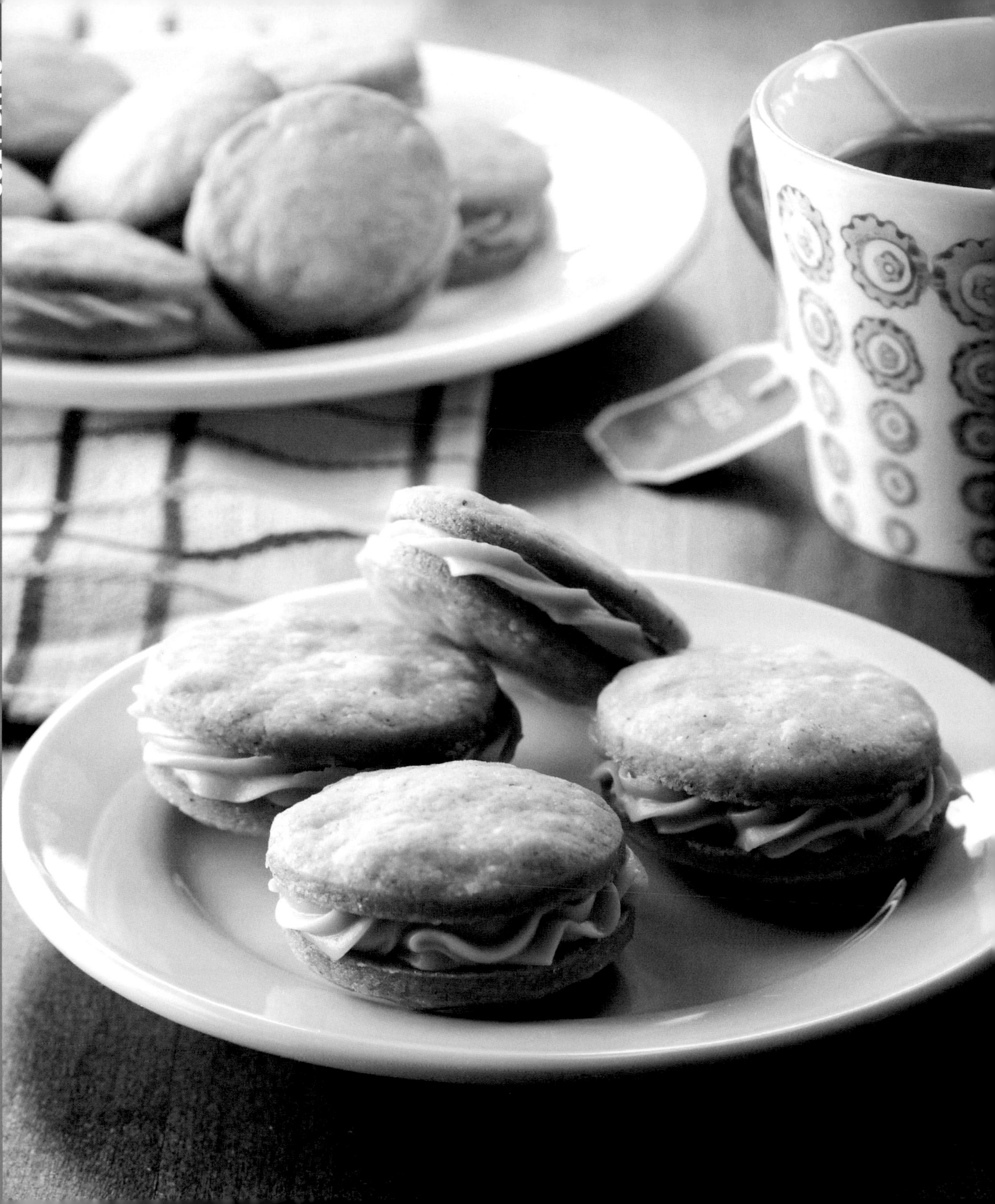

CHAI TEA SANDWICH COOKIES

Spiced cookies filled with creamy chai-flavored chocolate always impress. Serve them for afternoon tea or a morning treat.

—**LAUREN KNOELKE** MILWAUKEE, WI

PREP: 45 MIN. + CHILLING
BAKE: 10 MIN./BATCH + COOLING
MAKES: ABOUT 3½ DOZEN

- 8 ounces white baking chocolate, finely chopped
- ⅓ cup heavy whipping cream
- 2 chai-flavored black tea bags

COOKIES
- 2 cups all-purpose flour
- ½ cup sugar
- ½ teaspoon ground cinnamon
- ½ teaspoon ground cardamom
- ⅛ teaspoon salt
- ⅛ teaspoon pepper
- 1 cup cold butter, cut into 16 pieces
- 2 teaspoons vanilla extract

1. For ganache, place chocolate in a small bowl. In a small saucepan, bring cream just to a boil; remove from heat. Add tea bags; let stand 10 minutes. Discard the tea bags.

2. Reheat the cream just to a boil. Pour over chocolate; let stand 5 minutes. Stir with a whisk until smooth. Cool to room temperature or until ganache thickens to a spreading consistency, stirring occasionally, about 1 hour.

3. Meanwhile, in a large bowl, whisk flour, sugar, cinnamon, cardamom, salt and pepper; cut in butter with vanilla until crumbly. Knead until dough holds together when pressed. Shape into two disks; wrap each in plastic. Refrigerate for 15 minutes or until dough is firm enough to roll.

4. Preheat oven to 350°. On a lightly floured surface, gently roll dough to ⅛-in. thickness, lifting and rotating as needed. Cut with a 1½-in. round cookie cutter. Place cookies 1 in. apart on ungreased baking sheets. Bake for 10-12 minutes or until light brown. Remove from pans to wire racks to cool completely.

5. Spread 1 heaping teaspoon ganache on bottoms of half of the cookies; cover with remaining cookies. Let stand until set.

FREEZE OPTION *Prepare dough. Transfer wrapped disks to a resealable plastic freezer bag; freeze. To use, thaw dough in refrigerator until soft enough to roll. Make ganache. Prepare, bake and fill cookies as directed.*

CHEWY COCONUT MACAROONS

These chewy cookies are my husband's favorites, so he requests them often. I like to make the macaroons on cold winter days and keep them in an airtight bowl on the kitchen counter. They get scarfed up fast!

—**PEGGY KEY** GRANT, AL

PREP: 10 MIN. • **BAKE:** 20 MIN.
MAKES: 32 COOKIES

- 2½ cups flaked coconut
- ¾ cup all-purpose flour
- ⅛ teaspoon salt
- 1 can (14 ounces) fat-free sweetened condensed milk
- 1½ teaspoons almond extract

1. In a bowl, toss the coconut, flour and salt. Stir in milk and extract until blended (mixture will be thick and sticky).

2. Drop by rounded teaspoonfuls 3 in. apart on lightly greased baking sheets. Bake at 300° for 18-22 minutes or just until golden brown. Cool for 2 minutes

★ ★ ★ ★ ★ **READER REVIEW**

"These are very easy and everyone's favorite. My sister will not share these with anyone!"

MIJACINTO TASTEOFHOME.COM

flour, cocoa and baking soda; gradually add to the creamed mixture and mix well. Cover and refrigerate for 2 hours or until dough is stiff.

2. Meanwhile, for filling, heat chips and milk in a heavy saucepan over low heat until chips are melted, stirring constantly. Stir in nuts. Cover and refrigerate for 1 hour or until easy to handle.

3. Roll cookie dough into 1¼-in. balls. Place 2 in. apart on lightly greased baking sheets. Using the end of a wooden spoon handle, make an indentation in the center; smooth any cracks.

4. Roll filling into ½-in. balls; gently push one into each cookie. Bake at 375° for 8-10 minutes or until cookies are set. Remove to wire racks to cool.

WINTER FRUIT MACAROONS

I updated my mom's favorite coconut macaroon recipe to use sweetened condensed milk instead of egg whites. All you do is mix, drop and bake!

—VERONICA MILLER ALIQUIPPA, PA

....

PREP: 20 MIN. • **BAKE:** 10 MIN./BATCH
MAKES: ABOUT 7 DOZEN

- 1 **can (14 ounces) sweetened condensed milk**
- 2¼ **cups flaked coconut**
- 2¼ **cups coarsely chopped dates**
- 1½ **cups coarsely chopped walnuts**
- ¾ **cup dried cherries**
- ¾ **cup dried cranberries**
- ¾ **teaspoon vanilla extract**

1. Preheat oven to 350°. In a large bowl, mix all ingredients. Drop mixture by tablespoonfuls 2 in. apart onto parchment paper-lined baking sheets.

2. Bake 8-10 minutes or until light brown. Cool on pans 5 minutes. Remove to wire racks to cool. Store in an airtight container.

FREEZE OPTION *Freeze cookies, layered between waxed paper, in freezer containers. To use, thaw before serving.*

CHOCOLATE PUDDLES

The variations on this original recipe are almost endless. For double chocolate puddles, use semisweet chocolate chips for the white chips. Make peanut butter puddles by substituting peanut butter chips and peanuts for the white chips and mixed nuts.

—KATHIE GRIFFIN ANTELOPE, CA

....

PREP: 25 MIN. + CHILLING
BAKE: 10 MIN./BATCH
MAKES: ABOUT 5 DOZEN

- 1 **cup butter, softened**
- 1 **cup sugar**
- 1 **cup packed brown sugar**
- 2 **large eggs**
- 2 **teaspoons vanilla extract**
- 3 **cups all-purpose flour**
- ¾ **cup baking cocoa**
- 1 **teaspoon baking soda**

FILLING

- 1 **cup white baking chips**
- ½ **cup plus 2 tablespoons sweetened condensed milk**
- ¾ **cup finely chopped mixed nuts**

1. In a large bowl, cream butter and sugars until light and fluffy. Add the eggs, one at a time, beating well after each addition. Beat in vanilla. Combine the

SNOW-PUFFED MERINGUES

My family and friends like a nice pick-me-up dessert after a big meal, and these cookies are perfect! The feather-light morsels are ideal for winter parties, potlucks or simply snacks.
—LORRAINE CALAND SHUNIAH, ON

PREP: 20 MIN. • **BAKE:** 45 MIN. + COOLING
MAKES: ABOUT 3 DOZEN

- 4 large egg whites
- ½ teaspoon vanilla extract
- ¼ teaspoon salt
- ½ cup sugar
- 1 cup confectioners' sugar
- ⅓ cup Nutella

1. Place egg whites in a large bowl; let stand at room temperature 30 minutes.
2. Preheat oven to 225°. Add vanilla and salt to egg whites; beat on medium speed until foamy. Gradually add sugar, 1 tablespoon at a time, beating on high after each addition until the sugar is dissolved. Continue beating until stiff glossy peaks form. Fold in confectioners' sugar.
3. Cut a small hole in the tip of a pastry bag or in a corner of a food-safe plastic bag; insert a #96 star decorating tip. Transfer the meringue to the bag. Pipe 1½-in.-diameter cookies 2 in. apart onto parchment paper-lined baking sheets.
4. Bake 45-50 minutes or until firm to the touch. Turn oven off (do not open oven door); leave meringues in oven for 1½ hours. Remove from oven; cool completely on baking sheets.
5. Remove meringues from paper. Spread Nutella on the bottoms of half the cookies; cover with remaining cookies. Store in airtight containers at room temperature.
PEPPERMINT KISSES *Omit the Nutella. Crush 4 peppermint candy canes (two green and two red). Prepare and pipe meringue as directed. Sprinkle tops with crushed candy. Bake as directed.*

ITALIAN HONEY BALL COOKIES

My mother made these treats, known as *struffoli* in Italian, for neighbors, teachers and anyone who stopped by. The deep-fried delights are Easter, Christmas and special-occasion classics.

—SARAH KNOBLOCK HYDE PARK, IN

PREP: 45 MIN. + STANDING
COOK: 5 MIN./BATCH • **MAKES:** ABOUT 2 DOZEN

- 3 **cups all-purpose flour**
- ½ **teaspoon ground cinnamon**
- ½ **teaspoon aniseed, crushed**
- ⅛ **teaspoon salt**
- 4 **large eggs, lightly beaten**
- ⅓ **cup 2% milk**
  Oil for deep-fat frying
- 1 **cup honey**
- ¼ **cup sugar**
- ½ **cup pine nuts, toasted**
  Nonpareils, optional

1. Line 24 muffin cups with paper or foil liners. In a large bowl, whisk flour, cinnamon, aniseed and salt. Stir in eggs and milk. Turn dough onto a floured surface; knead until smooth and elastic, about 6-8 minutes. Shape into a disk; wrap in plastic. Let stand 1 hour.

2. Divide dough into six portions. Roll each portion into ½-in.-thick ropes; cut crosswise into ½-in. pieces. In an electric skillet or deep-fat fryer, heat oil to 350°. Fry pieces, a few at a time, for 2-3 minutes on each side or until golden brown. Drain on paper towels. Place dough pieces in a large heatproof bowl and keep warm in a 200° oven.

3. In a large heavy saucepan, combine honey and sugar. Bring to a boil over medium heat; boil 1 minute. Immediately remove from heat and drizzle over dough pieces. Stir to coat. Immediately spoon into prepared cups. Sprinkle with pine nuts and, if desired, nonpareils.

JANUARY 17
DAY OF ITALIAN CUISINES

NANNY'S FRUITCAKE COOKIES

My grandmother always made a holiday fruitcake. I took her recipe and turned it into a cookie that's perfect any time of day alongside a cup of tea.
—**AMANDA DIGGES** SOUTH WINDSOR, CT

PREP: 35 MIN. + CHILLING
BAKE: 15 MIN./BATCH
MAKES: ABOUT 4 DOZEN

1⅔ cups chopped pecans or walnuts
1⅓ cups golden raisins
1 cup pitted dried plums, chopped
⅔ cup dried apricots, finely chopped
½ cup dried cranberries
¼ cup Triple Sec
1 cup butter, softened
½ cup sugar
⅓ cup packed light brown sugar
½ teaspoon ground nutmeg
1 large egg
2⅔ cups all-purpose flour

1. Place the first five ingredients in a large bowl. Drizzle with Triple Sec and toss to combine. Let stand, covered, overnight.
2. In a large bowl, cream butter, sugars and nutmeg until light and fluffy. Beat in egg. Gradually beat in flour. Stir in fruit mixture.
3. Divide dough in half; shape each into a 12x3x1-in. rectangular log. Wrap in plastic; refrigerate overnight or until firm.
4. Preheat oven to 350°. Unwrap and cut dough crosswise into ½-in. slices. Place 2 in. apart on ungreased baking sheets. Bake 13-16 minutes or until edges are light brown. Remove from pans to wire racks to cool.

★ ★ ★ ★ ★ **READER REVIEW**

"These are a great twist on fruit cake. They are lovely on a plate. The recipe is simple and they are so good!"

RANDCBRUNS TASTEOFHOME.COM

FEBRUARY 2
HEDGEHOG
DAY

CHOCOLATE-PECAN HEDGEHOG COOKIES

Celebrate the European predecessor to Groundhog Day with these little cuties. German immigrants in Pennsylvania carried on the tradition of Europe's Hedgehog Day, substituting the more common groundhog.
—**PAM GOODLET** WASHINGTON ISLAND, WI

PREP: 30 MIN.
BAKE: 15 MIN./BATCH + COOLING
MAKES: 16 COOKIES

- ⅓ **cup butter, softened**
- ¼ **cup confectioners' sugar**
- ½ **teaspoon vanilla extract**
- ⅔ **cup all-purpose flour**
- ⅔ **cup ground pecans**
- ⅛ **teaspoon salt**
- ½ **cup 60% cacao bittersweet chocolate baking chips**
- ¼ **cup chocolate sprinkles**

1. Preheat oven to 325°. In a small bowl, cream butter and confectioners' sugar until light and fluffy. Beat in vanilla. Combine flour, pecans and salt; gradually add to creamed mixture and mix well. Shape 1 tablespoon of dough into a ball; pinch the dough to form a face. Repeat. Place 2 in. apart on a greased baking sheet.

2. Bake 12-15 minutes or until lightly browned. Let stand 5 minutes before removing to a wire rack to cool completely.

3. In a microwave, melt chocolate; stir until smooth. Holding a hedgehog cookie by the nose, spoon chocolate over the back (leave the face uncovered). Allow excess to drip off. Place on waxed paper; immediately coat the wet chocolate with sprinkles.

4. With a toothpick dipped in chocolate, make two eyes and a dot on the nose. Let stand until set. Store in an airtight container.

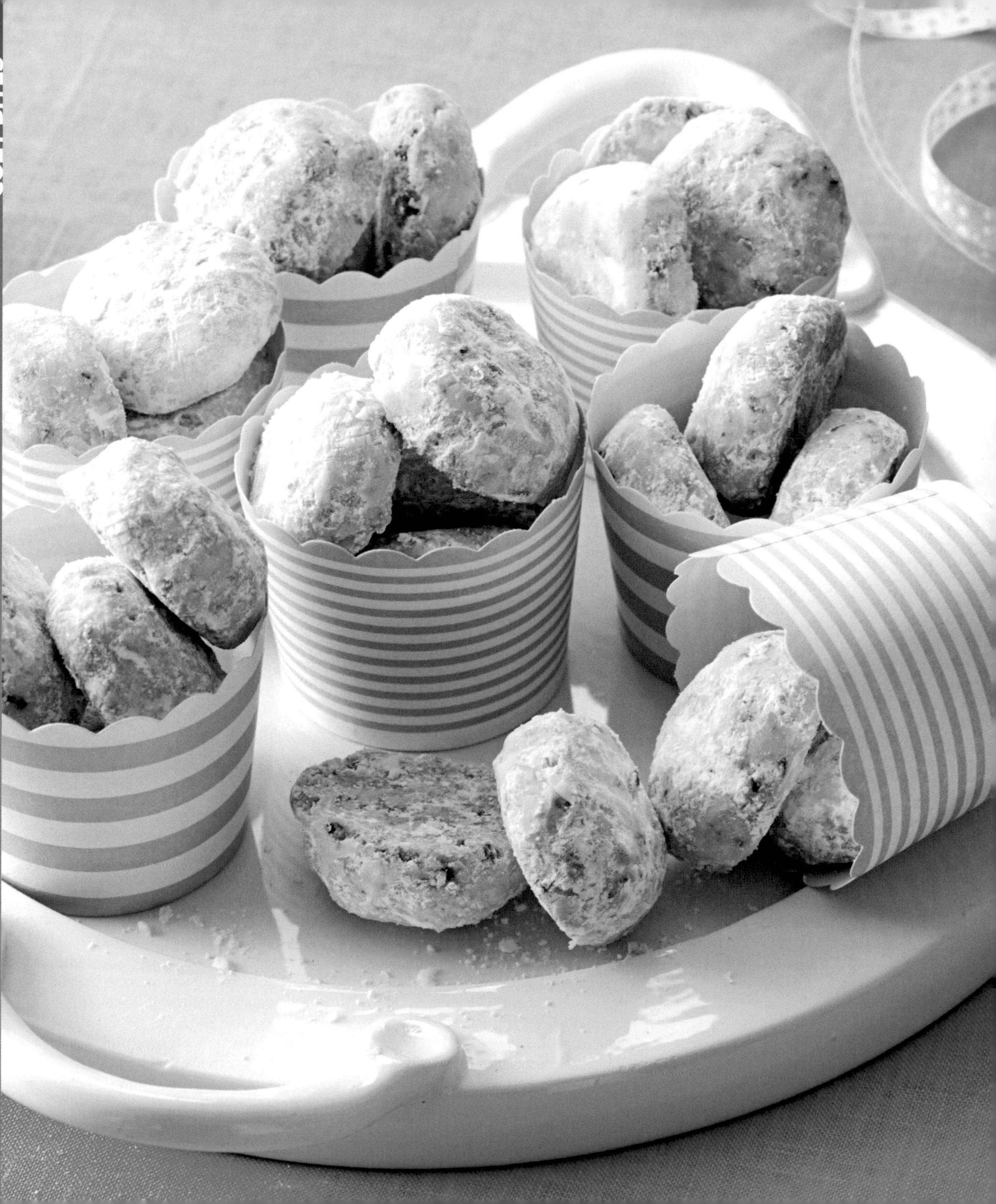

PECAN SANDIES

When Mother made these cookies, there never seemed to be enough! Even now when I make them, they disappear quickly. These melt-in-your mouth treats are great with a cold glass of milk or a steaming mug of hot chocolate.

—DEBBIE CARLSON SAN DIEGO, CA

PREP: 20 MIN.
BAKE: 20 MIN./BATCH + COOLING
MAKES: ABOUT 5 DOZEN

- 2 **cups butter, softened**
- 1 **cup confectioners' sugar**
- 2 **tablespoons water**
- 4 **teaspoons vanilla extract**
- 4 **cups all-purpose flour**
- 2 **cups chopped pecans**
  Additional confectioners' sugar

1. Preheat oven to 300°. In a large bowl, cream butter and sugar. Add water and vanilla; mix well. Gradually add flour; fold in pecans.
2. Roll dough into 1-in. balls. Place on ungreased baking sheets and flatten with your fingers.
3. Bake 20-25 minutes or until bottom edges are golden brown. Cool on a wire rack. When cool, dust with additional confectioners' sugar.

★ ★ ★ ★ ★ **READER REVIEW**

"These were truly amazing. My husband, a fan of pecan sandies, loved them. I had to make 2 batches to have enough for my office cookie exchange."

TONYAGJTASTEOFHOME.COM

TEXAS TUMBLEWEEDS

Tumbleweeds blow across the roads in some parts of Texas, and I think these cute stacks resemble them quite well. I've been making these sweets with my sister for years.

—KAREN LEMAY SEABROOK, TX

Short & Sweet

PREP: 20 MIN. + CHILLING
MAKES: ABOUT 4 DOZEN

- 1 **cup butterscotch chips**
- 1 **cup creamy peanut butter**
- 1 **can (9 ounces) potato sticks (about 6 cups)**

1. In a microwave or large metal bowl over simmering water, melt butterscotch chips and peanut butter; stir until smooth. Gently stir in potato sticks.
2. Drop by rounded tablespoonfuls onto waxed paper-lined baking sheets. Refrigerate 10-15 minutes or until set.

SNOWFLAKE COOKIES

Celebrate winter with these festive snowflake cookies.

—TASTE OF HOME TEST KITCHEN

PREP: 20 MIN. + CHILLING
BAKE: 10 MIN./BATCH + STANDING
MAKES: ABOUT 3 DOZEN

- 1 **cup butter, softened**
- 1 **cup confectioners' sugar**
- 1 **large egg**
- 1 **teaspoon vanilla extract**
- ½ **to 1 teaspoon almond extract**
- 2½ **cups all-purpose flour**
- ½ **teaspoon salt**

ROYAL ICING

- 2 **pounds confectioners' sugar**
- 6 **tablespoons meringue powder**
- ¾ **cup warm water**
  Sky blue gel food coloring
  White edible glitter and superfine sugar
  Ribbon

1. In a large bowl, cream butter and confectioners' sugar until light and fluffy. Beat in egg and extracts. Combine flour and salt; gradually add to creamed mixture and mix well.

2. Divide dough into fourths. Cover and refrigerate 1-2 hours or until easy to handle.

3. Preheat oven to 375°. On a lightly floured surface, roll out one portion to ⅛-in. thickness. (Refrigerate other portions until ready to use.) Using a variety of sizes of floured snowflake cookie cutters, cut out snowflakes.

4. Carefully place 1 in. apart on ungreased baking sheets. Using small decorating cutters, cut out desired shapes to create designs in some of the snowflakes. Use a toothpick to help remove the cutouts. With a plastic straw, poke a hole in the top of each small cookie.

5. Bake medium and large snowflakes 6½-7 minutes and small snowflakes 6 minutes or until bottoms are lightly browned. Remove to wire racks to cool. Repeat with remaining dough.

6. For royal icing, in a large bowl, combine confectioners' sugar and meringue powder. Add warm water; beat on low speed 1 minute. Beat on high 4-5 minutes or until stiff peaks form. Tint half blue. Leave remaining icing white; cover and set aside.

7. With blue icing and a round tip, outline half of the cookies; fill in centers with blue icing and let dry completely. With white icing and a round tip, outline each blue-colored cookie and create snowflake designs. Sprinkle with edible glitter and superfine sugar, then let dry completely.

8. On the remaining cookies, repeat process using white icing on white frosted cookies. Thread a ribbon through the hole in each small snowflake and through the cutout in each medium and large snowflake.

FEBRUARY 5
WORLD NUTELLA DAY

CHOCOLATE HAZELNUT TASSIES

Your taste buds will be delighted to find these delicious tassies not filled with the standard pecans but with dark chocolate and hazelnuts.

—**JOAN RANZINI** WAYNESBORO, VA

PREP: 25 MIN.
BAKE: 20 MIN./BATCH + COOLING
MAKES: 3 DOZEN

- 1 **cup butter, softened**
- 6 **ounces cream cheese, softened**
- 1 **tablespoon sugar**
- 2 **teaspoons grated lemon peel**
- 2 **cups all-purpose flour**

FILLING
- ¼ **cup Nutella**
- ½ **cup packed brown sugar**
- 1 **large egg**
- 1 **tablespoon butter, melted**
- 1 **teaspoon vanilla extract**
- ½ **cup finely chopped hazelnuts**
- ¼ **cup miniature semisweet chocolate chips**

1. In a large bowl, cream the butter, cream cheese, sugar and lemon peel. Beat in flour. Shape into 36 balls. With floured fingers, press onto the bottom and up the sides of ungreased miniature muffin cups.
2. For filling, in a small bowl, beat the Nutella, brown sugar, egg, butter and vanilla until blended. Stir in hazelnuts and chocolate chips. Fill prepared cups three-fourths full.
3. Bake at 375° for 16-18 minutes or until set. Cool on wire racks for 10 minutes. Carefully remove from pans to wire racks. Store in an airtight container.

CHOCOLATE CHAI SNICKERDOODLES

I used to think snickerdoodles could never be improved, but then I added chocolate. While they are baking, the aroma of chocolate mixed with warm spices reminds me of chai tea.

—KATHERINE WOLLGAST FLORISSANT, MO

PREP: 30 MIN. • **BAKE:** 10 MIN./BATCH
MAKES: ABOUT 3 DOZEN

- 2¼ cups sugar
- 1 teaspoon ground ginger
- 1 teaspoon ground cardamom
- 1 teaspoon ground cinnamon
- ½ teaspoon ground allspice
- ¼ teaspoon white pepper
- 1 cup butter, softened
- 2 large eggs
- 2 teaspoons vanilla extract
- 2¼ cups all-purpose flour
- ½ cup baking cocoa
- 2 teaspoons cream of tartar
- 1½ teaspoons baking powder
- ½ teaspoon salt

1. Preheat oven to 350°. In a large bowl, combine the first six ingredients. Remove ½ cup sugar mixture to a shallow dish.
2. Add butter to remaining sugar mixture; beat until light and fluffy. Beat in eggs and vanilla. In another bowl, whisk the flour, baking cocoa, cream of tartar, baking powder and salt; gradually beat into creamed mixture.
3. Shape dough into 1½-in. balls. Roll in reserved sugar mixture; place 2 in. apart on ungreased baking sheets. Flatten slightly with bottom of a glass. Bake for 10-12 minutes or until edges are firm. Remove to wire racks to cool.

★ ★ ★ ★ ★ **READER REVIEW**

"One of the best snickerdoodles I've ever had! The chocolate and cardamom push these over the top."

ALISONO TASTEOFHOME.COM

2. Using a cookie press fitted with a disk, press dough 1 in. apart onto ungreased baking sheets. Sprinkle with sprinkles. Bake 6-8 minutes or until set (do not brown). Remove from pans to wire racks to cool completely.

3. Spread about 1 teaspoon Biscoff on the bottoms of half of the cookies; top with remaining cookies.

FREEZE OPTION *Transfer dough to a resealable plastic freezer bag; freeze. To use, thaw dough in refrigerator overnight or until soft enough to press. Prepare and bake cookies as directed.*

RASPBERRY CREAM SUGAR COOKIES

We make sugar cookies and fill them with a tangy raspberry cream cheese. They taste best after they've been refrigerated for at least 45 minutes.

—HEIDI FARNWORTH RIVERTON, UT

PREP: 10 MIN. + CHILLING
BAKE: 10 MIN./BATCH + COOLING
MAKES: ABOUT 1½ DOZEN

- ½ **cup white baking chips**
- ¼ **cup heavy whipping cream**
- 6 **ounces cream cheese, softened**
- ¼ **cup red raspberry preserves**
- 1 **package sugar cookie mix**
- ½ **cup butter, softened**
- 1 **large egg**

1. Preheat oven to 350°. In a microwave, melt baking chips with cream; stir until smooth. In a large bowl, beat cream cheese and preserves until blended. Add melted baking chip mixture; beat until smooth. Refrigerate until assembling.

2. In a large bowl, mix cookie mix, butter and egg until blended. Shape into 1-in. balls; place 2 in. apart on ungreased baking sheets. Bake 7-9 minutes or until edges are light brown. Cool on pans 5 minutes. Remove to wire racks to cool completely.

3. Spread 1 tablespoon filling on the bottoms of half of the cookies; cover with remaining cookies. Refrigerate in an airtight container.

SPRITZ SANDWICH COOKIES

I prepare spritz cookies with Biscoff spread, which is made from ground Biscoff cookies.

—LINDA SWEET CORNWALL, NY

PREP: 40 MIN. • **BAKE:** 10 MIN./BATCH
MAKES: 5½ DOZEN

- 1½ **cups butter, softened**
- 1 **cup sugar**
- 1 **large egg**
- 2 **tablespoons 2% milk**
- 2 **teaspoons vanilla extract**
- 3½ **cups all-purpose flour**
- 1 **teaspoon baking powder**
- 1 **teaspoon ground cinnamon**
  Colored sprinkles
- ⅔ **cup Biscoff spread**

1. Preheat oven to 375°. In a large bowl, cream butter and sugar until light and fluffy. Beat in egg, milk and vanilla. In another bowl, whisk flour, baking powder and cinnamon; gradually beat into the creamed mixture.

SNOWMAN SUGAR COOKIES

Store-bought dough speeds up the preparation time of these cute cookies. They're so easy that the whole family—even little kids—can help decorate them.

—JEAN WARDRIP BURR HOPE MILLS, NC

PREP: 30 MIN.
BAKE: 10 MIN. + COOLING
MAKES: 2 DOZEN

Short & Sweet

- 1 **tube (18 ounces) refrigerated sugar cookie dough**
- ½ **cup shortening**
- ½ **cup butter, softened**
- 4 **cups confectioners' sugar**
- 1 **tablespoon whole milk**
- 1 **teaspoon vanilla extract**
- 48 **miniature semisweet chocolate chips**
- 24 **candy corn candies**
- ½ **cup Red Hots**

1. Cut cookie dough into ¼-in. slices. Place 2 in. apart on ungreased baking sheets. Bake at 350° for 8-12 minutes or until edges are lightly browned. Cool for 2 minutes before removing to wire racks to cool completely.

2. For frosting, in a small bowl, cream shortening and butter. Gradually beat in confectioners' sugar. Beat in milk and vanilla until smooth. Spread over the cookies. Decorate with chocolate chips, candy corn and Red Hots.

BE-MINE SANDWICH COOKIES

These simple cookies are the first thing to disappear from dessert tables. They're cute, colorful and extremely quick and easy.

—DARCIE CROSS NOVI, MI

Short & Sweet

START TO FINISH: 20 MIN.
MAKES: 50-55 COOKIES

- 6 **ounces white or milk chocolate candy coating, coarsely chopped**
- 50 **to 55 Oreo cookies**
  Assorted candy sprinkles or decorations

In a microwave, melt 2 oz. of candy coating at a time, stirring until smooth. Spread over cookie tops; decorate immediately. Place on waxed paper until set.

CHERRY-FILLED HEART COOKIES

These crisp, flaky cookies are a wonderful way to show you care. They take a little effort, but the smiles of satisfaction make it worthwhile.

—**AUDREY GROE** LAKE MILLS, IA

PREP: 50 MIN. • **BAKE:** 10 MIN./BATCH
MAKES: ABOUT 4½ DOZEN FILLED COOKIES

- ½ **cup butter, softened**
- ½ **cup shortening**
- 1 **cup sugar**
- 1 **large egg**
- ½ **cup milk**
- 1 **teaspoon vanilla extract**
- 3½ **cups all-purpose flour**
- 2 **teaspoons baking powder**
- 1 **teaspoon baking soda**
- ½ **teaspoon salt**

FILLING

- ½ **cup sugar**
- 4½ **teaspoons cornstarch**
- ½ **cup orange juice**
- ¼ **cup red maraschino cherry juice**
- 12 **red maraschino cherries, chopped**
- 1 **tablespoon butter**
  Additional sugar

1. In a bowl, cream the butter and shortening; gradually add the sugar. Add the egg, milk and vanilla. Combine dry ingredients; gradually add to creamed mixture. Mix well. Cover and refrigerate for at least 2 hours.

2. Meanwhile, for filling, combine sugar and cornstarch in small saucepan. Add juices, cherries and butter. Bring to a boil; boil and stir for 1 minute. Chill.

3. Roll out dough on a lightly floured surface to ⅛-in. thickness; cut with a 2½-in. heart-shaped cookie cutter dipped in flour.

4. Place half of the cookies on greased baking sheets; spoon ½ teaspoon filling in the center of each. Use a 1½-in. heart-shaped cutter to cut small hearts out of the other half of the cookies. (Bake small heart cutouts separately.) Place the remaining hearts over filled cookies; press edges together gently. Fill centers with additional filling if needed. Sprinkle with sugar.

5. Bake at 375° for 8-10 minutes or until lightly browned. Cool on wire racks.

LOLLIPOP COOKIES

Cookie lollipops are always a hit with kids (and their parents). Use your imagination with this recipe to create treats for any season—the possibilities are endless!

—JEAN EDWARDS INDIANAPOLIS, IN

PREP: 20 MIN. + CHILLING
BAKE: 10 MIN./BATCH + COOLING
MAKES: 3 DOZEN

- 1 cup butter, softened
- 1½ cups confectioners' sugar
- 1 large egg
- 1 teaspoon vanilla extract
- ¼ to ½ teaspoon almond extract
- 2½ cups all-purpose flour
- 1 teaspoon baking soda
- 1 teaspoon cream of tartar
- 2 ounces semisweet chocolate, melted

FROSTING
- 1 cup confectioners' sugar
- ¼ to ½ teaspoon almond extract
- ¼ teaspoon salt
- 1 to 2 teaspoons milk
  Red Hots and red sprinkles

1. In a large bowl, cream butter and confectioners' sugar until light and fluffy. Beat in egg and extracts. Combine the flour, baking soda and cream of tartar; gradually add to the creamed mixture and mix well. Divide dough in half; stir chocolate into one half. Refrigerate for 2 hours or until easy to handle.

2. On a lightly floured surface, roll out each portion to ⅛-in. thickness. Cut with a 2½-in. cookie cutter. Place 1 in. apart on lightly greased baking sheets.

3. Bake at 375° for 7-8 minutes or until lightly browned. Remove to wire racks to cool.

4. For frosting, combine confectioners' sugar, extract, salt and enough milk to achieve spreading consistency. Frost bottoms of chocolate cookies. Place a wooden stick on each cookie, leaving 3 in. for handle. Top each with a plain cookie. Frost tops; add candies and sprinkles.

FEBRUARY 14
HAPPY
VALENTINE'S
DAY!

OATMEAL ROLLOUT COOKIES

For special events, my mother would bring these cute cookies to my school. She decorated each cookie with a student's name written in frosting. Sweet and delicious, these are wonderful for Valentines Day.

—SALLY GORES ALMENA, WI

PREP: 30 MIN. + CHILLING
BAKE: 10 MIN./BATCH + COOLING
MAKES: 3½ DOZEN

- 1 cup butter, softened
- ¾ cup packed brown sugar
- ½ cup sugar
- 1 large egg
- 2 teaspoons vanilla extract
- 2½ cups all-purpose flour
- 1 cup quick-cooking oats
- 1 teaspoon baking soda
- ½ teaspoon salt

FROSTING
- ¼ cup butter, softened
- 1 package (8 ounces) cream cheese, softened
- 1 teaspoon vanilla extract
- 4 cups confectioners' sugar
  Colored sugar

1. In a large bowl, cream butter and sugars until light and fluffy. Beat in egg and vanilla. In another bowl, whisk flour, oats, baking soda and salt; gradually beat into creamed mixture.

2. Divide dough in half. Shape each into a disk; wrap in plastic. Refrigerate 1 hour or until firm enough to roll.

3. Preheat oven to 350°. On a lightly floured surface, roll each portion of dough to ¼-in. thickness. Cut with a floured 2¾-in. cookie cutter. Place 1 in. apart on greased baking sheets.

4. Bake 9-11 minutes or until edges are light brown. Remove from pans to wire racks to cool completely.

5. For frosting, in a small bowl, beat butter, cream cheese and vanilla until blended. Gradually beat in confectioners' sugar until smooth. Spread over cookies. Decorate with colored sugar. Store in airtight containers in the refrigerator.

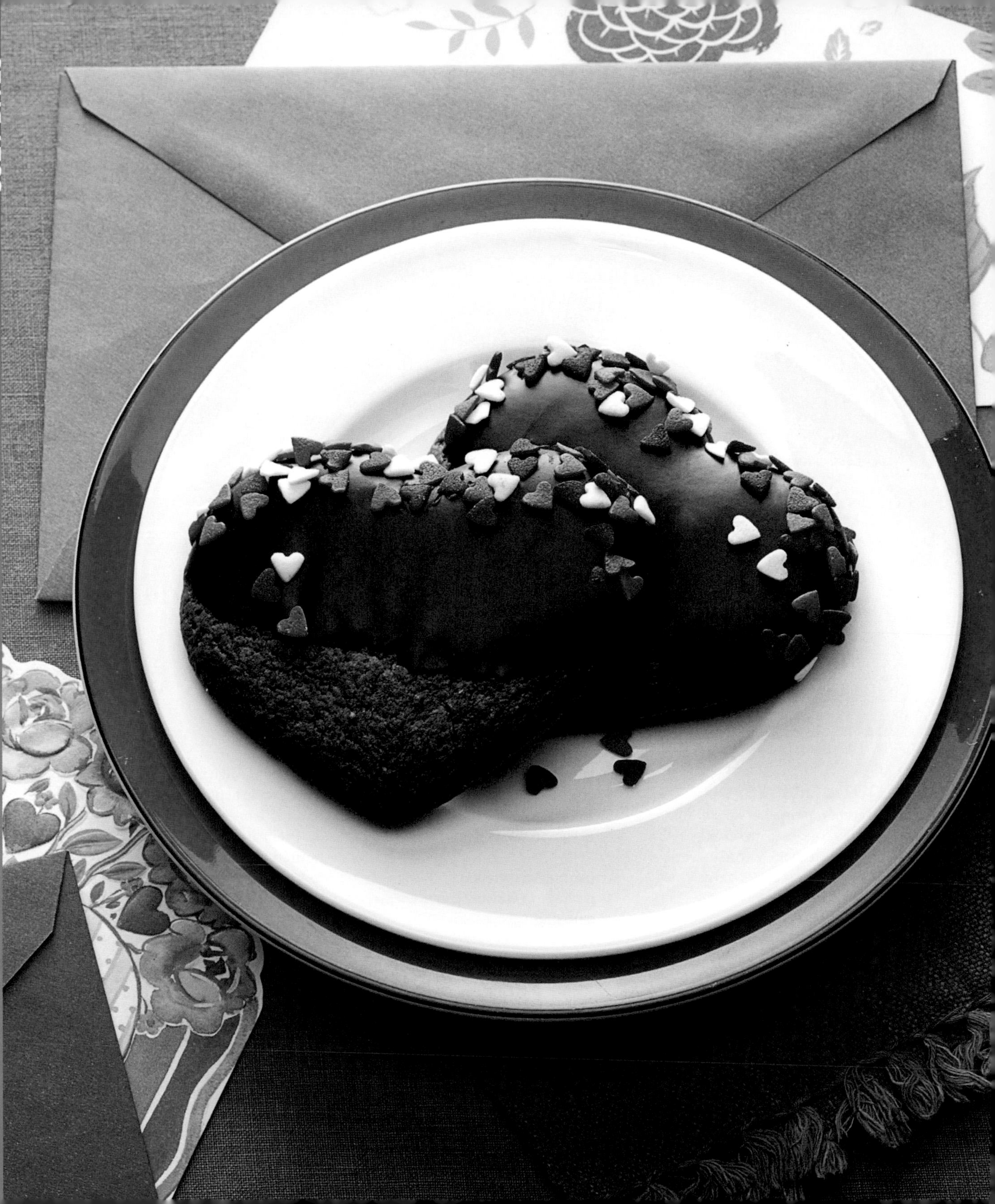

MINTY CHOCOLATE HEARTS

This is one of my all-time favorite cookies. The chocolate mint glaze really makes these a very special treat.

—SHERI LIVERMORE WAUKESHA, WI

PREP: 25 MIN. + CHILLING
BAKE: 10 MIN./BATCH + COOLING
MAKES: 2 DOZEN

- 1 package (10 ounces) mint chocolate chips, divided
- ¼ cup butter, softened
- ⅓ cup sugar
- 1 large egg
- ½ teaspoon vanilla extract
- 1¼ cups all-purpose flour
- ¾ teaspoon baking powder
- ¼ teaspoon salt
- ¼ teaspoon baking soda
- ¼ cup shortening
  Colored sprinkles, optional

1. In a microwave-safe bowl, melt ½ cup chocolate chips; stir. Cool slightly. In a small bowl, cream butter and sugar. Beat in the egg, vanilla and melted chocolate. Combine the flour, baking powder, salt and baking soda; gradually add to the creamed mixture and mix well.

2. Cover and refrigerate for 1-2 hours or until easy to handle. On a lightly floured surface, roll out dough to ¼-in. thickness. Cut with a floured 2½-in. heart-shaped cookie cutter. Place 2 in. apart on ungreased baking sheets. Bake at 350° for 7-10 minutes or until set. Remove to wire racks to cool completely.

3. In a microwave, melt shortening and remaining chocolate chips; stir until smooth. Dip each cookie halfway into chocolate mixture; allow excess to drip off. Sprinkle chocolate with sprinkles if desired. Place on waxed paper; refrigerate until set.

NO-BAKE COOKIE BALLS

I always go for these quick bites when I'm short on time or don't want to turn on the oven. I make them a day or two ahead to let the flavors blend.

—CARMELETTA DAILEY WINFIELD, TX

PREP: 25 MIN. • **MAKES:** 5 DOZEN

- 1 cup (6 ounces) semisweet chocolate chips
- 3 cups confectioners' sugar
- 1¾ cups crushed vanilla wafers (about 55 wafers)
- 1 cup chopped walnuts, toasted
- ⅓ cup orange juice
- 3 tablespoons light corn syrup
  Additional confectioners' sugar

1. In a large microwave-safe bowl, melt chocolate chips; stir until smooth. Stir in the confectioners' sugar, vanilla wafers, walnuts, orange juice and corn syrup.

2. Shape into 1-in. balls; roll in additional confectioners' sugar. Store in an airtight container.

COZY ⊛ BITES   **63**

GUMDROP COOKIES

These cookies were my mother's special treat. They are great for keeping children busy— they can cut up the gumdrops with a butter knife and eat all the black ones so they don't turn the dough gray.

—LETAH CHILSTON RIVERTON, WY

....

PREP: 15 MIN. + CHILLING
BAKE: 10 MIN./BATCH
MAKES: ABOUT 7 DOZEN

- 1½ **cups spice gumdrops**
- ¾ **cup coarsely chopped walnuts**
- ½ **cup golden raisins**
- 1¾ **cups all-purpose flour, divided**
- ½ **cup shortening**
- 1 **cup packed brown sugar**
- 1 **large egg**
- ¼ **cup buttermilk**
- ½ **teaspoon baking soda**
- ½ **teaspoon salt**

1. Cut gumdrops into small pieces; place in a bowl. Add walnuts, raisins and ¼ cup flour and toss to coat.
2. In a large bowl, beat shortening and brown sugar until blended. Beat in egg, then buttermilk. In another bowl, whisk remaining flour, baking soda and salt; gradually beat into shortening mixture. Stir in gumdrop mixture. Refrigerate, covered, 1 hour.
3. Preheat oven to 400°. Drop dough by rounded teaspoonfuls 2 in. apart onto ungreased baking sheets. Bake cookies 8-10 minutes or until golden brown. Cool on pans 2 minutes. Remove to wire racks to cool completely.

CHOCOLATE PEANUT BUTTER COOKIES

It's a snap to make a batch of tasty cookies using this recipe. My husband and son gobble them up.

—MARY PULYER PORT ST. LUCIE, FL

....

PREP: 10 MIN.
BAKE: 10 MIN./BATCH
MAKES: 4 DOZEN

Short & Sweet

- 1 **package devil's food cake mix (regular size)**
- 2 **large eggs**
- ⅓ **cup canola oil**
- 1 **package (10 ounces) peanut butter chips**

1. In a bowl, beat cake mix, eggs and oil (batter will be very stiff). Stir in chips.
2. Roll into 1-in. balls. Place on lightly greased baking sheets; flatten slightly. Bake at 350° for 10 minutes or until a slight indentation remains when lightly touched. Cool for 2 minutes before removing to a wire rack.

FEBRUARY 15
NATIONAL
GUMDROP
DAY!

PEANUT BUTTER PENGUINS

These little cuties are real show-stealers! Let the kids help out by sorting the M&M's and doing the decorating.

—**TASTE OF HOME** TEST KITCHEN

Short & Sweet

PREP: 1 HOUR + STANDING
MAKES: ABOUT 2½ DOZEN

- 1¼ **pounds dark chocolate candy coating, chopped**
- 1 **package (16 ounces) Nutter Butter cookies**
- 32 **bright white candy coating disks**
- 64 **candy eyes**
- 32 **orange M&M's minis**
- 64 **orange milk chocolate M&M's**

1. In a microwave, melt candy coating; stir until smooth. Dip one cookie in chocolate; allow excess to drip off. Place on waxed paper.

2. Attach a white coating disk for belly and two candy eyes. Add an M&M mini for beak and two regular M&M's for feet. Repeat. Let stand until set.

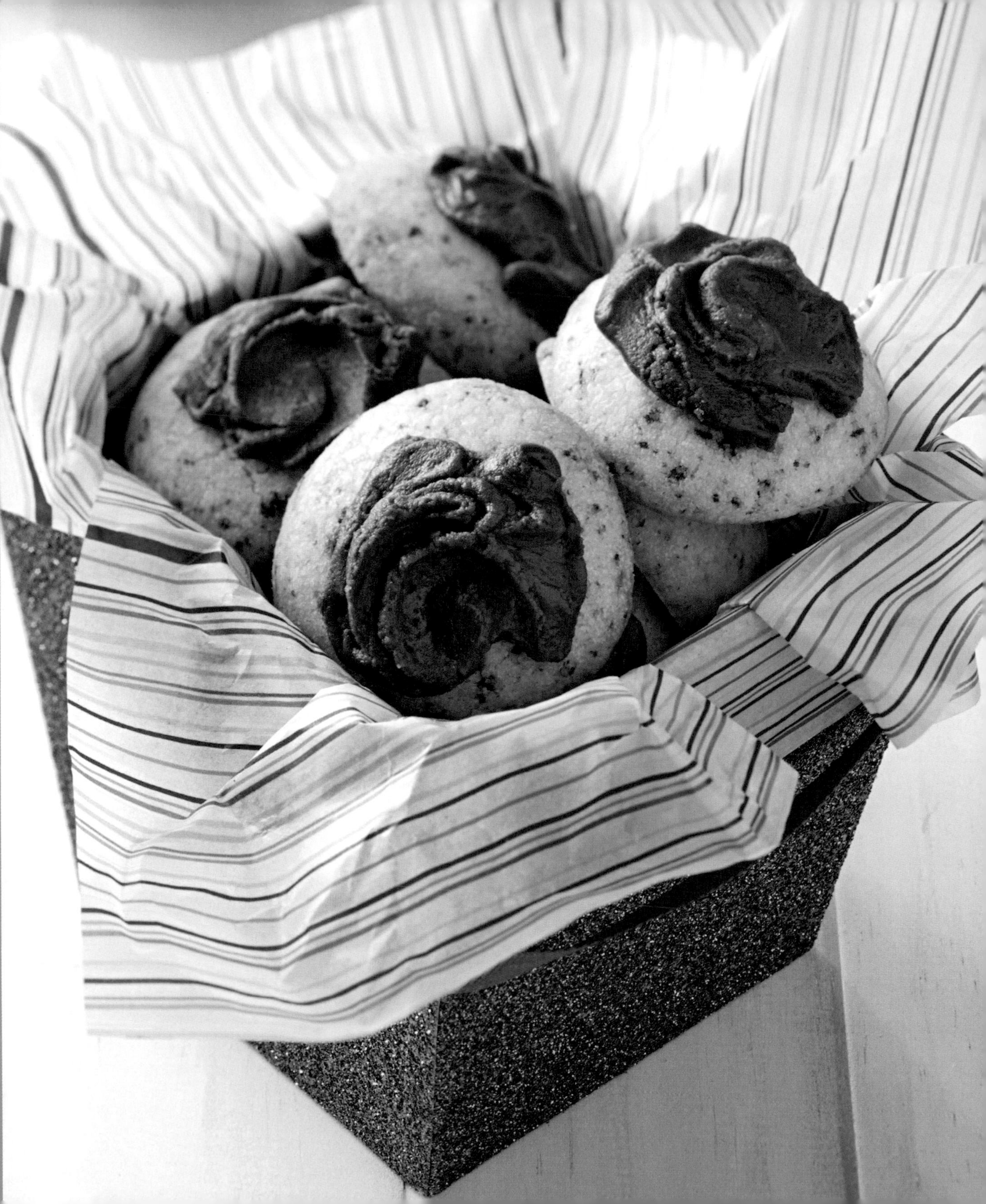

COFFEE BONBONS

When I first sampled this unique cookie, I decided it was the best cookie I'd ever tried. The coffee flavor and chocolate icing make it a delightful treat.

—LEITZEL MALZAHN FOX POINT, WI

PREP: 20 MIN. + CHILLING
BAKE: 20 MIN./BATCH • **MAKES:** 5 DOZEN

- 1 **cup butter, softened**
- ¾ **cup confectioners' sugar**
- ½ **teaspoon vanilla extract**
- 1 **tablespoon instant coffee granules**
- 1¾ **cups all-purpose flour**
CHOCOLATE GLAZE
- 1 **tablespoon butter**
- ½ **ounce unsweetened chocolate**
- 1 **cup confectioners' sugar**
- 2 **tablespoons milk**

1. In a bowl, cream butter and sugar until light and fluffy. Add vanilla. Combine coffee and flour; stir into the creamed mixture and mix well. Chill, then shape into ¾-in. balls and place on ungreased baking sheets. Bake at 350° for 18-20 minutes.

2. Meanwhile, for glaze, melt butter and chocolate together. Add melted mixture to sugar along with milk; beat until smooth. Frost cookies while still warm.

LOW-FAT PEANUT BUTTER COOKIES

When you bite into one of these yummy cookies, you'll never guess it's low in fat.

—MARIA REGAKIS SAUGUS, MA

PREP: 15 MIN. + FREEZING
BAKE: 10 MIN. + COOLING
MAKES: ABOUT 2 DOZEN

- 3 **tablespoons butter**
- 2 **tablespoons reduced-fat peanut butter**
- ½ **cup packed brown sugar**
- ¼ **cup sugar**
- 1 **large egg white**
- 1 **teaspoon vanilla extract**
- 1 **cup all-purpose flour**
- ¼ **teaspoon baking soda**
- ⅛ **teaspoon salt**

1. In a large bowl, cream the butter, peanut butter and sugars until light and fluffy. Add egg white; beat until blended. Beat in vanilla. Combine the flour, baking soda and salt; gradually add to creamed mixture and mix well. Shape into an 8-in. roll; wrap in plastic. Freeze for 2 hours or until firm.

2. Unwrap roll and cut into slices, just over ¼ in. thick. Place 2 in. apart on baking sheets coated with cooking spray; press with a fork to make crisscross pattern. Bake at 350° for 6-8 minutes for chewy cookies or 8-10 minutes for crisp cookies. Cool for 1-2 minutes before removing to wire racks; cool completely.

PEANUT BUTTER MAPLE COOKIES

I bake these crispy yet chewy peanut butter cookies often. My grandchildren, both near and far, can't wait to dig into the cookie jar.
—**LOIS BOWMAN** SWANTON, MD

PREP: 20 MIN. • **BAKE:** 15 MIN.
MAKES: ABOUT 5 DOZEN

- 1 **cup butter, softened**
- ½ **cup peanut butter**
- 1 **cup sugar**
- 1 **cup packed brown sugar**
- 2 **large eggs**
- 1 **tablespoon maple syrup**
- 2 **teaspoons vanilla extract**
- 2 **cups all-purpose flour**
- ¾ **cup quick-cooking oats**
- 1½ **teaspoons baking powder**
- 1 **teaspoon baking soda**
- 1 **teaspoon salt**
- 1 **package (10 ounces) peanut butter chips**

1. In a large bowl, cream the butter, peanut butter and sugars. Add the eggs, one at a time, beating well after each addition. Beat in syrup and vanilla. Combine the flour, oats, baking powder, baking soda and salt; add to the creamed mixture. Stir in peanut butter chips.
2. Drop by heaping tablespoonfuls 2 in. apart onto ungreased baking sheets. Bake at 325° for 15-18 minutes or until golden brown. Cool for 1 minute before removing to wire racks to cool completely.
NOTE *Reduced-fat peanut butter is not recommended for this recipe.*

CHOCOLATE CAKE COOKIES

I love these soft, chewy cookies. They take just a few minutes to make and are easy enough for kids to help.
—**MONICA STOUT** ANCHORAGE, AK

Short & Sweet

PREP: 30 MIN.
BAKE: 10 MIN./BATCH
MAKES: 7 DOZEN

- 1 **package chocolate fudge cake mix (regular size)**
- 2 **packages (3.9 ounces each) instant chocolate fudge pudding mix**
- 1½ **cups mayonnaise**
- 2 **cups (12 ounces) semisweet chocolate chips**
- ½ **cup chopped walnuts**

1. In a large bowl, combine cake mix, pudding mixes and mayonnaise; mix well. Stir in chocolate chips and walnuts.
2. Shape by teaspoonfuls into balls; place on greased baking sheets. Bake at 350° for 9-10 minutes or until cookies puff and surface cracks slightly. Cool for 5 minutes before removing from pans to wire racks.

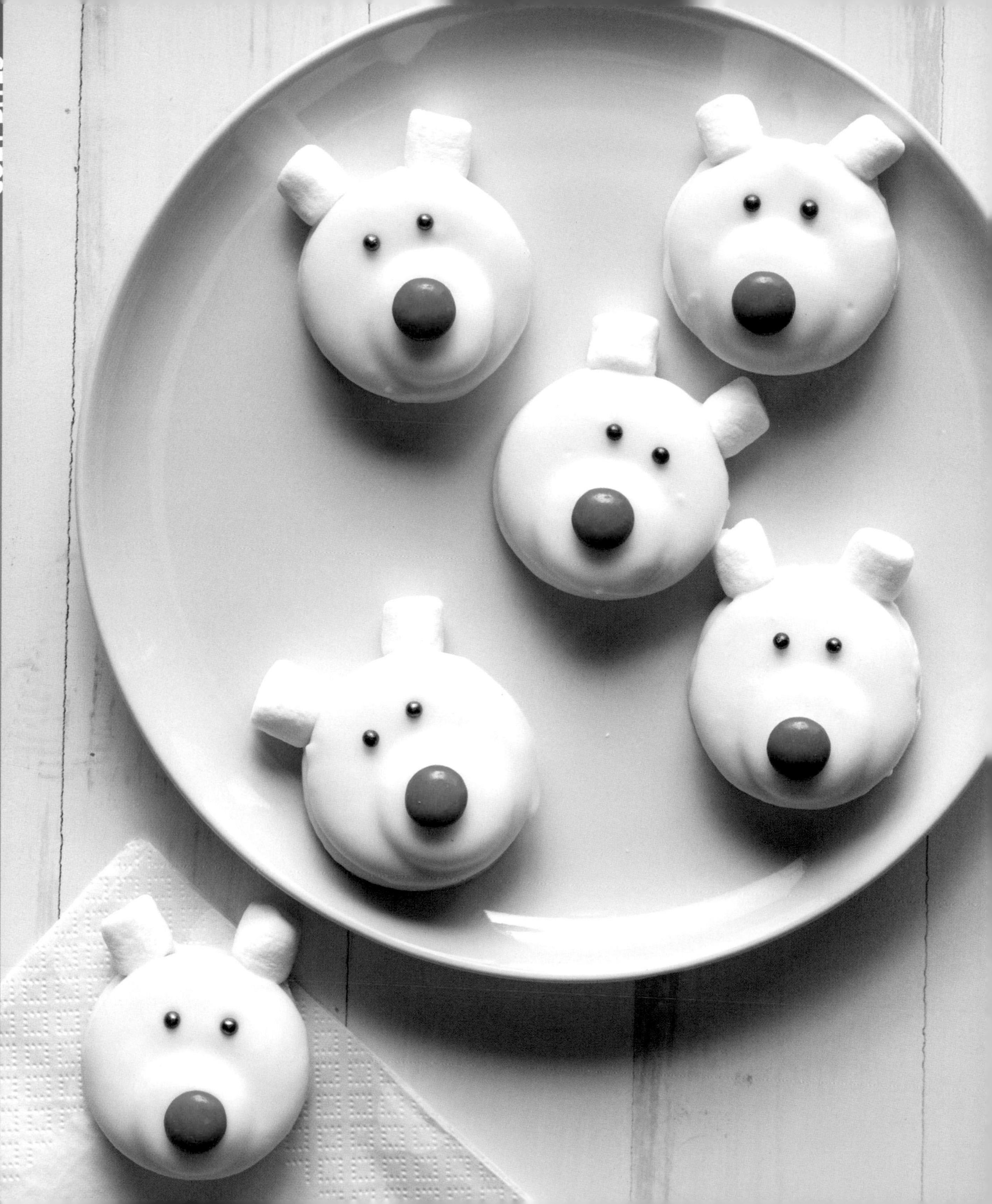

FROSTY POLAR BEARS

I love spending time in the kitchen with my nieces. This is the perfect recipe to make with the little ones. Dang cute, easy and portable!

—**EMILY TYRA** MILWAUKEE, WI

START TO FINISH: 25 MIN.
MAKES: 2½ DOZEN

- ¾ **cup creamy peanut butter**
- 60 **Ritz crackers**
- 24 **ounces white candy coating, melted**
- 60 **miniature marshmallows**
- 30 **mini Ritz crackers**
  Blue M&M's and black sugar pearls

1. Spread peanut butter on tops of half of the crackers; cover with remaining crackers. Dip sandwiches in melted candy coating; allow excess to drip off. Place on waxed paper. Dip marshmallows in the coating; allow excess to drip off. Place two marshmallows on each cookie for ears.

2. Dip mini crackers in melted candy coating; allow excess to drip off. Place on top of cookies for snouts. Decorate with M&M's for noses and sugar pearls for eyes. Let stand until set. Store in an airtight container in the refrigerator.

NUTTY RICE KRISPIE COOKIES

My mom and I used to make these treats for Christmas every year. Making them with just the microwave means they're super easy.

—**SAVANNA CHAPDELAINE** ORLANDO, FL

START TO FINISH: 15 MIN.
MAKES: ABOUT 2 DOZEN

- 1 **package (10 to 12 ounces) white baking chips**
- ¼ **cup creamy peanut butter**
- 1 **cup miniature marshmallows**
- 1 **cup Rice Krispies**
- 1 **cup salted peanuts**

In a large microwave-safe bowl, melt the baking chips; stir until smooth. Stir in peanut butter until blended. Add mini marshmallows, Rice Krispies and salted peanuts. Drop by heaping tablespoonfuls onto wax paper-lined baking sheets. Cool completely. Store in an airtight container.

PEANUT BUTTER SPRITZ FINGERS

My family loves these cookies because they satisfy the need for chocolate and for something crunchy, sweet and nutty, all in just one bite!

—**IRMA LOWERY** REEDSBURG, WI

PREP: 25 MIN. + CHILLING
BAKE: 10 MIN./BATCH + COOLING
MAKES: ABOUT 4 DOZEN

- ½ **cup butter, softened**
- ½ **cup creamy peanut butter**
- ½ **cup sugar**
- ½ **cup packed brown sugar**
- 1 **large egg**
- 1 **teaspoon vanilla extract**
- 1½ **cups all-purpose flour**
- ¾ **teaspoon baking soda**
- ½ **teaspoon baking powder**
- ¼ **teaspoon salt**
- 3 **milk chocolate candy bars (4 ounces each), chopped**
- 1 **cup finely chopped unsalted peanuts**

1. In a large bowl, cream the butter, peanut butter and sugars until light and fluffy. Beat in egg and vanilla. Combine the flour, baking soda, baking powder and salt; gradually add to creamed mixture and mix well. Cover and refrigerate for 30 minutes or until easy to handle.
2. Using a cookie press fitted with a star disk, press dough 2 in. apart into long strips on ungreased baking sheets. Cut each strip into 2-in. pieces (do not separate pieces).
3. Bake at 350° for 7-9 minutes or until golden brown. Remove to wire racks to cool completely.
4. In a microwave, melt candy bars; stir until smooth. Dip one end of each cookie into chocolate; allow excess to drip off. Coat with peanuts. Place on waxed paper; let stand until set.

PECAN GOODY CUPS

These miniature tarts feature pretty pecans, caramel filling and a buttery cream cheese crust that melts in your mouth.

—**JANICE HOSE** HAGERSTOWN, MD

PREP: 35 MIN. + CHILLING
BAKE: 20 MIN./BATCH • **MAKES:** 4 DOZEN

- ¾ **cup butter, softened**
- 6 **ounces cream cheese, softened**
- 2 **cups all-purpose flour**

FILLING
- 1½ **cups packed brown sugar**
- 2 **large eggs**
- 1 **tablespoon butter, melted**
- 48 **pecan halves**

1. In a large bowl, beat butter and cream cheese until light and fluffy. Gradually add flour, beating until mixture forms a ball. Cover and refrigerate for 15 minutes. For filling, in a small bowl, combine the brown sugar, eggs and butter.
2. Roll dough into 1-in. balls. Press onto the bottoms and up the sides of greased miniature muffin cups. Spoon filling into cups; top each with a pecan half.
3. Bake at 350° for 20-25 minutes or until golden brown. Cool for 2-3 minutes before removing from pans to wire racks.

CHOCOLATE-MINT COOKIE CUPS

Peppermint adds a fresh bite to these pretty chocolate cookies. They're my holiday party go-to. If you don't have mini muffin pans, use disposable foil baking cups.

—PAM CORRELL BROCKPORT, PA

PREP: 45 MIN. + CHILLING
BAKE: 10 MIN./BATCH • **MAKES:** 4 DOZEN

- ½ **cup butter, softened**
- 1 **cup sugar**
- 1 **large egg**
- 1 **teaspoon peppermint extract**
- 1½ **cups all-purpose flour**
- ½ **cup baking cocoa**
- ¼ **teaspoon baking soda**
- ¼ **teaspoon baking powder**
- ¼ **teaspoon salt**

TOPPING

- 1 **cup (6 ounces) semisweet chocolate chips**
- ½ **cup heavy whipping cream**
- ¼ **cup white baking chips**
  Green paste food coloring, optional

1. Preheat oven to 350°. In a large bowl, cream butter and sugar until light and fluffy. Beat in egg and extract. Combine flour, cocoa, baking soda, baking powder and salt; gradually add to the creamed mixture and mix well.

2. Shape into 1-in. balls; place in paper-lined miniature muffin cups. Bake 8-10 minutes or until set. Remove to wire racks. Cool completely.

3. Place chocolate chips in a small bowl. In a small saucepan, bring cream just to a boil. Pour over chocolate; whisk until smooth. Cool to room temperature, stirring occasionally. Refrigerate until ganache reaches a piping consistency, about 20 minutes. Pipe over cookies.

4. In a microwave-safe bowl, melt white baking chips at 50% power 1 minute; stir until smooth. If desired, tint with green food coloring. Pipe over tops.

FEBRUARY 19
NATIONAL CHOCOLATE MINT DAY

CHOCOLATE-DIPPED ALMOND MACAROONS

My mother taught my daughter how to make these chocolaty macaroons. When my daughter was 10 years old, she entered a batch in the county fair and won a ribbon.

—TRACI BOOE VEEDERSBURG, IN

PREP: 40 MIN.
BAKE: 10 MIN./BATCH + COOLING
MAKES: 6 DOZEN

- 3 **large egg whites**
  Dash salt
- 1½ **cups confectioners' sugar**
- 2½ **cups unblanched almonds, finely ground**

CHOCOLATE BUTTERCREAM
- 7 **tablespoons sugar**
- 7 **tablespoons water**
- 4 **large egg yolks, lightly beaten**
- ⅔ **cup unsalted butter, softened**
- 1 **tablespoon baking cocoa**

CHOCOLATE DIP
- 9 **ounces semisweet chocolate, chopped and melted**

1. Place egg whites in a small bowl; let stand at room temperature 30 minutes. Line baking sheets with parchment paper.
2. Preheat oven to 350°. Add salt to egg whites; beat on medium speed until soft peaks form. Gradually add confectioners' sugar, 1 tablespoon at a time, beating on high until stiff glossy peaks form and sugar is dissolved. Fold in almonds.
3. Drop by rounded teaspoonfuls 2 in. apart onto prepared baking sheets. Bake 8-12 minutes or until firm to the touch. Cool 5 minutes before removing to wire racks to cool completely.
4. For buttercream, combine sugar and water in a small heavy saucepan. Bring to a boil; cook over medium-high heat until sugar is dissolved. Remove from heat. Whisk a small amount of the hot mixture into egg yolks; return all to pan, stirring constantly. Cook 2 minutes or until the mixture is thickened and reaches 160°, stirring constantly. Remove from heat. Cool to room temperature.
5. In a small bowl, beat butter until fluffy, about 5 minutes. Gradually beat in cooked sugar mixture. Beat in cocoa until smooth. If necessary, refrigerate until buttercream reaches spreading consistency.
6. Spread buttercream over bottom of each cooled cookie. Refrigerate until firm, about 15 minutes. Dip bottom of each cookie in melted chocolate, allowing excess to drip off. Place on waxed paper; let stand until set. Store in an airtight container in the refrigerator.

FROM THE COOKIE JAR

Unsalted butter is often used for baking cookies. Although unsalted butter may be specifically called for in a recipe, it can usually be substituted for salted butter if that's what you have on hand.

FULL-OF-GOODNESS OATMEAL COOKIES

I love to bake, and I bring in extra treats to leave in the faculty lounge for my colleagues. To avoid being blamed for ruining their diets, I came up with this healthier version of the classic oatmeal cookie. It makes snacking on these a good choice instead of a guilty indulgence.

—SHARON BALESTRA BLOOMFIELD, NY

PREP: 35 MIN. • **BAKE:** 10 MIN./BATCH
MAKES: 6 DOZEN

- 2 **tablespoons hot water**
- 1 **tablespoon ground flaxseed**
- 1 **cup pitted dried plums, chopped**
- 1 **cup chopped dates**
- ½ **cup raisins**
- ⅓ **cup butter, softened**
- ¾ **cup packed brown sugar**
- 1 **large egg**
- 2 **teaspoons vanilla extract**
- ½ **cup unsweetened applesauce**
- ¼ **cup maple syrup**
- 1 **tablespoon grated orange peel**
- 3 **cups quick-cooking oats**
- 1 **cup all-purpose flour**
- ½ **cup whole wheat flour**
- 1 **teaspoon baking soda**
- 1 **teaspoon ground cinnamon**
- ½ **teaspoon salt**
- ¼ **teaspoon ground nutmeg**
- ¼ **teaspoon ground cloves**

1. In a small bowl, combine water and flaxseed. In a large bowl, combine the plums, dates and raisins. Cover with boiling water. Let flaxseed and plum mixtures stand for 10 minutes.

2. Meanwhile, in a large bowl, cream butter and brown sugar until light and fluffy. Beat in egg and vanilla. Beat in the applesauce, maple syrup and orange peel. Combine the oats, flours, baking soda, cinnamon, salt, nutmeg and cloves; gradually add to creamed mixture and mix well. Drain plum mixture; stir plum mixture and flaxseed into dough.

3. Drop by rounded teaspoonfuls 2 in. apart onto lightly greased baking sheets. Bake at 350° for 8-11 minutes or until set. Cool for 2 minutes before removing from pans to wire racks.

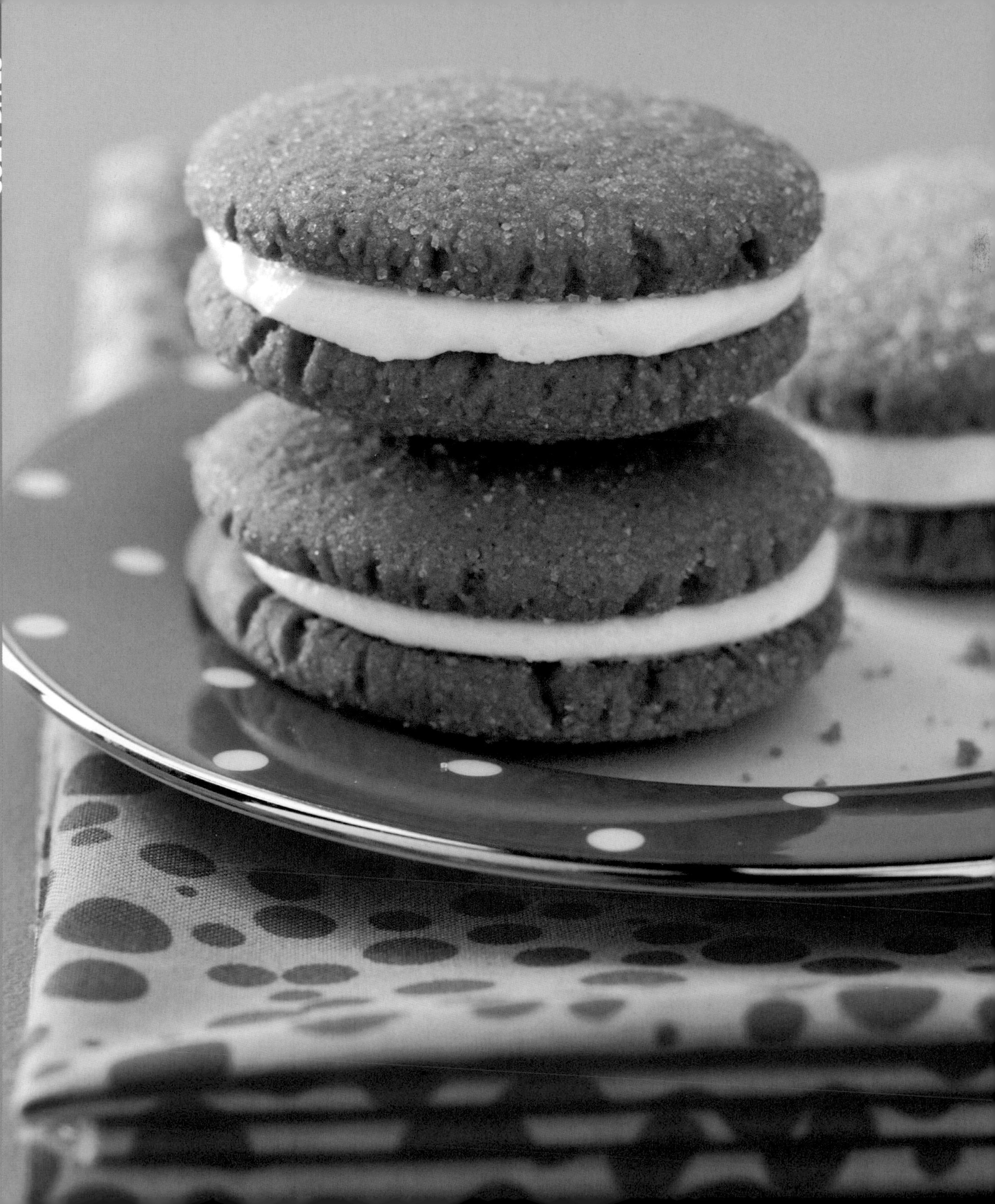

LEMONY GINGERBREAD WHOOPIE PIES

These whoopie pies are spiced just right. They combine two popular flavors in one fun treat. Rolling the chewy cookies in sugar before baking gives them a sweet crunch.
—**JAMIE JONES** MADISON, GA

PREP: 25 MIN. + CHILLING
BAKE: 10 MIN./BATCH + COOLING
MAKES: ABOUT 2 DOZEN

- ¾ cup butter, softened
- ¾ cup packed brown sugar
- ½ cup molasses
- 1 large egg
- 3 cups all-purpose flour
- 2 teaspoons ground ginger
- 1 teaspoon ground cinnamon
- 1 teaspoon baking soda
- ¼ teaspoon salt
- ½ cup sugar

FILLING

- ¾ cup butter, softened
- ¾ cup marshmallow creme
- 1½ cups confectioners' sugar
- ¾ teaspoon lemon extract

1. In a large bowl, cream butter and brown sugar until light and fluffy. Beat in molasses and egg. Combine flour, ginger, cinnamon, baking soda and salt; gradually add to creamed mixture and mix well. Cover and refrigerate at least 3 hours.
2. Preheat oven to 350°. Shape into 1-in. balls; roll in sugar. Place 3 in. apart on ungreased baking sheets. Flatten to ½-in. thickness with a glass dipped in sugar. Bake 8-10 minutes or until set. Cool 2 minutes before removing from pans to wire racks to cool completely.
3. For filling, in a small bowl, beat butter and marshmallow creme until light and fluffy. Gradually beat in confectioners' sugar and extract.
4. Spread filling on the bottoms of half of the cookies, about 1 tablespoon on each; top with remaining cookies.

RASPBERRY & PINK PEPPERCORN MERINGUES

Here, classic meringue gets an update with the subtle flavor of raspberry, a drizzle of chocolate and a fun sprinkling of pink peppercorns. Yum!
—**TASTE OF HOME** TEST KITCHEN

PREP: 15 MIN. • **BAKE:** 20 MIN. + COOLING
MAKES: 4 DOZEN

- 3 large egg whites
- ¼ teaspoon cream of tartar
  Pinch salt
- ¾ cup sugar
- 1 teaspoon raspberry extract
- 5 to 8 drops food coloring, optional
- ¼ cup semisweet chocolate chips
- 1 teaspoon shortening
- 2 tablespoons whole pink peppercorns, crushed

1. Place egg whites in a large bowl; let stand at room temperature 30 minutes. Add cream of tartar and salt; beat on medium speed until soft peaks form. Gradually add sugar, 1 tablespoon at a time, beating on high until stiff glossy peaks form and sugar is dissolved. Beat in extract and, if desired, food coloring.
2. Cut a small hole in the corner of a pastry or plastic bag; insert a large star tip. Fill bag with egg white mixture. Pipe 1¼-in.-diameter cookies onto parchment paper-lined baking sheets. Bake at 300° for 20-25 minutes or until set and dry. (Turn oven off; leave meringues in oven for 1 hour.) Remove to wire racks. In a microwave, melt chocolate chips and shortening; stir until smooth. Drizzle over cookies; sprinkle with peppercorns. Store in an airtight container.

CELEBRATE
SPRING

Relish the excitement of spring with sweet sensations that bake up in a pinch. Starring sweet honey and tangy fruits, these cookies brighten up any day. You'll also find coconut bites perfect for sharing, thin and crispy sugar cookies and treats featuring berries. Shaped cookies make cute Easter goodies, and a variety of biscotti and tea cookies perfectly complement an afternoon break. Celebrate with any of these treats, and they're sure to become new family favorites.

LOOK FOR THE SPECIAL DAYS IN THIS CHAPTER:

Put a spring in your step! St. Patrick's Day, Easter, Waffle Day and National Jelly Bean Day are just a few reasons to bake up some fun this season.

APRIL 10
NATIONAL CINNAMON CRESCENT DAY

BUTTERSWEETS

With cream cheese, cherries and a sweet topping, this recipe turns chocolate chip cookies into something special. What a nice combination of pretty and tasty!

—LEEANN McCUE WEST SPRINGFIELD, MA

PREP: 20 MIN.
BAKE: 10 MIN./BATCH + COOLING
MAKES: 32 COOKIES

Short & Sweet

- 1 tube (18 ounces) refrigerated chocolate chip cookie dough
- 3 ounces cream cheese, softened
- ¾ cup confectioners' sugar
- ¼ cup chopped maraschino cherries
- 1 drop red food coloring, optional
- ½ cup semisweet chocolate chips
- 2 tablespoons butter

1. With a sharp knife, cut cookie dough into eight equal slices. Cut each slice into quarters; roll into balls. Place 2 in. apart on ungreased baking sheets. Bake at 375° for 10 minutes or until cookies are golden brown. Immediately make a deep impression in the center of each cookie using the back of a small melon baller or small spoon. Cool 5 minutes; remove to wire racks to cool completely.

2. Meanwhile, in a bowl, cream the cream cheese and sugar. Pat cherries dry with paper towels. Stir cherries and, if desired, food coloring into the cream cheese mixture.

3. Place a teaspoonful of filling into the center of each cookie. In a heavy saucepan over low heat, melt chocolate chips and butter, stirring occasionally. Drizzle mixture over cookies. Store in the refrigerator.

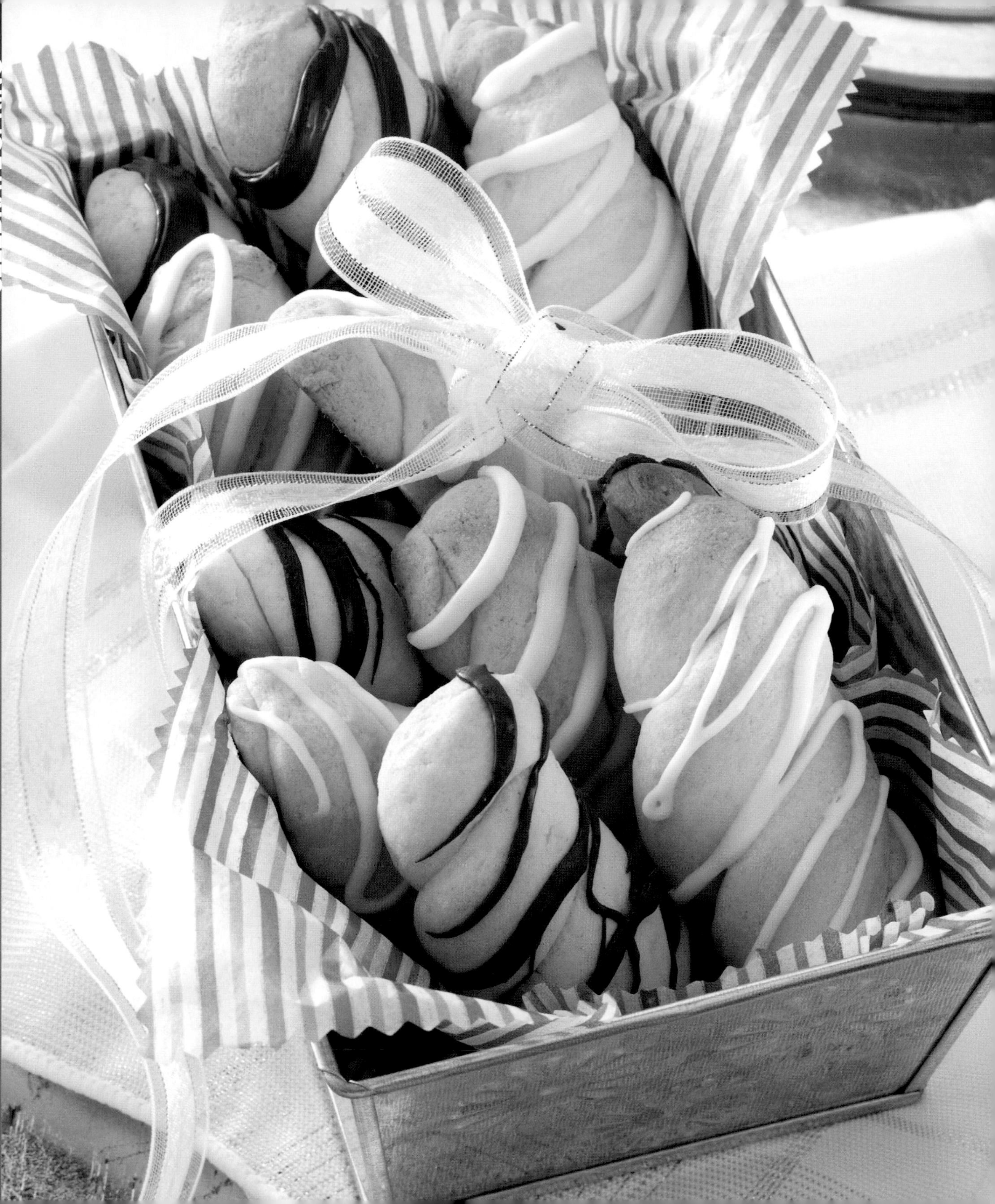

ALMOND-RICOTTA TWISTS

A dear friend gave me this recipe, so I make these to remind me of our time together. I like to drizzle melted white chocolate or chocolate chips on the baked cookies.

—PAULA PRECHTL BROCKPORT, PA

PREP: 45 MIN. + CHILLING
BAKE: 15 MIN./BATCH + COOLING
MAKES: ABOUT 6½ DOZEN

- 1 **cup sugar**
- 1 **cup butter, melted and cooled**
- 2 **large eggs**
- 1 **cup ricotta cheese**
- 2 **teaspoons almond extract**
- 4 **cups all-purpose flour**
- 2 **teaspoons baking powder**
- 1 **teaspoon baking soda**
- 1 **teaspoon salt**
- 1 **cup white baking chips, melted**
- 1 **cup semisweet chocolate chips, melted**

1. In a large bowl, beat sugar and butter until blended. Beat in eggs, then ricotta cheese and extract. In another bowl, whisk flour, baking powder, baking soda and salt; gradually beat into creamed mixture. Refrigerate, covered, 2 hours or until firm enough to shape.

2. Preheat the oven to 350°. Using 1 tablespoon of dough for each cookie, divide in half and shape each into a 3-in. rope. (If dough is soft, work in batches and keep remaining dough chilled until ready to shape.) Twist the two ropes around each other, pinching and tucking under ends. Place cookies 2 in. apart on ungreased baking sheets.

3. Bake 12-15 minutes or until golden brown. Cool 1 minute before removing to wire racks to cool completely.

4. Drizzle melted baking chips over cookies; let stand until set. Store in airtight containers.

DEVIL'S FOOD SANDWICH COOKIES

These cookies freeze really well, so it's good to keep some on hand for last-minute munching. In summer, I often make them larger and use them for ice cream sandwiches.

—MARY REMPEL ALTONA, MB

Short & Sweet

PREP: 15 MIN.
BAKE: 10 MIN./BATCH + COOLING
MAKES: ABOUT 6 DOZEN

- 2 **packages devil's food cake mix (regular size)**
- 1 **cup canola oil**
- 4 **large eggs**

FILLING

- 8 **ounces cream cheese, softened**
- ¼ **cup butter, softened**
- 2½ **cups confectioners' sugar**
- 1 **teaspoon vanilla extract**

1. In a large bowl, combine the cake mixes, oil and eggs until well blended. Roll dough into 1-in. balls. Place 2 in. apart on ungreased baking sheets. Do not flatten.

2. Bake at 350° for 8-10 minutes or until set. Cool for 5 minutes before removing to wire racks. (The cookies will flatten as they cool.)

3. In a small bowl, beat the cream cheese and butter until fluffy. Beat in sugar and vanilla until smooth. Spread or pipe filling on the bottoms of half of the cookies; top with remaining cookies. Store in the refrigerator.

APRICOT THUMBPRINT COOKIES

I enjoy experimenting with cake mixes to make new cookie recipes. I love apricot, but feel free to fill the thumbprint in the center of these goodies with any fruit preserve you like.

—**NANCY A JOHNSON** LAVERNE, OK

PREP: 30 MIN.
BAKE: 15 MIN./BATCH + COOLING
MAKES: ABOUT 7 DOZEN

Short & Sweet

- 2 **packages yellow cake mix (regular size)**
- ½ **cup all-purpose flour**
- 1 **cup canola oil**
- 6 **large eggs**
- 1 **teaspoon ground cinnamon**
- ½ **teaspoon ground ginger**
- 3 **tablespoons water**
- 4 **cups finely chopped pecans, divided**
- ⅔ **cup apricot preserves**

ICING
- 2 **cups confectioners' sugar**
- 3 **to 5 tablespoons water**

1. Preheat oven to 350°. In a large bowl, beat cake mix, flour, oil, 4 eggs, cinnamon and ginger until well blended.
2. In a shallow bowl, whisk water and remaining eggs. Place half of the pecans in another shallow bowl. Shape dough into 1-in. balls. Dip in egg mixture then coat with pecans, adding remaining pecans to bowl as needed. Place cookies 2 in. apart on greased baking sheets.
3. Press a deep indentation in center of each cookie with the end of a wooden spoon handle. Fill each with preserves. Bake 12-14 minutes or until golden brown. Remove from pans to wire racks to cool completely.
4. In a medium bowl, combine the confectioners' sugar and enough water to achieve a drizzling consistency. Drizzle over cookies. Let stand until set.
FREEZE OPTION *Freeze drizzled cookies, layered between waxed paper, in freezer containers. To use, thaw in covered containers.*

CRISPY POTATO CHIP COOKIES

Give this cookie a try the next time you're looking for a sweet and salty treat. They quickly bake to a crispy golden brown, and they disappear even faster!

—**MONNA LU BAUER** LEXINGTON, KY

PREP: 15 MIN. • **BAKE:** 10 MIN./BATCH
MAKES: 4 DOZEN

- 1 cup butter-flavored shortening
- ¾ cup sugar
- ¾ cup packed brown sugar
- 2 large eggs
- 2 cups all-purpose flour
- 1 teaspoon baking soda
- 2 cups crushed potato chips
- 1 cup butterscotch chips

1. Preheat oven to 375°. In a large bowl, cream shortening and sugars until light and fluffy. Beat in eggs. In another bowl, whisk flour and baking soda; gradually beat into creamed mixture. Stir in potato chips and butterscotch chips.

2. Drop dough by tablespoonfuls 2 in. apart onto ungreased baking sheets. Bake 10-12 minutes or until golden brown. Cool on pans 1 minute. Remove to wire racks to cool.

★ ★ ★ ★ ★ **READER REVIEW**

"One of the best cookies I've ever tasted. I like to leave the crushed potato chips just a little coarse for more crunch. Good for a potluck crowd."

MARYKAUHI TASTEOFHOME.COM

BEST-EVER SUGAR COOKIES

What makes these cookies the best ever? A delicious cream cheese dough flavored with vanilla, almond and a hint of nutmeg!

—**CHRISTY HINRICHS** PARKVILLE, MO

PREP: 30 MIN. + CHILLING
BAKE: 10 MIN./BATCH + COOLING
MAKES: 4 DOZEN

- 1 **cup butter, softened**
- 3 **ounces cream cheese, softened**
- 1 **cup sugar**
- 1 **large egg yolk**
- ½ **teaspoon vanilla extract**
- ¼ **teaspoon almond extract**
- 2¼ **cups all-purpose flour**
- ½ **teaspoon salt**
- ¼ **teaspoon baking soda**
- ⅛ **teaspoon ground nutmeg**

ICING

- 3¾ **cups confectioners' sugar**
- ⅓ **cup water**
- 4 **teaspoons meringue powder**
  Assorted colors of liquid food coloring

1. In a large bowl, cream the butter, cream cheese and sugar until light and fluffy. Beat in egg yolk and extracts. Combine the flour, salt, baking soda and nutmeg; gradually add to creamed mixture. Cover and refrigerate 3 hours or until easy to handle.

2. On a lightly floured surface, roll out dough to ⅛-in. thickness. Cut with floured 2½-in. cookie cutters.

3. Place 1 in. apart on ungreased baking sheets. Bake at 375° for 8-10 minutes or until the edges begin to brown. Cool for 2 minutes before removing from pans to wire racks to cool completely.

4. For icing, in a small bowl, combine the confectioners' sugar, water and meringue powder; beat on low speed just until combined. Beat on high for 4 minutes or until soft peaks form. Cover icing with plastic wrap or damp paper towels between uses.

5. Working quickly, spread or pipe icing over cookies; let dry at room temperature for several hours or until firm-set. Use toothpicks or new small paintbrushes and food coloring to make designs on the cookies. Let stand until set. Store in an airtight container.

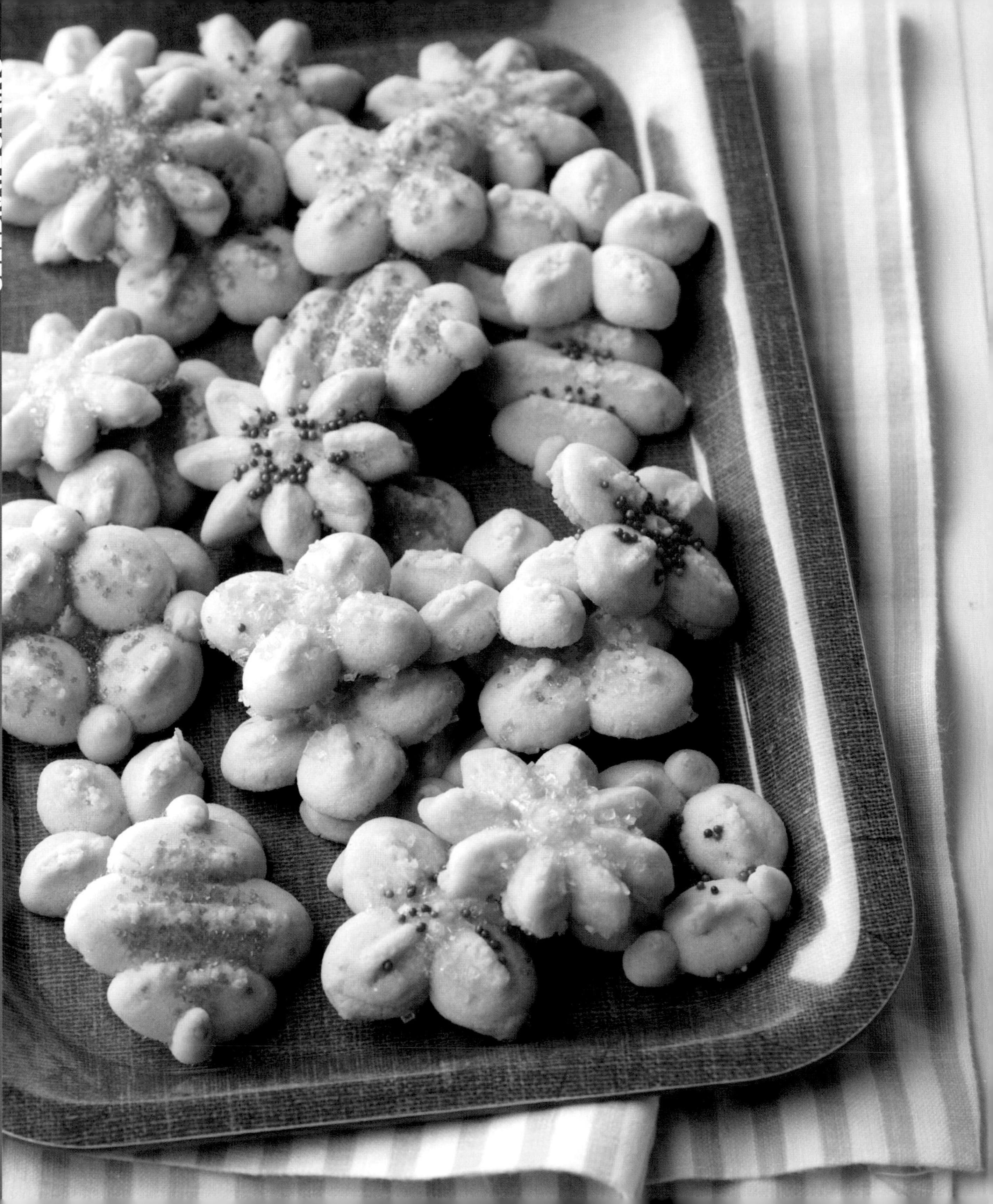

ORANGE SPRITZ COOKIES

Spritz cookies don't have to be reserved for Christmas. This variation has a rich, buttery shortbread taste and texture with a hint of orange flavor. They are a delightful addition to my baking lineup.

—SEAN FLEMING ST. CHARLES, IL

PREP: 25 MIN. • **BAKE:** 10 MIN./BATCH
MAKES: ABOUT 5½ DOZEN

- ½ cup butter, softened
- 3 ounces cream cheese, softened
- ½ cup packed brown sugar
- 2 teaspoons grated orange peel
- ½ teaspoon orange or vanilla extract
- 1½ cups all-purpose flour
- ¼ teaspoon salt
- Colored sugar

1. In a large bowl, cream the butter, cream cheese and brown sugar until light and fluffy. Beat in orange peel and extract. Combine flour and salt; gradually add to creamed mixture.

2. Using a cookie press fitted with the disk of your choice, press cookies 1 in. apart onto ungreased baking sheets. Sprinkle with colored sugar. Bake at 375° for 6-9 minutes or until lightly browned. Cool for 2 minutes before removing to wire racks.

LEMON SLICE SUGAR COOKIES

Here's a light, refreshing variation of my grandmother's sugar cookie recipe. Lemon pudding mix and a citrus icing add subtle tartness that tingles the taste buds.

—MELISSA TURKINGTON
CAMANO ISLAND, WA

PREP: 15 MIN. + CHILLING
GBAKE: 10 MIN. + COOLING
MAKES: 2 DOZEN

- ½ cup unsalted butter, softened
- 1 package (3.4 ounces) instant lemon pudding mix
- ½ cup sugar
- 1 large egg
- 2 tablespoons 2% milk
- 1½ cups all-purpose flour

- 1 teaspoon baking powder
- ¼ teaspoon salt

ICING
- ⅔ cup confectioners' sugar
- 2 to 4 teaspoons lemon juice

1. In a large bowl, cream butter, pudding mix and sugar until light and fluffy. Beat in egg and milk. In another bowl, whisk flour, baking powder and salt; gradually beat into creamed mixture.

2. Divide dough in half. On a lightly floured surface, shape each into a 6-in.-long roll. Wrap in plastic; refrigerate for 3 hours or until firm.

3. Preheat oven to 375°. Unwrap and cut dough crosswise into ½-in. slices. Place 1 in. apart on ungreased baking sheets. Bake 8-10 minutes or until edges are light brown. Cool on pans 2 minutes. Remove to wire racks to cool completely.

4. In a small bowl, mix confectioners' sugar and enough lemon juice to reach a drizzling consistency. Drizzle over cookies. Let stand until set.

TO MAKE AHEAD *This dough can be made 2 days in advance. Wrap in plastic and place in a resealable bag. Store in the refrigerator.*

FREEZE OPTION *Place wrapped logs in a resealable plastic freezer bag and freeze. To use, unwrap frozen logs and cut into slices. Bake as directed, increasing time by 1-2 minutes.*

CAPPUCCINO FLATS

These coffee-flavored cookies are so delicious, most people can't believe they're made in my kitchen instead of a gourmet bakery. You've got to give them a try!

—JACQUELINE CLINE DRUMMOND, WI

PREP: 20 MIN. + CHILLING
BAKE: 10 MIN./BATCH + STANDING
MAKES: 4½ DOZEN

- ½ cup butter, softened
- ½ cup shortening
- ½ cup sugar
- ½ cup packed brown sugar
- 1 tablespoon instant coffee granules
- 1 teaspoon warm water
- 1 large egg
- 2 ounces unsweetened chocolate, melted and cooled
- 2 cups all-purpose flour
- 1 teaspoon ground cinnamon
- ¼ teaspoon salt

GLAZE
- 1½ cups semisweet chocolate chips
- 3 tablespoons shortening

1. In a large bowl, cream butter, shortening and sugars until light and fluffy. Dissolve coffee in water; add to creamed mixture with egg and melted chocolate until blended. Combine the flour, cinnamon and salt; gradually add to creamed mixture and mix well (dough will be sticky). Shape into two 6½-in. rolls; wrap each in plastic. Refrigerate for 4 hours or until firm.

2. Unwrap rolls and cut into ¼-in. slices. Place 2 in. apart on ungreased baking sheets. Bake at 350° for 10-12 minutes or until firm. Remove to wire racks to cool completely.

3. In a microwave, melt chocolate chips and shortening; stir until smooth. Dip each cookie halfway in chocolate; allow excess to drip off. Place on waxed paper; let stand until set.

MELT-IN-YOUR-MOUTH LEMON CUTOUTS

Full of flavor, these cookies are great for any time of year and always popular with family and friends.

—PATRICIA QUINN OMAHA, NE

PREP: 35 MIN.
BAKE: 10 MIN./BATCH + COOLING
MAKES: 5 DOZEN

- 1 **cup shortening**
- 1½ **cups sugar**
- 2 **large eggs**
- 1½ **teaspoons lemon extract**
- ½ **teaspoon vanilla extract**
- 3½ **cups all-purpose flour**
- 2 **teaspoons baking powder**
- ½ **teaspoon salt**

FROSTING

- 1 **package (8 ounces) cream cheese, softened**
- ½ **cup shortening**
- 1 **teaspoon lemon extract**
- 1 **teaspoon vanilla extract**
- 2 **cups confectioners' sugar**
  Yellow colored sugar

1. In a large bowl, cream shortening and sugar until light and fluffy. Beat in eggs and extracts. In another bowl, whisk flour, baking powder and salt; gradually beat into creamed mixture.

2. Preheat oven to 375°. Divide dough in half. On a lightly floured surface, roll each portion to ⅛-in. thickness. Cut with a floured 3-in. flower-shaped cookie cutter. Place 1 in. apart on greased baking sheets.

3. Bake 6-8 minutes or until edges are light brown. Cool on pans 2 minutes. Remove to wire racks to cool completely.

4. For frosting, in a bowl, beat cream cheese, shortening and extracts until blended. Gradually beat in confectioners' sugar until smooth. Spread over cookies; sprinkle with colored sugar. Let stand until set. Store in airtight containers in the refrigerator.

BUTTERFINGER COOKIES

These simple cookies don't last long, so you might want to bake a double batch!

—**CAROL KITCHENS** RIDGELAND, MS

PREP: 15 MIN. • **BAKE:** 30 MIN.
MAKES: 4 DOZEN

- ½ cup butter, softened
- ¾ cup sugar
- ⅔ cup packed brown sugar
- 2 large egg whites
- 1¼ cups chunky peanut butter
- 1½ teaspoons vanilla extract
- 1 cup all-purpose flour
- ½ teaspoon baking soda
- ¼ teaspoon salt
- 5 Butterfinger candy bars (2.1 ounces each), chopped

1. In a large bowl, cream butter and sugars until light and fluffy. Beat in egg whites. Beat in the peanut butter and vanilla. Combine the flour, baking soda and salt; gradually add to the creamed mixture. Stir in candy bars.

2. Shape into 1½-in. balls; place 2 in. apart on greased baking sheets. Bake at 350° for 10-12 minutes or until golden brown. Remove to wire racks to cool.

HOW TO ROLL COOKIE DOUGH INTO BALLS

A 1-in. ball takes about 2 teaspoons of dough. If the dough is sticky, lightly flour your hands, then roll the dough between your palms until a ball forms.

MARCH 17
HAPPY ST. PATRICK'S DAY!

2. Divide dough in half; shape each half into a 7½-in.-long roll. Roll in chopped pistachios. Wrap in plastic. Refrigerate 2 hours or until firm.

3. Preheat oven to 375°. Unwrap and cut crosswise into ¼-in. slices. Place 1 in. apart on ungreased baking sheets. Press a whole pistachio into the center of each cookie.

4. Bake 7-9 minutes or until edges are lightly browned. Remove from pans to wire racks to cool.

OREO COOKIE BITES

For cute and easy treats, I roll Oreos and cream cheese into balls and dunk them in white chocolate. Topped with colored sugar or sprinkles, they're a pretty sight in one bite.
—CARLA GIORGIO NEW YORK, NY

Short & Sweet

PREP: 30 MIN. + CHILLING
MAKES: ABOUT 3 DOZEN

- 1 package (14.3 ounces) Oreo cookies
- 1 package (8 ounces) cream cheese, softened
- 1 package (10 to 12 ounces) white baking chips
  Colored sugar or sprinkles, optional

1. Pulse cookies in a food processor until fine crumbs form. Add cream cheese; pulse just until blended. Refrigerate, covered, until easy to handle. Shape into 1-in. balls; freeze for several hours or overnight.

2. Microwave baking chips on high until melted; stir until smooth. Dip balls in melted chips; allow excess to drip off. Place on waxed paper. Drizzle with remaining chocolate or, if desired, decorate with sugar. Let stand until set. Refrigerate until serving.

PISTACHIO CREAM CHEESE COOKIES

My son-in-law is a big fan of pistachios, so he loves these buttery cookies. They're lovely in spring, but I bake these for him all year long.
—LILY JULOW LAWRENCEVILLE, GA

PREP: 30 MIN. + CHILLING
BAKE: 10 MIN./BATCH • **MAKES:** 5 DOZEN

- ½ cup butter, softened
- 3 ounces cream cheese, softened
- 1½ cups confectioners' sugar
- 1 large egg
- 3 teaspoons grated lemon peel
- 1½ teaspoons vanilla extract
- 1 to 2 drops green food coloring
- 2½ cups all-purpose flour
- ½ teaspoon baking powder
- ½ teaspoon salt
- ½ cup finely chopped pistachios
- 60 shelled pistachios (about ⅓ cup)

1. In a large bowl, beat butter, cream cheese and confectioners' sugar until blended. Beat in egg, lemon peel, vanilla and food coloring. In another bowl, whisk flour, baking powder and salt; gradually beat into creamed mixture.

NO-BAKE CHOCOLATE MINT TREATS

At our house, everyone lends a hand to make these simple chocolate-covered cookies. Decorate them with sprinkles to match any occasion, holiday or season.

—**LILY JULOW** LAWRENCEVILLE, GA

Short & Sweet

PREP: 15 MIN. + FREEZING
MAKES: ABOUT 3 DOZEN

- 3 **cups crushed chocolate wafers (about 65 wafers)**
- 6 **ounces cream cheese, softened**
  Sugar
- 1 **pound chocolate mint candy coating disks, chopped**
- 2 **tablespoons shortening**
  Green and white sprinkles, optional

1. In a large bowl, combine chocolate wafer crumbs and cream cheese. Shape into 1-in. balls. Coat bottom of a glass with cooking spray, then dip in sugar; flatten balls to ¼-in. thickness. (Re-dip glass in sugar as needed.) Freeze 30 minutes or until firm.

2. In a microwave, melt candy coating disks and shortening; stir until smooth. Dip cookies in coating mixture; allow excess to drip off. Place on waxed paper; if desired, decorate immediately with sprinkles. Store between layers of waxed paper in an airtight container in the refrigerator.

NOTE *Chocolate candy coating disks are sometimes called chocolate melts. Look for them in the baking aisle at the supermarket.*

OATMEAL GINGERSNAPS

I always get compliments on these delicious, chewy cookies. The aroma fills my kitchen when they're baking and never fails to set a happy mood.
—SHERRY HARKE SOUTH BEND, IN

PREP: 20 MIN. • **BAKE:** 10 MIN./BATCH
MAKES: ABOUT 3½ DOZEN

- ½ **cup shortening**
- 1 **cup sugar**
- 1 **large egg**
- ¼ **cup molasses**
- 1½ **cups all-purpose flour**
- ¾ **cup quick-cooking oats**
- 1 **teaspoon baking soda**
- 1 **teaspoon ground ginger**
- ¼ **teaspoon salt**
- ¼ **teaspoon ground cloves**
  Additional sugar

1. In a large bowl, cream shortening and sugar until light and fluffy. Beat in egg and molasses. Combine the dry ingredients; gradually add to creamed mixture and mix well. Roll into 1-in. balls; roll balls in the additional sugar.

2. Place 2 in. apart on greased baking sheets. Flatten with a glass dipped in sugar. Bake at 350° for 10 minutes or until set (do not overbake). Remove to wire racks to cool.

NO-BAKE FRUITY PEBBLES COOKIES

Keep your kitchen cool with these freezer cookies made with fruity cereal. They're extra-sweet, and kids have fun helping assemble them.
—*TASTE OF HOME* TEST KITCHEN

PREP: 15 MIN. + FREEZING
MAKES: ABOUT 2 DOZEN

- 4 cups Fruity Pebbles cereal
- 6 ounces cream cheese, softened
  Sugar
- 8 ounces white candy coating
- 2 tablespoons shortening
- ⅛ teaspoon lemon extract, optional
  Sprinkles, optional

1. Place cereal in a food processor; process until finely crushed. Add cream cheese; process until blended. Shape into 1-in. balls. Coat bottom of a glass with cooking spray, then dip in sugar. Press cookies with bottom of glass to flatten, re-dipping in sugar as needed. Flatten to ¼-in. thickness with bottom of glass. Freeze 30 minutes or until firm.

2. In a microwave, melt candy coating and shortening; stir until smooth. Stir in lemon extract if desired. Dip cookies in coating mixture; allow excess to drip off. Place on waxed paper-lined baking sheets. If desired, immediately decorate with sprinkles. Store between layers of waxed paper in an airtight container in the refrigerator.

GINGERSNAP COCONUT CREAMS

I switch up a holiday classic with a lovely coconut filling. It's a fun change-of-pace treat!

—DARLENE BRENDEN SALEM, OR

....

PREP: 35 MIN.
BAKE: 10 MIN./BATCH + COOLING
MAKES: 4 DOZEN

- ⅓ **cup butter, softened**
- ⅓ **cup packed brown sugar**
- 1 **large egg**
- ⅓ **cup molasses**
- 1½ **cups all-purpose flour**
- 1 **teaspoon baking soda**
- ½ **teaspoon ground ginger**
- ½ **teaspoon ground cinnamon**
- ¼ **teaspoon ground cloves**

FILLING
- ¼ **cup butter, softened**
- ¾ **cup confectioners' sugar**
- ½ **teaspoon orange extract**
- ¼ **cup flaked coconut**

1. Preheat oven to 375°. In a large bowl, cream butter and brown sugar until light and fluffy. Beat in egg and molasses. In another bowl, whisk flour, baking soda and spices; gradually beat into creamed mixture.

2. Drop dough by level teaspoonfuls 1 in. apart onto parchment paper-lined baking sheets. Bake 6-8 minutes or just until edges begin to brown. Remove from pans to wire racks to cool completely.

3. For filling, in a small bowl, mix butter, confectioners' sugar and extract until blended; stir in coconut. Spread on bottoms of half of the cookies; cover with remaining cookies.

FROM THE COOKIE JAR

Store gingerbread cookies in a container separate from other cookies. The ingredients and spices used in gingerbread can often affect the flavor and aroma of other cookies stored with them.

CANNOLI WAFER SANDWICHES

My family loves to visit a local Italian place that has a wonderful dessert buffet. Their cannoli are among our favorites, so I just had to come up with my own version. These cookies are best if served the same day so the wafers stay crisp.

—NICHI LARSON SHAWNEE, KS

PREP: 35 MIN. + STANDING
MAKES: 3½ DOZEN

- 1 cup whole-milk ricotta cheese
- ¼ cup confectioners' sugar
- 1 tablespoon sugar
- ¼ teaspoon vanilla extract
- 1 package (12 ounces) vanilla wafers
- 12 ounces white candy coating, melted
- ½ cup miniature semisweet chocolate chips
  Additional confectioners' sugar

1. In a small bowl, mix the ricotta cheese, confectioners' sugar, sugar and vanilla until blended. Spread 1 scant teaspoon of the filling on bottoms of half of the wafers, cover with remaining wafers.

2. Dip each sandwich cookie halfway into candy coating; allow excess to drip off. Place on waxed paper; sprinkle with mini chocolate chips. Let stand until set, about 10 minutes.

3. Serve within 2 hours or refrigerate until serving. Dust with additional confectioners' sugar just before serving.

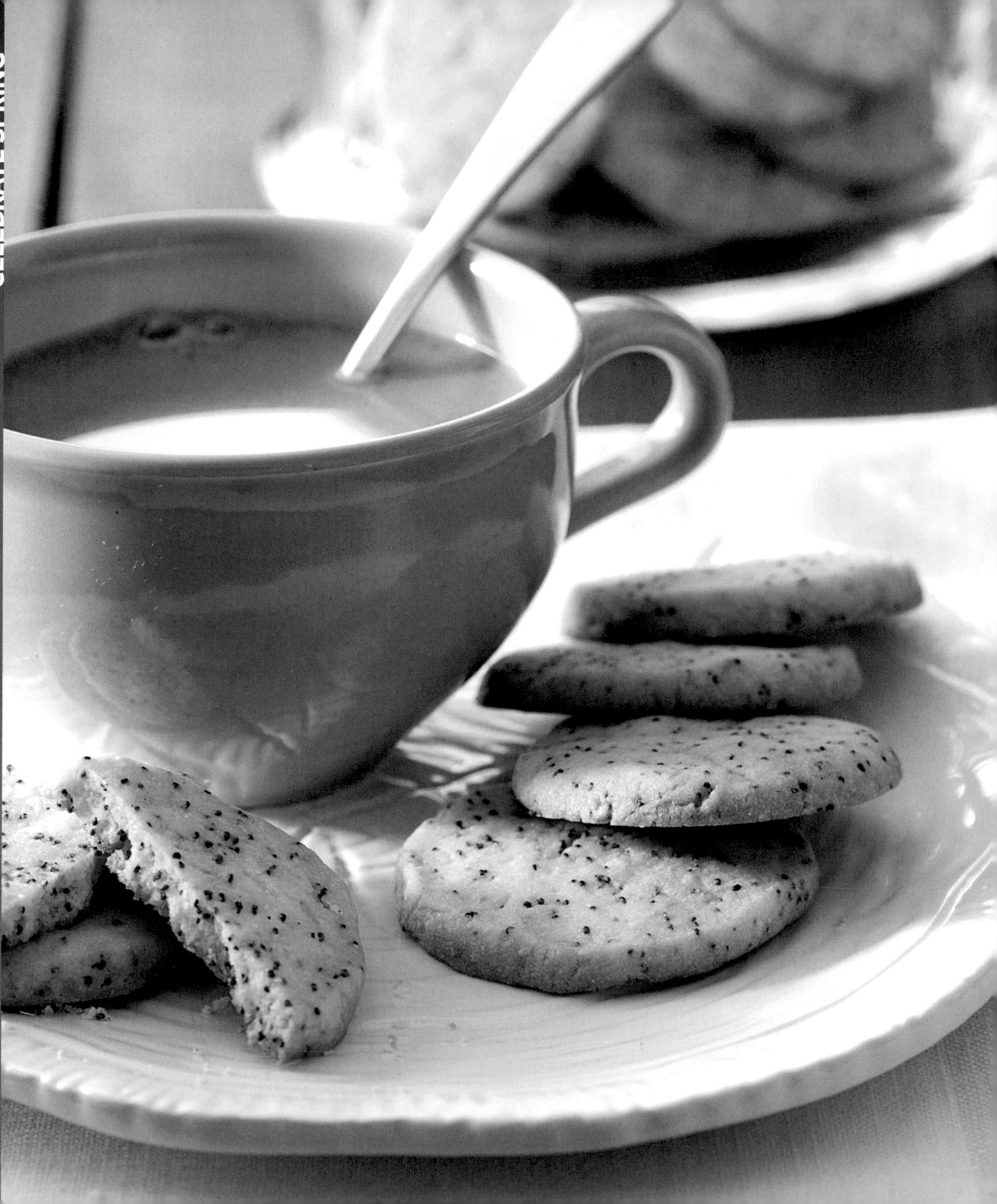

LEMON POPPY SEED SLICES

My mom taught me to bake, and I use lots of recipes from her abundant collection, including this one.
—**PAULINE PIRAINO** BAY SHORE, NY

PREP: 10 MIN. + CHILLING
BAKE: 10 MIN./BATCH • **MAKES:** 5½ DOZEN

- ¾ cup butter, softened
- 1 cup sugar
- 1 large egg
- 1 tablespoon 2% milk
- 2 teaspoons finely grated lemon peel
- ½ teaspoon vanilla extract
- ½ teaspoon lemon extract, optional
- 2½ cups all-purpose flour
- ¼ cup poppy seeds

1. In a large bowl, cream butter and sugar until light and fluffy. Beat in egg, milk, lemon peel and extracts. Gradually add flour and mix well. Stir in poppy seeds. Shape into two 8-in. rolls; wrap each in plastic. Refrigerate 3 hours or until firm.

2. Preheat oven to 350°. Unwrap and cut rolls into ¼-in. slices. Place 2 in. apart on ungreased baking sheets. Bake for 10-12 minutes or until edges are golden. Cool 2 minutes before removing to wire racks to cool completely.

CHOCOLATE MALTED COOKIES

The next best thing to malted milk shakes! With malted milk powder and chocolate syrup plus plenty of chocolate chips, these are the yummiest cookies I've ever tasted... and with six kids, I've made a lot of them over the years.
—**TERI RASEY** CADILLAC, MI

START TO FINISH: 30 MIN.
MAKES: ABOUT 1½ DOZEN

- 1 cup butter-flavored shortening
- 1¼ cups packed brown sugar
- ½ cup malted milk powder
- 2 tablespoons chocolate syrup
- 1 tablespoon vanilla extract
- 1 large egg
- 2 cups all-purpose flour
- 1 teaspoon baking soda
- ½ teaspoon salt
- 1½ cups semisweet chocolate chunks
- 1 cup milk chocolate chips

1. In a large bowl, beat the shortening, brown sugar, malted milk powder, chocolate syrup and vanilla for 2 minutes. Add the egg.

2. Combine the flour, baking soda and salt; gradually add to creamed mixture, mixing well after each addition. Stir in chocolate chunks and chips.

3. Shape dough into 2-in. balls; place 3 in. apart on ungreased baking sheets. Bake at 375° for 12-14 minutes or until golden brown. Cool for 2 minutes before removing to a wire rack.

CHOCOLATE-COVERED RAISIN COOKIES

My family loves these chewy cookies. While the moist bites are a wonderful change of pace from traditional Christmas cookies, they also make a terrific year-round treat.
—**KAREN BOURNE** MAGRATH, AB

PREP: 15 MIN. • **BAKE:** 10 MIN./BATCH
MAKES: ABOUT 6 DOZEN

- 1 **cup butter, softened**
- 1 **cup sugar**
- 1 **cup packed brown sugar**
- 3 **large eggs**
- 1 **teaspoon vanilla extract**
- 2 **cups all-purpose flour**
- 2 **cups quick-cooking oats**
- 2 **teaspoons baking powder**
- 1 **teaspoon baking soda**
- ½ **teaspoon salt**
- 2 **cups Rice Krispies**
- 1½ **cups chocolate-covered raisins**
- 1 **cup flaked coconut**

In a bowl, cream butter and sugars. Add the eggs, one at a time, beating well after each addition. Beat in vanilla. Combine the flour, oats, baking powder, baking soda and salt; add to the creamed mixture and mix well. Stir in cereal, raisins and coconut. Drop by tablespoonfuls 2 in. apart onto ungreased baking sheets. Bake at 350° for 10-12 minutes or until lightly browned. Cool for 5 minutes before removing to wire racks.

★ ★ ★ ★ ★ **READER REVIEW**

"Very good cookies. I used mini chocolate chips because it was what I had. Everyone liked them. Yummy."

ANQ TASTEOFHOME.COM

CATHEDRAL COOKIES

Kids love the colorful marshmallows in my no-bake slices, which mimic the appearance of stained glass. Part cookie, part candy, these treats light up snack time.
—**CAROL SHAFFER** CAPE GIRARDEAU, MO

PREP: 10 MIN. + FREEZING
COOK: 10 MIN. + CHILLING
MAKES: ABOUT 5 DOZEN

- 1 **cup (6 ounces) semisweet chocolate chips**
- 2 **tablespoons butter**
- 1 **large egg, lightly beaten**
- 3 **cups pastel miniature marshmallows**
- ½ **cup chopped pecans or walnuts**
- 1 **cup flaked coconut**

1. In a heavy saucepan, melt chocolate chips and butter over low heat, stirring occasionally. Stir a small amount into the egg, then return all to pan. Cook and stir over low heat for 2 minutes. Pour into a bowl; let cool for 15 minutes. Gently stir in the marshmallows and nuts. Chill for 30 minutes.
2. On a sheet of waxed paper, shape the mixture into a 1½-in.-diameter log. Place coconut on another sheet of waxed paper. Gently roll log over coconut to coat sides. Wrap up tightly, twisting ends to seal.
3. Freeze for 4 hours or overnight. Remove waxed paper. Cut into ¼-in. slices. Store in an airtight container in the refrigerator.

MARCH 24
NATIONAL
CHOCOLATE
COVERED
RAISINS
DAY

BUTTER PECAN BISCOTTI

Here's a crunchy cookie that is perfect for dunking. These biscotti have a pleasant coffee flavor and subtle sweetness.

—*TASTE OF HOME* TEST KITCHEN

Short & Sweet

PREP: 25 MIN. • **BAKE:** 40 MIN. + COOLING
MAKES: ABOUT 2 DOZEN

- 1   package butter pecan cake mix (regular size)
- 1   cup all-purpose flour
- ½   cup butter, melted
- 2   large eggs
- 3   tablespoons maple syrup
- 2½ teaspoons instant coffee granules
- 1   teaspoon vanilla extract
- 1   cup white baking chips
- 1   cup confectioners' sugar
- 2   tablespoons brewed coffee
- 1   cup finely chopped pecans

1. In a large bowl, beat the cake mix, flour, butter, eggs, syrup, coffee granules and vanilla until well blended (dough will be very thick). Fold in baking chips. Divide dough in half.

2. On an ungreased baking sheet, shape each portion into a 12x2-in. rectangle. Bake at 350° for 30-35 minutes or until golden brown.

3. Place pans on wire racks. When cool enough to handle, transfer to a cutting board; cut diagonally with a serrated knife into ¾-in. slices. Place cut side down on ungreased baking sheets.

4. Bake for 10-15 minutes or until firm. Remove to wire racks to cool completely.

5. Combine confectioners' sugar and coffee in a small bowl. Drizzle over the biscotti; sprinkle with pecans. Let stand until set. Store in an airtight container.

CRISP LEMON SHORTBREAD

Buttery, crispy shortbread squares get a tangy twist of citrus when you mix in lemon juice and zest. Sprinkling on coarse sugar adds a bit of sparkle.

—MARCIA WHITNEY GAINESVILLE, FL

PREP: 20 MIN. • **BAKE:** 20 MIN.
MAKES: 2 DOZEN

- ¾ **cup butter, softened**
- ½ **cup confectioners' sugar**
- 1 **teaspoon grated lemon peel**
- 1 **tablespoon lemon juice**
- 1½ **cups all-purpose flour**
- 2 **teaspoons coarse sugar**

1. Preheat oven to 325°. In a bowl, beat butter, confectioners' sugar and lemon peel until blended. Beat in lemon juice. Gradually beat in flour.

2. Divide dough into four portions. On a lightly floured surface, roll each portion of the dough into a 5x3½-in. rectangle. Transfer to ungreased baking sheets. Cut each rectangle into six squares, but do not separate. Prick tops with a fork. Sprinkle with sugar.

3. Bake 20-25 minutes or until light brown. Cool on pans 10 minutes. Transfer shortbread to a cutting board; recut into squares. Cool on a wire rack.

★ ★ ★ ★ ★ 5 STAR TIP

The key to melt-in-your-mouth shortbread cookies is to avoid overmixing the dough. That's why most recipes call for the butter to be softened but not melted. Similarly, beating the butter and sugar together first means you don't have to work the dough as hard when adding the flour.

DUTCH WAFFLE COOKIES

My mom taught me how to make these waffle-iron cookies. Now I have my friends bring their waffle irons to my house, and we make big batches.

—RACHEL SETALA SURREY, BC

PREP: 40 MIN. • **COOK:** 5 MIN./BATCH
MAKES: ABOUT 6 DOZEN

- 1 **cup butter, softened**
- 1 **cup sugar**
- 2 **large eggs**
- ½ **cup 2% milk**
- 1 **tablespoon vanilla extract**
- 4 **cups all-purpose flour**
- 1¾ **teaspoons baking powder**
- ¾ **teaspoon baking soda**
  Confectioners' sugar, optional

1. In large bowl, beat butter and sugar until blended. Beat in eggs, milk and vanilla. In another bowl, whisk flour, baking powder and baking soda; gradually beat into butter mixture.

2. Shape level tablespoons of dough into balls; place 2 in. apart on a preheated waffle iron coated with cooking spray. Bake on medium heat 3-4 minutes or until cookies are golden brown. Remove to wire racks to cool. If desired, dust with confectioners' sugar.

FREEZE OPTION *Freeze cookies, layered between waxed paper, in freezer containers. To use, thaw in covered containers. If desired, dust with additional confectioners' sugar.*

MARCH 25
WAFFLE DAY

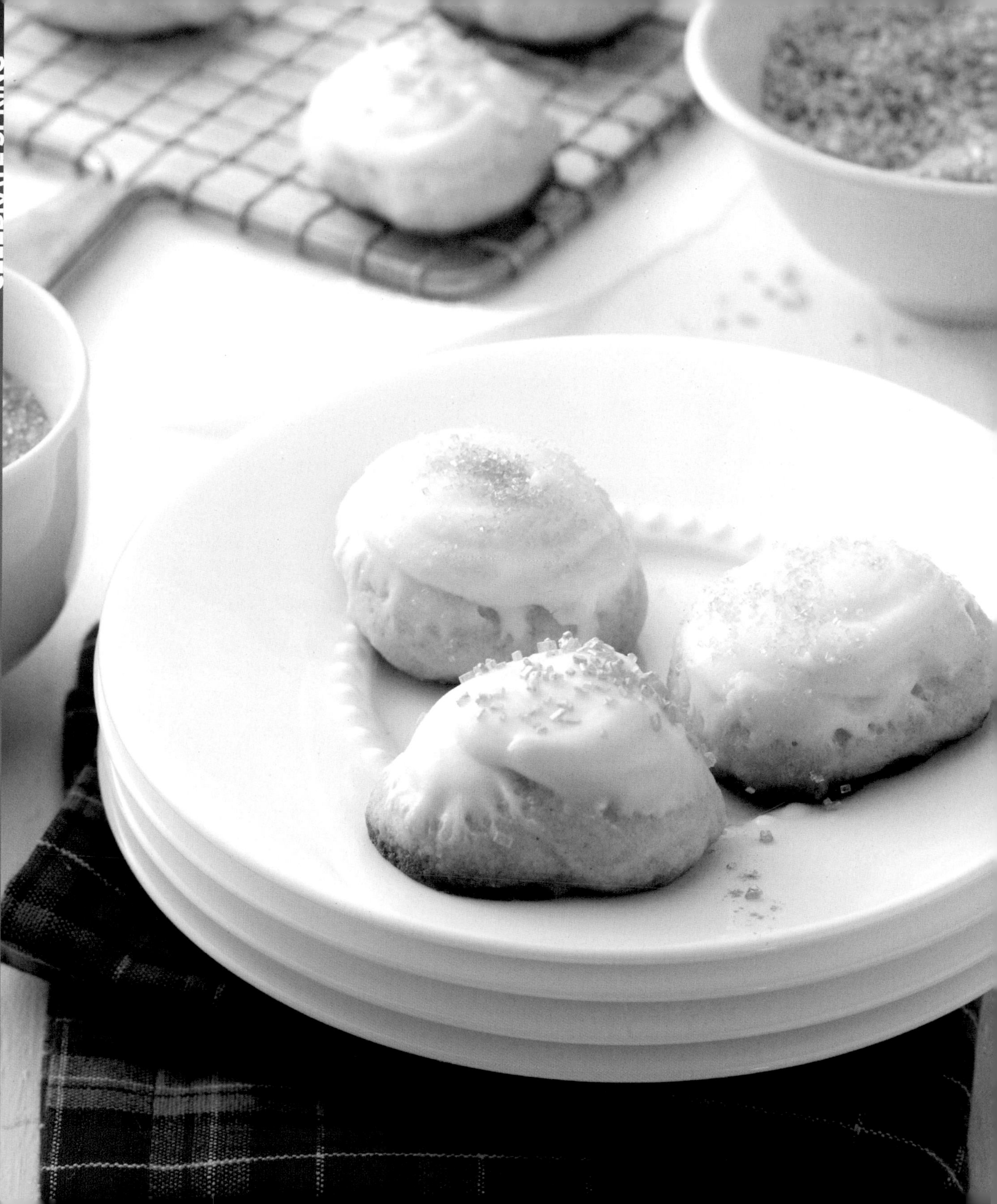

RICOTTA DROP COOKIES

A single batch of these mouthwatering cookies is never enough. I usually make one to give away and two more to keep at home. Adding ricotta cheese to the batter makes the morsels extra soft.

—**DORIS MARSHALL** STRASBURG, PA

PREP: 25 MIN.
BAKE: 10 MIN./BATCH + COOLING
MAKES: 8½ DOZEN

- 1 **cup butter, softened**
- 2 **cups sugar**
- 3 **large eggs**
- 1 **carton (15 ounces) ricotta cheese**
- 2 **teaspoons vanilla extract**
- 4 **cups all-purpose flour**
- 1 **teaspoon salt**
- 1 **teaspoon baking soda**

FROSTING

- ¼ **cup butter, softened**
- 3 **to 4 cups confectioners' sugar**
- ½ **teaspoon vanilla extract**
- 3 **to 4 tablespoons milk**
   Colored sprinkles

1. In a bowl, cream butter and sugar. Add the eggs, one at a time, beating well after each addition. Beat in ricotta and vanilla. Combine flour, salt and baking soda; gradually add to creamed mixture.

2. Drop by rounded teaspoonfuls 2 in. apart onto greased baking sheets. Bake at 350° for 10-12 minutes or until lightly browned. Remove to wire racks to cool.

3. In a large bowl, cream softened butter, confectioners' sugar, vanilla and enough milk to reach spreading consistency. Frost cooled cookies and immediately decorate with sprinkles. Store in the refrigerator.

ICE CREAM KOLACHKES

These sweet pastries have Polish and Czech roots; the ice cream provides a unique twist.
—**DIANE TURNER** BRUNSWICK, OH

PREP: 1 HOUR + CHILLING
BAKE: 15 MIN./BATCH • **MAKES:** 10 DOZEN

- 2 **cups butter, softened**
- 1 **pint vanilla ice cream, softened**
- 4 **cups all-purpose flour**
- 2 **tablespoons sugar**
- 2 **cans (12 ounces each) apricot and/or raspberry cake and pastry filling**
- 1 **to 2 tablespoons confectioners' sugar, optional**

1. In the bowl of a heavy-duty stand mixer, beat butter and ice cream until blended (mixture will appear curdled). Add flour and sugar; mix well. Divide dough into four portions; cover and refrigerate 2 hours or until easy to handle.

2. Preheat oven to 350°. On a lightly floured surface, roll one portion of dough into a 12x10-in. rectangle; cut into 2-in. squares. Place a teaspoonful of filling in the center of each square. Overlap two opposite corners of dough over filling; pinch tightly to seal. Place 2 in. apart on ungreased baking sheets. Repeat with remaining dough and filling.

3. Bake 11-14 minutes or until bottoms are lightly browned. Cool for 1 minute before removing from pans to wire racks. Sprinkle with the confectioners' sugar if desired.

ROYAL ICING

- 1½ cups confectioners' sugar
- 2 tablespoons water
- 3¼ teaspoons meringue powder
  - Dash cream of tartar
  - Food coloring, optional

1. Preheat oven to 350°. Beat cookie dough and flour until blended. On a lightly floured surface, roll out dough to ¼-in. thickness. Cut out with cookie cutters of your choice dipped in flour.

FOR LOLLIPOP COOKIES *Place lollipop sticks or pretzel sticks on foil-lined baking sheets. Top each with cutout dough; press down gently. Bake until lightly browned, 9-11 minutes. Carefully remove to wire racks to cool.*

FOR CUTOUTS WITH CANDY CENTERS *Place cutouts 1 in. apart on foil-lined baking sheets. Cut out center of each cookie. Bake 9-11 minutes. Add crushed candy to the centers; bake until lightly browned, 3-5 minutes longer. Cool completely before carefully removing to wire racks to cool.*

FOR FROSTED COOKIES *Transfer cutouts to foil-lined baking sheets. Bake until lightly browned, 9-11 minutes. Remove to wire racks to cool.*

2. Meanwhile, for royal icing, combine confectioners' sugar, water, meringue powder and cream of tartar; beat on low speed just until combined. Beat on high until stiff peaks form, 4-5 minutes. Tint with food coloring if desired. Cut a small hole in the tip of a pastry bag or in a corner of a food-safe plastic bag. Transfer icing to bag. Keep unused icing covered at all times with a damp cloth (if necessary, beat again on high speed to restore texture.

3. Outline each cookie with plain icing; let dry. Fill center of each cookie with tinted icing; spread with a toothpick. Let dry completely. Attach candies and decorations with additional icing.

CORNMEAL LIME COOKIES

Want to add something new to your bake-sale favorites? My cornmeal cookies feature a tart lime glaze that really stands out!
—**WENDY RUSCH** CAMERON, WI

PREP: 45 MIN. + FREEZING
BAKE: 15 MIN./BATCH • **MAKES:** 8 DOZEN

- 1 cup butter, softened
- ½ cup sugar
- ½ cup packed brown sugar
- 1 large egg
- ¼ cup lime juice
- 4½ teaspoons grated lime peel
- 2 cups all-purpose flour
- 1 cup yellow cornmeal

GLAZE
- 2 cups confectioners' sugar
- 3 tablespoons lime juice
  - Holiday sprinkles

1. In a large bowl, cream butter and sugars until light and fluffy. Beat in egg, lime juice and peel. Combine flour and cornmeal; gradually add to creamed mixture and mix well.

2. Shape into two 12-in. rolls; wrap each in plastic. Refrigerate 30 minutes. Shape each roll into a square-shaped log. Freeze 1 hour or until firm.

3. Preheat oven to 350°. Unwrap logs and cut into ⅜-in. slices. Place 1 in. apart on parchment paper-lined baking sheets. Bake 11-14 minutes or until set. Remove to wire racks to cool completely.

4. Combine confectioners' sugar and lime juice; spread over cookies. Decorate with sprinkles. Let stand until set.

COOKIE POPS

Using packaged cookie dough gives you more time to decorate these cute pops!
—*TASTE OF HOME* TEST KITCHEN

Short & Sweet

PREP: 1 HOUR
BAKE: 15 MIN. + COOLING
MAKES: 2 DOZEN

- 1 tube (16½ ounces) refrigerated sugar cookie dough
- ⅔ cup all-purpose flour
  - Lollipop sticks or pretzel sticks
  - Jolly Rancher hard candies, coarsely crushed

ORANGE SUGAR COOKIES

I make these citrusy cookies for spring parties, and we always gobble up the ones that don't come out perfectly. Eventually I had to start making extra little "mistakes" just to keep my family happy!

—MYRRH WERTZ MILWAUKEE, WI

PREP: 25 MIN. + CHILLING
BAKE: 10 MIN./BATCH + COOLING
MAKES: 2½ DOZEN

- 1 **cup butter, softened**
- 1 **cup sugar**
- ½ **teaspoon salt**
- 1 **large egg**
- 4 **teaspoons grated orange peel**
- ⅓ **cup orange juice**
- 1½ **teaspoons lemon extract**
- 2½ **cups all-purpose flour**

ICING

- 1 **cup confectioners' sugar**
- 2 **tablespoons 2% milk**
- 3 **drops orange food coloring, optional**

1. In a large bowl, cream butter, sugar and salt until light and fluffy. Beat in egg, orange peel, orange juice and extract. Gradually beat in flour.

2. Divide dough in half. Shape each half into a disk; wrap in plastic. Refrigerate 1 hour or until firm enough to roll.

3. Preheat oven to 375°. On a floured surface, roll each portion of dough to ¼-in. thickness. Cut with a floured 2½-in. cookie cutter. Place 1 in. apart on greased baking sheets.

4. Bake 8-10 minutes or until edges are light brown. Remove from pans to wire racks to cool completely.

5. In a small bowl, mix confectioners' sugar, milk and, if desired, food coloring until smooth. Pipe or spread over cookies; let stand until set.

NO-BAKE CORNFLAKE COOKIES

I grew up on a farm where we hand-milked cows and had plenty of milk and cream to use for baking. Sometimes we'd substitute light cream for the evaporated milk in this recipe. We'd rarely let these cookies cool before sampling them, and a batch never lasted more than a day!

—DENISE MARNELL HEREFORD, TX

....

START TO FINISH: 25 MIN.
MAKES: 3-4 DOZEN

- 4 cups cornflakes
- 1½ cups flaked coconut
- ¾ cup chopped pecans
- ½ cup light corn syrup
- 1½ cups sugar
  Dash salt
- ½ cup evaporated milk
- ¼ cup butter

In a large bowl, combine cornflakes, coconut and pecans; set aside. Place the remaining ingredients in a 1-qt. saucepan. Bring mixture to 240° (soft-ball stage), stirring constantly. Add syrup mixture to dry ingredients; stir well. Drop mixture by tablespoonfuls onto waxed paper.

FROM THE COOKIE JAR

When following a cookie recipe that calls for a dash of seasoning, add the ingredient with a quick downward stroke of the hand—usually a scant ⅛ of a teaspoon.

MEXICAN CRINKLE COOKIES

When it's cookie time, my family lobbies for these Mexican specialties. You can replace an ounce of unsweetened chocolate with 3 tablespoons of cocoa powder plus 1 tablespoon of shortening, butter or oil.

—**KIM KENYON** GREENWOOD, MO

PREP: 25 MIN. + CHILLING
BAKE: 10 MIN./BATCH
MAKES: ABOUT 2 DOZEN

- ¾ **cup butter, cubed**
- 2 **ounces unsweetened chocolate, chopped**
- 1 **cup packed brown sugar**
- ¼ **cup light corn syrup**
- 1 **large egg**
- 2 **cups all-purpose flour**
- 2 **teaspoons baking soda**
- 1½ **teaspoons ground cinnamon, divided**
- ¼ **teaspoon salt**
- ½ **cup confectioners' sugar**

1. In a microwave, melt butter and chocolate; stir until smooth. Beat in brown sugar and corn syrup until blended. Beat in egg. In another bowl, whisk flour, baking soda, 1 teaspoon cinnamon and salt; gradually beat into brown sugar mixture. Refrigerate, covered, until firm, about 1 hour.

2. Preheat oven to 350°. In a shallow bowl, mix confectioners' sugar and remaining cinnamon. Shape dough into 1½-in. balls; roll in confectioners' sugar mixture. Place 2 in. apart on greased baking sheets.

3. Bake until set and tops are cracked, 10-12 minutes. Cool on pans 2 minutes. Remove to wire racks to finish cooling.

LEMON OATMEAL SUGAR COOKIES

This is an especially fun recipe to make with kids because they can roll the dough into balls and flatten them on the baking sheets. The lemon and oatmeal are a nice addition to traditional sugar cookies.

—**SUSAN MARSHALL**
COLORADO SPRINGS, CO

PREP: 30 MIN. + CHILLING
BAKE: 10 MIN./BATCH • **MAKES:** 6 DOZEN

- 1 **cup butter, softened**
- 2 **cups sugar**
- 2 **large eggs**
- 2 **teaspoons grated lemon peel**
- 3 **tablespoons lemon juice**
- 2¾ **cups all-purpose flour**
- 1 **cup quick-cooking oats**
- 2 **teaspoons baking powder**
- ¼ **teaspoon salt**
  Additional sugar

1. In a large bowl, cream butter and sugar until light and fluffy. Beat in eggs, lemon peel and lemon juice. In another bowl, whisk flour, oats, baking powder and salt; gradually beat into creamed mixture. Refrigerate, covered, 2 hours or until firm enough to shape.

2. Preheat oven to 375°. Shape level tablespoons of dough into balls; place 2 in. apart on parchment paper-lined baking sheets. Coat the bottom of a glass with cooking spray, then dip in sugar. Press cookies with bottom of glass to flatten, redipping in sugar as needed.

3. Bake 6-8 minutes or until edges are light brown. Remove from pans to wire racks to cool.

CITRUS COOKIES

Turn convenient refrigerated cookie dough into these cute treats. The sweet orange and lemon cookies taste like the sunny citrus slices they resemble.

—TASTE OF HOME TEST KITCHEN

PREP: 20 MIN. + CHILLING
BAKE: 10 MIN./BATCH
MAKES: ABOUT 2 DOZEN

- 1 tube (18 ounces) refrigerated sugar cookie dough
- 2 teaspoons grated orange peel
- 2 teaspoons orange extract
  Orange and yellow paste food coloring
- 2 teaspoons grated lemon peel
- 2 teaspoons lemon extract
  Sugar
- ½ cup vanilla frosting
  Orange and yellow colored sugar

1. Divide cookie dough in half. Place one half in a small bowl. Add the orange peel, orange extract and orange food coloring and mix well. Stir the lemon peel, lemon extract and yellow food coloring into the remaining dough and mix well. Cover and refrigerate for 2 hours or until firm.

2. Roll dough into 1-in. balls. Place 2 in. apart on ungreased baking sheets. Coat the bottom of a glass with cooking spray, then dip in granulated sugar.

3. Flatten the dough balls with the glass, redipping glass in sugar as needed. Bake at 375° for 8-10 minutes or until edges are golden brown. Remove to wire racks to cool completely.

4. Cut a small hole in the corner of a small plastic bag; add frosting. Pipe circle of frosting on cookie tops; dip in colored sugar. Pipe lines of frosting for citrus sections.

MARCH 31

NATIONAL ORANGES & LEMONS DAY

Short & Sweet

PIGGY POPS

My mother-in-law and I made these cute cookie pops for a bake sale. Wrap them in little cellophane bags and tie off with a piece of pink crafting pipe cleaner. You can curl the pipe cleaner around a pencil to make a squiggly pig's tail.

—LORRI REINHARDT BIG BEND, WI

Short & Sweet

PREP: 1 HOUR + COOLING
MAKES: 32 POPS

- 16 **large pink and/or white marshmallows**
- 1 **tablespoon sugar**
- 2 **packages (10 to 12 ounces each) white baking chips**
- 2 **tablespoons shortening**
- 3 **to 4 drops red food coloring, optional**
- 32 **double-stuffed Oreo cookies**
- 32 **Popsicle sticks or craft sticks**
- 64 **miniature semisweet chocolate chips (about 1 tablespoon)**
- 64 **M&M's miniature baking bits (about 2 tablespoons)**

1. Cut marshmallows into thirds horizontally; cut the center portion of each into four wedges for ears. Roll cut sides of ears in sugar to prevent sticking together. Set ears and remaining portions of marshmallows aside.

2. In a microwave, melt baking chips and shortening; stir until smooth. Stir in food coloring if desired.

3. Twist apart sandwich cookies. Dip the end of a wooden pop stick into melted baking chip mixture and place on a cookie half; replace cookie top. Repeat. Place pops on waxed paper-lined baking sheets; refrigerate for 10 minutes or until set.

4. Reheat baking chip mixture if necessary; dip a pop in mixture and allow excess to drip off. Return to waxed paper-lined baking sheet. While wet, position a marshmallow slice on the cookie for a snout. Add ears on top edge of cookie; hold for a few seconds or until set. Add chocolate chip eyes. Place two baking bits on snout, securing with a dab of baking chip mixture. Repeat. Let stand until set.

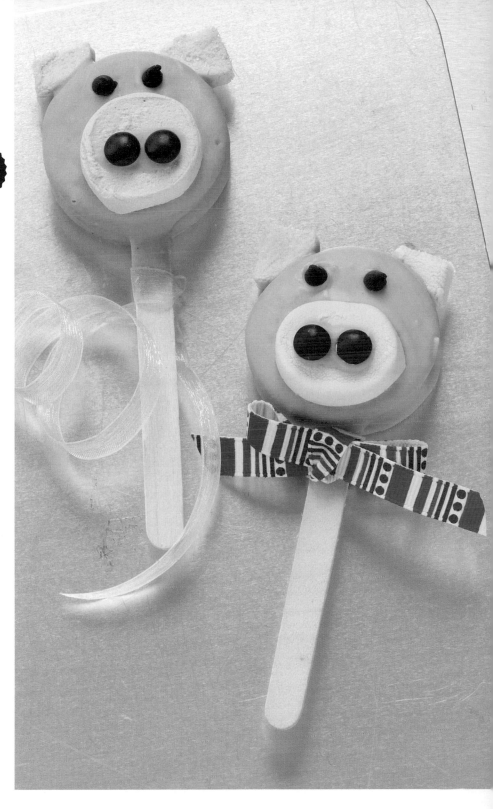

PEANUT CHOCOLATE WHIRLS

The mouthwatering combination of chocolate and peanut butter is irresistible in these tender swirl cookies. My daughters and I have such fun making and sharing these yummy snacks.

—JOANNE WOLOSCHUK YORKTON, SK

PREP: 20 MIN. + CHILLING
BAKE: 10 MIN./BATCH
MAKES: ABOUT 3 DOZEN

- ½ cup shortening
- ½ cup creamy peanut butter
- 1 cup sugar
- 1 large egg
- 2 tablespoons milk
- 1 teaspoon vanilla extract
- 1¼ cups all-purpose flour
- ½ teaspoon baking soda
- ½ teaspoon salt
- 1 cup (6 ounces) semisweet chocolate chips

1. In a large bowl, cream the shortening, peanut butter and sugar until light and fluffy. Beat in the egg, milk and vanilla. Combine the flour, baking soda and salt; gradually add to creamed mixture and mix well.
2. Cover and refrigerate for 1 hour or until easy to handle. Turn onto a lightly floured surface; roll into a 16x12-in. rectangle.
3. In a microwave, melt chocolate chips; stir until smooth. Cool slightly. Spread over dough to within ½ in. of edges. Tightly roll up jelly-roll style, starting with a short side. Wrap the roll in plastic. Refrigerate for up to 30 minutes.
4. Unwrap and cut into ¼-in. slices with a serrated knife. Place slices 1 in. apart on ungreased baking sheets. Bake at 350° for 8-10 minutes or until lightly browned. Remove to wire racks to cool.

QUADRUPLE CHOCOLATE CHUNK COOKIES

Of all the recipes I have in my repertoire, these are the biggest hit. After all, when cookies include Oreos, candy bars and chocolate chips, you're all but guaranteed a winning treat. Indeed, these cookies have placed in a contest!

—JEFF KING DULUTH, MN

PREP: 25 MIN. • **BAKE:** 10 MIN./BATCH
MAKES: 8 DOZEN

- 1 cup butter, softened
- 1 cup sugar
- 1 cup packed brown sugar
- 2 large eggs
- 2 teaspoons vanilla extract
- 2½ cups all-purpose flour
- ¾ cup Dutch-processed cocoa
- 1 teaspoon baking soda
- ¼ teaspoon salt
- 1 cup white baking chips, chopped
- 1 cup semisweet chocolate chips, chopped
- 1 cup chopped Oreo cookies (about 10 cookies)
- 1 Hershey's cookies and cream candy bar (1.55 ounces), chopped

1. Preheat oven to 375°. In a large bowl, cream butter, sugar and brown sugar until light and fluffy. Beat in eggs and vanilla. In another bowl, whisk flour, cocoa, baking soda and salt; gradually beat into creamed mixture. Stir in remaining ingredients.
2. Drop by tablespoonfuls 2 in. apart onto greased baking sheets. Bake for 6-8 minutes or until set. Cool on pans 1 minute. Remove to wire racks to cool completely. Store in an airtight container.

GRANDMA BRUBAKER'S ORANGE COOKIES

At least two generations of my family have enjoyed the recipe for these light, delicate, orange-flavored cookies.
—**SHERI DEBOLT** HUNTINGTON, IN

START TO FINISH: 30 MIN.
MAKES: ABOUT 6 DOZEN

- 1 **cup shortening**
- 2 **cups sugar**
- 2 **large eggs, separated**
- 1 **cup buttermilk**
- 5 **cups all-purpose flour**
- 2 **teaspoons baking powder**
- 2 **teaspoons baking soda**
  Pinch salt
  Juice and grated peel of 2 medium navel oranges

ICING
- 2 **cups confectioners' sugar**
- ¼ **cup orange juice**
- 1 **tablespoon butter**
- 1 **tablespoon grated orange peel**

1. In a bowl, cream shortening and sugar. Beat in egg yolks and buttermilk. Sift together flour, baking powder, soda and salt; add alternately with orange juice and peel to creamed mixture. Add egg whites and beat until smooth.

2. Drop by rounded teaspoonfuls onto greased cookie sheets. Bake at 325° for 10 minutes.

3. For icing, combine all ingredients and beat until smooth. Frost cookies when cool.

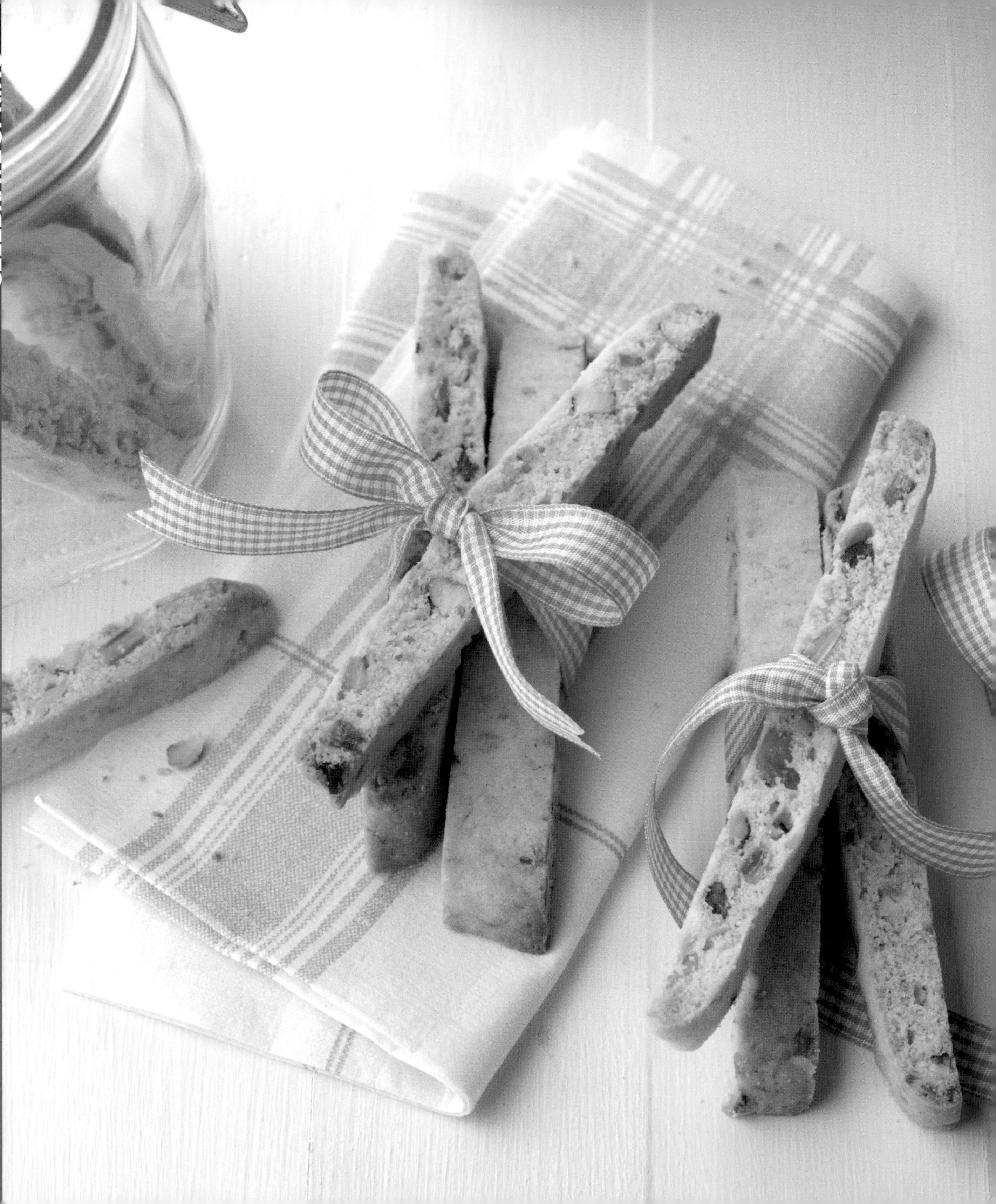

TONI'S TROPICAL BISCOTTI

I wish I could take credit for these delightful change-of-pace treats, but they come from a family member. She had an idea to bake something with pistachios and dried papaya, and these biscotti were the results!

—**BONNIE HAUSCHILD** WELLINGTON, FL

PREP: 25 MIN. • **BAKE:** 25 MIN. + COOLING
MAKES: ABOUT 4 DOZEN

- ¾ cup unsalted butter, softened
- 1 cup sugar
- 2 large eggs
- 4 teaspoons grated orange peel
- 1 tablespoon vanilla extract
- 2½ cups all-purpose flour
- ¾ teaspoon baking powder
- ½ teaspoon salt
- ½ cup flaked coconut, toasted
- ½ cup chopped dried mangoes
- ½ cup pistachios, toasted and chopped

1. Preheat oven to 350°. In a large bowl, cream butter and sugar until light and fluffy. Beat in eggs, orange peel and vanilla. In a small bowl, whisk flour, baking powder and salt; gradually beat into creamed mixture. Stir in coconut, mangoes and pistachios.

2. Divide dough in half. On ungreased baking sheets, shape each half into a 12x4-in. rectangle. Bake 15-20 minutes or until firm to the touch.

3. Cool on pans on wire racks until cool enough to handle. Transfer baked rectangles to a cutting board. Using a serrated knife, cut crosswise into ½ in. slices. Place on ungreased baking sheets, cut side down. Bake 6-7 minutes longer or until golden brown. Remove from pans to wire racks to cool.

APRIL 1
HAPPY APRIL FOOLS' DAY!

BURGER COOKIES

Surprise! My husband loves peppermint patties, and our son is crazy for vanilla wafers. So I put the two together to make a cool cookie that looks just like a burger. Both my guys give these snacks a thumbs up!

—**JULIE WELLINGTON** YOUNGSTOWN, OH

START TO FINISH: 30 MIN.
MAKES: 20 COOKIES

Short & Sweet

- ½ cup vanilla frosting
  Red and yellow paste or gel food coloring
- 40 vanilla wafers
- 20 peppermint patties
- 1 teaspoon corn syrup
- 1 teaspoon sesame seeds

Place ¼ cup frosting in each of two small bowls. Tint one red and the other yellow. Spread yellow frosting on the bottoms of 20 vanilla wafers; top with a peppermint patty. Spread with red frosting. Brush tops of the remaining vanilla wafers with corn syrup; sprinkle with sesame seeds. Place over red frosting.

★ ★ ★ ★ ★ **READER REVIEW**

"My family has been making these for years, and they're always a hit. We add green-tinted coconut for lettuce."

BRYT_EZY TASTEOFHOME.COM

WHITE CHOCOLATE-MACADAMIA NUT COOKIES

Making dessert is my kind of cooking. Your family is sure to delight in these bites— a nice change from the classic chocolate chip.
—**SHANA BOUNDS** MAGEE, MS

PREP: 20 MIN. + CHILLING • **BAKE:** 15 MIN.
MAKES: ABOUT 2½ DOZEN COOKIES

- ½ cup butter, softened
- ½ cup shortening
- ¾ cup sugar
- ½ cup packed brown sugar
- 1 large egg
- 2 teaspoons vanilla extract
- 1¾ cups all-purpose flour
- 1 teaspoon baking soda
- ½ teaspoon salt
- 10 ounces white chocolate, coarsely chopped
- ½ cup coarsely chopped macadamia nuts, lightly toasted

1. In a large bowl, cream the butter, shortening and sugars until light and fluffy. Beat in egg and vanilla. Combine the flour, baking soda and salt; gradually add to creamed mixture and mix well. Stir in white chocolate and nuts. Cover and chill dough for 1 hour.
2. Drop by heaping tablespoonfuls about 3 in. apart on ungreased baking sheets. Bake at 350° for 12-14 minutes or until lightly browned. Let stand a few minutes before removing to a wire rack to cool.

FROM THE COOKIE JAR

Butter and shortening have properties that affect the texture and flavor of baked goods differently. By combining them, you get the wonderful flavor of butter, while shortening helps cookies retain their shape.

SLICE & BAKE COCONUT SHORTBREAD COOKIES

Light and buttery, these delicate shortbread cookies are melt-in-your-mouth good. The coconut flavor makes them extra-special. They were made to nestle beside a teacup.
—**ROBERTA OTTO** DULUTH, MN

PREP: 15 MIN. + CHILLING
BAKE: 20 MIN./BATCH • **MAKES:** 4 DOZEN

- 1 cup butter, softened
- ¾ cup sugar
- 1 teaspoon vanilla extract
- 1¾ cups all-purpose flour
- 1 cup flaked coconut

1. In a large bowl, cream butter and sugar until light and fluffy. Beat in vanilla. Gradually beat flour into creamed mixture. Stir in coconut.
2. Using a sheet of waxed paper, shape dough into a 12x3x1-in. rectangle. Wrap dough in waxed paper; refrigerate 3 hours or overnight.
3. Preheat oven to 300°. Unwrap and cut dough crosswise into ¼-in. slices. Place 1 in. apart on ungreased baking sheets. Bake 18-20 minutes or until edges are light golden. Cool on pans 5 minutes. Remove to wire racks to cool.

CHERRY BONBON COOKIES

This is a very old recipe from my grandma. The sweet cherry filling surprises folks trying them for the first time.

—PAT HABIGER SPEARVILLE, KS

PREP: 15 MIN. • **BAKE:** 20 MIN. + COOLING
MAKES: 2 DOZEN

- ½ cup butter, softened
- ¾ cup confectioners' sugar
- 2 tablespoons milk
- 1 teaspoon vanilla extract
- 1½ cups all-purpose flour
- ⅛ teaspoon salt
- 24 maraschino cherries

GLAZE

- 1 cup confectioners' sugar
- 1 tablespoon butter, melted
- 2 tablespoons maraschino cherry juice
  Additional confectioners' sugar

1. Preheat oven to 350°. In a large bowl, cream butter and sugar until light and fluffy. Add milk and vanilla. Combine flour and salt; gradually add to the creamed mixture.

2. Divide dough into 24 portions; shape each portion around a cherry, forming a ball. Place on ungreased baking sheets. Bake 18-20 minutes or until lightly browned. Remove to wire racks to cool.

3. For glaze, combine sugar, butter and cherry juice until smooth. Drizzle over cookies. Dust with confectioners' sugar.

ITALIAN RAINBOW COOKIES

My family has made these classic Italian cookies for generations.

—CINDY CASAZZA HOPEWELL, NJ

PREP: 35 MIN.
BAKE: 10 MIN./BATCH + CHILLING
MAKES: 11 DOZEN

- 4 **large eggs**
- 1 **cup sugar**
- 3½ **ounces almond paste, cut into small pieces**
- 1 **cup all-purpose flour**
- 1 **cup butter, melted and cooled**
- ½ **teaspoon salt**
- ½ **teaspoon almond extract**
- 6 **to 8 drops red food coloring**
- 6 **to 8 drops green food coloring**
- ¼ **cup seedless raspberry jam**

GLAZE
- 1 **cup (6 ounces) semisweet chocolate chips**
- 1 **teaspoon shortening**

1. Preheat oven to 375°. In a large bowl, beat eggs and sugar 2-3 minutes or until thick and lemon-colored. Gradually add almond paste; mix well. Gradually add flour, butter, salt and extract.

2. Divide batter into thirds. Tint one portion red and one portion green; leave remaining portion plain. Spread one portion into each of three well-greased 11x7-in. baking dishes.

3. Bake 7-11 minutes or until a toothpick inserted in center comes out clean and edges begins to brown. Cool 10 minutes before removing from pans to wire racks to cool completely.

4. Place red layer on waxed paper; spread with 2 tablespoons jam. Top with plain layer and remaining jam. Add green layer; press down gently.

5. For glaze, in a microwave, melt chocolate chips and shortening; stir until smooth. Spread half over green layer. Refrigerate 20 minutes or until set. Turn over; spread remaining glaze over red layer. Refrigerate 20 minutes or until set.

6. With a sharp knife, trim edges. Cut rectangle lengthwise into fourths. Cut each portion into ¼-in. slices.

RASPBERRY SPARKLE COOKIES

Sugar-free gelatin gives these cute cookies their sweetness. You can alter the gelatin flavor and color to your liking.

—BETTY BINDER WILLIAMSTOWN, MI

PREP: 20 MIN. • **BAKE:** 10 MIN./BATCH
MAKES: 1½ DOZEN

- ¼ **cup shortening**
- ¼ **cup butter, softened**
- ⅓ **cup sugar blend**
- 1 **large egg**
- ½ **teaspoon vanilla extract**
- 1 **cup all-purpose flour**
- ¼ **teaspoon baking powder**
- ¼ **teaspoon baking soda**
- 1 **teaspoon sugar-free raspberry gelatin**

1. In a small bowl, beat the shortening, butter and sugar until well blended. Beat in egg and vanilla. Combine the flour, baking powder and baking soda; gradually add to butter mixture and mix well.

2. Shape into 1-in. balls; dip tops in gelatin. Place 2 in. apart on baking sheets coated with cooking spray. Bake at 350° for 8-10 minutes or until edges are golden brown. Cool for 1 minute before removing from pans to wire racks. Store in an airtight container.

NOTE *This recipe was tested with Splenda sugar blend.*

HOW TO ENSURE EVEN BAKING

Preheat the oven while preparing the dough. Set cookies at least 2 in. apart on the baking sheet, and leave at least 2 in. around the edges of the sheet to allow the heat to circulate.

APRIL 10

NATIONAL
CINNAMON
CRESCENT
DAY

CINNAMON CRESCENTS

We've been enjoying these crispy cinnamon sugar goodies for years. The crescents are easy to make, and my family considers them a real treat.

—**EMILY ENGEL** QUILL LAKE, , SK

PREP: 30 MIN. • **BAKE:** 20 MIN.
MAKES: 3 DOZEN

- 2½ cups all-purpose flour
- 1 teaspoon baking powder
- 1 cup cold butter
- ½ cup milk
- 1 large egg, beaten
- 1 cup sugar
- 4 teaspoons ground cinnamon
- **OPTIONAL GLAZE**
- 1 cup confectioners' sugar
- 1 to 2 teaspoons ground cinnamon
- 4 teaspoons 2% milk

1. Combine flour and baking powder in a large bowl; cut in butter until crumbly. Stir in milk and egg. Divide into three portions; shape each portion into a ball.
2. Combine sugar and cinnamon, sprinkle a third over a pastry board or other clean surface. Roll one ball into a 12-in. circle; cut into 12 wedges. Roll up from wide edge. Repeat with remaining dough and cinnamon sugar. Place rolls with point side down on lightly greased baking sheets; form into crescent shapes. Bake at 350° for 16-18 minutes or until lightly browned (do not overbake).
3. For optional glaze, combine the confectioners' sugar, cinnamon and milk until smooth. Drizzle over the cooled cinnamon crescents.

CHOCOLATE CHIP CHERRY OATMEAL COOKIES

Chocolate-covered-cherry lovers have to try these! My husband and I just love homemade cookies, so I concocted these oatmeal treats with chocolate chips and dried cherries.

—**DENISE FRITZ** ORMOND BEACH, FL

PREP: 20 MIN. • **BAKE:** 15 MIN./BATCH
MAKES: 15 COOKIES

- ½ cup butter, softened
- ⅔ cup packed brown sugar
- ⅓ cup sugar
- 1 large egg
- 1 teaspoon vanilla extract
- 1 cup all-purpose flour
- ¾ cup quick-cooking oats
- ¾ teaspoon baking soda
- ½ teaspoon salt
- ⅔ cup dried cherries, chopped
- ½ cup semisweet chocolate chips

1. In a small bowl, cream butter and sugars until light and fluffy. Beat in egg and vanilla. Combine the flour, oats, baking soda and salt; gradually add to creamed mixture and mix well. Stir in cherries and chocolate chips.
2. Drop by scant ¼ cupfuls 3 in. apart onto ungreased baking sheets. Bake at 350° for 14-16 minutes or until golden brown. Cool for 1 minute before removing from baking sheets to wire racks. Store in an airtight container.

CREAM CHEESE CUTOUTS

Decorating cookies always puts me in a happy mood. These treats are perfect for decorating because they don't rise a lot or lose their shape.
—**JULIE DAWSON** GALENA, OH

PREP: 15 MIN. + CHILLING
BAKE: 10 MIN./BATCH + COOLING
MAKES: ABOUT 7 DOZEN

- 1 cup butter, softened
- 3 ounces cream cheese, softened
- 1 cup sugar
- ¼ teaspoon salt
- 1 large egg
- 1 teaspoon vanilla extract
- 2½ cups all-purpose flour

FROSTING

- 3 cups confectioners' sugar
- ⅓ cup butter, softened
- 1½ teaspoons vanilla extract
- 2 to 3 tablespoons 2% milk
  Food coloring, optional
  Assorted sprinkles or candies

1. In a large bowl, cream butter, cream cheese, sugar and salt until light and fluffy. Beat in egg and vanilla. Gradually beat in flour. Refrigerate, covered, 1-2 hours or until firm enough to roll.
2. Preheat oven to 375°. On a lightly floured surface, roll dough to ⅛-in. thickness. Cut with floured cookie cutters. Place 1 in. apart on ungreased baking sheets.
3. Bake 7-8 minutes or until edges are lightly browned. Cool on pans 1 minute. Remove to wire racks to cool completely.
4. In a small bowl, beat confectioners' sugar, butter, vanilla and enough milk to reach desired consistency. If desired, add food coloring. Decorate cookies with frosting and sprinkles.

★ ★ ★ ★ ★ **5 STAR TIP**

"I make my cutout cookies ahead and freeze them without frosting. They keep better that way. Before a party or potluck, I just thaw the cookies and frost them. They taste and look freshly baked." —**Jean M., Scandinavia, WI**

HONEY-PEANUT BUTTER COOKIES

It's not unusual for my husband to request these cookies by name. You'll love 'em.
—**LUCILE PROCTOR** PANGUITCH, UT

PREP: 15 MIN. • **BAKE:** 10 MIN./BATCH
MAKES: 5 DOZEN

- ½ cup shortening
- 1 cup creamy peanut butter
- 1 cup honey
- 2 large eggs, lightly beaten
- 3 cups all-purpose flour
- 1 cup sugar
- 1½ teaspoons baking soda
- 1 teaspoon baking powder
- ½ teaspoon salt

1. Preheat oven to 350°. In a bowl, mix shortening, peanut butter and honey. Add eggs; mix well. Combine flour, sugar, baking soda, baking powder and salt; add to peanut butter mixture and mix well.

2. Roll into 1- to 1½-in. balls and place on ungreased baking sheets. Flatten with a fork dipped in flour. Bake 8-10 minutes or until set. Remove to wire racks to cool.

SOUR CREAM SUGAR COOKIES

I make these cookies for my family and our neighbors every year. The treats stay soft for at least a week, and they look so pretty. Best of all, you can use different cutters to suit any occasion!

—CAROLYN WALTON SMOOT, WY

PREP: 70 MIN. + CHILLING
BAKE: 10 MIN./BATCH + COOLING
MAKES: ABOUT 4½ DOZEN

- 1 **cup shortening**
- 1 **cup sugar**
- 1 **large egg**
- 1 **cup (8 ounces) sour cream**
- 1½ **teaspoons vanilla extract**
- 4 **cups all-purpose flour**
- 1½ **teaspoons baking soda**
- ¼ **teaspoon salt**

FROSTING
- 1 **cup butter, softened**
- 9 **cups confectioners' sugar**
- 3 **teaspoons vanilla extract**
- ⅔ **to ¾ cup 2% milk**
  Paste food coloring

1. In a large bowl, cream shortening and sugar until light and fluffy. Beat in egg, sour cream and vanilla. Combine the flour, baking soda and salt; gradually add to creamed mixture and mix well. Cover and refrigerate for 1 hour or until easy to handle.

2. On a lightly floured surface, roll dough to ¼-in. thickness. Cut with a floured 3-in. cookie cutter of your choice.

3. Place 1 in. apart on baking sheets lightly coated with cooking spray. Bake at 350° for 8-10 minutes or until set. Cool for 1 minute before removing to wire racks to cool completely.

4. For frosting, in a large bowl, cream butter until light and fluffy. Beat in confectioners' sugar and vanilla. Add enough milk to achieve the desired consistency. Tint with food coloring. Decorate cookies as desired.

NOTE *To create the look in the photo, use #10 and #4 round pastry tips.*

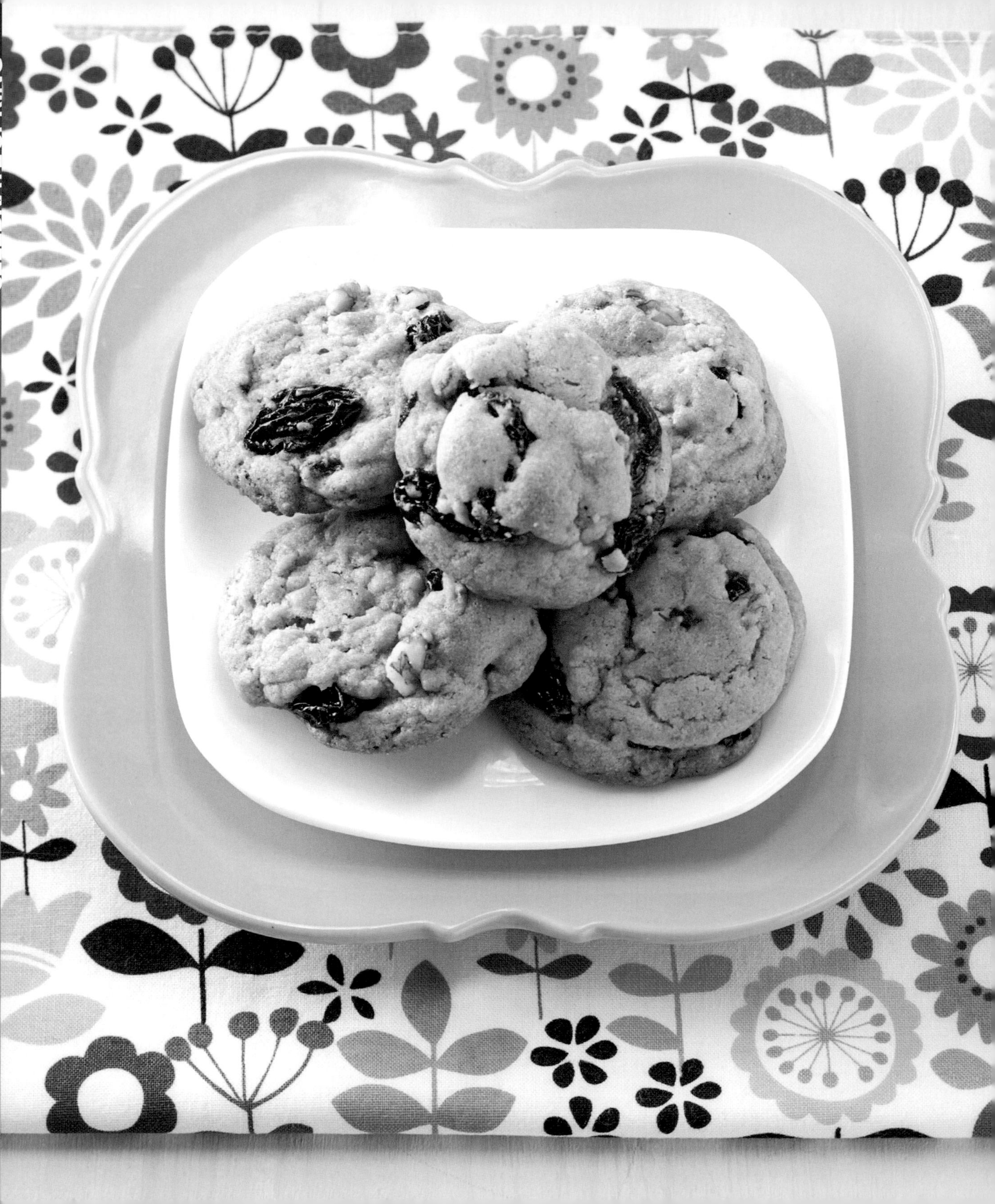

MOM'S SOFT RAISIN COOKIES

With four sons in the service during World War II, my mother sent these favorite cookies as a taste of home to her boys in different parts of the world. These days, my grand-children are enjoying them as we did, along with my stories of long ago.
—**PEARL COCHENOUR** WILLIAMSPORT, OH

PREP: 25 MIN. • **BAKE:** 15 MIN./BATCH
MAKES: 6 DOZEN

- 1 cup water
- 2 cups raisins
- 1 cup shortening
- 1¾ cups sugar
- 2 large eggs
- 1 teaspoon vanilla extract
- 3½ cups all-purpose flour
- 1 teaspoon baking powder
- 1 teaspoon baking soda
- 1 teaspoon salt
- ½ teaspoon ground cinnamon
- ½ teaspoon ground nutmeg
- ½ cup chopped walnuts

1. Combine water and raisins in a small saucepan; bring to a boil. Cook for 3 minutes; remove from the heat and let cool (do not drain).

2. Preheat oven to 350°. In a large bowl, cream shortening and sugar until light and fluffy. Beat in eggs and vanilla. Combine flour, baking powder, baking soda, salt and spices; gradually add to creamed mixture and mix well. Stir in nuts and raisins.

3. Drop by teaspoonfuls 2 in. apart onto greased baking sheets. Bake 12-14 minutes or until golden brown. Remove to wire racks to cool.

COCONUT KISSES

Chewy on the inside and crisp on the outside, these meringue cookies are a sweet reward. They add a light touch to spring dessert buffets, and they make fun treats at parties and celebrations all year long.
—**DOROTHY BEAUDRY** ALBERTVILLE, MN

PREP: 15 MIN. • **BAKE:** 20 MIN.
MAKES: 1 DOZEN

- 1 large egg white
- ½ cup confectioners' sugar
- 1 cup flaked coconut

1. Place the egg white in a small bowl; let stand at room temperature for 30 minutes. Beat on medium speed until soft peaks form. Gradually beat in confectioners' sugar, 1 tablespoon at a time, on high until stiff peaks form. Fold in coconut.

2. Drop by rounded tablespoonfuls 2 in. apart onto a parchment paper-lined baking sheet. Bake at 325° 18-20 minutes or until firm to the touch. Cool 1 minute before removing to a wire rack. Store in an airtight container.

MERINGUE BUNNIES

These cute characters make a smile-fetching addition to your Easter table! Enlist the kids to help decorate them.

—TASTE OF HOME TEST KITCHEN

PREP: 30 MIN. • **BAKE:** 1½ HOURS + COOLING
MAKES: 1 DOZEN

- 2 **large egg whites**
- ⅛ **teaspoon cream of tartar**
- ½ **cup sugar**
- ¼ **cup pink candy coating disks**
- 36 **heart-shaped red decorating sprinkles**

1. Place egg whites in a small bowl; let stand at room temperature 30 minutes.
2. Preheat oven to 225°. Add cream of tartar to egg whites; beat on medium speed until foamy. Gradually add sugar, 1 tablespoon at a time, beating on high after each addition until sugar is dissolved. Continue beating until stiff glossy peaks form.
3. Cut a small hole in the tip of a pastry bag or in a corner of a food-safe plastic bag. Transfer meringue to bag. Pipe 4¾-in. bunny shapes onto parchment paper-lined baking sheets. Bake 1½ hours or until firm. Remove to wire racks to cool completely.
4. In a microwave, melt candy coating; stir until smooth. Place in another pastry or plastic bag; cut a small hole in the tip of the bag. Pipe ears, whiskers and mouths on bunnies with melted candy coating. Attach hearts for eyes and nose.

FROM THE COOKIE JAR

Meringue recipes often call for beating egg whites until stiff peaks form. Beat the egg whites until the volume increases and the mixture thickens. When you lift the beaters, the peaks should stand up straight.

SUGAR DOVES

I enjoy making these beautiful cookies and love to spend relaxing evenings decorating them. The pretty little birds are sure to get a lot of attention.

—PEGGY PRESTON FENTON, IA

PREP: 30 MIN. + CHILLING
AKE: 10 MIN./BATCH + COOLING
MAKES: 7½ DOZEN

- 1 **cup butter, softened**
- 2 **cups sugar**
- 2 **large eggs**
- 2 **tablespoons milk**
- 2 **teaspoons vanilla extract**
- 4¼ **cups all-purpose flour**
- 2 **teaspoons baking powder**
- ¼ **teaspoon salt**

FROSTING
- ½ **cup shortening**
- 3¾ **cups confectioners' sugar**
- 2 **tablespoons milk**
- 1 **teaspoon almond extract**
- ½ **teaspoon vanilla extract**
- 1 **to 2 tablespoons water**
- 4½ **cups sliced almonds**
- 3½ **cups finely chopped walnuts**
   Miniature semisweet chocolate chips

1. In a large bowl, cream butter and sugar until light and fluffy. Add eggs, one at a time, beating well after each addition. Beat in milk and vanilla.
2. In another bowl, whisk flour, baking powder and salt; gradually beat into creamed mixture. Refrigerate, covered, 2 hours or until easy to handle.
3. Preheat oven to 350°. On a lightly floured surface, roll out dough to ⅛-in. thickness. Cut with a 3-in. bird-shaped cookie cutter. Place 1 in. apart on greased baking sheets. Bake 7-9 minutes or until set. Remove from pans to wire racks to cool completely.
4. For frosting, in a small bowl, combine shortening, confectioners' sugar, milk, extracts and enough water to achieve spreading consistency.
5. Frost cookies. Arrange walnuts over the bodies and almonds for feathers. Add chocolate chip eyes.

HAPPY EASTER!

1. In a small resealable plastic bag, combine the coconut, water and food coloring. Seal bag and shake until blended; set aside.

2. For bunny ears, cut each marshmallow in half horizontally. Cut each Laffy Taffy into small oval pieces. Press one candy piece onto the cut side of each marshmallow half; set aside.

3. In a microwave-safe bowl, melt candy coating; stir until smooth. Dip one cookie into candy coating. Let excess drip off and place on waxed paper. Immediately sprinkle coconut onto the bottom of cookie. Gently press jelly beans into coconut. Using kitchen scissors, cut bottom ends of marshmallow ears; press onto cookie. Add M&M's for eyes.

4. Repeat for remaining bunnies. Pipe pink icing for noses and whiskers. Let stand for 15 minutes or until set.

MEXICAN CINNAMON COOKIES

My extended family shares a meal every Sunday. The aunts and uncles take turns bringing everything from main dishes to desserts like this traditional Mexican cinnamon cookie called *reganadas*.
—**ADAN FRANCO** MILWAUKEE, WI

PREP: 25 MIN. + STANDING
BAKE: 10 MIN./BATCH • **MAKES:** 12 DOZEN

- 1 large egg, separated
- 2 cups lard
- 4 cups all-purpose flour
- 3 teaspoons baking powder
- 1½ teaspoons ground cinnamon
  Dash salt
- ¾ cup sugar

COATING
- ⅔ cup sugar
- 4 teaspoons ground cinnamon
  Confectioners' sugar, optional

1. Place egg white in a small bowl; let stand at room temperature 30 minutes.

2. Preheat oven to 375°. In a large bowl, beat lard until creamy. In another bowl, whisk flour, baking powder, cinnamon and salt; gradually beat into lard.

3. Beat egg white on high speed until stiff peaks form. Gently whisk in sugar and egg yolk. Gradually beat into lard mixture. Turn onto a lightly floured surface; knead gently 8-10 times.

4. Divide dough into six portions. On a lightly floured surface, roll each portion into a 24-in.-long rope; cut diagonally into 1-in. pieces. Place 1 in. apart on ungreased baking sheets. Bake 8-10 minutes or until edges are light brown. Cool on pans 2 minutes.

5. In a small bowl, mix sugar and cinnamon. Roll the warm cookies in cinnamon sugar mixture or, if desired, confectioners' sugar. Cool on wire racks.

★ ★ ★ ★ ★ **READER REVIEW**

"These are so delicious. I like the cinnamon sugar version a little better but both are excellent. The yield is 144 cookies, so there's not really much saturated fat per cookie."

LINDAS_WI TASTEOFHOME.COM

EASTER BUNNY COOKIES

Kids will love these sweet little bunnies, particularly if they get to help decorate. What a cute Easter treat!
—**SUE GRONHOLZ** BEAVER DAM, WI

PREP: 1½ HOURS + STANDING
MAKES: 1 DOZEN

Short & Sweet

- 1 cup flaked coconut
- ½ teaspoon water
- 6 drops green food coloring
- 1 drop yellow food coloring
- 12 large marshmallows
- 4 pink Laffy Taffy candies
- 12 ounces white candy coating disks
- 12 Nutter Butter cookies
- 36 small jelly beans
- 24 brown M&M's miniature baking bits
  Pink decorating icing

ROSEMARY-LEMON SLICE & BAKE COOKIES

Tart lemon and fresh rosemary make these luscious treats a sweet surprise for friends and family.

—MALORIE HARRIS WILDOMAR, CA

PREP: 25 MIN. + FREEZING
BAKE: 10 MIN./BATCH • **MAKES:** 8 DOZEN

- 1 **cup butter, softened**
- ½ **cup sugar**
- 3 **tablespoons lemon juice**
- 1 **teaspoon grated lemon peel**
- ½ **teaspoon vanilla extract**
- 2 **cups all-purpose flour**
- 4½ **teaspoons minced fresh rosemary**
- ¼ **teaspoon salt**

1. In a large bowl, cream butter and sugar until light and fluffy. Beat in the lemon juice, peel and vanilla. Combine the flour, rosemary and salt; gradually add to creamed mixture and mix well.

2. Shape into two 12-in. rolls; wrap each in plastic. Freeze for 30 minutes or until firm. Cut into ¼-in. slices. Place 2 in. apart on ungreased baking sheets. Bake at 350° for 8-10 minutes or until edges begin to brown. Cool for 2 minutes before removing from pans to wire racks. Store in an airtight container.

DROP-COOKIE DOUGH

The dough for drop cookies is often quite thick. If your mixer begins to strain, use a wooden spoon to stir in the last of the dry ingredients by hand.

APRIL 22
NATIONAL
JELLY
BEAN
DAY

JELLY BEAN COOKIES

It's a tradition for my grandmother and I to make these colorful cookies every year.
—**CHEYENNE FINK** PLEASANTVILLE, PA

PREP: 15 MIN. • **BAKE:** 10 MIN./BATCH
MAKES: ABOUT 2½ DOZEN

- ½ cup shortening
- ¾ cup sugar
- 1 large egg
- 2 tablespoons 2% milk
- 1 teaspoon vanilla extract
- 1½ cups all-purpose flour
- 1¼ teaspoons baking powder
- ½ teaspoon salt
- ¾ cup small jelly beans

1. Preheat oven to 350°. In a large bowl, cream shortening and sugar until blended. Beat in egg, milk and vanilla. In another bowl, whisk flour, baking powder and salt; gradually beat into creamed mixture. Stir in jelly beans.
2. Drop dough by tablespoonfuls 1½ in. apart onto greased or parchment paper-lined baking sheets. Bake for 8-10 minutes or until edges are light golden brown. Cool on pans 2 minutes. Remove to wire racks to cool.
NOTE *Hold back a few jelly beans from the dough and press them into the tops of the cookies before baking. That way, you'll have a few colorful spots right on top of each cookie.*

FROM THE COOKIE JAR

Always allow cookies to cool completely before storing them, and store crisp cookies apart from soft ones. Otherwise, crispy treats can lose their crunch due to moisture from their softer counterparts.

LIME & GIN COCONUT MACAROONS

I took these lime and coconut macaroons to our annual cookie exchange, where we name a cookie queen. I won the crown!
—**MILISSA KIRKPATRICK** ANGEL FIRE, NM

PREP: 20 MIN.
BAKE: 15 MIN./BATCH + COOLING
MAKES: 2½ DOZEN

- 4 large egg whites
- ⅔ cup sugar
- 3 tablespoons gin
- 1½ teaspoons grated lime peel
- ¼ teaspoon salt
- ¼ teaspoon almond extract
- 1 package (14 ounces) flaked coconut
- ½ cup all-purpose flour
- 8 ounces white baking chocolate, melted

1. Preheat oven to 350°. In a small bowl, whisk the first six ingredients until blended. In a large bowl, toss coconut with flour; stir in egg white mixture.
2. Drop by tablespoonfuls 2 in. apart onto greased baking sheets. Bake for 15-18 minutes or until tops are light brown. Remove from pans to wire racks to cool completely.
3. Dip bottoms of macaroons into melted chocolate, allowing excess to drip off. Place on waxed paper; let stand until set. Store in an airtight container.

HONEY-LIME ALMOND COOKIES

Decades ago my grandmother passed this buttery lime cookie recipe to me. Through years of baking, our cookie memories keep the family connected although we're miles apart.

—PAULA MARCHESI LENHARTSVILLE, PA

PREP: 25 MIN. + CHILLING
BAKE: 10 MIN./BATCH + COOLING
MAKES: ABOUT 3 DOZEN

- 1 **cup butter, softened**
- ½ **cup sugar**
- 3 **tablespoons honey**
- 1 **large egg yolk**
- 1 **tablespoon grated lime peel**
- 1 **teaspoon lime juice**
- 2 **cups all-purpose flour**
- 1 **cup slivered almonds, finely chopped**
  Confectioners' sugar, optional

1. In a large bowl, cream butter and sugar until light and fluffy. Beat in honey, egg yolk, lime peel and lime juice. Gradually beat in flour. Stir in almonds.

2. Divide dough in half; shape each into a 5-in.-long roll. Wrap in plastic; refrigerate 1 hour or until firm.

3. Preheat oven to 350°. Unwrap and cut dough crosswise into ¼-in. slices. Place 1 in. apart on ungreased baking sheets. Bake 10-12 minutes or until edges are light brown.

4. Cool on pans 2 minutes. Remove to wire racks to cool completely. If desired, dust with confectioners' sugar.

FREEZE OPTION *Freeze cookies in freezer containers. To use, thaw before serving. If desired, dust with additional confectioners' sugar.*

MAY 11
NATIONAL EAT WHAT YOU WANT DAY

KITCHEN SINK COOKIES

Crisp on the outside and soft inside, these cookies are packed with oats, coconut, chocolate and lots of flavor.

—**BRITTNEY MUSGROVE** DALLAS, GA

PREP: 25 MIN. • **BAKE:** 10 MIN./BATCH
MAKES: 5 DOZEN

- 1   cup butter, softened
- 1¼ cups packed brown sugar
- 2   large eggs
- 3   teaspoons vanilla extract
- 2   teaspoons 2% milk
- 2   cups quick-cooking oats
- 1¾ cups all-purpose flour
- 1   teaspoon baking soda
- ½   teaspoon salt
- ¼   teaspoon ground nutmeg
- 1   cup (6 ounces) semisweet chocolate chips
- ⅓   cup Reese's Pieces
- ⅓   cup flaked coconut
- ⅓   cup chopped walnuts
- ⅓   cup milk chocolate M&M's

1. In a large bowl, cream butter and brown sugar until light and fluffy. Beat in the eggs, vanilla and milk. Combine the oats, flour, baking soda, salt and nutmeg; gradually add to creamed mixture and mix well. Stir in remaining ingredients.
2. Drop by rounded tablespoonfuls 3 in. apart onto ungreased baking sheets. Flatten slightly with the bottom of a glass coated with cooking spray.
3. Bake at 375° for 8-10 minutes or until golden brown. Cool for 1 minute before removing from pans to wire racks.

★ ★ ★ ★ ★ **5 STAR TIP**

When making drop cookies such as these, fill a tablespoon with dough, then use another spoon or small rubber spatula to push the mound of dough off the spoon onto the cool baking sheet.

FOLDED HAZELNUT COOKIES

We first made these cookies when my boys were little. They would always end up covered in flour and with Nutella all over their faces. Such good memories! Try them if you have little ones in your family!

—PAULA MARCHESI LENHARTSVILLE, PA

PREP: 30 MIN. • **BAKE:** 10 MIN./BATCH
MAKES: ABOUT 2 DOZEN

- 1 **tablespoon finely chopped hazelnuts**
- 1 **tablespoon sugar**
- 1½ **cups all-purpose flour**
- ½ **cup confectioners' sugar**
- ¼ **cup cornstarch**
- ¾ **cup cold butter, cubed**
- 2 **tablespoons Nutella**
- 1 **large egg, lightly beaten**

1. Preheat oven to 350°. In a small bowl, mix hazelnuts and sugar. In a large bowl, whisk flour, confectioners' sugar and cornstarch. Cut in butter until crumbly. Transfer to a clean work surface. Knead gently until mixture forms a smooth dough, about 2 minutes (dough will be crumbly but will come together).

2. Divide dough in half. On a lightly floured surface, roll each portion to ⅛-in. thickness. Cut with a floured 2-in. round cookie cutter. Place ¼ teaspoon Nutella in center. Fold dough partially in half, just enough to cover filling.

3. Place 1 in. apart on greased baking sheets. Brush with beaten egg; sprinkle with hazelnut mixture. Bake for 10-12 minutes or until bottoms are light brown. Remove from pans to wire racks to cool.

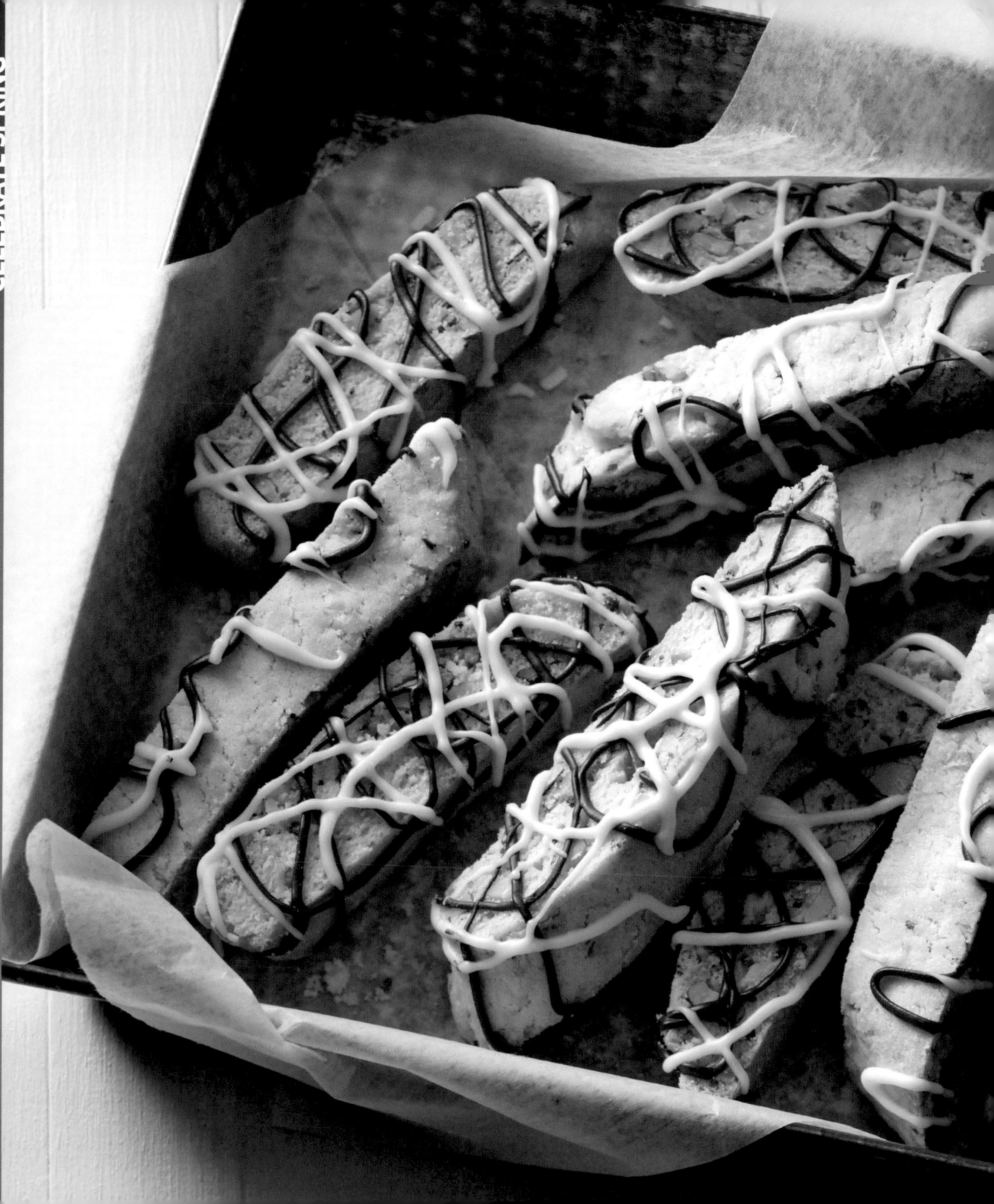

DOUBLE-DRIZZLED BISCOTTI

Semisweet and white chocolate drizzles give this biscotti a pretty look. They don't bake as long as some biscotti, so they're a little softer.
—**CHERYL LUDEMANN** BOONVILLE, NY

PREP: 25 MIN. • **BAKE:** 30 MIN. + COOLING
MAKES: ABOUT 3 DOZEN

- ¾ cup butter, softened
- 1 cup sugar
- 3 large eggs
- 1 teaspoon almond extract
- 1 teaspoon vanilla extract
- 3 cups all-purpose flour
- 2 tablespoons aniseed
- 1½ teaspoons baking powder
- ¼ teaspoon salt
- 1 cup chopped walnuts
- ⅓ cup semisweet chocolate chips
- 2 teaspoons shortening, divided
- ⅓ cup white baking chips

1. Preheat oven to 350°. In a large bowl, cream butter and sugar until light and fluffy. Beat in eggs and extracts. In a small bowl, whisk flour, aniseed, baking powder and salt; gradually beat into creamed mixture. Stir in walnuts.

2. Divide dough in half. On an ungreased baking sheet, shape each dough half into a 14x2-in. rectangle. Bake 15 20 minutes or until firm to the touch.

3. Cool on pans on wire racks until cool enough to handle. Transfer baked rectangles to a cutting board. Using a serrated knife, cut diagonally into ½-in. slices. Place on ungreased baking sheets, cut side down. Bake 6-7 minutes on each side or until golden brown. Remove from pans to wire racks to cool completely.

4. In a microwave, melt semisweet chips and 1 teaspoon shortening; stir until smooth. Drizzle over the biscotti. In a microwave, melt the white chips and remaining shortening; stir until smooth. Drizzle over biscotti.

AUSTRIAN NUT COOKIES

These are my family's favorite cookies. If you arrange the slivered almonds in pinwheel fashion, it looks like a poinsettia for Christmas.
—**MARIANNE WEBER** SOUTH BEACH, OR

PREP: 30 MIN. + CHILLING
BAKE: 10 MIN./BATCH + COOLING
MAKES: 20 SANDWICH COOKIES

- 1 cup all-purpose flour
- ⅔ cup finely chopped almonds
- ⅓ cup sugar
- ½ cup cold butter
- ½ cup raspberry jam

FROSTING
- 1 ounce unsweetened chocolate, melted and cooled
- ⅓ cup confectioners' sugar
- 2 tablespoons butter, softened
  Slivered almonds

1. In a bowl, combine flour, chopped almonds and sugar. Cut in butter until mixture resembles coarse crumbs. Form into a ball; cover and refrigerate for 1 hour.

2. On a floured surface, roll the dough to ⅛-in. thickness. Cut with a 2-in. round cutter and place 1 in. apart on greased baking sheets. Bake at 375° 7-10 minutes or until the edges are lightly browned. Remove to wire racks to cool completely. Spread ½ teaspoon jam on half of the cookies; top with another cookie.

3. For frosting, combine chocolate, confectioners' sugar and butter. Spread on tops of cookies. Decorate as desired with slivered almonds.

STRAWBERRY TUILE CANNOLI

My mom and I created this recipe by combining two different ones. The cute cookies are crispy on the outside yet light and fluffy inside. You could also bake them flat and serve the filling as a cookie dip.

—**CRYSTAL BRIDDICK** COLFAX, IL

PREP: 40 MIN. • **BAKE:** 5 MIN./BATCH
MAKES: ABOUT 2 DOZEN

- 4 **ounces cream cheese, softened**
- ¼ **cup sugar**
- 2 **tablespoons seedless strawberry jam**
- ¼ **cup heavy whipping cream, whipped**
- 1 **to 3 drops red food coloring, optional**

BATTER

- ½ **cup sugar**
- ⅓ **cup all-purpose flour**
- 2 **large egg whites**
- ¼ **teaspoon vanilla extract**
- ⅛ **teaspoon salt**
- ¼ **cup butter, melted and cooled**
  Chopped fresh strawberries, optional

1. For filling, in a small bowl, beat cream cheese, sugar and jam until blended. Fold in whipped cream and, if desired, food coloring. Chill.

2. In a small bowl, whisk the sugar, flour, egg whites, vanilla and salt until smooth. Whisk in the butter until blended.

3. Line baking sheets with parchment paper. Preparing four cookies at a time, drop batter by 1½ teaspoonfuls 4 in. apart onto prepared pans. Bake at 400° for 5-8 minutes or until the edges are lightly browned.

4. Loosen each cookie from pan and curl around a wooden spoon handle. Press lightly to seal and hold until set, about 20 seconds. Remove and place on waxed paper to cool. Continue with remaining cookies. If cookies become too cool to shape, return to oven for 1 minute to soften.

5. Just before serving, pipe or spoon filling into cookie shells. Dip ends of cookies into chopped strawberries if desired. Refrigerate leftovers.

ICED COCONUT CRESCENTS

Crescents get a tropical twist when you add refreshing orange juice and coconut. Bake these goodies any time of year and decorate them to suit the season or occasion.

—**MARIA BENBROOK** PORT MONMOUTH, NJ

PREP: 15 MIN. • **BAKE:** 10 MIN./BATCH
MAKES: 4 DOZEN

- ½ **cup butter, softened**
- ¾ **cup sugar**
- 3 **large eggs**
- ½ **cup orange juice**
- 1½ **teaspoons vanilla extract**
- 3 **cups all-purpose flour**
- 3 **teaspoons baking powder**
- 1⅔ **cups flaked coconut**

ICING

- 2 **cups confectioners' sugar**
- ¼ **cup 2% milk**
  Assorted sprinkles of your choice

1. Preheat oven to 350°. In a large bowl, cream butter and sugar until light and fluffy. Beat in eggs, orange juice and vanilla. Combine flour and baking powder; gradually add to creamed mixture and mix well. Stir in coconut.

2. Shape tablespoonfuls of dough into crescent shapes. Place 2 in. apart on ungreased baking sheets. Bake 8-10 minutes or until edges are lightly browned. Cool 1 minute before removing to wire racks to cool.

3. Combine confectioners' sugar and milk in a small bowl. Decorate with icing and sprinkles. Let stand until set.

GRANDMA'S SUGAR COOKIES

This is one of my great-grandmother's recipes that I received years ago from one of my great-aunts. We bake these cookies for lots of special occasions.

—KRISTY DELOACH BATON ROUGE, LA

....

PREP: 15 MIN. + CHILLING
BAKE: 10 MIN./BATCH
MAKES: 6 DOZEN 2½-INCH COOKIES OR 1½ DOZEN 4¼-INCH COOKIES

- 2 **cups sugar**
- 1 **cup butter, softened**
- 1 **teaspoon vanilla extract**
- ½ **teaspoon salt**
- 2 **large eggs, lightly beaten**
- 3 **cups all-purpose flour**
- 2 **teaspoons baking powder**
- ¾ **teaspoon baking soda**

ICING

- 4 **cups confectioners' sugar**
- ¼ **teaspoon almond extract**
- ½ **to ⅔ cup evaporated milk**
    Assorted food coloring and decorations of your choice

1. In a large bowl, cream the sugar, butter, vanilla and salt. Add eggs and mix well. Combine the flour, baking powder and baking soda; add to creamed mixture. Chill until firm, about 1 hour.

2. On a floured surface, roll dough to ¼-in. thickness. Cut shapes with cookie cutters; place on greased baking sheets. Bake at 375° for 7-12 minutes (depending on size) or until light golden brown. Remove to wire racks to cool completely.

3. In a large bowl, combine the confectioners' sugar, extract and enough milk to achieve desired consistency. Tint with food coloring. Decorate cookies as desired.

HAPPY
MOTHER'S
DAY!

BLACK-EYED SUSAN COOKIES

Black-eyed Susans attract butterflies when planted in masses, and you'll draw a crowd when you make these cookies. They may be a little more time-consuming than some cookies, but their sunny faces and gumdrop centers are worth it.

—**GRACE PACK** BEAVER, WV

PREP: 25 MIN. + CHILLING
BAKE: 10 MIN./BATCH + COOLING
MAKES: 21 COOKIES

- 1 **cup butter, softened**
- 1¼ **cups sugar**
- 2 **large eggs**
- 1 **teaspoon orange extract**
- 2½ **cups all-purpose flour**
- 1 **teaspoon baking powder**
- ½ **teaspoon salt**

GLAZE

- 2 **cups confectioners' sugar**
- ¼ **cup milk**
- ½ **teaspoon orange extract**
- 2 **to 3 drops yellow food coloring, optional**
  Additional confectioners' sugar
  Black gumdrops

1. In a large bowl, cream butter and sugar until light and fluffy. Beat in the eggs and orange extract. Combine the flour, baking powder and salt; gradually add to creamed mixture. Divide dough in half so that one portion is slightly larger than the other; shape each into a disk. Wrap in plastic; refrigerate for 1-2 hours or until dough is easy to handle.

2. On a lightly floured surface, roll larger portion of dough to ⅛-in. thickness. Cut with a floured 3-in. round or scalloped cookie cutter to make flower bottoms. Place 1 in. apart on greased baking sheets. Repeat with remaining dough using a floured 2¾-in. flower or a scalloped cookie cutter to make an equal number of flower tops.

3. Bake larger cookies at 350° for 8-10 minutes or until golden brown; bake smaller cookies for 5-7 minutes or until golden brown. Remove to wire racks to cool completely.

4. In a bowl, combine the confectioners' sugar, milk, extract and, if desired, food coloring; mix until smooth. Immediately spread over cooled cookies. Stir additional confectioners' sugar into remaining glaze to thicken; spread a small amount on bottom of smaller cookies; place cookies over larger cookies. Top with gumdrops.

MOM'S SOFT SUGAR COOKIES

This delicious recipe has been passed down in our family for 75 years. Try it and you'll see why it remains our very favorite cookie!

—ARNITA SCHROEDER HOAGLAND, IN

....

PREP: 20 MIN. + CHILLING
BAKE: 10 MIN./BATCH
MAKES: ABOUT 7½ DOZEN

- 4 cups all-purpose flour
- 1 teaspoon baking powder
- ½ teaspoon nutmeg
- 1 cup butter, softened
- 1¾ cups sugar
- ¾ teaspoon salt
- 4 large egg yolks
- 2 large eggs
- 1 teaspoon baking soda
- 2 tablespoons hot water
- 1 cup (8 ounces) sour cream
  Optional toppings: colored or granulated sugar

1. In a large bowl, whisk flour, baking powder and nutmeg. In another bowl, cream butter, sugar and salt until light and fluffy. Beat in egg yolks and eggs. Dissolve baking soda in hot water. Add sour cream and dissolved baking soda to creamed mixture. Gradually beat in flour mixture (dough will be sticky). Refrigerate, covered, overnight.

2. Preheat oven to 350°. Working with one-third of the batch at a time, roll out dough on a well-floured surface to ¼-in. thickness. (Cover and refrigerate the remaining dough until ready to roll.) Cut with a floured 2½-in. round or other shaped cookie cutter. Place 1 in. apart on greased baking sheets. If desired, sprinkle tops with sugar.

3. Bake 8-10 minutes or until cookies are set but not browned. Remove from pans to wire racks to cool.

PEANUT BUTTER COOKIES

It is amazing how much flavor these simple cookies have. I make them often because I always have the three ingredients on hand. It's nice that the recipe makes a small batch.

—MAGGIE SCHIMMEL WAUWATOSA, WI

START TO FINISH: 30 MIN.
MAKES: 2 DOZEN

Short & Sweet

- 1 **large egg, beaten**
- 1 **cup sugar**
- 1 **cup creamy peanut butter**

1. In a large bowl, mix all ingredients. Scoop level tablespoonfuls and roll into balls. Place on ungreased baking sheets and flatten with a fork.

2. Bake at 350° for about 18 minutes or until set. Remove to wire racks to cool.

NOTE *This recipe does not contain flour.*

PIZZELLE CANNOLI

We made two Italian treats into one with beautiful pizzelle cookies wrapped around a rich, chocolaty cannoli filling. Chopped pistachios are an attractive touch.

—TASTE OF HOME TEST KITCHEN

PREP: 45 MIN. + COOLING
COOK: 5 MIN./BATCH
MAKES: 12 FILLED COOKIES

- 1 large egg
- ¼ cup sugar
- ¼ cup butter, melted
- ½ teaspoon vanilla extract
- ¼ teaspoon grated lemon peel
- ⅛ teaspoon almond extract
- ½ cup all-purpose flour
- ¼ teaspoon baking powder

FILLING
- ¾ cup sugar
- 3 tablespoons cornstarch
- 1 cup milk
- 1⅛ teaspoons vanilla extract
- 1 drop cinnamon oil, optional
- 1¾ cups ricotta cheese
- 1 milk chocolate candy bar with almonds (4¼ ounces), chopped
- ½ cup chopped pistachios

1. In a large bowl, beat the egg, sugar, butter, vanilla, lemon peel and almond extract until blended. Combine flour and baking powder; stir into egg mixture and mix well.

2. Bake in a preheated pizzelle iron according to manufacturer's directions until golden brown. Remove cookies and immediately shape into tubes. Place on wire racks to cool.

3. In a small saucepan, combine sugar and cornstarch. Stir in milk until smooth. Bring to a boil; cook and stir for 2 minutes or until thickened. Stir in the vanilla and, if desired, cinnamon oil. Cool completely.

4. In a large bowl, beat ricotta cheese until smooth. Gradually beat in custard mixture. Fold in chocolate. Spoon or pipe into shells. Dip each end into pistachios. Serve immediately. Refrigerate leftovers.

HAPPY MEMORIAL DAY! ☆

PATRIOTIC SUGAR COOKIES

One thing I especially love about these sugar cookies is that they ship well, so they're a wonderful treat to send overseas to troops. Get a group together to have a baking, decorating and packing party!

—**SUSAN WHETZEL** PEARISBURG, VA

PREP: 1¼ HOURS + CHILLING
BAKE: 10 MIN./BATCH + COOLING
MAKES: 10 DOZEN

- 1 **cup butter, softened**
- ½ **cup cream cheese, softened**
- 2 **cups sugar**
- 4 **large eggs**
- 1½ **teaspoons vanilla extract**
- 1 **teaspoon lemon extract**
- 5 **cups all-purpose flour**
- 2 **teaspoons baking powder**
- 1 **teaspoon salt**
  Decorating icing and/or colored sugars

1. In a large bowl, cream the butter, cream cheese and sugar until light and fluffy. Beat in eggs and extracts. Combine flour, baking powder and salt; gradually add to creamed mixture and mix well. Cover and refrigerate for 2 hours or until easy to handle.

2. On a lightly floured surface, roll out dough to ¼-in. thickness. Cut with floured 2- to 3-in. cookie cutters. Place 1 in. apart on ungreased baking sheets. Sprinkle with colored sugars as desired.

3. Bake at 350° for 9-11 minutes or until set. Cool 2 minutes before removing from pans to wire racks to cool completely. Decorate with icing and additional sugars if desired.

NOTE *If shipping these cookies, consider decorating with royal icing.*

FESTIVE SANDWICH COOKIES

Here's a simple picnic dessert that's ready in a snap and won't melt in the summer heat.

—JERRY GULLEY PLEASANT PRAIRIE, WI

START TO FINISH: 15 MIN.
MAKES: 3 DOZEN

Short & Sweet

- 4 **ounces white or milk chocolate candy coating, coarsely chopped**
- 1 **package (14.3 ounces) Oreo cookies**
  Patriotic sprinkles

In a microwave, melt 2 oz. of candy coating, stirring until smooth. Spread over tops of half of the cookies; decorate as desired with sprinkles. Place on waxed paper until set. Repeat with remaining coating, cookies and toppings.

PISTACHIO MACARONS

These macarons call for pistachios instead of almonds and feature a chocolate filling.
—*TASTE OF HOME* TEST KITCHEN

PREP: 35 MIN.
BAKE: 10 MIN./BATCH + COOLING
MAKES: ABOUT 1½ DOZEN

- 3 **large egg whites**
- 1¼ **cups confectioners' sugar**
- ¾ **cup pistachios**
  Dash salt
- ¼ **cup sugar**

CHOCOLATE FILLING

- 4 **ounces bittersweet chocolate, chopped**
- ½ **cup heavy whipping cream**
- 2 **teaspoons corn syrup**
- 1 **tablespoon butter**

1. Place egg whites in a small bowl; let stand at room temperature for 30 minutes. Line baking sheets with parchment paper; set aside. Place the confectioners' sugar and pistachios in a food processor. Cover and process until pistachios become a fine powder.

2. Preheat oven to 350°. Add salt to egg whites; beat on medium speed until soft peaks form. Add sugar, 1 tablespoon at a time, beating on high until stiff peaks form. Fold in pistachio mixture.

3. Place mixture in a heavy-duty resealable plastic bag; cut a small hole in a corner of the bag. Pipe 1-in.-diameter cookies 1 in. apart onto prepared baking sheets. Bake for 10-12 minutes or until lightly browned and firm to the touch. Cool completely on pans on wire racks.

4. Place chocolate in a small bowl. In a small saucepan, bring cream and corn syrup just to a boil. Pour over chocolate; whisk until smooth. Whisk in butter. Cool, stirring occasionally, to room temperature or until filling reaches a spreading consistency, about 45 minutes. Spread on the bottoms of half of the cookies; top with remaining cookies.

CHOCOLATE AMARETTI

I enjoy baking, especially Italian cookies, and these classic almond-paste treats are like those you'd find in an Italian bakery. My husband and children are always excited when I include them in my baking lineup.
—**KATHY LONG** WHITEFISH BAY, WI

PREP: 15 MIN. • **BAKE:** 20 MIN./BATCH
MAKES: 3 DOZEN

- 1¼ cups almond paste
- ¾ cup sugar
- 2 large egg whites
- ½ cup confectioners' sugar
- ¼ cup baking cocoa

1. In a large bowl, beat the almond paste, sugar and egg whites until combined. Combine confectioners' sugar and cocoa; gradually add to almond mixture and mix well.

2. Drop by tablespoonfuls 2 in. apart onto parchment paper-lined baking sheets. Bake at 350° for 17-20 minutes or until the tops are cracked. Cool for 1 minute before removing the cookies from pans to wire racks. Store in an airtight container.

APRICOT ALMOND BLONDIES

My mom shared this recipe with me after sampling these cookies at a bed-and-breakfast. For a little variation, I sometimes substitute cranberries and pecans for the apricots and almonds.

—AMY FORKNER CHEYENNE, WY

PREP: 10 MIN. • **BAKE:** 10 MIN./BATCH
MAKES: 6 DOZEN

- ¾ **cup butter, softened**
- 1 **cup packed brown sugar**
- 1 **large egg**
- 1 **teaspoon vanilla extract**
- 1⅔ **cups all-purpose flour**
- ½ **teaspoon baking soda**
- ¼ **teaspoon salt**
- 1 **package (10 to 12 ounces) vanilla or white chips**
- ¾ **cup chopped almonds**
- ¾ **cup chopped dried apricots**

1. In a large bowl, cream butter and brown sugar until light and fluffy. Beat in egg and vanilla. Combine the flour, baking soda and salt; gradually add to creamed mixture and mix well. Stir in vanilla chips, almonds and apricots.

2. Drop by heaping tablespoonfuls 2 in. apart onto ungreased baking sheets. Bake at 350° for 7-9 minutes or until lightly browned. Remove to wire racks to cool.

★ ★ ★ ★ ★ **READER REVIEW**

"Loved these...easy and you can substitute different dried fruits and nuts. I used craisins and pecans. Delicious!"

ADGIRL22 TASTEOFHOME.COM

TENDER ITALIAN SUGAR COOKIES

These traditional cookies are moist and tender. To tie into the colors of the Italian flag, you could tint the icing red, green and white.

—**WEDA MOSELLIE** PHILLIPSBURG, NJ

PREP: 20 MIN.
BAKE: 10 MIN./BATCH + COOLING
MAKES: 3 DOZEN

- ¾ cup shortening
- ¾ cup sugar
- 3 large eggs
- 1 teaspoon vanilla extract
- 3 cups all-purpose flour
- 3 teaspoons baking powder
- ⅛ teaspoon salt

ICING
- ¼ cup milk
- 2 tablespoons butter, melted
- ½ teaspoon vanilla extract
- 2½ cups confectioners' sugar
  Food coloring and coarse sugar, optional

1. Preheat oven to 400°. In a large bowl, cream shortening and sugar until light and fluffy. Beat in eggs and vanilla. Combine flour, baking powder and salt; gradually add to creamed mixture and mix well.

2. Shape dough into 1½-in. balls. Place 1 in. apart on ungreased baking sheets. Bake for 8-10 minutes or until lightly browned. Remove to wire racks to cool.

3. For icing, in a small bowl, combine milk, butter, vanilla and confectioners' sugar until smooth. Tint with food coloring if desired. Dip tops of cookies in icing; allow excess to drip off. Sprinkle with coarse sugar if desired. Place on waxed paper; let stand until set.

OLD-FASHIONED OATMEAL COOKIES

I'm the fourth generation of cooks in my family to bake these cookies. When my grandmother sent a batch for my birthday one year, I asked her for the recipe. That's when I learned it was originally my great-grandmother's recipe…and it's one I will definitely make sure gets passed on!

—**LORETTA PAKULSKI** INDIAN RIVER, MI

PREP: 10 MIN. • **BAKE:** 15 MIN./BATCH
MAKES: 4 DOZEN

- 1 cup shortening
- 2 cups packed brown sugar
- 2 large eggs
- 2 tablespoons milk
- 2½ cups all-purpose flour
- 2 cups old-fashioned oats
- 1 teaspoon baking soda
- 1 teaspoon salt
- 1 teaspoon ground cinnamon

In a bowl, cream shortening and brown sugar. Add eggs and milk; mix well. Combine flour, oats, baking soda, salt and cinnamon; add to the creamed mixture. Drop by rounded teaspoonfuls 2 in. apart onto lightly greased baking sheets. Bake at 350° for 12-15 minutes or until done.

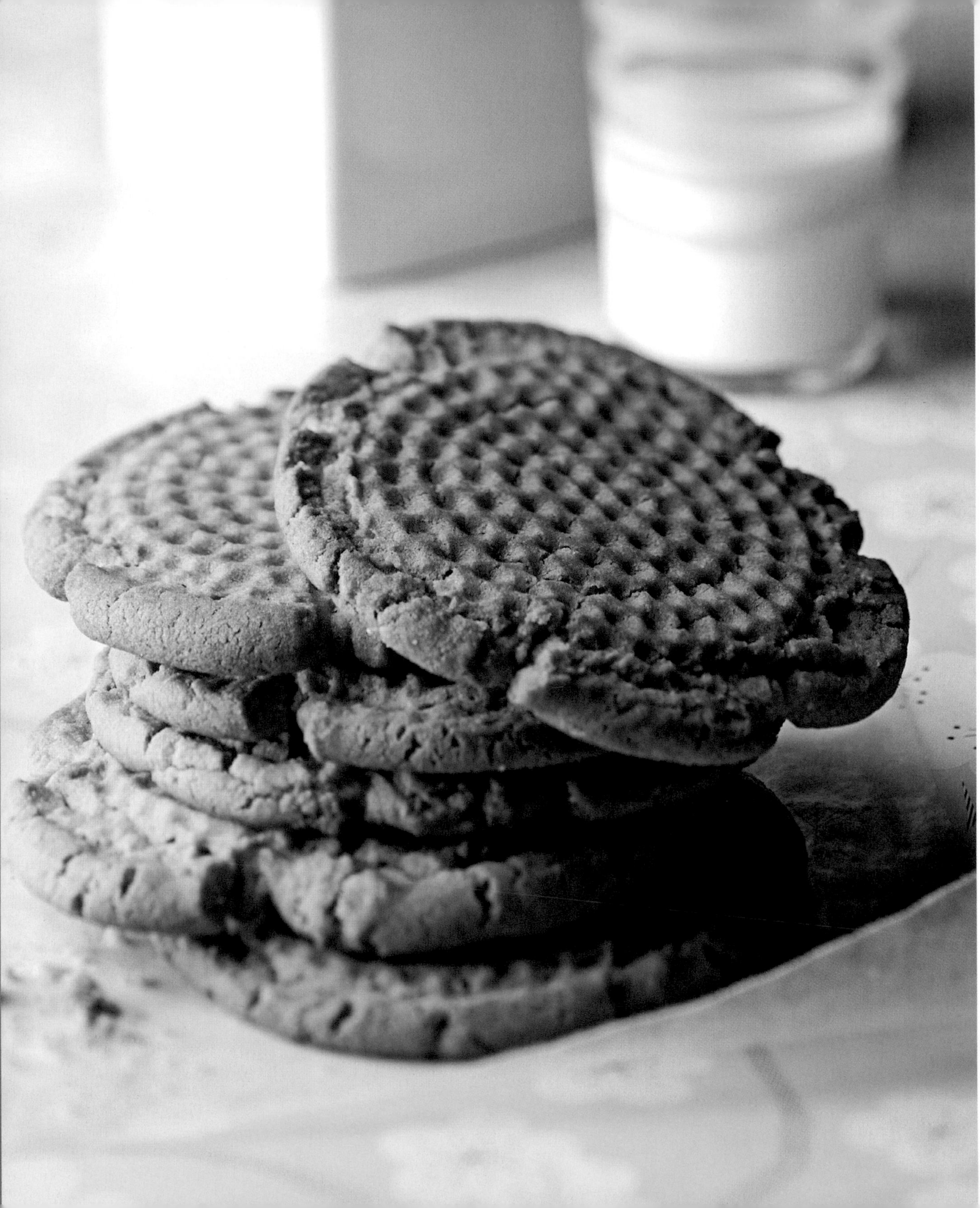

PIONEER PEANUT BUTTER COOKIES

This treasured recipe is the only one my grandmother ever wrote down! When my mother was married, she insisted her mother write down one recipe for her. That was a real effort, because Grandma was a pioneer-type cook who used a little of this or that 'til it felt right.

—**JANET HALL** CLINTON, WI

PREP: 15 MIN. • **BAKE:** 10 MIN./BATCH
MAKES: 3 DOZEN

- 1 **cup shortening**
- 1 **cup peanut butter**
- 1 **cup sugar**
- 1 **cup packed brown sugar**
- 3 **large eggs**
- 3 **cups all-purpose flour**
- 2 **teaspoons baking soda**
- ¼ **teaspoon salt**

1. Preheat oven to 375°. In a large bowl, cream shortening, peanut butter and sugars until light and fluffy. Add eggs, one at a time, beating well after each addition. Combine flour, baking soda and salt; add to creamed mixture and mix well.
2. Roll into 1½-in. balls. Place 3 in. apart on ungreased baking sheets. Flatten with a fork or meat mallet if desired. Bake 10-15 minutes. Remove to wire racks to cool.

★ ★ ★ ★ ★ **READER REVIEW**

"Great cookies ! Lots of recipes that called for 'a little bit of this and a little bit of that' were lost. Glad Janet's mom saved this one."

TSUOP TASTEOFHOME.COM

CHOCOLATE ALMOND BISCOTTI

During college, I came across a chocolate biscotti recipe and played around with it until I achieved these decadent bites. They're great for dunking into tea or coffee.

—**LORI HINZE** MCCOOK, NE

PREP: 30 MIN. • **BAKE:** 50 MIN. + COOLING
MAKES: 13 COOKIES

- ¼ **cup butter, softened**
- ⅔ **cup sugar**
- 1 **large egg**
- 2 **tablespoons beaten egg**
- 1 **ounce semisweet chocolate, melted and cooled**
- ½ **teaspoon instant coffee granules**
- ½ **teaspoon hot water**
- 1¼ **cups all-purpose flour**
- 2 **tablespoons baking cocoa**
- 1½ **teaspoons baking powder**
- ¼ **teaspoon salt**
- ⅓ **cup slivered almonds, toasted**
- 3 **ounces white baking chocolate, melted**

1. In a small bowl, cream butter and sugar until light and fluffy. Beat in eggs and semisweet chocolate until blended. Dissolve coffee granules in hot water; beat into the chocolate mixture. Combine the flour, cocoa, baking powder and salt; gradually add to chocolate mixture.
2. Turn dough onto a floured surface; knead in almonds. On a baking sheet coated with cooking spray, shape dough into a 12x3-in. rectangle. Bake at 350° for 28-30 minutes or until lightly browned. Cool for 10 minutes.
3. Transfer to a cutting board; cut diagonally with a serrated knife into 13 slices. Place cut side down on a baking sheet coated with cooking spray. Bake for 20-25 minutes or until firm and crisp, turning once. Remove biscotti to a wire rack to cool.
4. Drizzle white chocolate over the biscotti; let stand until set. Store in an airtight container.

BUTTERMILK BLUEBERRY SCOOKIES

The "scookie" idea came when I made cookie shapes out of scone dough. Light and crispy right from the oven, they are just sweet enough. We love them!

—**ALLY PHILLIPS** MURRELLS INLET, SC

START TO FINISH: 25 MIN.
MAKES: 1 DOZEN

- 2 **cups all-purpose flour**
- ½ **cup plus 1 tablespoon sugar, divided**
- 2 **teaspoons baking powder**
- 1 **teaspoon baking soda**
- ½ **cup cold butter, cubed**
- ½ **cup buttermilk**
- 1 **large egg, lightly beaten**
- 1 **cup fresh or frozen blueberries, thawed**

1. Preheat oven to 375°. In a large bowl, whisk flour, ½ cup sugar, baking powder and baking soda. Cut in butter until mixture resembles coarse crumbs. In another bowl, whisk buttermilk and egg until blended; stir into crumb mixture just until moistened.

2. Drop dough by scant ¼ cupfuls 2 in. apart onto a parchment paper-lined baking sheet. Form a ½-in.-deep indentation in center of each with the back of a spoon coated with cooking spray. Gently press blueberries into indentations; sprinkle with remaining sugar.

3. Bake 11-14 minutes or until golden brown. Serve warm.

PIGNOLI COOKIES

Cookies are the crown jewels of Italian confections. I can't let a special occasion go by without baking these traditional almond sweets rolled in mild pine nuts.

—**MARIA REGAKIS** SAUGUS, MA

PREP: 30 MIN. • **BAKE:** 15 MIN./BATCH
MAKES: 2½ DOZEN

- 1¼ **cups (12 ounces) almond paste**
- ½ **cup sugar**
- 4 **large egg whites, divided**
- 1 **cup confectioners' sugar**
- 1½ **cups pine nuts**

1. In a small bowl, beat almond paste and sugar until crumbly. Beat in 2 egg whites. Gradually add the confectioners' sugar; mix well.

2. Whisk remaining egg whites in a shallow bowl. Place pine nuts in another shallow bowl. Shape dough into 1-in. balls. Roll in egg whites and coat with pine nuts. Place 2 in. apart on parchment paper-lined baking sheets. Flatten slightly.

3. Bake at 325° for 15-18 minutes or until lightly browned. Cool for 1 minute before removing from pans to wire racks. Store in an airtight container.

MAY 30
NATIONAL
SCONE
DAY

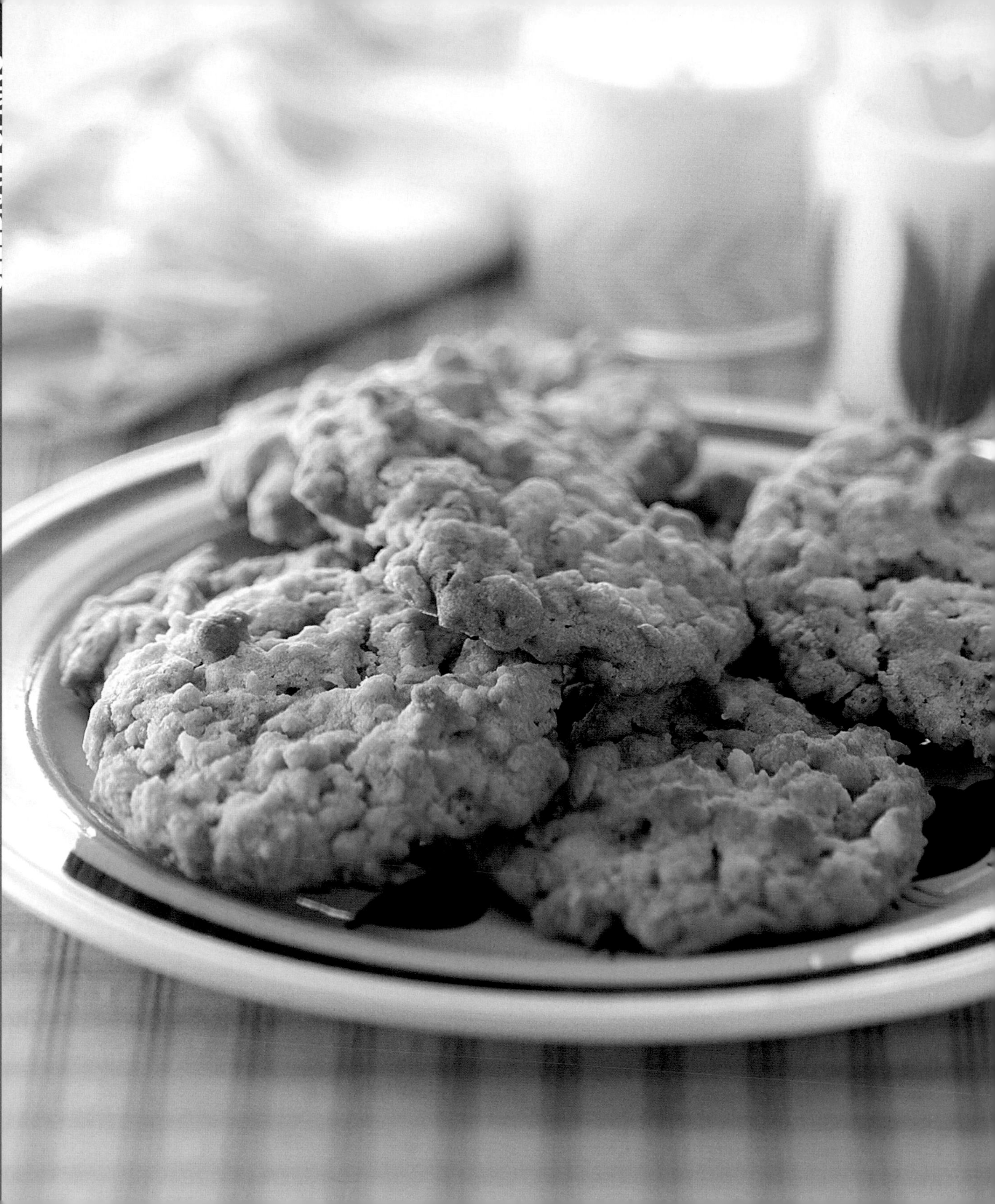

RANGER COOKIES

These golden brown cookies are crispy on the outside and cake-like on the inside. Their tasty blend of oats, rice cereal, coconut and brown sugar have made them a favorite with our family. You won't be able to eat just one.

—MARY LOU BOYCE WILMINGTON, DE

PREP: 25 MIN. • **BAKE:** 10 MIN./BATCH
MAKES: 7½ DOZEN

- 1 **cup shortening**
- 1 **cup sugar**
- 1 **cup packed brown sugar**
- 2 **large eggs**
- 1 **teaspoon vanilla extract**
- 2 **cups all-purpose flour**
- 1 **teaspoon baking soda**
- ½ **teaspoon baking powder**
- ½ **teaspoon salt**
- 2 **cups quick-cooking oats**
- 2 **cups crisp rice cereal**
- 1 **cup flaked coconut**

1. Preheat oven to 350°. In a large bowl, cream shortening and sugars until light and fluffy. Beat in the eggs and vanilla. Combine the flour, baking soda, baking powder and salt; gradually add to the creamed mixture and mix well. Stir in the oats, cereal and coconut.

2. Drop by rounded tablespoonfuls 2 in. apart onto ungreased baking sheets. Bake for 7-9 minutes or until golden brown. Remove to wire racks to cool.

PEANUT BUTTER RANGER COOKIES
Before creaming the shortening and sugars, add 1 cup peanut butter.

FROM THE COOKIE JAR

Ranger Cookies are great for shipping because they're a sturdy drop cookie. Wrap them in bundles of two with plastic wrap, placing the bottom sides together. Line the cookie tin or box with crumpled waxed paper to cushion the treats.

CHOCOLATE PECAN KISSES

A good friend gave me this recipe and, in turn, I have shared it with many others. It's a very easy recipe to make and makes a lot of cookies. I learned that these sometimes are called forgotten cookies because you can bake them at night and leave them in the oven until the next morning.

—JOSEPHINE BEALS ZIONSVILLE, IN

PREP: 15 MIN. + STANDING
BAKE: 40 MIN. + STANDING • **MAKES:** 1½ DOZEN

- 1 **large egg white**
- ⅓ **cup sugar**
- ½ **cup miniature semisweet chocolate chips**
- ½ **cup chopped pecans**

1. Place egg white in a small bowl; let stand at room temperature 30 minutes. Beat whites on medium speed until soft peaks form. Gradually beat in the sugar, 1 tablespoon at a time, on high until stiff peaks form. Fold in chocolate chips and chopped pecans.

2. Drop by rounded teaspoonfuls 2 in. apart onto parchment paper-lined baking sheets. Bake at 250° for 40-45 minutes or until firm to the touch. Turn oven off and let cookies dry in the oven for 1½ hours.

3. Carefully remove cookies from the parchment paper. Store in an airtight container.

COOKIES IN A JIFFY

You'll be amazed and delighted with how quickly you can whip up a batch of these homemade cookies.
—**CLARA HIELKEMA** WYOMING, MI

Short & Sweet

START TO FINISH: 20 MIN.
MAKES: 2 DOZEN

- 1 **package (9 ounces) yellow cake mix**
- ⅔ **cup quick-cooking oats**
- ½ **cup butter, melted**
- 1 **large egg**
- ½ **cup milk chocolate M&M's or butterscotch chips**

1. In a large bowl, beat the first four ingredients until well blended. Stir in the M&M's or butterscotch chips.

2. Drop by tablespoonfuls 2 in. apart onto ungreased baking sheets. Bake at 375° for 10-12 minutes or until lightly browned. Immediately remove to wire racks to cool.

LEMONY MACAROONS

These chewy gems have refreshing lemon flavor. They freeze well and thaw quickly, so you can cure a craving anytime.

—KARLA JOHNSON EAST HELENA, MT

PREP: 15 MIN.
BAKE: 15 MIN./BATCH + COOLING
MAKES: ABOUT 3 DOZEN

- 4 **large egg whites**
  Dash cream of tartar
  Dash salt
- 1 **can (14 ounces) sweetened condensed milk**
- ¼ **cup lemon juice**
- 1½ **teaspoons grated lemon peel**
- ½ **teaspoon baking powder**
- 3 **packages (7 ounces each) sweetened shredded coconut**

1. Preheat oven to 325°. In a bowl, beat egg whites, cream of tartar and salt until stiff peaks form. In another bowl, beat milk and lemon juice on high speed until thickened, about 3 minutes. Stir in lemon peel, baking powder and coconut. Fold in egg whites.

2. Drop mixture by tablespoonfuls 2 in. apart onto parchment paper-lined baking sheets. Bake 15-18 minutes or until golden brown. Cool on pans 2 minutes. Remove to wire racks to cool.

FREEZE OPTION *Freeze cookies, layered between waxed paper, in freezer containers. To use, thaw before serving.*

BREAKFAST COOKIES

I like to give my family a hearty start in the morning, especially when they have to eat in a hurry. These easy bacon-and-cheese cookies are perfect for breakfast on the run and really appeal to the kid in all of us.

—WANDA COX ROSCOMMON, MI

PREP: 25 MIN. • **BAKE:** 15 MIN.
MAKES: 3 DOZEN

- ⅔ **cup butter, softened**
- ⅔ **cup sugar**
- 1 **large egg, lightly beaten**
- 1 **teaspoon vanilla extract**
- ¾ **cup all-purpose flour**
- ½ **teaspoon baking soda**
- ½ **teaspoon salt**
- 1½ **cup old-fashioned oats**
- ½ **cup toasted wheat germ**
- 1 **cup shredded cheddar cheese**
- 6 **bacon strips, cooked and crumbled**

In a bowl, cream butter and sugar. Add egg and vanilla; mix well. Combine flour, baking soda and salt; add to creamed mixture and mix well. Stir in oats and wheat germ. Fold in cheese and bacon. Drop by rounded teaspoonfuls onto ungreased baking sheets. Bake at 350° for 15-17 minutes or until light brown.

ICED COOKIES

Grated lemon peel gives these soft bites a bright citrus flavor, and the yogurt keeps them tender. They are the perfect cookies to dunk in milk.

—BETTY THOMPSON LA PORTE, TX

PREP: 15 MIN. • **BAKE:** 10 MIN.
MAKES: ABOUT 3 DOZEN

- 7 **tablespoons butter, softened**
- ½ **cup sugar**
- 1 **large egg**
- 1¾ **cups all-purpose flour**
- 1 **teaspoon baking powder**
- ½ **teaspoon salt**
- ⅓ **cup honey**
- ¼ **cup plain yogurt**
- 2 **teaspoons grated lemon peel**
- ½ **teaspoon lemon extract**

ICING

- 1 **cup confectioners' sugar**
- 2 **tablespoons lemon juice**
- 2 **teaspoons grated lemon peel**

1. In a small bowl, cream butter and sugar until light and fluffy. Beat in egg. Combine the flour, baking powder and salt. Combine honey, yogurt, lemon peel and lemon extract. Add dry ingredients to creamed mixture alternately with honey mixture, mixing well after each addition.

2. Drop by tablespoonfuls 2 in. apart onto greased baking sheets. Bake at 350° for 10-12 minutes or until golden brown. Remove to wire racks.

3. Combine the confectioners' sugar and lemon juice in a small bowl until smooth. Brush over the warm cookies; sprinkle with lemon peel.

BANANA CHOCOLATE CHIP COOKIES

These soft cookies have a cake-like texture and lots of banana flavor that folks seem to love.

—VICKI RAATZ WATERLOO, WI

....

PREP: 20 MIN. • **BAKE:** 10 MIN./BATCH
MAKES: 3 DOZEN

- ⅓ **cup butter, softened**
- ½ **cup sugar**
- 1 **large egg**
- ½ **cup mashed ripe banana**
- ½ **teaspoon vanilla extract**
- 1 **cup all-purpose flour**
- 1 **teaspoon baking powder**
- ¼ **teaspoon salt**
- ⅛ **teaspoon baking soda**
- 1 **cup (6 ounces) semisweet chocolate chips**

1. In a small bowl, cream butter and sugar until light and fluffy. Beat in the egg, banana and vanilla. Combine the flour, baking powder, salt and baking soda; gradually add to creamed mixture and mix well. Stir in chocolate chips.

2. Drop by tablespoonfuls 2 in. apart onto baking sheets coated with cooking spray. Bake at 350° for 9-11 minutes or until edges are lightly browned. Remove to wire racks to cool.

★ ★ ★ ★ ★ **READER REVIEW**

"Banana lovers will eat these up! Easy and quick to pull together, my kids love them so much that I also make them into mini muffins."

MAMAKNOWSBEST
TASTEOFHOME.COM

SUMMER FUN

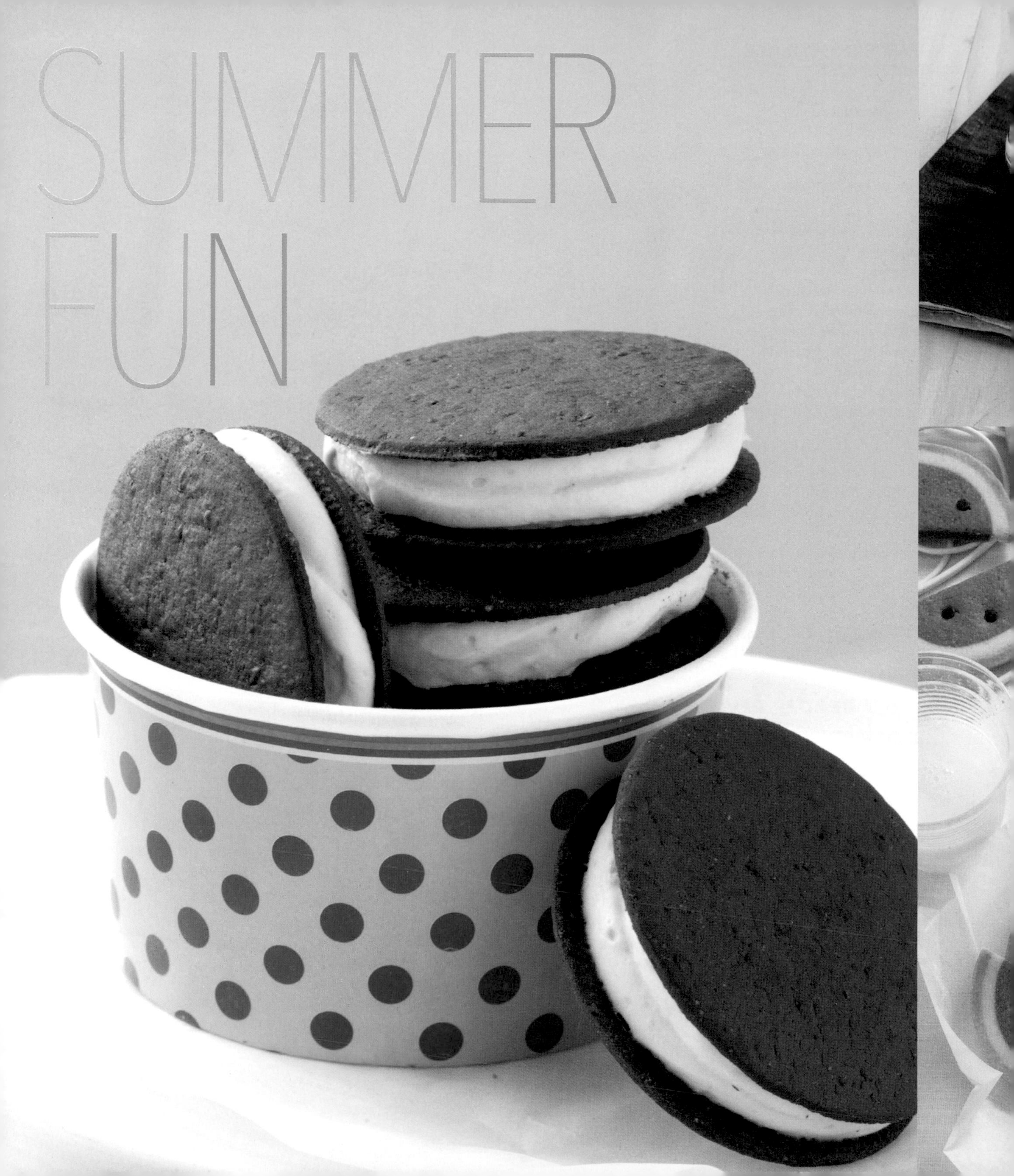

Block parties, baby showers and backyard barbecues...these are just a few of the hot spots where sweet treats are in demand. When these parties hit your summer calendar, turn here for cookies that won't eat up your time. You'll find ice cream sandwiches, icebox cookies and no-bakes perfect for warm-weather fun. In fact, this section offers 90 cookies ideal for summer snacking. Pack up enough to share before heading to the park, going to watch fireworks or planning a campfire getaway.

LOOK FOR THE SPECIAL DAYS IN THIS CHAPTER:

There's so much to celebrate in summer! Add these fun and funny days to your lineup, and bring the kids into the kitchen to help bake up a sweet treat!

JULY 12
NATIONAL PECAN PIE DAY

GOOEY CARAMEL-TOPPED GINGERSNAPS

Making these cookies is therapeutic for me. The gingersnaps are quite popular at fundraisers. If you'd like, you can switch things up by changing the cookie base or varying the nuts.
—**DEIRDRE COX** KANSAS CITY, MO

Short & Sweet

PREP: 30 MIN. + STANDING
MAKES: 3½ DOZEN

- 42 **gingersnap cookies**
- 1 **package (14 ounces) caramels**
- ¼ **cup 2% milk or heavy whipping cream**
- 1 **cup chopped honey-roasted peanuts**
- 12 **ounces white or dark chocolate candy coating, melted**
  Chocolate jimmies or finely chopped honey-roasted peanuts

1. Arrange cookies in a single layer on waxed paper-lined baking sheets. In a microwave, melt caramels with milk; stir until smooth. Stir in 1 cup chopped peanuts. Spoon about 1 teaspoon of the caramel mixture over each cookie; refrigerate until set.

2. Dip each cookie halfway into candy coating; allow excess to drip off. Return to baking sheet; sprinkle with jimmies. Refrigerate until set.

JUNE 1
WORLD MILK DAY

MALTED MILK COOKIES

My family loves anything made with malt or chocolate malted milk balls, so these cookies are some of their favorites!

—**NANCY FOUST** STONEBORO, PA

PREP: 40 MIN.
BAKE: 10 MIN./BATCH + COOLING
MAKES: 4 DOZEN

- 1 cup butter, softened
- 2 cups packed brown sugar
- 2 large eggs
- ⅓ cup sour cream
- 2 teaspoons vanilla extract
- 4¾ cups all-purpose flour
- ¾ cup malted milk powder
- 2 teaspoons baking powder
- ½ teaspoon baking soda
- ½ teaspoon salt

FROSTING

- 3 cups confectioners' sugar
- ½ cup malted milk powder
- ⅓ cup butter, softened
- 1½ teaspoons vanilla extract
- 3 to 4 tablespoons 2% milk
- 2 cups coarsely chopped malted milk balls

1. Preheat oven to 350°. In a large bowl, cream butter and brown sugar until light and fluffy. Beat in eggs, sour cream and vanilla. In another bowl, whisk flour, malted milk powder, baking powder, baking soda and salt; gradually beat into creamed mixture.

2. Divide dough into three portions. On a lightly floured surface, roll each portion of dough to ¼-in. thickness. Cut with a floured 2½-in. round cookie cutter. Place 2 in. apart on parchment paper-lined baking sheets.

3. Bake 10-12 minutes or until edges are light brown. Remove from pans to wire racks to cool completely.

4. For frosting, in a bowl, beat the confectioners' sugar, malted milk powder, butter, vanilla and enough milk to reach a good spreading consistency. Spread over cookies. Sprinkle with chopped candies.

BLUE MOON CRESCENT COOKIES

I love my grandma's vanilla crescent cookies, but I wanted to add my own twist. These have a touch of lemon and cinnamon, plus flecks of dried blueberries.
—CRYSTAL SCHLUETER NORTHGLENN, CO

PREP: 15 MIN.
BAKE: 15 MIN./BATCH + COOLING
MAKES: ABOUT 2½ DOZEN

- 1 cup butter, softened
- ½ cup sugar
- 2 teaspoons grated lemon peel
- 1 teaspoon lemon juice
- ½ teaspoon vanilla extract
- ½ teaspoon ground cinnamon
- ¼ teaspoon salt
- 2 cups all-purpose flour
- 1 cup dried blueberries
  Confectioners' sugar

1. Preheat oven to 350°. In a large bowl, cream butter and sugar until light and fluffy. Beat in lemon peel, juice, vanilla, cinnamon and salt. Gradually beat flour into creamed mixture; stir in blueberries. Shape tablespoonfuls of the dough into crescent shapes. Place crescents 2 in. apart on ungreased baking sheets. Bake for 15-18 minutes or until the edges are lightly browned.

2. Cool on pans 2 minutes. Remove to wire racks to cool completely. Dust cookies with confectioners' sugar.

★ ★ ★ ★ ★ 5 STAR TIP

If the cookie dough is too sticky to successfully shape, dust your hands with a little flour or set the dough in the refrigerator to firm up a bit.

CRISP BUTTON COOKIES

Almost too cute to eat but always too sweet to resist, these clever cookies take minutes to make—and they'll disappear even faster!

—**BONNIE BUCKLEY** KANSAS CITY, MO

PREP: 20 MIN. + CHILLING
BAKE: 10 MIN./BATCH
MAKES: ABOUT 3 DOZEN

- ¾ **cup butter, softened**
- 1 **cup confectioners' sugar**
- 1 **large egg**
- 1 **teaspoon vanilla extract**
- 2½ **cups all-purpose flour**
- ¼ **teaspoon salt**
- ¼ **teaspoon ground cardamom**
  Assorted food coloring, optional
  Multicolored pull-and-peel licorice

1. In a large bowl, cream butter and confectioners' sugar until light and fluffy. Beat in egg and vanilla. In another bowl, whisk flour, salt and cardamom; gradually beat into creamed mixture. If desired, divide dough into portions and tint with food coloring. Refrigerate, covered, for 2 hours or until easy to handle.
2. Preheat oven to 350°. On a lightly floured surface, roll dough to ¼-in. thickness. Cut with a floured 2½-in. round cookie cutter. Place 1 in. apart on ungreased baking sheets. With the top of a ¼-cup measuring cup dipped in flour, press an indented edge into each cookie. Using a plastic straw, cut out four holes near the center of the cookie.
3. Bake 10-15 minutes or until edges are lightly browned. Remove to wire racks to cool. Lace licorice through the holes in each button; trim licorice.

WHOOPIE PIES

These cupcake-like treats have been a favorite for years. They're especially fun to assemble with kids when they're out of school.

—**RUTH ANN STELFOX** RAYMOND, AB

PREP: 15 MIN. • **BAKE:** 5 MIN./BATCH + COOLING
MAKES: 1½ DOZEN

- 1 **cup butter, softened**
- 1½ **cups sugar**
- 2 **large eggs**
- 2 **teaspoons vanilla extract**
- 4 **cups all-purpose flour**
- ¾ **cup baking cocoa**
- 2 **teaspoons baking soda**
- ½ **teaspoon salt**
- 1 **cup water**
- 1 **cup buttermilk**

FILLING

- 2 **cups confectioners' sugar**
- 2 **cups marshmallow creme**
- ½ **cup butter, softened**
- 2 **teaspoons vanilla extract**

1. In a large bowl, cream butter and sugar until light and fluffy. Beat in eggs and vanilla. Combine the flour, cocoa, baking soda and salt; add to creamed mixture alternately with water and buttermilk, beating well after each addition.
2. Drop by tablespoonfuls 2 in. apart onto greased baking sheets. Bake at 375° for 5-7 minutes or until set. Remove to wire racks to cool completely.
3. In a bowl, beat filling ingredients until fluffy. Spread on the bottoms of half of the cookies; top with remaining cookies.

JUNE 2
NATIONAL ROCKY ROAD DAY

ROCKY ROAD COOKIE CUPS

Traditional rocky road ice cream has nuts, marshmallows and chocolate. Using prepared cookie dough makes it easy to put those flavors together.

—CHARLOTTE MCDANIEL
JACKSONVILLE, AL

PREP: 20 MIN.
BAKE: 15 MIN. + COOLING
MAKES: 2 DOZEN

- 1 tube (16½ ounces) refrigerated chocolate chip cookie dough
- ¾ cup miniature marshmallows
- 2 tablespoons miniature semisweet chocolate chips
- ¼ cup sliced almonds, toasted

1. Preheat oven to 350°. Shape dough into 1¼-in. balls; press evenly onto bottom and up sides of 24 greased mini-muffin cups.

2. Bake 10-12 minutes or until edges are golden. Using the back of a measuring teaspoon, make an indentation in each cup. Immediately place 3 marshmallows and ¼ teaspoon chocolate chips in each cup; sprinkle with almonds. Return to the oven; bake 1 minute longer. Cool completely in pans on wire racks.

NOTE *To toast nuts, evenly spread in a 15x10x1-in. baking pan. Bake at 350° for 5-10 minutes or until lightly browned, stirring occasionally. Or, place in a nonstick skillet and heat over low heat until lightly browned, stirring the nuts occasionally.*

CHERRY COOKIE TARTS

A tender, almond-flavored dough, cherry filling and thin glaze make these so special.

—JANICE CHRISTOFFERSON
EAGLE RIVER, WI

PREP: 45 MIN. + CHILLING
BAKE: 15 MIN./BATCH + COOLING
MAKES: 3 DOZEN

- ¾ cup unsalted butter, softened
- ¾ cup sugar
- 1 large egg
- 2 tablespoons 2% milk

- 1 teaspoon almond extract
- 2½ cups all-purpose flour
- ¼ teaspoon baking soda
- ¼ teaspoon salt
- ¾ cup cherry preserves
- 1 large egg white, lightly beaten

GLAZE
- 1 cup confectioners' sugar
- 2 tablespoons 2% milk
- ½ teaspoon vanilla extract

1. In a large bowl, cream butter and sugar until light and fluffy. Beat in egg, milk and extract. In another bowl, whisk flour, baking soda and salt; gradually beat into creamed mixture. Divide dough in half. Shape each into a disk; wrap in plastic. Refrigerate for 1 hour or until easy to handle.

2. Preheat oven to 350°. On a lightly floured surface, roll one portion of dough to ⅛-in. thickness. Cut with a floured 2-in. round cookie cutter.

3. Place half of the cutouts 2 in. apart on greased baking sheets. Top each with a heaping teaspoonful of preserves; top with remaining cutouts. Crimp edges together with a fork to seal. With a sharp knife, cut an X in the top of each cookie. Brush tops with egg white.

4. Bake 12-15 minutes or until edges are light brown. Remove to wire racks to cool completely.

5. In a small bowl, mix glaze ingredients; spread over cooled cookies. Let stand until set.

Short & Sweet

MINT CREME COOKIES

A minty filling sandwiched between rich chocolate cookies—what's not to love?

—GAYLENE ANDERSON SANDY, UT

PREP: 20 MIN. • **BAKE:** 10 MIN. + COOLING
MAKES: 4 DOZEN

- 1½ cups packed brown sugar
- ¾ cup butter, cubed
- 2 tablespoons water
- 2 cups (12 ounces) semisweet chocolate chips
- 2 large eggs
- 3 cups all-purpose flour
- 1¼ teaspoons baking soda
- 1 teaspoon salt

FILLING
- ⅓ cup butter, softened
- 3 cups confectioners' sugar
- 3 to 4 tablespoons milk
- ⅛ teaspoon peppermint extract
  Dash salt

1. In a small saucepan, combine the brown sugar, butter and water. Cook and stir over medium heat until sugar is dissolved. Remove from the heat; stir in the chocolate chips until melted and smooth. Transfer to a bowl; cool slightly.
2. Add eggs, one at a time, beating well after each addition. Combine the flour, baking soda and salt; gradually add to chocolate mixture and mix well.
3. Drop by rounded teaspoonfuls onto greased baking sheets. Bake at 350° for 8-10 minutes or until set. Remove to wire racks; flatten slightly. Cool completely.
4. Combine filling ingredients; spread on the bottoms of half of the cookies; top with the remaining cookies. Store in the refrigerator.

★ ★ ★ ★ ★ **5 STAR TIP**

These delightful sandwich cookies are refreshing for summer, but feel free to make them all year long! Add a drop or two of food coloring to the filling for a lovely Valentine's Day pink, St. Patrick's Day green, fun Easter yellow or deep red for Christmas.

AUNT IONE'S ICEBOX COOKIES

Whenever we went to visit my Aunt Ione in Georgia, her icebox cookies were our favorite treat.

—**JENNY HILL** MERIDIANVILLE, AL

PREP: 20 MIN. + CHILLING
BAKE: 10 MIN./BATCH
MAKES: ABOUT 17 DOZEN

- 6 **cups all-purpose flour**
- 1½ **teaspoons baking powder**
- 1 **teaspoon baking soda**
- 1 **teaspoon ground nutmeg**
- 1 **teaspoon ground cinnamon**
- 2 **cups butter, softened**
- 1 **cup sugar**
- 1 **cup packed brown sugar**
- 3 **large eggs**
- 1 **teaspoon vanilla extract**
- 1 **teaspoon lemon extract**
- 2 **cups chopped nuts**

1. Sift together first five ingredients; set aside. In a bowl, cream butter and sugars. Add eggs, vanilla and lemon extract; beat well. Add dry ingredients; mix well. Stir in nuts.

2. Divide dough into four parts and shape into 11x1½-in. rolls. Wrap in foil and chill overnight.

3. Slice the cookies ⅜ in. thick. Bake on greased baking sheets at 350° for about 10 minutes.

WATERMELON SLICE COOKIES

When I made these cute butter cookies for a party, a neighbor thought they were so adorable that she actually froze one to show her friends.

—SUE ANN BENHAM VALPARAISO, IN

PREP: 25 MIN. + CHILLING
BAKE: 10 MIN./BATCH
MAKES: ABOUT 3 DOZEN

- ¾ **cup butter, softened**
- ¾ **cup sugar**
- 1 **large egg**
- ½ **teaspoon almond extract**
- 2 **cups all-purpose flour**
- ¼ **teaspoon baking powder**
- ⅛ **teaspoon salt**
  Red and green gel food coloring
- ⅓ **cup miniature semisweet chocolate chips or raisins, chopped**
- 1 **teaspoon sesame seeds, optional**

1. In a large bowl, cream butter and sugar until light and fluffy. Beat in egg and extract. In another bowl, whisk flour, baking powder and salt; gradually beat into creamed mixture. Reserve 1 cup dough.

2. Tint remaining dough red; shape into a 3½-in.-long roll. Wrap in plastic. Tint ⅓ cup of reserved dough green; wrap in plastic. Wrap remaining plain dough. Refrigerate 2 hours or until firm.

3. On a lightly floured surface, roll plain dough into an 8½x3½-in. rectangle. Unwrap red dough and place on a short end of the plain dough; roll up.

4. Roll green dough into a 10x3½-in. rectangle. Place red and plain roll on a short end of the green dough; roll up. Wrap in plastic; refrigerate the dough overnight.

5. Preheat oven to 350°. Unwrap and cut dough into ³⁄₁₆-in. slices (just less than ¼ in.). Place 2 in. apart on ungreased baking sheets. Lightly press chocolate chips and, if desired, sesame seeds into red dough to resemble watermelon seeds.

6. Bake for 9-11 minutes or until firm. Immediately cut cookies in half, then remove to wire racks to cool.

CRISP GRAHAM COOKIES

I was delighted to find the recipe for these fun cookies. The peanut butter makes them extra special.

—LORI DANIELS BEVERLY, WV

PREP: 25 MIN. • **BAKE:** 10 MIN.
MAKES: 7 DOZEN

- ½ cup butter-flavored shortening
- ½ cup packed brown sugar
- 1 large egg
- 1½ teaspoons vanilla extract
- 1 can (14 ounces) sweetened condensed milk
- 3 tablespoons creamy peanut butter
- 1½ cups all-purpose flour
- 1 cup graham cracker crumbs
- 1 teaspoon baking soda
- 1 teaspoon salt
- ½ cup chopped pecans
- 1 package (12.6 ounces) milk chocolate M&M's

1. In a bowl, cream shortening and brown sugar; beat in egg. Add vanilla and milk. Blend in peanut butter. Combine dry ingredients; add to the creamed mixture. Stir in the pecans and M&M's.
2. Drop by teaspoonfuls 1 in. apart on ungreased baking sheets. Bake at 350° for 10-12 minutes or until golden brown. Cool on wire racks.

★ ★ ★ ★ ★ **READER REVIEW**

"Very delicious cookie! I'm throwing away my favorite cookie recipe. This is my new No. 1."

LORIHAGEL TASTEOFHOME.COM

PINWHEEL POPS

My mom used to make pinwheels every year, and I still love them. They are so colorful, and they're perfect for sharing as gifts.

—JILL HEATWOLE PITTSVILLE, MD

PREP: 30 MIN. + CHILLING
BAKE: 10 MIN./BATCH • **MAKES:** 2 DOZEN

- 1¼ cups butter, softened
- 1 cup packed brown sugar
- ½ cup sugar
- 2 large eggs
- 1 teaspoon vanilla, orange, almond, lemon or coconut extract
- 4 cups all-purpose flour
- 1 teaspoon salt
- 1 teaspoon baking powder
- ¼ teaspoon baking soda
  Pink, orange and yellow gel food coloring
  Sprinkles
  Wooden skewers or pop sticks

1. In a large bowl, cream butter and sugars until light and fluffy. Beat in eggs and vanilla. In another bowl, whisk flour, salt, baking powder and baking soda; gradually beat into creamed mixture.

2. Divide dough into three portions. Tint each portion as desired with food coloring; wrap in plastic. Refrigerate 30 minutes or until easy to handle.

3. Between pieces of waxed paper, roll each portion into a 12x6-in. rectangle. Remove pieces of waxed paper. Stack colored rectangles on top of each other to form one thick rectangle. Wrap in plastic; refrigerate 30 minutes or until firm.

4. Preheat oven to 375°. Unwrap and slice stacked rectangles crosswise, into 6x½-in. strips. Taper the ends of each strip; wrap strips around themselves to form coils. Place 1 in. apart on ungreased baking sheets. Decorate with sprinkles along cookie edges. Bake 8-10 minutes or until set.

5. Remove to wire racks to cool. While cookie is still soft, insert a wooden skewer or pop stick into each cookie.

WHITE CHOCOLATE NUT CRACKLES

My aunt and I would bake together when I was growing up, and we had a similar recipe for a white cookie. After some experimenting, I added the macadamia nuts and white chocolate chips. My family and co-workers rave over these treats.

—JOYCE GETHING PAMPA, TX

....

PREP: 25 MIN. + CHILLING
BAKE: 10 MIN./BATCH • **MAKES:** 5½ DOZEN

- ½ **cup butter, softened**
- ½ **cup shortening**
- ½ **cup sugar**
- ½ **cup packed brown sugar**
- 1 **large egg**
- 1 **teaspoon vanilla extract**
- 2 **cups all-purpose flour**
- 1 **teaspoon baking soda**
- 1 **teaspoon cream of tartar**
- ½ **teaspoon salt**
- 6 **ounces white baking chocolate, coarsely chopped**
- ½ **cup coarsely chopped macadamia nuts, toasted**
  Additional sugar

1. In a large bowl, cream the butter, shortening and sugars until light and fluffy. Beat in egg and vanilla. Combine the flour, baking soda, cream of tartar and salt; gradually add to the creamed mixture and mix well. Stir in chocolate and nuts. Cover and refrigerate for 1 hour or until easy to handle.

2. Roll into 1-in. balls. Dip each ball halfway in water, then in sugar. Place sugar side up 2 in. apart on ungreased baking sheets; flatten slightly.

3. Bake at 400° for 8-10 minutes or until golden brown. Remove to wire racks to cool.

LOADED-UP PRETZEL COOKIES

Coconut, M&M's and salty, crunchy pretzels make these loaded cookies unlike any you've ever tasted—or resisted.

—JACKIE RUCKWARDT
COTTAGE GROVE, OR

....

PREP: 20 MIN. • **BAKE:** 15 MIN./BATCH
MAKES: 2 DOZEN

- 1 **cup butter, softened**
- 1 **cup sugar**
- 1 **cup packed brown sugar**
- 2 **large eggs**
- 2 **teaspoons vanilla extract**
- 2½ **cups all-purpose flour**
- 1 **teaspoon baking powder**
- 1 **teaspoon baking soda**
- 1 **teaspoon salt**
- 2 **cups miniature pretzels, broken**
- 1½ **cups flaked coconut**
- 1½ **cups milk chocolate M&M's**

1. Preheat oven to 350°. In a large bowl, cream butter and sugars until light and fluffy. Beat in eggs and vanilla. In another bowl, whisk flour, baking powder, baking soda and salt; gradually beat into creamed mixture. Stir in remaining ingredients.

2. Shape ¼ cupfuls of dough into balls; place 3 in. apart on ungreased baking sheets. Bake 12-14 minutes or until golden brown. Carefully remove from pans to wire racks to cool.

NOTE *To make smaller cookies, shape rounded tablespoons of dough into balls. Bake as directed.*

CHIPPY PEANUT BUTTER COOKIES

"Hey, these are good!" is the remark I hear most often when I bake these for the family. As simple as it may seem, all I do is follow the directions. Works like a charm.

—**IAN BADEER** HICKMAN, NE

PREP: 25 MIN. • **BAKE:** 15 MIN./BATCH
MAKES: ABOUT 4 DOZEN

- 1 cup butter, softened
- 1 cup creamy peanut butter
- 1 cup sugar
- 1 cup packed brown sugar
- 2 large eggs
- 1 teaspoon vanilla extract
- 2¼ cups all-purpose flour
- 2 teaspoons baking soda
- ¼ teaspoon salt
- 1 package (11 ounces) peanut butter and milk chocolate chips

1. In a large bowl, cream the butter, peanut butter and sugars until light and fluffy. Beat in eggs and vanilla. Combine the flour, baking soda and salt; gradually add to creamed mixture and mix well. Stir in chips.

2. Drop by rounded tablespoonfuls onto ungreased baking sheets. Bake at 350° for 12-15 minutes or until golden brown. Cool for 2 minutes before removing to wire racks.

FROM THE COOKIE JAR

Don't forget to wash out your cookie jar on a regular basis. Miscellaneous crumbs at the bottom of the jar can affect both the taste and texture of fresh cookies, so be sure to clean it out before loading it back up!

DOUBLE CHOCOLATE PECAN COOKIES

Chock-full of chocolate, these crispy cookies produce a tantalizing aroma while they bake. They'll surely satisfy any sweet tooth.

—**MARILYN SPANGLER** OAK CREEK, WI

PREP: 15 MIN. • **BAKE:** 10 MIN./BATCH
MAKES: 4 DOZEN

- 1 cup butter, softened
- 2 cups sugar
- 2 large eggs
- 4 ounces unsweetened chocolate, melted and cooled
- 2 teaspoons vanilla extract
- 2¼ cups all-purpose flour
- 1 teaspoon baking soda
- 1 teaspoon salt
- ¼ teaspoon ground cinnamon
- 1 cup (6 ounces) semisweet chocolate chips
- 1 cup chopped pecans

1. In a large bowl, cream butter and sugar until light and fluffy. Add eggs, one at a time, beating well after each addition. Beat in chocolate and vanilla. Combine the flour, baking soda, salt and cinnamon; gradually add to the creamed mixture. Stir in chocolate chips and pecans.

2. Drop by tablespoonfuls 2 in. apart onto ungreased baking sheets. Bake at 375° for 10-12 minutes or until tops are cracked. Remove to wire racks to cool.

JUNE 12
NATIONAL
PEANUT
BUTTER
COOKIE
DAY

STRAWBERRY SHORTCAKE COOKIES

Strawberry shortcake is one of my favorite desserts. I thought it would be great to capture that wonderful flavor in a cookie. The pastry-like cookie is topped with pink strawberry frosting and fresh berries.

—ALLISON ANDERSON AVONDALE, AZ

PREP: 35 MIN. + CHILLING
BAKE: 15 MIN./BATCH + COOLING
MAKES: 2 DOZEN

- 2 **cups all-purpose flour**
- ½ **cup sugar**
  Dash salt
- ⅔ **cup cold butter**
- 2 **tablespoons water**
- 1 **teaspoon vanilla extract**

FROSTING

- ½ **cup butter, softened**
- ¾ **cup fresh strawberries, sliced**
- 2 **tablespoons 2% milk**
- 5 **cups confectioners' sugar**
  Additional sliced fresh strawberries, optional

1. In a large bowl, combine the flour, sugar and salt. Cut in butter until mixture resembles coarse crumbs. Combine water and vanilla; stir into crumb mixture just until moistened. Cover and refrigerate for 1-2 hours or until firm.

2. On a lightly floured surface, roll out to ¼-in. thickness; cut with a floured 3-in. round cookie cutter. Place cookies 1 in. apart on greased baking sheets.

3. Bake at 325° for 15-18 minutes or until lightly browned. Cool for 2 minutes before removing to wire racks to cool completely.

4. In a large bowl, beat the butter, strawberries and milk until combined. Gradually add confectioners' sugar; beat until blended. Spread over the cookies; garnish with additional sliced strawberries if desired.

HAZELNUT CRUNCHERS

These cookies make a great addition to any snack-time lineup!

—RUTH SAYLES PENDLETON, OR

START TO FINISH: 25 MIN.
MAKES: ABOUT 2 DOZEN

- ½ cup butter, softened
- ½ cup packed dark brown sugar
- ⅓ cup sugar
- 1 large egg
- ½ teaspoon vanilla extract
- 1 cup plus 2 tablespoons all-purpose flour
- ½ teaspoon baking soda
  Pinch salt
- 1 cup vanilla or white chips
- 1 cup chopped hazelnuts, toasted

In a large bowl, cream butter and sugars. Add egg and vanilla; mix well. Combine dry ingredients; add to creamed mixture and mix well. Stir in chips and nuts. Shape into 1½-in. balls; place on greased baking sheets. Flatten to ½-in. thickness with a glass dipped in sugar. Bake at 350° for 10-12 minutes or until lightly browned. Remove to a wire rack to cool.

PAPA'S SUGAR COOKIES

My grandchildren love these crisp sugar cookies. Their subtle macadamia nut, cinnamon and orange peel flavors go perfectly together.

—**LEE DOVERSPIKE** NORTH RIDGEVILLE, OH

PREP: 20 MIN. + CHILLING
BAKE: 10 MIN./BATCH • **MAKES:** 8 DOZEN

- 1 **cup butter, softened**
- 1 **cup canola oil**
- 1 **cup sugar**
- 1 **cup confectioners' sugar**
- 2 **large eggs**
- 2 **tablespoons butter flavoring**
- 1 **tablespoon grated orange peel**
- 1 **tablespoon vanilla extract**
- 5½ **cups all-purpose flour**
- ¼ **cup ground macadamia nuts**
- 1½ **teaspoons baking soda**
- 1 **teaspoon salt**
- 1 **teaspoon cream of tartar**
- 1 **teaspoon ground cinnamon**
  Additional granulated sugar

1. In a large bowl, beat the butter, oil and sugars until well blended. Add eggs, one at a time, beating well after each addition. Beat in the butter flavoring, orange peel and vanilla.

2. Combine the flour, nuts, baking soda, salt, cream of tartar and cinnamon; gradually add to butter mixture and mix well. Cover and refrigerate for 1 hour or until easy to handle.

3. Roll into 1-in. balls, then roll in additional sugar. Place 2 in. apart on ungreased baking sheets. Flatten with a glass dipped in additional sugar.

4. Bake at 350° for 10-12 minutes or until edges begin to brown. Remove to wire racks to cool.

HAPPY
FATHER'S
DAY!

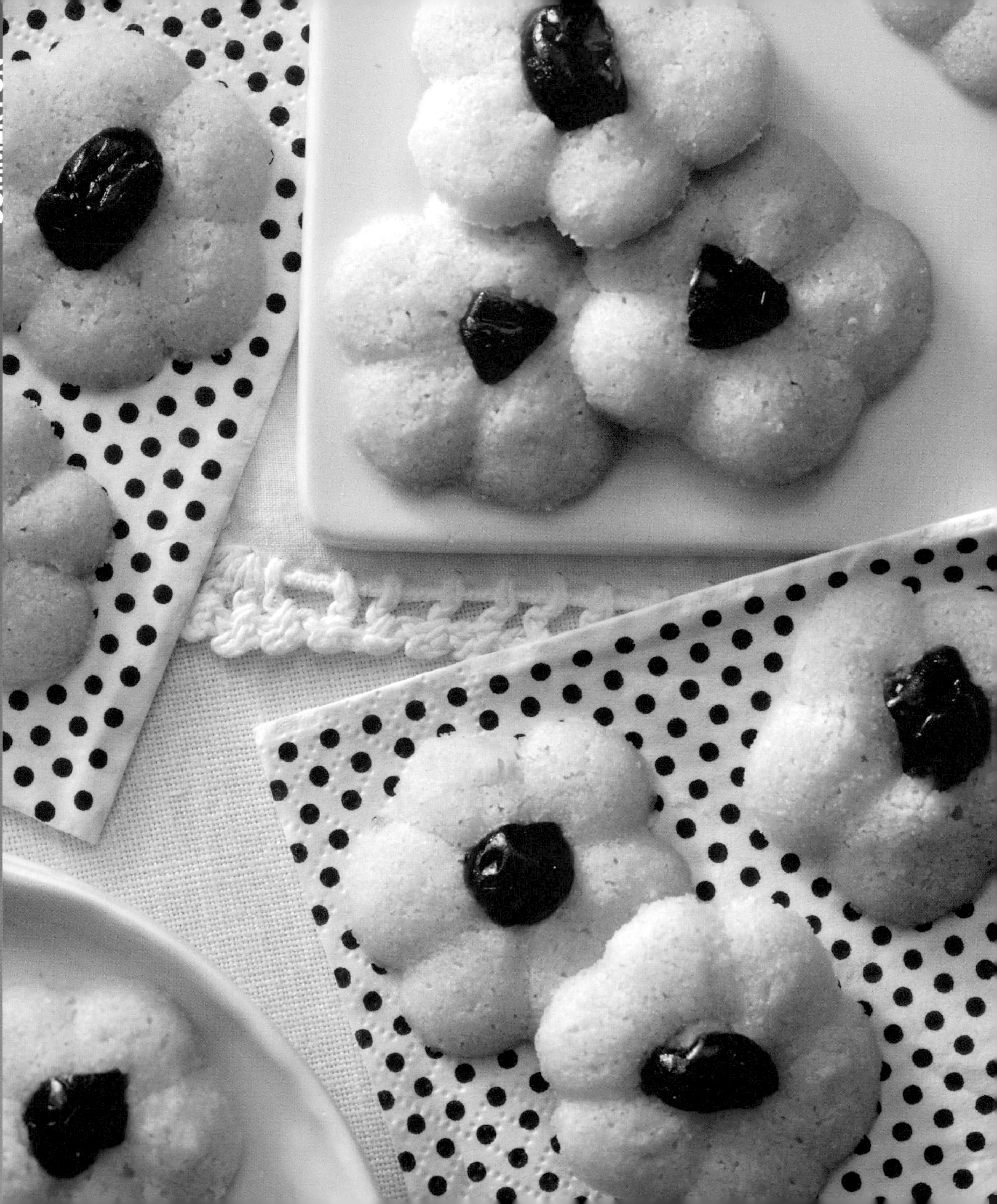

ITALIAN CORNMEAL SPRITZ COOKIES

A chef at a local culinary school gave me this recipe, and I've been using it for years. Italian cornmeal cookies are from the Piedmont region of northern Italy. They're not too sweet, and the glazed cherries add just the right touch.

—KRISTINE CHAYES SMITHTOWN, NY

PREP: 35 MIN. • **BAKE:** 10 MIN./BATCH
MAKES: 5½ DOZEN

- ⅔ **cup butter, softened**
- ½ **cup sugar**
- 2 **large eggs**
- 1 **teaspoon vanilla extract**
- ½ **teaspoon almond extract**
- 1 **cup all-purpose flour**
- ⅔ **cup yellow cornmeal**
  Red candied cherries, quartered

1. Preheat oven to 325°. In a large bowl, cream butter and sugar until light and fluffy. Beat in eggs and extracts. In another bowl, whisk flour and cornmeal; gradually beat into creamed mixture.
2. Using a cookie press fitted with a flower or star disk, press dough 1 in. apart onto ungreased baking sheets. Top with candied cherries.
3. Bake 9-11 minutes or until set. Remove from pans to wire racks to cool.

BANANA SPLIT COOKIES

This banana-shaped cookie is garnished with homemade frosting, a chocolate drizzle and nuts and cherries. It really looks like a banana split.

—TASTE OF HOME TEST KITCHEN

PREP: 40 MIN.
BAKE: 10 MIN./BATCH + COOLING
MAKES: 5 DOZEN

- ½ **cup butter, softened**
- 6 **tablespoons sugar**
- 6 **tablespoons packed brown sugar**
- 1 **large egg**
- 1 **medium ripe banana, mashed**
- ¼ **cup sour cream**
- ½ **teaspoon vanilla extract**
- 1¼ **cups all-purpose flour**
- ½ **teaspoon baking soda**
- ¼ **teaspoon salt**
- 1 **cup (6 ounces) semisweet chocolate chips**
- 6 **tablespoons chopped walnuts**
- ¼ **cup dried cherries, chopped**

BUTTERCREAM FROSTING
- ⅓ **cup butter, softened**
- 3 **cups confectioners' sugar**
- 1 **teaspoon vanilla extract**
- 3 **to 4 tablespoons 2% milk**

GLAZE
- ⅓ **cup butter, cubed**
- 2 **ounces unsweetened chocolate**
- 2 **cups confectioners' sugar**
- 1½ **teaspoons vanilla extract**
- 3 **to 6 tablespoons hot water**
- 10 **red candied cherries, chopped**
- 2 **tablespoons chopped walnuts**

1. In a large bowl, cream butter and sugars until light and fluffy. Beat in the egg, banana, sour cream and vanilla. Combine the flour, baking soda and salt; gradually add to creamed mixture and mix well. Fold in the chocolate chips, walnuts and dried cherries.
2. Place dough in a heavy-duty resealable plastic bag; cut a ¾-in. hole in one corner of bag. Pipe 2-in. strips about 2 in. apart onto greased baking sheets. Bake at 375° for 6-8 minutes or until lightly browned. Remove to wire racks.
3. In a large bowl, cream butter until light and fluffy. Beat in the confectioners' sugar, vanilla and enough milk to achieve desired consistency. Pipe three mounds over each cookie.
4. For the glaze, in a small saucepan, combine butter and chocolate. Cook and stir over low heat until smooth. Remove from the heat. Stir in the confectioners' sugar, vanilla and enough water to achieve a drizzling consistency. Drizzle over tops; sprinkle with candied cherries and chopped walnuts.

SALTED CARAMEL & NUT CUPS

These indulgent cookie cups, with four kinds of nuts, have helped make many of my get-togethers even more special.
—**ROXANNE CHAN** ALBANY, CA

PREP: 30 MIN. + CHILLING
BAKE: 20 MIN. + COOLING • **MAKES:** 1½ DOZEN

- ½ cup butter, softened
- 3 ounces cream cheese, softened
- 2 tablespoons sugar
- 1 cup all-purpose flour
- 1 large egg
- ¼ cup hot caramel ice cream topping
- ¼ to ½ teaspoon ground allspice
- ¼ cup chopped pecans
- ¼ cup chopped slivered almonds
- ¼ cup chopped macadamia nuts
- ¼ cup chopped pistachios
  Coarse sea salt
  Sweetened whipped cream, optional

1. In a small bowl, beat butter, cream cheese and sugar until blended. Gradually beat in flour. Refrigerate, covered, for 30 minutes or until firm.

2. Preheat oven to 350°. Shape level tablespoons of dough into balls; press evenly onto bottoms and up the sides of greased mini-muffin cups.

3. In a small bowl, whisk egg, caramel topping and allspice until blended. Stir in nuts. Place about 2 teaspoons mixture in each cup.

4. Bake 20-22 minutes or until the edges are golden and filling is set. Immediately sprinkle tops with salt. Cool in pans 10 minutes. Remove to wire racks to cool. If desired, serve with whipped cream.

TOASTED OATMEAL COOKIES

These down-home cookies are a family favorite. Toasting the oats gives them an extra nutty flavor. The cookies freeze well and remain crisp even after thawing.
—**MARILYN KRUEGER** MILWAUKEE, WI

PREP: 20 MIN. + STANDING • **BAKE:** 10 MIN.
MAKES: 3½ DOZEN

- ¾ cup butter, cubed
- 2½ cups rolled oats
- ¾ cup all-purpose flour
- 1 teaspoon baking soda
- 1 cup packed brown sugar
- 2 large eggs, beaten
- 1 teaspoon vanilla extract
- ½ cup salted peanuts, coarsely chopped

In a large skillet over medium heat, melt the butter until lightly browned. Add the oats, stirring constantly until golden, 8-10 minutes. Remove from heat; cool. Combine flour and baking soda; set aside. In a large bowl, beat brown sugar, eggs and vanilla until light. Stir in dry ingredients and peanuts until well blended. Let stand for about 15 minutes. Drop by rounded teaspoonfuls onto greased baking sheets. Bake at 375° for 10 minutes or until golden. Remove to wire rack to cool.

JUNE 16
NATIONAL FUDGE DAY

FUDGE PUDDLES

I was inspired to make these cookies after trying them at a cafe. I changed a few things when I got home, and the little cups became an instant hit with my family. Any leftover filling goes great with ice cream!

—**KIMARIE MAASSEN** AVOCA, IA

PREP: 25 MIN. + CHILLING
BAKE: 15 MIN./BATCH + COOLING
MAKES: 4 DOZEN

- ½ cup butter, softened
- ½ cup creamy peanut butter
- ½ cup sugar
- ½ cup packed light brown sugar
- 1 large egg
- ½ teaspoon vanilla extract
- 1¼ cups all-purpose flour
- ¾ teaspoon baking soda
- ½ teaspoon salt

FUDGE FILLING

- 1 cup milk chocolate chips
- 1 cup semisweet chocolate chips
- 1 can (14 ounces) sweetened condensed milk
- 1 teaspoon vanilla extract
  Chopped peanuts

1. In a large bowl, cream butter, peanut butter and sugars until blended. Beat in egg and vanilla. In a small bowl, whisk flour, baking soda and salt; gradually beat into creamed mixture. Refrigerate, covered, 1 hour or until easy to handle.
2. Preheat oven to 325°. Shape into forty-eight 1-in. balls. Place in greased mini muffin cups. Bake 14-16 minutes or until light brown. Immediately press a ½-in.-deep indentation in center of each cookie with the end of a wooden spoon handle. Cool in pans 5 minutes. Remove to wire racks to cool completely.
3. For filling, in a microwave, melt the chocolate and semisweet chips; stir until smooth. Whisk in milk and vanilla until smooth. Fill each cookie with filling; sprinkle with peanuts. (If desired, refrigerate remaining filling.)

NO-BAKE FUDGY COCONUT COOKIES

My daughter works at a summer camp, so I send treats. Instead of a cookie jar we use a coffee can and call it the Wrangler Feeding Trough. Campers ask for this no-bake treat every summer.

—**SUE KLEMM** RHINELANDER, WI

PREP: 30 MIN. + CHILLING • **MAKES:** 3½ DOZEN

- 1½ cups sugar
- ⅔ cup 2% milk
- ½ cup baking cocoa
- ½ cup butter, cubed
- ½ teaspoon salt
- ⅓ cup creamy peanut butter
- 1 teaspoon vanilla extract
- 2 cups quick-cooking oats
- 1 cup flaked coconut
- ½ cup white baking chips
- 1 teaspoon shortening

1. In a large saucepan, combine the first five ingredients. Bring to a boil, stirring constantly. Cook and stir 3 minutes.
2. Remove from heat; stir in peanut butter and vanilla until blended. Stir in oats and coconut. Drop mixture by tablespoonfuls onto waxed paper-lined baking sheets.
3. In a microwave, melt baking chips and shortening; stir until smooth. Drizzle over cookies; refrigerate until set. Store in airtight containers.

S'MOOKIES

S'mores are one of my favorite desserts. I wanted to use a cookie to replace the graham cracker—that's when my s'mookie was born! It's just as delicious as the classic.
—MARIA DAVIS HERMOSA BEACH, CA

PREP: 15 MIN. + CHILLING
BAKE: 10 MIN. + COOLING
MAKES: 10 COOKIES

- 1 **cup all-purpose flour**
- ½ **cup old-fashioned or quick-cooking oats**
- ⅓ **cup packed brown sugar**
- 2 **teaspoons grated lemon peel**
- ½ **teaspoon grated whole nutmeg or 1 teaspoon ground nutmeg**
- ½ **teaspoon salt**
- ¾ **cup cold butter, cubed**
- 2 **tablespoons heavy cream**
- 1 **teaspoon vanilla extract**
- ½ **cup cinnamon baking chips**
- 10 **tablespoons Biscoff creamy cookie spread**
- 20 **large marshmallows**

1. Place the first six ingredients in a food processor; process until blended. Add butter, cream and vanilla; pulse until dough comes together (do not overmix). Stir in cinnamon chips. Divide dough in half. Shape each into a disk; wrap in plastic. Refrigerate for 30 minutes or until firm enough to roll.

2. Preheat oven to 350°. On a lightly floured surface, roll each portion of dough to ¼-in. thickness. Cut with a floured 2½-in. square cookie cutter. Place 1 in. apart on ungreased baking sheets. Bake 10-12 minutes or until the cookies begin to brown (do not overbake). Remove from pans to wire racks to cool completely.

3. Preheat broiler. Spread 1 tablespoon cookie spread on bottoms of half of the cookies. Set aside. Place a marshmallow on bottoms of the remaining cookies; transfer to a baking sheet. Broil 5-6 in. from heat for 30-45 seconds or until marshmallows are golden brown. Cover with the cookie-spread halves; press down gently.

LEMON ZUCCHINI DROPS

When we lived on the East Coast, a nearby fruit and vegetable stand had a bakery featuring soft, cakey cookies like these. We missed every summery bite after we moved away, so I developed this recipe to capture that delightful flavor.

—**BARBARA FRANKLIN** TUCSON, AZ

PREP: 20 MIN.
BAKE: 10 MIN./BATCH + COOLING
MAKES: 3½ DOZEN

- ½ **cup butter, softened**
- 1 **cup sugar**
- 1 **large egg**
- 1 **cup finely shredded zucchini**
- 1 **teaspoon grated lemon peel**
- 2 **cups all-purpose flour**
- 1 **teaspoon baking soda**
- 1 **teaspoon baking powder**
- 1 **teaspoon ground cinnamon**
- ½ **teaspoon salt**
- ½ **cup raisins**
- ½ **cup chopped walnuts**

LEMON GLAZE

- 2 **cups confectioners' sugar**
- 2 **to 3 tablespoons lemon juice**

1. In a large bowl, cream butter and sugar until light and fluffy. Beat in egg, zucchini and lemon peel. Combine the flour, baking soda, baking powder, cinnamon and salt; gradually add to the creamed mixture and mix well. Stir in raisins and chopped walnuts.
2. Drop by tablespoonfuls 3 in. apart onto lightly greased baking sheets. Bake at 375° for 8-10 minutes or until lightly browned. Remove to wire racks to cool.
3. For glaze, combine sugar and enough lemon juice to achieve a thin spreading consistency. Spread or drizzle over cooled cookies.

OATMEAL KISS COOKIES

This is a nice change from the usual peanut butter kiss cookie. Kids can join in the fun by unwrapping the chocolate kisses for these mouthwatering morsels.

—**ANNA MARY KNIER** MOUNT JOY, PA

PREP: 35 MIN. • **BAKE:** 10 MIN./BATCH
MAKES: 6 DOZEN

- ½ **cup butter, softened**
- ½ **cup shortening**
- 1 **cup sugar**
- 1 **cup packed brown sugar**
- 2 **large eggs**
- 2 **cups all-purpose flour**
- 1 **teaspoon baking soda**
- 1 **teaspoon salt**
- 2¼ **cups quick-cooking oats**
- 1 **cup chopped nuts**
- 72 **milk chocolate kisses**

1. In a large bowl, cream the butter, shortening and sugars until light and fluffy. Add eggs, one at a time, beating well after each addition. Combine the flour, baking soda and salt; gradually add to creamed mixture and mix well. Stir in oats and nuts. Roll into 1-in. balls. Place 2 in. apart on ungreased baking sheets.
2. Bake at 375° for 10-12 minutes or until lightly browned. Immediately press a chocolate kiss in the center of each cookie. Remove to wire racks.

★ ★ ★ ★ ★ **5 STAR TIP**

Quick-cooking oats and old-fashioned oats are interchangeable, but quick-cooking oats are often better for baking. This is because they're smaller, so they cook faster and give cookies a more delicate texture. If, however, you want a heartier texture, then old-fashioned oats are the way to go.

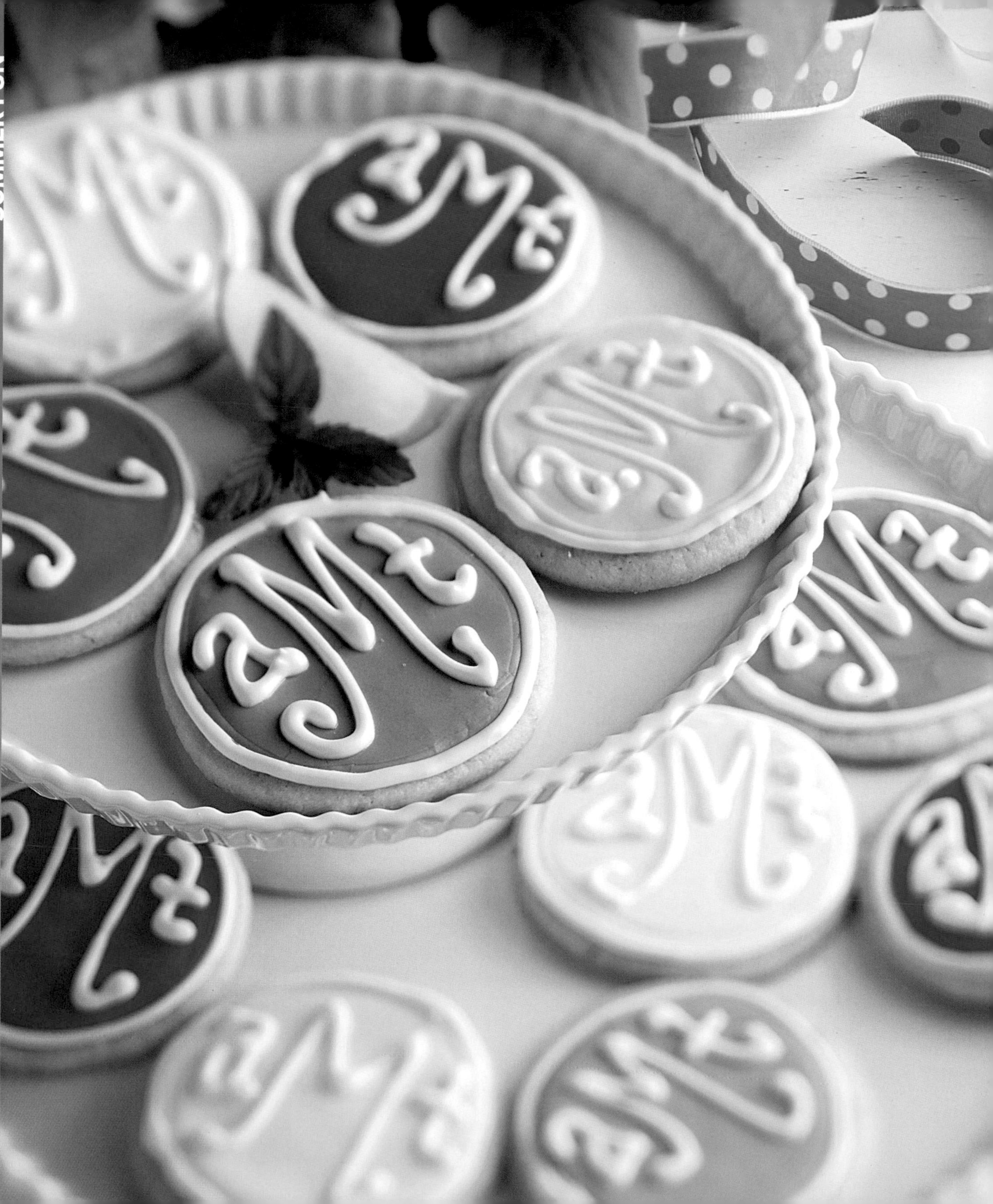

MONOGRAMMED COOKIES

Mint and lime zest bring fresh flavor to these crisp sugar cookies. For a fun wedding shower dessert, simply frost and adorn the tops with the bride's monogram.

—TASTE OF HOME TEST KITCHEN

PREP: 40 MIN. + CHILLING
BAKE: 10 MIN./BATCH • **MAKES:** 4 DOZEN

- 1 **cup butter, softened**
- 3 **ounces cream cheese, softened**
- 1 **cup sugar**
- 1 **large egg yolk**
- 3 **tablespoons minced fresh mint**
- 1 **teaspoon grated lime peel**
- 1 **teaspoon rum extract**
- 1 **teaspoon vanilla extract**
- 2¼ **cups all-purpose flour**
- ½ **teaspoon salt**
- ¼ **teaspoon baking soda**

ROYAL ICING

- 4 **cups confectioners' sugar**
- 6 **tablespoons warm water**
- 3 **tablespoons meringue powder**
  Paste food coloring

WEDDING SEASON

1. In a large bowl, cream the butter, cream cheese and sugar until light and fluffy. Beat in the egg yolk, mint, lime peel and extracts. Combine the flour, salt and baking soda; gradually add to creamed mixture and mix well. Cover dough and refrigerate for 3 hours or until it is easy to handle.

2. On a lightly floured surface, roll out dough to ⅛-in. thickness. Cut with a floured 2½-in. round cookie cutter. Place 1 in. apart on ungreased baking sheets. Bake at 375° for 8-10 minutes or until edges begin to brown. Cool for 2 minutes before removing from pans to wire racks to cool completely.

3. For icing, in a large bowl, combine the confectioners' sugar, water and meringue powder; beat on low speed just until combined. Beat on high for 4-5 minutes or until stiff peaks form. Tint as desired with food coloring. (Keep unused icing covered at all times with a damp cloth. If necessary, beat again on high speed to restore texture.)

4. Frost and decorate cookies as desired. For writing, use a #1 or #2 round pastry tip. Let dry at room temperature for several hours or until firm. Store cookies in an airtight container.

MEXICAN WEDDING CAKES

As part of a Mexican tradition, I tucked these sugar-dusted cookies into small gift boxes for the guests at my sister's wedding. Most folks said the cookies never made it home! We bake them around the holidays, too.

—SARITA JOHNSTON SAN ANTONIO, TX

PREP: 30 MIN. • **BAKE:** 15 MIN.
MAKES: ABOUT 6 DOZEN

- 2 **cups butter, softened**
- 1 **cup confectioners' sugar**
- 1 **teaspoon vanilla extract**
- 4 **cups all-purpose flour**
- 1 **cup finely chopped pecans**
  Additional confectioners' sugar

1. Preheat oven to 350°. Cream butter and 1 cup confectioners' sugar until light and fluffy; beat in vanilla. Gradually beat in flour. Stir in pecans.

2. Shape tablespoons of dough into 2-in. crescents. Place 2 in. apart on ungreased baking sheets.

3. Bake until light brown, 12-15 minutes. Roll cookies in additional confectioners' sugar while warm; cool on wire racks.

★ ★ ★ ★ ★ **READER REVIEW**

"Whether you call them Mexican wedding cakes, pecan puffs or Russian tea cakes, this is one recipe to save."

SUEFALK TASTEOFHOME.COM

LAVENDER COOKIES

I am a wedding and event planner, and one of my brides served these unusual cookies at her reception. I just had to have the recipe. You can guess what her wedding color was!

—**GLENNA TOOMAN** BOISE, ID

PREP: 30 MIN. • **BAKE:** 10 MIN./BATCH
MAKES: ABOUT 6 DOZEN

- ½ cup shortening
- ½ cup butter, softened
- 1¼ cups sugar
- 2 large eggs
- 1 teaspoon vanilla extract
- ½ teaspoon almond extract
- 2¼ cups all-purpose flour
- 4 teaspoons dried lavender flowers
- 1 teaspoon baking powder
- ½ teaspoon salt

1. In a large bowl, cream the shortening, butter and sugar until light and fluffy. Add eggs, one at a time, beating well after each addition. Beat in extracts. Combine the flour, lavender, baking powder and salt; gradually add to creamed mixture and mix well.

2. Drop by rounded teaspoonfuls 2 in. apart onto baking sheets lightly coated with cooking spray.

3. Bake at 375° for 8-10 minutes or until golden brown. Cool for 2 minutes before removing to wire racks. Store in an airtight container.

NOTE *Look for dried lavender flowers in spice shops. If using lavender from the garden, make sure it hasn't been treated with chemicals.*

FROM THE COOKIE JAR

Lavender Cookies are the perfect bite for summer snacking. Be sure to store them separately, as the lavender in these cookies can affect the flavor of other cookies and baked goods.

PASTELITOS DE BODA

In Mexico, these rich cookies are called Little Wedding Cakes and are usually served with hot chocolate. Having moved from the Midwest to a location that's closer to Mexico, I've enjoyed trying to replicate authentic recipes. These treats are a sharp departure from the Iowa favorites I grew up with!

—**TERRI LINS** SAN DIEGO, CA

PREP: 20 MIN. + CHILLING
BAKE: 15 MIN./BATCH
MAKES: ABOUT 3 DOZEN

- ¾ cup butter, softened
- ½ cup confectioners' sugar
- 2 teaspoons vanilla
- 2 cups sifted all-purpose flour
- ¼ teaspoon salt
- 1 cup finely chopped walnuts
- ¼ cup heavy whipping cream
  Additional confectioners' sugar

1. In a large bowl, cream butter and sugar until light and fluffy; add vanilla. Combine flour, salt and nuts; gradually add to the creamed mixture and mix well. Add the cream; knead lightly.

2. Shape into a roll 2½ in. in diameter. Wrap in plastic. Refrigerate several hours or overnight.

3. Preheat oven to 375°. Unwrap and cut into ¼-in. slices. Place 2 in. apart on ungreased baking sheets. Bake 15 minutes or until delicately browned around edges. Remove to wire rack. While warm, roll in additional confectioners' sugar.

LEMON CRISP COOKIES

Here's a quick-to-fix treat that's perfect for when you've forgotten to make a potluck or bake-sale item. This only takes 10 minutes to whip up—and the sunny yellow color, big lemon flavor and delightful crunch are sure to bring smiles.

—JULIA LIVINGSTON FROSTPROOF, FL

START TO FINISH: 30 MIN.
MAKES: ABOUT 4 DOZEN

- 1 package lemon cake mix (regular size)
- 1 cup crisp rice cereal
- ½ cup butter, melted
- 1 large egg, lightly beaten
- 1 teaspoon grated lemon peel

1. Preheat oven to 350°. In a large bowl, combine all the ingredients (dough will be crumbly). Shape into 1-in. balls. Place 2 in. apart on ungreased baking sheets.
2. Bake 10-12 minutes or until set. Cool 1 minute; remove from pan to a wire rack to cool completely.

★ ★ ★ ★ ★ **READER REVIEW**

"I made these at the last minute to take to our church, and four of the ladies who work in the kitchen asked me to give them the recipe. So easy, and the lemon is so refreshing!"

DANARENEE TASTEOFHOME.COM

SPRITZ BUTTER BLOSSOMS

With food coloring and colored sugar, it's a snap to customize these pretty cookies to match a wedding's theme. You can also decorate them to suit any holiday or party. Go ahead...get creative!

—CHRISTINE OMAR HARWICH PORT, MA

PREP: 30 MIN. • **BAKE:** 10 MIN./BATCH
MAKES: ABOUT 6½ DOZEN

- ¾ cup sugar
- ½ cup blanched almonds, toasted
- 1 cup butter, softened
- 1 large egg
- 1 teaspoon almond extract
- 1 teaspoon vanilla extract
- 2 cups all-purpose flour
- ¼ teaspoon salt
  Sprinkles or colored sugar

1. Place sugar and almonds in a food processor; cover and process until almonds are finely ground.
2. In a large bowl, cream butter and sugar mixture until light and fluffy. Beat in the egg and extracts. Combine flour and salt; gradually add to creamed mixture and mix well.
3. Using a cookie press fitted with the disk of your choice, press dough 2 in. apart onto ungreased baking sheets. Decorate with sprinkles or colored sugar.
4. Bake at 375° for 7-9 minutes. Remove the cookies to wire racks. Store in an airtight container.

FROSTED CHOCOLATE DELIGHTS

These simple chocolate drop cookies are crowned with a creamy vanilla frosting.

—PATRICIA RAMCZYK APPLETON, WI

PREP: 20 MIN.
BAKE: 15 MIN./BATCH + COOLING
MAKES: 5½ DOZEN

- ½ cup shortening
- 1 cup packed brown sugar
- 1 large egg
- ½ cup milk
- 1 teaspoon vanilla extract
- 2 ounces unsweetened chocolate, melted and cooled
- 1¾ cups all-purpose flour
- 1 teaspoon baking powder
- ½ teaspoon salt
- ¼ teaspoon baking soda
- ½ cup chopped walnuts

FROSTING

- 9 tablespoons butter, softened
- 4½ cups confectioners' sugar
- 1½ teaspoons vanilla extract
- 6 to 8 tablespoons milk

1. In a large bowl, cream shortening and brown sugar. Beat in the egg, milk and vanilla. Beat in chocolate until blended. Combine the flour, baking powder, salt and baking soda; gradually add to the creamed mixture. Stir in the chopped walnuts.

2. Drop by tablespoonfuls 2 in. apart onto ungreased baking sheets. Bake at 350° for 11-13 minutes or until firm. Remove to wire racks to cool.

3. For frosting, in a bowl, cream butter and sugar. Beat in vanilla and enough milk to achieve spreading consistency. Frost cooled cookies.

SOFT BLUEBERRY BUTTON COOKIES

I have fond memories of picking blueberries and enjoying icy cold lemonade at my aunt's house. This cookie marries those two memorable flavors.
—**RENEE MURBY** JOHNSTON, RI

PREP: 30 MIN. • **BAKE:** 15 MIN./BATCH
MAKES: ABOUT 2½ DOZEN

- ½ cup butter, softened
- ½ cup sugar
- ½ cup packed brown sugar
- 1½ teaspoons grated lemon peel
- 1 large egg
- ½ cup fat-free lemon Greek yogurt
- ⅓ cup blueberry juice cocktail
- 1 teaspoon almond extract
- 2 cups all-purpose flour
- 1½ teaspoons ground cinnamon
- 1 teaspoon baking powder
- ¼ teaspoon salt
- ¼ teaspoon baking soda
- 1 to 1½ cups fresh blueberries

GLAZE
- 1 cup confectioners' sugar
- 2 tablespoons blueberry juice cocktail
- 1 tablespoon butter, melted

1. Preheat oven to 350°. In a large bowl, cream butter, sugars and lemon peel until light and fluffy. Beat in egg. Beat in yogurt, juice and extract until blended. In another bowl, whisk the flour, cinnamon, baking powder, salt and baking soda; gradually beat into creamed mixture.

2. Drop dough by rounded tablespoonfuls 2 in. apart onto ungreased baking sheets. Press four blueberries into each cookie to resemble a button.

3. Bake 13-15 minutes or until edges begin to brown. Remove from pans to wire racks to cool slightly.

4. In a small bowl, mix glaze ingredients until smooth. Spoon over warm cookies. Let stand until set. Store in airtight containers.

CHERRY-COCONUT SLICES

My mother got this recipe from a woman named Emmie Oddie, a well-known home economist in Canada who had a column in a farming newspaper. She would test reader recipes in her own kitchen and write about them. These tasty bites are so rich that you only need a small one.

—**JUDY OLSON** WHITECOURT, AB

PREP: 15 MIN. + CHILLING
COOK: 5 MIN. + COOLING • **MAKES:** 32 BARS

- 3 cups graham cracker crumbs
- 1½ cups miniature marshmallows
- 1 cup unsweetened finely shredded coconut
- ½ cup chopped maraschino cherries
- 1 can (14 ounces) sweetened condensed milk
- 1 teaspoon maple flavoring

FROSTING

- 1 cup packed brown sugar
- ⅓ cup butter, cubed
- ¼ cup 2% milk
- 1 cup confectioners' sugar

1. In a large bowl, mix cracker crumbs, marshmallows, coconut and cherries; stir in condensed milk and flavoring. Press into a greased 8-in. square baking pan.

2. For frosting, in a small saucepan, combine brown sugar, butter and milk. Bring to a boil, stirring constantly; cook and stir 3 minutes. Transfer mixture to a small bowl; cool until lukewarm, about 15 minutes. Stir in confectioners' sugar until smooth. Spread over crumb mixture; refrigerate until set, about 1½ hours.

3. Cut into bars. Store in an airtight container in the refrigerator.

NOTE *Look for unsweetened coconut in the baking or health food section.*

NO-BAKE CHOCOLATE HAZELNUT THUMBPRINTS

Years ago, a friend gave me a recipe for treats that didn't require baking. I thought it was a quick and clever way to whip up a batch of snacks without heating up the kitchen in the summer. I began making different variations, and this one includes luscious Nutella and crunchy hazelnuts.

—**LISA SPEER** PALM BEACH, FL

PREP: 30 MIN. + CHILLING
MAKES: ABOUT 3½ DOZEN

- 1 carton (8 ounces) spreadable cream cheese
- 1 cup (6 ounces) semisweet chocolate chips, melted
- ½ cup Nutella
- 2¼ cups graham cracker crumbs
- 1 cup finely chopped hazelnuts
- 1 cup whole hazelnuts, toasted

1. Beat cream cheese, melted chocolate and Nutella until blended. Stir in cracker crumbs. Refrigerate until firm enough to roll, about 30 minutes.

2. Shape mixture into 1-in. balls; roll in chopped hazelnuts. Make an indentation in the center of each ball with the end of a wooden spoon handle. Fill each with a hazelnut. Store in an airtight container in the refrigerator, separating layers with waxed paper.

NOTE *To toast nuts, bake in a shallow pan in a 350° oven for 5-10 minutes or cook in a skillet over low heat until lightly browned, stirring occasionally.*

JULY 1
NATIONAL GINGERSNAP DAY

OLD-FASHIONED GINGERSNAPS

I discovered this recipe many years ago, and it's been a favorite among our family and friends since. Who doesn't like cookies?
—**FRANCIS STOOPS** STONEBORO, PA

PREP: 15 MIN. + CHILLING
BAKE: 10 MIN./BATCH + COOLING
MAKES: ABOUT 4 DOZEN

- 1 **cup butter, softened**
- 1 **cup sugar**
- 1 **large egg**
- ¼ **cup molasses**
- 2 **cups all-purpose flour**
- 2 **teaspoons baking soda**
- 1 **teaspoon ground cinnamon**
- 1 **teaspoon ground cloves**
- 1 **teaspoon ground ginger**
- ¼ **teaspoon salt**
  Additional sugar

1. In a bowl, cream butter and sugar. Beat in egg and molasses. Combine the flour, baking soda, cinnamon, cloves, ginger and salt; gradually add to creamed mixture. Chill.
2. Roll into 1¼-in. balls and dip into sugar. Place 2 in. apart on ungreased baking sheets. Bake at 375° for about 10 minutes or until cookies are set and surface cracks. Cool on wire racks.

★ ★ ★ ★ ★ **READER REVIEW**

"Phenomenal! Easy to make, incredible taste and came out as the recipe said. Mine looked exactly like the picture!"

ELFIEPOO TASTEOFHOME.COM

FROZEN STRAWBERRY SANDWICH COOKIES

It takes only three ingredients to make these chilled sandwich cookies with their pretty pink filling. What a cute summer treat!
—**MARY ANN IRVINE** LOMBARD, IL

Short & Sweet

PREP: 10 MIN. + FREEZING
MAKES: 8 SANDWICH COOKIES

- ½ **cup spreadable strawberry cream cheese**
- ¼ **cup strawberry yogurt**
- 16 **chocolate wafers**

In a small bowl, beat cream cheese and yogurt until blended. Spread on bottoms of half of the chocolate wafers; top with remaining wafers. Place on a baking sheet. Freeze 30 minutes or until firm. Serve right away, or wrap in plastic and return to freezer for serving later.

FROZEN BLUEBERRY SANDWICH COOKIES *Use blueberry spreadable cream cheese and yogurt instead of strawberry cream cheese and yogurt.*

BROWNIE MOUNDS

If you crave brownies but not the long baking time, try these quick chocolaty cookies. They're perfect any time of year. If you don't like nuts, you can just leave those out.

—MARY TURNER BLOUNTVILLE, TN

PREP: 15 MIN. • **BAKE:** 20 MIN.
MAKES: 3 DOZEN

- ⅓ **cup butter, softened**
- ¾ **cup sugar**
- ⅓ **cup light corn syrup**
- 1 **large egg**
- 3 **ounces unsweetened chocolate, melted**
- 1 **teaspoon vanilla extract**
- 1⅔ **cups all-purpose flour**
- ½ **teaspoon baking powder**
- ¼ **teaspoon salt**
- ½ **cup chopped walnuts**

1. In a large bowl, cream butter and sugar until light and fluffy. Add corn syrup and egg; beat well. Stir in melted chocolate and vanilla. Combine the flour, baking powder and salt; add to chocolate mixture and beat well. Stir in chopped walnuts.

2. Drop by tablespoonfuls 2 in. apart onto greased baking sheets. Bake at 350° for 10-12 minutes or until edges are firm. Remove to wire racks to cool.

SAND DOLLAR COOKIES

Before the military relocated our family, my children had never lived near the ocean. I came up with this special treat with a beach theme—it made our move even more fun!

—MICHELLE DUNCAN CALLAWAY, FI

PREP: 15 MIN. + CHILLING
BAKE: 15 MIN./BATCH
MAKES: ABOUT 1½ DOZEN

- 1½ cups butter, softened
- ⅔ cup confectioners' sugar
- 3 tablespoons sugar
- 4 teaspoons almond extract
- 2⅔ cups all-purpose flour
- ½ teaspoon salt
- 2 large eggs, lightly beaten
  Slivered almonds
  Cinnamon sugar

1. In a large bowl, cream butter and sugars until light and fluffy. Beat in extract. Combine the flour and salt; gradually add to creamed mixture and mix well. Divide dough in half. Shape each half into a disk; wrap in plastic. Refrigerate for 1 hour or until firm enough to roll.

2. Preheat oven to 325°. Roll each portion of dough between waxed paper to ⅛-in. thickness. Cut with a 3½-in. round cookie cutter dipped in flour. Using a floured spatula, place cookies 1 in. apart on ungreased baking sheets.

3. Brush with egg. Decorate with almonds to resemble sand dollars and sprinkle with cinnamon sugar.

4. Bake 12-16 minutes or until edges begin to brown. Cool for 2 minutes before removing to wire racks.

CUTE PIG COOKIES

I created this recipe for a party my friend had for National Pig Day, which is March 1. Not only were they a big hit at the party, they've also been popular at my son's school.

—BECKY BALDWIN ANNVILLE, PA

PREP: 35 MIN.
BAKE: 10 MIN./BATCH + COOLING
MAKES: 6 DOZEN

- 1 cup butter, softened
- 1½ cups sugar
- 2 large eggs
- 1 cup (8 ounces) sour cream
- 1 teaspoon vanilla extract
- 3 cups all-purpose flour
- 1 teaspoon baking powder
- ½ teaspoon salt

FROSTING/DECORATIONS

- 4 cups confectioners' sugar
- ½ cup butter, melted
- 6 tablespoons milk
- 2 teaspoons vanilla extract
- 3 to 4 drops red food coloring
  Pink sugar wafer cookies
- 36 large marshmallows, halved
  Butterscotch chips and miniature semisweet chocolate chips

1. In a large bowl, cream butter and sugar until light and fluffy. Beat in the eggs, sour cream and vanilla. Combine dry ingredients; gradually add to creamed mixture and mix well.

2. Drop dough by tablespoonfuls onto ungreased baking sheets. Bake at 375° for 10-12 minutes or until edges are lightly browned. Remove from pans to wire racks to cool completely.

3. For frosting, in a large bowl, combine the confectioners' sugar, butter, milk, vanilla and food coloring. Frost cookies.

4. Cut sugar wafers into triangles; place two on each cookie for ears. With a toothpick, poke two holes in each marshmallow half for nostrils; press butterscotch chips into holes. Place noses on cookies; add chocolate chip eyes.

BLACK FOREST SANDWICH COOKIES

Speed up prep time for these sandwich cookies by using chocolate wafers from the cookie aisle. You can even make them ahead of time. What a great addition to your next pool party!

—TASTE OF HOME TEST KITCHEN

Short & Sweet

PREP: 30 MIN. + CHILLING
MAKES: 2 DOZEN

- ½ cup mascarpone cheese
- 1 tablespoon confectioners' sugar
- 1 teaspoon cherry brandy
- 1½ cups cherry pie filling
- 48 chocolate wafers

In a small bowl, combine the cheese, confectioners' sugar and brandy. Spread 1 tablespoonful over a wafer; top with 1 tablespoonful pie filling and a second wafer. Repeat. Refrigerate for at least 2 hours before serving.

SUPER CHUNKY COOKIES

Chocolate lovers will go crazy over these bites that feature loads of chocolate! When friends ask me to make "those cookies," I know exactly which recipe they mean.

—**REBECCA JENDRY** SPRING BRANCH, TX

PREP: 15 MIN. • **BAKE:** 10 MIN./BATCH
MAKES: 6½ DOZEN

- ½ cup butter-flavored shortening
- ½ cup butter, softened
- 1 cup packed brown sugar
- ¾ cup sugar
- 2 large eggs
- 2 teaspoons vanilla extract
- 2½ cups all-purpose flour
- 1 teaspoon baking soda
- ⅛ teaspoon salt
- 1 cup miniature semisweet chocolate chips
- 1 cup milk chocolate chips
- 1 cup vanilla or white chips
- 4 ounces bittersweet chocolate, coarsely chopped
- ¾ cup English toffee bits or almond brickle chips
- ½ cup chopped pecans

1. In a large bowl, cream the shortening, butter and sugars until light and fluffy. Add eggs, one at a time, beating well after each addition. Beat in vanilla. Combine the flour, baking soda and salt; gradually add to the creamed mixture and mix well. Stir in the remaining ingredients.

2. Drop by tablespoonfuls 3 in. apart on ungreased baking sheets. Bake at 350° for 10-12 minutes or until lightly browned. Cool for 2-3 minutes before removing to wire racks to cool completely.

OATMEAL COOKIE ICE CREAM SANDWICHES

If you're tight on time, you can use store-bought cookies, but I highly recommend making these oatmeal chocolate cookies from scratch. Dessert sandwiches are just pure fun. Sometimes I decorate the sides of the sandwiches with colorful jimmies, too.

—DIANE HALFERTY CORPUS CHRISTI, TX

PREP: 35 MIN. • **BAKE:** 10 MIN. + FREEZING
MAKES: 10 SERVINGS

- ½ cup butter, softened
- ⅓ cup sugar
- ⅓ cup packed dark brown sugar
- 1 large egg
- 2 teaspoons vanilla extract
- ⅔ cup all-purpose flour
- ½ teaspoon baking soda
- ¼ teaspoon salt
- ¼ teaspoon ground cinnamon
- 1½ cups quick-cooking oats
- ½ cup finely chopped semisweet chocolate
- 3 cups dulce de leche ice cream, softened if necessary
- ¼ cup brickle toffee bits

1. Preheat oven to 350°. In a large bowl, cream butter and sugars until light and fluffy. Beat in egg and vanilla. In another bowl, whisk flour, baking soda, salt and cinnamon; gradually beat into creamed mixture. Stir in oats and semisweet chocolate.

2. Shape dough into twenty 1¼-in. balls. Place 2½ in. apart on ungreased baking sheets; flatten slightly with bottom of a glass dipped in sugar, smoothing edges if necessary. Bake 10-13 minutes or until golden brown. Transfer from pans to wire racks to cool completely.

3. To assemble, place about ¼ cup ice cream on bottom of a cookie; sprinkle with 1 teaspoon toffee bits. Top with a second cookie, pressing gently to flatten ice cream. Place on a baking sheet; freeze overnight or until firm. Repeat with remaining cookies and ice cream. For longer storage, wrap frozen sandwiches individually and return to freezer.

HAPPY
FOURTH
OF JULY!

LEMON STAR COOKIES

Family and friends will yell, "hooray!" when they see these star-spangled sweets. Make the treats all year by using different cookie cutters and food coloring.

—TASTE OF HOME TEST KITCHEN

PREP: 25 MIN. + CHILLING
BAKE: 10 MIN./BATCH + COOLING
MAKES: ABOUT 5½ DOZEN

- 1 **cup butter, softened**
- 2 **cups confectioners' sugar**
- 2 **large eggs**
- 2 **tablespoons lemon juice**
- 4 **teaspoons half-and-half cream**
- 2 **teaspoons grated lemon peel**
- 3¾ **cups all-purpose flour**
- ½ **cup ground almonds**
- ½ **teaspoon baking soda**
- ⅛ **teaspoon salt**

GLAZE

- 2 **cups confectioners' sugar**
- ¼ **cup light corn syrup**
- 2 **tablespoons lemon juice**
  Red and blue food coloring

1. In a large bowl, cream butter and confectioners' sugar until light and fluffy. Add eggs, one at a time, beating well after each addition. Beat in the lemon juice, cream and lemon peel.

2. Combine the flour, almonds, baking soda and salt; gradually add to creamed mixture. Cover and refrigerate for 2 hours or until easy to handle.

3. On a lightly floured surface, roll out dough to ⅛-in. thickness. Cut with a floured star-shaped cookie cutter. Place 1 in. apart on ungreased baking sheets. Bake at 350° for 8-10 minutes or until lightly browned. Remove cookies to wire racks to cool completely.

4. For glaze, in a small bowl, combine the confectioners' sugar, corn syrup and lemon juice until smooth. Divide into three bowls. Tint one portion red and one portion blue; leave the third portion white. Spread over cookies; let stand overnight for glaze to harden.

CRISP CHOCOLATE CHIP COOKIES

A friend gave me this recipe quite a while ago, and I make them for my five children and 18 grandkids. Be warned—if you don't want these cookies to disappear quickly, you'd better hide them!

—MANDY FALKNER GREENACRES, WA

PREP: 20 MIN. • **BAKE:** 15 MIN.
MAKES: ABOUT 3 DOZEN

- 1 **cup butter, softened**
- 1 **cup sugar**
- 1 **cup packed brown sugar**
- 1 **cup canola oil**
- 1 **large egg**
- 1 **teaspoon vanilla extract**
- 3½ **cups all-purpose flour**
- 3 **teaspoons baking soda**
- ½ **teaspoon salt**
- 2 **cups (12 ounces) chocolate chips**
- 1 **cup quick-cooking or old-fashioned oats**
- 1 **cup cornflakes or crisp rice cereal**

1. In a large bowl, cream butter and sugars until light and fluffy. Add the oil, egg and vanilla. Combine flour, baking soda and salt; gradually add to the creamed mixture.

2. Stir in chocolate chips, oats, and cornflakes. Drop by tablespoonfuls onto greased baking sheets. Bake at 350° for 12-14 minutes. Remove to wire racks to cool.

★ ★ ★ ★ ★ **5 STAR TIP**
When preparing these crispy cookies, consider adding ¼ cup of baking cocoa to the flour mixture. It's a great way to add a little chocolate flair and give these cookies a whole new look!

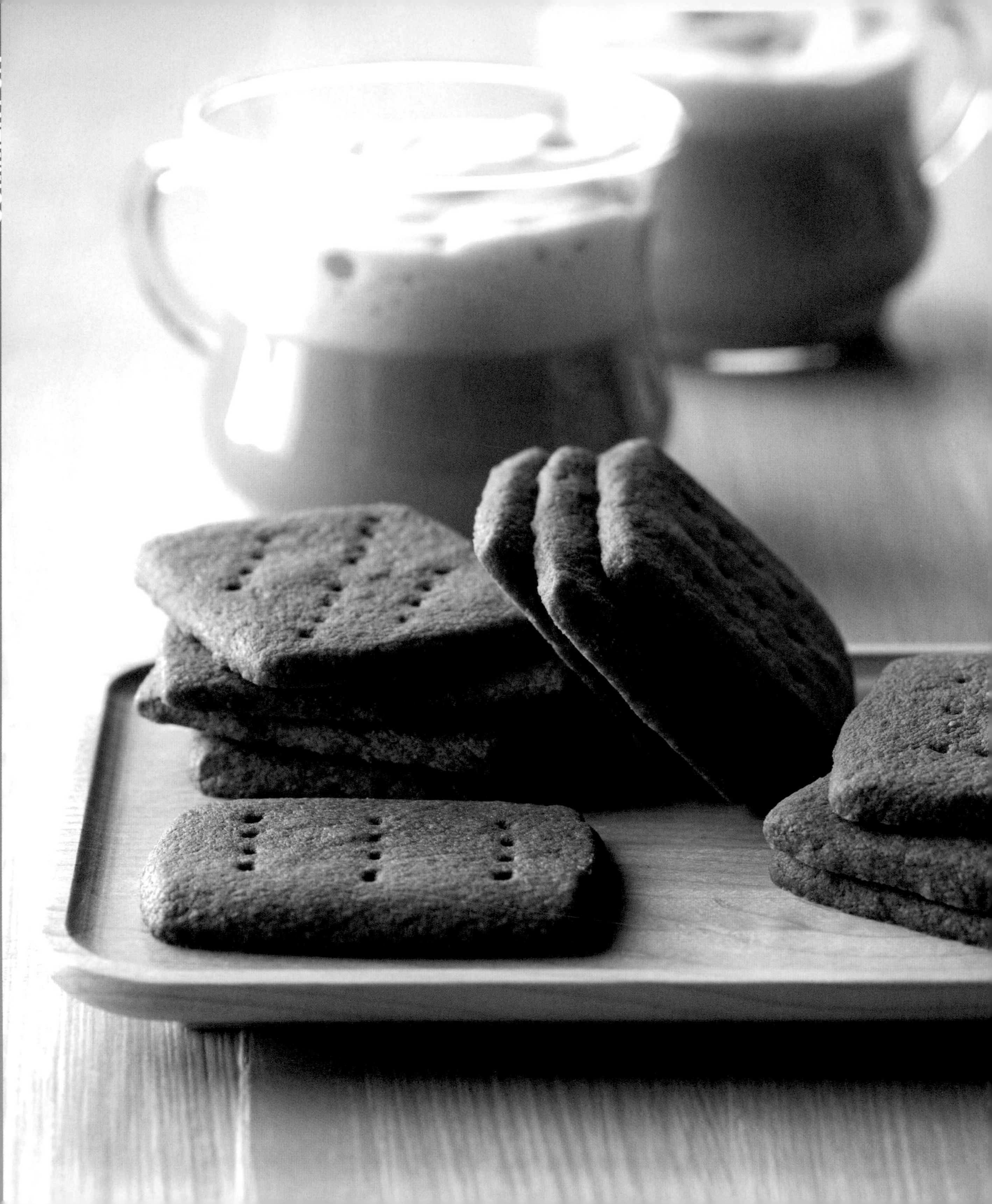

CHOCOLATE SHORTBREAD

This recipe has been in my files for a long time...probably from when I first learned to bake. Any chocolate lover will appreciate these melt-in-your-mouth cookies. I make variations of them year-round. They're even richer with a thin coat of icing or as a sandwich cookie with frosting in the middle.

—SARAH BUECKERT AUSTIN, MB

PREP: 10 MIN. • **BAKE:** 20 MIN. + COOLING
MAKES: 1 DOZEN

- ¼ **cup butter, softened**
- ¼ **teaspoon vanilla extract**
- ½ **cup all-purpose flour**
- ¼ **cup confectioners' sugar**
- 1 **to 2 tablespoons baking cocoa**

1. In a small bowl, cream butter until light and fluffy. Beat in vanilla. Combine the flour, sugar and cocoa; add to creamed mixture. Beat until dough holds together, about 3 minutes.

2. Pat dough into a 9x4-in. rectangle. Cut into 2x1½-in. strips. Place 1 in. apart on ungreased baking sheets. Prick strips with a fork.

3. Bake at 300° for 20-25 minutes or until set. Cool for 5 minutes before removing from pan to a wire rack to cool completely.

HAZELNUT ESPRESSO MACARONS

You don't have to be an expert in French baking to whip up these sandwich cookies. The crisp, chewy macarons are simple—and simply a delight.

—TASTE OF HOME TEST KITCHEN

PREP: 30 MIN. • **BAKE:** 10 MIN./BATCH
MAKES: 5 DOZEN

- 6 **large egg whites**
- 1½ **cups hazelnuts**
- 2½ **cups confectioners' sugar**
  Dash salt
- ½ **cup superfine sugar**

ESPRESSO FILLING

- 1 **cup sugar**
- 6 **tablespoons water**
- 6 **large egg yolks**
- 4 **teaspoons instant espresso powder**

- 1 **teaspoon vanilla extract**
- 1½ **cups butter, softened**
- 6 **tablespoons confectioners' sugar**

1. Place egg whites in a small bowl; let stand at room temperature for 30 minutes.

2. Preheat oven to 350°. Place hazelnuts in a 15x10x1-in. baking pan and bake for 7-10 minutes or until lightly toasted and fragrant. Transfer to a clean kitchen towel; cool. Rub briskly with the towel to remove the skins.

3. Place confectioners' sugar and toasted hazelnuts in a food processor. Cover and process until hazelnuts are ground.

4. Add salt to egg whites; beat on medium speed until soft peaks form. Gradually add superfine sugar, 1 tablespoon at a time, beating on high until stiff peaks form. Fold in hazelnut mixture.

5. Place the mixture in a heavy-duty resealable plastic bag; cut a small hole in a corner of bag. Pipe 1-in.-diameter cookies 2 in. apart onto parchment paper-lined baking sheets. Bake at 350° 9-12 minutes or until lightly browned and firm to the touch. Cool completely on pans on wire racks.

6. For filling, in a heavy saucepan, bring the sugar and water to a boil; cook over medium-high heat until the sugar is dissolved. Remove from the heat. Add a small amount of hot mixture to egg yolks; return all to the pan, stirring constantly. Cook for 2-3 minutes or until mixture thickens, stirring constantly. Remove from heat; stir in espresso powder and vanilla. Cool to room temperature.

7. In a stand mixer fitted with a whisk attachment, beat butter until creamy, about 3 minutes. Gradually beat in cooked sugar mixture. Beat in confectioners' sugar until fluffy. Refrigerate until filling reaches spreading consistency, about 10 minutes.

8. Spread on the bottoms of half of the cookies; top with remaining cookies. Store in the refrigerator.

SPUMONI SLICES

My sweet rectangles get their name from the old-fashioned tricolor ice cream. Our whole family prefers the change-of-pace cookies.

—MARY CHUPP CHATTANOOGA, TN

....

PREP: 40 MIN. + CHILLING
BAKE: 10 MIN./BATCH
MAKES: ABOUT 7 DOZEN

- 1 **cup butter, softened**
- 1½ **cups confectioners' sugar**
- 1 **large egg**
- 1 **teaspoon vanilla extract**
- 2½ **cups all-purpose flour**
- 2 **ounces semisweet chocolate, melted**
- ½ **cup chopped pecans**
- 3 **to 5 drops green food coloring**
- ¼ **cup finely chopped candied red cherries**
- ½ **teaspoon almond extract**
- 3 **to 5 drops red food coloring**

1. In a large bowl, cream butter and sugar until light and fluffy. Beat in egg and vanilla. Gradually add flour and mix well. Divide dough in three portions. Stir chocolate into one portion. Add pecans and green food coloring to the second portion. Add cherries, almond extract and red food coloring to the third portion.

2. Roll each portion between two pieces of waxed paper into an 8x6-in. rectangle. Remove waxed paper. Place the chocolate rectangle on a piece of plastic wrap. Top with the green and pink rectangles; press together lightly. Wrap with plastic and chill overnight.

3. Cut chilled dough in half lengthwise. Return one rectangle to the refrigerator. Cut remaining rectangle into ⅛-in. slices. Place 1 in. apart on ungreased baking sheets.

4. Bake at 375° for 5-7 minutes or until set. Cool 2 minutes before removing to wire racks. Repeat with the remaining cookie dough.

ANGEL SUGAR CRISPS

What a great sugar cookie! Whenever I've taken these to church coffees, I've had women come into the kitchen and ask me to share the recipe. I'm always happy to oblige.
—**ANNABEL COX** OLIVET, SD

PREP: 25 MIN. • **BAKE:** 10 MIN.
MAKES: 4 DOZEN

- ½ **cup butter, softened**
- ½ **cup shortening**
- ½ **cup sugar**
- ½ **cup packed brown sugar**
- 1 **large egg**
- 1 **teaspoon vanilla extract**
- 2 **cups all-purpose flour**
- 1 **teaspoon baking soda**
- 1 **teaspoon cream of tartar**
- ½ **teaspoon salt**
  Water
  Additional white or colored sugar

In a bowl, cream butter, shortening, sugars, egg and vanilla until light and fluffy. Sift together flour, soda, cream of tartar and salt. Add to creamed mixture; mix until blended. Shape into large marble-size balls. Dip half of ball into water, then in sugar. Place, sugared side up, on ungreased baking sheets. Bake at 400° for 6 minutes or until done. Cool.

★ ★ ★ ★ ★ **READER REVIEW**

"Oh my goodness! These are delicious. I followed the recipe, but instead of using large marble-size balls, I used my teaspoon melon scooper and dipped them alternately in red and green sugar."

GRANMIK TASTEOFHOME.COM

CHOCOLATE BUTTERSCOTCH HAYSTACKS

My grandmother made haystacks like these. She snuck them to my cousin Vonnie and me when our parents didn't want us to have any more sweets!
—**CHRISTINE SCHWESTER** DIVIDE, CO

PREP: 25 MIN. + CHILLING
MAKES: 3 DOZEN

- 2 **cups (12 ounces) semisweet chocolate chips**
- 1 **package (10 to 11 ounces) butterscotch chips**
- 4 **cups crispy chow mein noodles**

1. In a microwave or large metal bowl over simmering water, melt chocolate chips and butterscotch chips; stir until smooth. Gently stir in noodles.
2. Drop by rounded tablespoonfuls onto waxed paper-lined baking sheets. Refrigerate 10-15 minutes or until set.

JULY 9
NATIONAL
SUGAR
COOKIE
DAY

CARDAMOM-BLACKBERRY LINZER COOKIES

These cookies are a miniature version of an Austrian classic, the Linzer torte. The fruity jam goes well with the cardamom.

—CHRISTIANNA GOZZI ASTORIA, NY

PREP: 50 MIN. + CHILLING
BAKE: 10 MIN./BATCH + COOLING
MAKES: ABOUT 2 DOZEN

- 2 **cups all-purpose flour**
- 1 **cup roasted salted almonds**
- 2 **to 3 teaspoons ground cardamom**
- ¼ **teaspoon salt**
- 1 **cup unsalted butter, softened**
- ½ **cup plus 1 teaspoon sugar, divided**
- 1 **large egg**
- 1 **jar (10 ounces) seedless blackberry spreadable fruit**
- 1 **tablespoon lemon juice**
- 3 **tablespoons confectioners' sugar**

1. In a food processor, combine ½ cup of the flour and the almonds; pulse until the almonds are finely ground. Add the cardamom, salt and remaining flour; pulse until combined.

2. In a large bowl, cream butter and ½ cup sugar until light and fluffy. Beat in egg. Gradually beat in flour mixture. Divide dough in half. Shape each into a disk; wrap in plastic. Refrigerate 1 hour or until firm enough to roll.

3. Preheat oven to 350°. On a lightly floured surface, roll each portion to ⅛-in. thickness. Cut with a floured 2-in. round cookie cutter. Using a floured 1-in. round cookie cutter, cut out the centers of half of the cookies. Place the solid and the window cookies 1 in. apart on greased baking sheets.

4. Bake 10-12 minutes or until light brown. Remove from pans to wire racks to cool completely.

5. In a small bowl, mix spreadable fruit, lemon juice and remaining sugar. Spread filling on bottoms of solid cookies; top with window cookies. Dust with confectioners' sugar.

LIME COCONUT BISCOTTI

Dunk this biscotti into your morning cup of coffee, enjoy it as an afternoon snack or try it for dessert.

—DIANA BURRINK CRETE, IL

PREP: 25 MIN. • **BAKE:** 30 MIN. + COOLING
MAKES: 32 BISCOTTI

- ¾ cup sugar
- ¼ cup canola oil
- 2 large eggs
- ¼ cup lime juice
- 1 teaspoon vanilla extract
- ¼ teaspoon coconut extract
- 1¾ cups all-purpose flour
- ⅔ cup cornmeal
- 1½ teaspoons baking powder
- ¼ teaspoon salt
- 1 cup flaked coconut
- 1 teaspoon grated lime peel

1. In a small bowl, beat sugar and oil until blended. Beat in the eggs, lime juice and extracts. Combine the flour, cornmeal, baking powder and salt; gradually add to sugar mixture and mix well (dough will be sticky). Stir in coconut and lime peel.

2. Divide the dough in half. With lightly floured hands, shape each half into a 12x2-in. rectangle on a parchment paper-lined baking sheet. Bake at 350° for 20-25 minutes or until set.

3. Place pan on a wire rack. When cool enough to handle, transfer loaves to a cutting board; cut diagonally with a serrated knife into ¾-in. slices. Place cut side down on ungreased baking sheets.

4. Bake for 5-6 minutes on each side or until golden brown. Remove to wire racks to cool. Store in an airtight container.

CHERRY CHEESE WINDMILLS

These pretty cookies look fancy, but they're really not much work. They're perfect for any occasion throughout the year.

—HELEN MCGIBBON DOWNERS GROVE, IL

PREP: 25 MIN. + CHILLING
BAKE: 10 MIN./BATCH + COOLING
MAKES: 32 COOKIES

- ⅓ cup butter, softened
- ⅓ cup shortening
- ¾ cup sugar
- 1 large egg
- 1 tablespoon milk
- 1 teaspoon vanilla extract
- 2 cups all-purpose flour
- 1½ teaspoons baking powder
- ¼ teaspoon salt

FILLING

- 3 ounces cream cheese, softened
- ¼ cup sugar
- ¼ teaspoon almond extract
- ½ cup finely chopped maraschino cherries
- ¼ cup sliced almonds, toasted and chopped

1. In a large bowl, cream the butter, shortening and sugar until light and fluffy. Beat in the egg, milk and vanilla. Combine the flour, baking powder and salt; gradually add to creamed mixture and mix well. Divide dough in half. Cover and refrigerate for 3 hours or until easy to handle.

2. In a small bowl, beat cream cheese, sugar and extract until smooth. Fold in cherries. On a floured surface, roll each portion of dough into a 10-in. square. With a sharp knife or pastry wheel, cut into 2½-in. squares. Place 2 in. apart on ungreased baking sheets. Make 1-in. cuts from each corner toward the center of the dough.

3. Drop teaspoonfuls of filling in the center of each square; sprinkle with almonds. Fold alternating points to the center to form a windmill; moisten points with water and pinch gently at center to seal. Bake at 350° for 8-10 minutes or until set. Cool on wire racks.

PECAN PIE THUMBPRINTS

The buttery dough and nutty filling take time to make, but the result is so worth it. After trying one of these, I think you'll agree.
—**PEGGY KEY** GRANT, AL

PREP: 30 MIN. + CHILLING
BAKE: 10 MIN./BATCH + COOLING
MAKES: 4½ DOZEN

- 1 cup butter, softened
- ½ cup sugar
- 2 large eggs, separated
- ½ cup dark corn syrup
- 2½ cups all-purpose flour

FILLING

- ¼ cup plus 2 tablespoons confectioners' sugar
- 3 tablespoons butter
- 2 tablespoons dark corn syrup
- ¼ cup plus 2 tablespoons finely chopped pecans

1. In a large bowl, cream butter and sugar until light and fluffy. Beat in egg yolks and corn syrup. Gradually beat in flour. Refrigerate, covered, 30 minutes or until firm enough to roll.

2. For the filling, in a small saucepan, combine confectioners' sugar, butter and corn syrup. Bring to a boil over medium heat, stirring occasionally. Remove from heat; stir in pecans. Remove from pan; refrigerate 30 minutes or until cold.

3. Preheat oven to 375°. Shape dough into 1-in. balls; place 2 in. apart on parchment paper-lined baking sheets. In a small bowl, whisk egg whites; brush over tops.

4. Bake 5 minutes. Remove from oven. Gently press an indentation in center of each cookie with the end of a wooden spoon handle. Fill each with a scant ½ teaspoon of the pecan mixture. Bake 4-5 minutes longer or until the edges are light brown.

5. Cool on pans 5 minutes. Remove to wire racks to cool.

JULY 12
NATIONAL PECAN PIE DAY

RASPBERRY CRESCENTS

These delicate, puffy turnover cookies, spiked with raspberry and almond, are delightful with afternoon tea.

—LINDA HOBBS ALBION, NY

PREP: 25 MIN. + CHILLING
BAKE: 15 MIN. • **MAKES:** 4 DOZEN

- 2 **cups sifted all-purpose flour**
- 1 **cup cold butter**
- 1 **cup (8 ounces) plus 2 tablespoons cream-style cottage cheese**
  Raspberry jam

GLAZE
- 1 **cup confectioners' sugar**
- ⅛ **teaspoon almond extract**
  Milk

1. Place flour in a medium bowl; cut in butter as for pie crust. Blend in cottage cheese until mixture forms a ball (can use a food processor). Chill 1 hour.

2. On a floured surface, roll dough to ⅛-in. thickness. Cut with a 3-in. round cutter. Place a level ¼ teaspoon of jam in center of reach cookie. Moisten edges and fold in half; seal tightly with a fork. Place on lightly greased baking sheets; prick tops with fork.

3. Bake at 400° for 15 minutes or until lightly browned. Cool on wire racks. For glaze, combine the sugar, extract and enough milk to create a thin spreading consistency; drizzle over cooled crescents.

BEARY CUTE COOKIES

I make bear-shaped cookies for picnics and other fun gatherings. Use assorted candies for the eyes and noses to keep things simple and playful.

—SUSAN SCHULLER BRAINERD, MN

PREP: 25 MIN. • **BAKE:** 10 MIN./BATCH
MAKES: 2½ DOZEN

- ¾ cup shortening
- ½ cup sugar
- ½ cup packed brown sugar
- 1 large egg
- 1 teaspoon vanilla extract
- 2 cups all-purpose flour
- 1 teaspoon salt
- ½ teaspoon baking soda
  Additional sugar
- 30 miniature milk chocolate kisses
- 60 M&M's miniature baking bits
  Colored decorating icing, optional

1. Preheat oven to 375°. In a large bowl, cream shortening and sugars until light and fluffy. Beat in egg and vanilla. In another bowl, whisk the flour, salt and baking soda; gradually beat into creamed mixture (dough will be crumbly).
2. Set aside about ½ cup dough for ears. Shape remaining dough into 1-in. balls; roll in additional sugar. Place 3 in. apart on ungreased baking sheets. Flatten to about ½-in. thickness. Roll reserved dough into ½-in. balls; roll in sugar. Place two smaller balls about 1 in. apart touching each flattened ball (do not flatten smaller balls).
3. Bake 10-12 minutes or until set and edges are lightly browned. Remove from oven; immediately press one kiss and two baking bits into each cookie for nose and eyes. Cool on pans 5 minutes. Remove to wire racks to cool completely. If desired, pipe with colored icing.

SNICKERDOODLE ICE CREAM SANDWICH MINIS

My husband absolutely loves ice cream sandwiches and snickerdoodles, so I combined them into one fun treat. Here's how we build this cool dessert.

—HEATHER PILON WINSLOW, ME

PREP: 40 MIN. + FREEZING
BAKE: 10 MIN. + COOLING
MAKES: ABOUT 16 SERVINGS

- ½ cup butter, softened
- ¾ cup plus 3 tablespoons sugar, divided
- 1 large egg
- 1½ cups all-purpose flour
- 1 teaspoon cream of tartar
- ½ teaspoon baking soda
- ⅛ teaspoon salt
- 1 tablespoon brown sugar
- 2 teaspoons ground cinnamon
- 2 cups vanilla ice cream

1. Preheat oven to 400°. In a bowl, beat butter and ¾ cup sugar until blended. Beat in egg. In another bowl, whisk flour, cream of tartar, baking soda and salt; gradually beat into creamed mixture.
2. In a small bowl, mix brown sugar, cinnamon and remaining sugar until blended. Shape rounded tablespoons of dough into 1-in. balls; roll in brown sugar mixture. Place 2 in. apart on ungreased baking sheets.
3. Bake 7-9 minutes or until set and edges are lightly browned. Remove from pans to wire racks to cool completely.
4. Using a scoop, place 2 tablespoons ice cream on bottom of a cookie; top with a second cookie, pressing gently to flatten ice cream. Wrap in plastic and freeze. Repeat. Freeze the ice cream sandwiches overnight.

RAINBOW S'MOREO COOKIES

Homemade Oreo cookies are pretty great on their own, but add crunchy graham cracker crumbs to the dough, stuff the cookies with marshmallow creme and roll them in sprinkles, and you've got a fantastic summer dessert that will have everyone talking.

—COLLEEN DELAWDER HERNDON, VA

PREP: 15 MIN. • **BAKE:** 10 MIN./BATCH
MAKES: ABOUT 2 DOZEN

- ½ cup unsalted butter, softened
- 1 cup sugar
- 1 large egg
- 1 teaspoon vanilla extract
- ½ cup baking cocoa
- ¾ cup graham cracker crumbs
- ½ cup all-purpose flour
- 1 teaspoon baking powder
- ¼ teaspoon kosher salt
- 1 jar (7 ounces) marshmallow creme
  Rainbow sprinkles

1. Preheat oven to 350°. Cream butter and sugar until light and fluffy. Beat in egg and vanilla. Beat in cocoa. In another bowl, whisk cracker crumbs, flour, baking powder and salt; gradually beat into creamed mixture.

2. Shape dough into ½-in. balls. Place 2 in. apart on parchment paper-lined baking sheets. Flatten with bottom of a glass. Bake until set, 6-8 minutes. Cool on pans 3 minutes. Remove to wire racks to cool completely.

3. Spread marshmallow creme over half of cookies; top with remaining cookies. Roll sides in sprinkles.

SOFT HONEY COOKIES

This old-fashioned cookie has a pleasant honey-cinnamon flavor and a tender texture that resembles cake. It has been a family favorite for years. I love sharing the recipe.
—**ROCHELLE FRIEDMAN** BROOKLYN, NY

PREP: 15 MIN. + CHILLING • **BAKE:** 10 MIN.
MAKES: 16 COOKIES

- ¼ **cup sugar**
- 2 **tablespoons canola oil**
- 1 **large egg**
- 3 **tablespoons honey**
- ¾ **teaspoon vanilla extract**
- 1 **cup plus 2 tablespoons all-purpose flour**
- ¼ **teaspoon baking powder**
- ¼ **teaspoon ground cinnamon**
- ⅛ **teaspoon salt**

1. In a small bowl, beat sugar and oil until blended. Beat in egg; beat in honey and vanilla extract. Combine the flour, baking powder, cinnamon and salt; gradually add to sugar mixture and mix well (dough will be stiff). Cover and refrigerate for at least 2 hours.

2. Drop dough by tablespoonfuls 2 in. apart onto a greased baking sheet. Bake at 350° for 8-10 minutes or until bottoms are lightly browned. Cool for 1 minute before removing from pan to a wire rack. Store in an airtight container.

FROM THE COOKIE JAR

It's best to set sticky cookie dough in the fridge for a few hours before proceeding with the recipe. Cooling the dough will generally make it easier to work with.

OATMEAL RAISIN COOKIES

I was given this recipe by a friend many years ago, and these cookies are as delicious as Mom used to make. The secret is to measure exactly (no guessing on the amounts) and to avoid overbaking.
—**WENDY COALWELL** ABBEVILLE, GA

START TO FINISH: 30 MIN.
MAKES: ABOUT 3½ DOZEN

- 1 **cup shortening**
- 1 **cup sugar**
- 1 **cup packed light brown sugar**
- 3 **large eggs**
- 1 **teaspoon vanilla extract**
- 2½ **cups all-purpose flour**
- 2 **teaspoons baking soda**
- 1 **teaspoon salt**
- 1 **teaspoon ground cinnamon**
- 2 **cups old-fashioned oats**
- 1 **cup raisins**
- 1 **cup coarsely chopped pecans, optional**

1. In a large bowl, cream the shortening and sugars until light and fluffy. Beat in eggs, one at a time, beating well after each addition. Beat in the vanilla. Combine the flour, baking soda, salt and cinnamon. Add to creamed mixture, mixing just until combined. Stir in the oats, raisins and, if desired, pecans.

2. Shape into 1-in. balls. Place 2 in. apart on ungreased baking sheets. Flatten with a greased glass bottom.

3. Bake at 350° for 10-11 minutes or until golden brown. Do not overbake. Remove to a wire rack to cool.

HOMEMADE FORTUNE COOKIES

Our home is frequently filled with guests, so I'm always baking up something new. I prepared these five-ingredient cookies when I was looking to surprise my husband. Have fun thinking of different fortunes to tuck inside!
—**SUSAN BETTINGER** BATTLE CREEK, MI

PREP: 45 MIN. • **BAKE:** 5 MIN.
MAKES: 10 COOKIES

- 3 **tablespoons butter, softened**
- 3 **tablespoons sugar**
- 1 **large egg white**
- ½ **teaspoon vanilla extract**
- ⅓ **cup all-purpose flour**

1. Preheat oven to 400°. Write fortunes on small strips of paper (3½x¼-in.); set aside. Line a baking sheet with parchment paper. Using a pencil, draw two 3½-in. circles on a sheet of parchment paper. Place paper, pencil mark down, on a baking sheet; set aside.
2. In a small bowl, beat butter, sugar, egg white and vanilla. Add flour; mix well. Spread 1 tablespoon batter over each circle. Bake 4-5 minutes or until lightly browned.
3. Slide parchment paper onto a work surface. Cover one cookie with a kitchen towel. Place a fortune in the center of the other cookie; loosen cookie from the parchment paper with a thin spatula. Fold cookie in half over fortune strip so the edges meet; hold edges together for 3 seconds.
4. Place center of cookie over the rim of a glass; gently press ends down to bend cookie in middle. Cool 1 minute before removing to a wire rack. Repeat with second cookie. If cookies become too cool to fold, return to oven to soften for 1 minute. Repeat with remaining batter and fortunes.

JULY 20
NATIONAL FORTUNE COOKIE DAY

MACADAMIA NUT COOKIES

I host a mainland luau every year. These rich cookies—filled with chocolate chips and Hawaiian macadamia nuts—are always a delectable ending to the meal.

—MARY GAYLORD BALSAM LAKE, WI

PREP: 20 MIN. + CHILLING
BAKE: 10 MIN./BATCH
MAKES: ABOUT 6 DOZEN

- 1 **cup butter, softened**
- ¾ **cup sugar**
- ¾ **cup packed brown sugar**
- 2 **large eggs**
- 1 **teaspoon vanilla extract**
- 2¼ **cups all-purpose flour**
- 1 **teaspoon baking soda**
- 1 **teaspoon salt**
- 2 **jars (3½ ounces each) macadamia nuts, chopped**
- 2 **cups (12 ounces) semisweet chocolate chips**
- 1 **cup (6 ounces) white baking chips**

1. In a large bowl, cream butter and sugars until light and fluffy. Add eggs and vanilla; beat on medium speed for 2 minutes. Combine the flour, baking soda and salt; add to creamed mixture and beat for 2 minutes. Stir in nuts and chips. Cover and refrigerate several hours or overnight.

2. Drop by tablespoonfuls 2 in. apart onto ungreased baking sheets. Bake at 375° for 10-12 minutes or until golden brown. Cool on pans for 1 minute before removing to wire racks; cool completely.

NOTE *Two cups of chopped almonds may be substituted for the macadamia nuts.*

AMISH SUGAR COOKIES

These easy-to-make cookies simply melt in your mouth! I've passed the recipe around to many friends. After I gave it to my sister, she entered the cookies in a local fair and won the top prize!

—**SYLVIA FORD** KENNETT, MO

PREP: 10 MIN. • **BAKE:** 10 MIN./BATCH
MAKES: ABOUT 5 DOZEN

- 1 **cup butter, softened**
- 1 **cup vegetable oil**
- 1 **cup sugar**
- 1 **cup confectioners' sugar**
- 2 **large eggs**
- 1 **teaspoon vanilla extract**
- 4½ **cups all-purpose flour**
- 1 **teaspoon baking soda**
- 1 **teaspoon cream of tartar**

1. In a large bowl, beat the butter, oil and sugars. Beat in the eggs until well blended. Beat in vanilla. Combine the flour, baking soda and cream of tartar; gradually add to creamed mixture.

2. Drop by small teaspoonfuls onto ungreased baking sheets. Bake at 375° for 8-10 minutes or until lightly browned. Remove to wire racks to cool.

BAKING SHEETS

When baking cookies, use heavy-gauge, dull aluminum baking sheets with low sides. If your pan is dark, the cookies may over-brown.

BABY SHOWER

SNOWBALL SURPRISE COOKIES

Is it a boy or a girl? Candy coating disks hidden inside these tender cookies reveal the gender of the baby-to-be. Since the disks come in a variety of colors, you can also make these cookies to match any holiday or theme.
—**JAN WHITWORTH** ROEBUCK, SC

PREP: 25 MIN. + CHILLING
BAKE: 15 MIN./BATCH
MAKES: ABOUT 3 DOZEN

- 1 **cup butter, softened**
- 1½ **cups confectioners' sugar, divided**
- 2 **teaspoons vanilla extract**
- 2 **cups all-purpose flour**
- ¼ **teaspoon salt**
- ⅓ **cup each finely chopped pecans, walnuts and almonds, toasted**
- 39 **pink or blue candy coating disks**

1. In a large bowl, cream butter, ½ cup confectioners' sugar and vanilla until light and fluffy. In another bowl, whisk flour and salt; gradually beat into creamed mixture. Stir in nuts. Refrigerate 1 hour or until firm.

2. Preheat oven to 350°. Shape dough into 1-in. balls; place them 1 in. apart on ungreased baking sheets. Insert a candy disk into the center of each cookie, reshaping dough into a ball and covering disk completely.

3. Bake 12-15 minutes or until bottoms are light brown. Cool on pans 2 minutes. Place remaining confectioners' sugar in a shallow bowl. Roll warm cookies in confectioners' sugar. Cool on wire racks. Re-roll cookies in confectioners' sugar if needed.

ROCKING HORSE COOKIES

These precious ponies are perfect baby shower favors. The 3-D cookies stand nicely and even rock back-and-forth.

—LORRI REINHARDT BIG BEND, WI

PREP: 2 HOURS + CHILLING
BAKE: 10 MIN./BATCH + STANDING
MAKES: 20 ROCKING HORSES

- 1 **cup butter, softened**
- 1 **cup sugar**
- ½ **cup packed brown sugar**
- 1 **large egg**
- 1 **teaspoon vanilla extract**
- 2¼ **cups all-purpose flour**
- ½ **cup baking cocoa**
- 1 **teaspoon baking soda**

ASSEMBLY

- 1 **cup (6 ounces) semisweet chocolate chips**
- 40 **chocolate-covered graham cracker cookies**
- 4 **cups confectioners' sugar**
- 4½ **teaspoons meringue powder**
- 3 **to 4 teaspoons warm water**
  Paste food coloring
- 20 **Riesen's chewy chocolate-covered caramels**
  Thin crafting ribbon, optional

1. In a large bowl, cream butter and sugars until light and fluffy. Beat in egg and vanilla. Combine flour, cocoa and baking soda; gradually add to creamed mixture and mix well. Cover and refrigerate at least 2 hours or until easy to handle.

2. Preheat oven to 375°. On a lightly floured surface, roll dough to ¼-in. thickness. Cut with a floured 3½-in. rocking-horse-shaped cookie cutter. Place on greased baking sheets, flipping half of cutouts so they face in the opposite direction (two cutouts will form each rocking horse cookie).

3. Bake 7-9 minutes or until set. Cool 2-3 minutes before removing from pans to wire racks to cool completely.

4. Flip cutouts so their flat sides are up. Melt chips; stir until smooth. Spread the top of a graham cracker cookie with some chocolate; attach to body area of cutout.

Repeat with the remaining cutouts. Let stand until set. Set aside the remaining chocolate.

5. For icing, in a large bowl, beat the confectioners' sugar, meringue powder and warm water on low speed just until combined. Beat on high for 4-5 minutes or until stiff peaks form. Tint as desired with food coloring. Keep unused icing covered at all times with a damp cloth.

6. Flip cutouts right-side up; decorate as desired with icing. Let stand at room temperature for several hours or until icing is firm.

7. To assemble horses, reheat chips until melted. Place a caramel candy on a work surface in front of you; brush the long sides with chocolate. Pair up two cutouts so they align, forming a rocking horse.

8. Brush graham cracker cookies with chocolate; set the cutouts on either side of the caramel candy. Press the cutouts together, forming a rocking horse. (The rocking horse halves are attached in the center by the graham cracker cookies, which join the body, and the caramel candy, which supports the rocker.)

9. Gently place rocking horse on its side; let stand at room temperature for several hours or until firm. Repeat for remaining rocking horses. With ribbon, tie bows around rocking horses' necks if desired.

3. Drop by rounded tablespoonfuls 2 in. apart onto ungreased baking sheets. Bake at 350° for 12-14 minutes or until edges are lightly browned. Cool for 1 minute before removing from pans to wire racks.

CHOCOLATE-PEANUT BUTTER CUP COOKIES

If you want to enjoy one of these soft, fully loaded treats the day after you make them, you'd better find a good hiding spot.
—JENNIFER KREY CLARENCE, NY

PREP: 25 MIN. • **BAKE:** 10 MIN./BATCH
MAKES: 4 DOZEN

- 1 cup butter, softened
- ¾ cup creamy peanut butter
- 1 cup packed brown sugar
- ½ cup sugar
- 2 large egg yolks
- ¼ cup 2% milk
- 2 teaspoons vanilla extract
- 2⅓ cups all-purpose flour
- ⅓ cup baking cocoa
- 1 teaspoon baking soda
- 1 cup milk chocolate chips
- 1 cup peanut butter chips
- 6 packages (1½ ounces each) peanut butter cups, chopped

1. Preheat oven to 350°. In a large bowl, cream butter, peanut butter and sugars until light and fluffy. Beat in egg yolks, milk and vanilla. Combine flour, cocoa and baking soda; gradually add to the creamed mixture and mix well. Stir in chips and peanut butter cups.
2. Drop heaping tablespoonfuls 2 in. apart onto ungreased baking sheets. Bake 8-10 minutes or until set (do not overbake). Cool for 2 minutes before removing from pans to wire racks. Store in an airtight container.

CHERRY CHOCOLATE CHIP COOKIES

We run a cherry orchard, so I'm always dreaming up new cherry recipes. These cookies are one of my family's favorites.
—PAMELA ALEXANDER PROSSER, WA

PREP: 15 MIN. • **BAKE:** 15 MIN./BATCH
MAKES: ABOUT 3½ DOZEN

- 1 cup dried cherries, chopped
- ⅓ cup hot water
- 6 tablespoons shortening
- 6 tablespoons butter, softened
- 1½ cups packed brown sugar
- ½ cup sugar
- 2 large eggs
- 3 teaspoons grated orange peel
- 1½ teaspoons vanilla extract
- 3 cups quick-cooking oats
- 1¾ cups all-purpose flour
- ¾ teaspoon baking soda
- ¾ teaspoon ground cinnamon
- ½ teaspoon salt
- 1 cup (6 ounces) semisweet chocolate chips

1. In a small bowl, soak cherries in hot water for at least 10 minutes.
2. Meanwhile, in a large bowl, cream the shortening, butter and sugars until light and fluffy. Beat in the eggs, orange peel and vanilla. Combine the oats, flour, baking soda, cinnamon and salt; gradually add to creamed mixture and mix well. Stir in the chocolate chips and cherries with liquid.

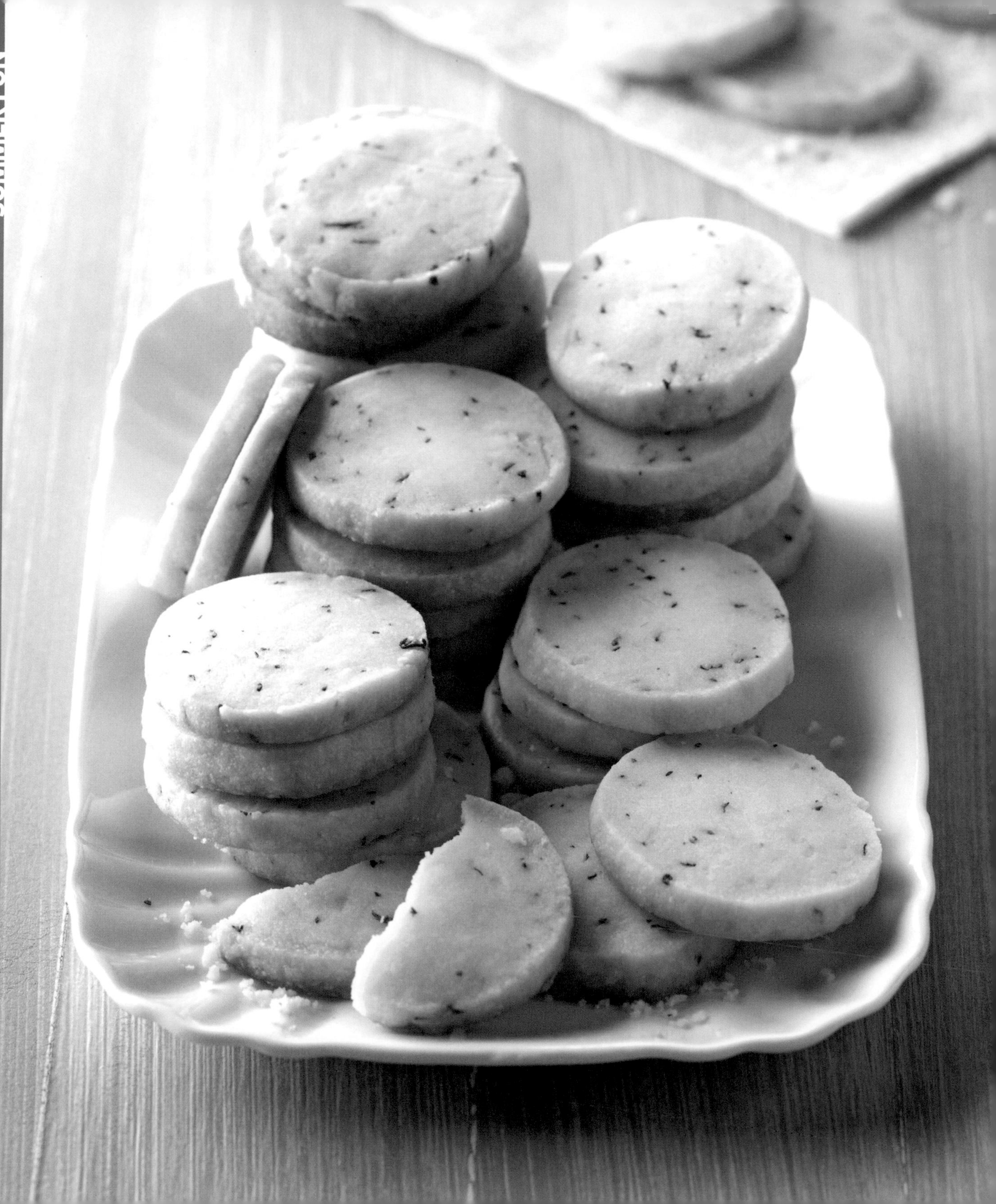

ROSEMARY SHORTBREAD COOKIES

I love these five-ingredient treats because you can make the dough ahead of time and store it in the refrigerator, then just slice and bake! The rosemary makes them a nice change-of-pace cookie.

—AMAVIDA COFFEE ROSEMARY BEACH, FL

PREP: 30 MIN. + CHILLING
BAKE: 15 MIN./BATCH • **MAKES:** 5½ DOZEN

- 1 **cup butter, softened**
- ½ **cup confectioners' sugar**
- 2 **cups all-purpose flour**
- 2 **tablespoons minced fresh rosemary**
- ½ **teaspoon sea salt**

1. In a large bowl, cream butter and confectioners' sugar until light and fluffy. Combine the flour, rosemary and salt; gradually add to creamed mixture and mix well.

2. Shape into two 8¼-in. rolls; wrap each in plastic. Refrigerate overnight. Cut into ¼-in. slices. Place 2 in. apart on ungreased baking sheets.

3. Bake at 350° for 11-13 minutes or until edges begin to brown. Cool for 1 minute before removing from pans to wire racks. Store in an airtight container.

BIG & BUTTERY CHOCOLATE CHIP COOKIES

My version of the classic cookie is based on a recipe from a bakery in California called Hungry Bear. It's big, thick and chewy—perfect for dunking.

—IRENE YEH MEQUON, WI

PREP: 35 MIN. + CHILLING
BAKE: 10 MIN./BATCH
MAKES: ABOUT 2 DOZEN

- 1 **cup butter, softened**
- 1 **cup packed brown sugar**
- ¾ **cup sugar**
- 2 **large eggs**
- 1½ **teaspoons vanilla extract**
- 2⅔ **cups all-purpose flour**
- 1¼ **teaspoons baking soda**
- 1 **teaspoon salt**
- 1 **package (12 ounces) semisweet chocolate chips**

AUGUST 4
NATIONAL CHOCOLATE CHIP COOKIE DAY

- 2 **cups coarsely chopped walnuts, toasted**

1. In a large bowl, beat butter and sugars until blended. Beat in eggs and vanilla. In a small bowl, whisk flour, baking soda and salt; gradually beat into butter mixture. Stir in chocolate chips and walnuts.

2. Shape ¼ cupfuls of dough into balls. Flatten each to ¾-in. thickness (2½-in. diameter), smoothing edges as necessary. Place in an airtight container, separating layers with waxed or parchment paper; refrigerate, covered, overnight.

3. To bake, place dough portions 2 in. apart on parchment paper-lined baking sheets; let stand at room temperature 30 minutes before baking. Preheat oven to 400°.

4. Bake 10-12 minutes or until edges are golden brown (centers will be light). Cool on pans 2 minutes. Remove to wire racks to cool completely.

NOTE *To toast nuts, bake in a shallow pan in a 350° oven for 5-10 minutes or cook in a skillet over low heat until lightly browned, stirring occasionally.*

★ ★ ★ ★ ★ **READER REVIEW**

"This is the best recipe I have found for chocolate chip cookies! They were delicious and stayed nice and soft."

KMT01 TASTEOFHOME.COM

THICK SUGAR COOKIES

Thicker than the norm, this sugar cookie is like one you might find at a bakery. My children often request these for their birthdays and are always happy to help me decorate them.

—HEATHER BIEDLER MARTINSBURG, WV

PREP: 25 MIN. + CHILLING
BAKE: 10 MIN./BATCH + COOLING
MAKES: ABOUT 3 DOZEN

- 1 **cup butter, softened**
- 1 **cup sugar**
- 2 **large eggs**
- 3 **large egg yolks**
- 1½ **teaspoons vanilla extract**
- ¾ **teaspoon almond extract**
- 3½ **cups all-purpose flour**
- 1½ **teaspoons baking powder**
- ¼ **teaspoon salt**

FROSTING
- 4 **cups confectioners' sugar**
- ½ **cup butter, softened**
- ½ **cup shortening**
- 1 **teaspoon vanilla extract**
- ½ **teaspoon almond extract**
- 2 **to 3 tablespoons 2% milk**
  Assorted colored nonpareils, optional

1. In a large bowl, cream butter and sugar until light and fluffy. Beat in eggs, egg yolks and extracts. In another bowl, whisk flour, baking powder and salt; gradually beat into creamed mixture. Shape dough into a disk; wrap in plastic. Refrigerate for 1 hour or until firm enough to roll.

2. Preheat oven to 375°. On a lightly floured surface, roll dough to ½-in. thickness. Cut with a floured 2-in. cookie cutter. Place 1 in. apart on ungreased baking sheets.

3. Bake 10-12 minutes or until edges begin to brown. Cool on pans 5 minutes. Remove to wire racks to cool completely.

4. For frosting, in a large bowl, beat confectioners' sugar, butter, shortening, extracts and enough milk to reach desired consistency. Spread over cookies. If desired, sprinkle with nonpareils.

OATMEAL SANDWICH COOKIES

These fun treats are perfect to snack on and to pack in lunch boxes. They always sell out at bake sales.

—JAN WOODALL INDIANAPOLIS, IN

PREP: 25 MIN.
BAKE: 10 MIN./BATCH + COOLING
MAKES: ABOUT 4½ DOZEN

- 1½ cups shortening
- 2⅔ cups packed brown sugar
- 4 large eggs
- 2 teaspoons vanilla extract
- 2¼ cups all-purpose flour
- 2 teaspoons ground cinnamon
- 1½ teaspoons baking soda
- 1 teaspoon salt
- ½ teaspoon ground nutmeg
- 4 cups old-fashioned oats

FILLING
- ¾ cup shortening
- 3 cups confectioners' sugar
- 1 jar (7 ounces) marshmallow creme
- 1 to 3 tablespoons 2% milk

1. In a large bowl, cream shortening and brown sugar until light and fluffy. Beat in the eggs and vanilla. Combine the flour, cinnamon, baking soda, salt and nutmeg; gradually add to creamed mixture and mix well. Stir in oats.

2. Drop by rounded teaspoonfuls 2 in. apart onto lightly greased baking sheets. Bake at 350° for 10-12 minutes or until golden brown. Remove cookies to wire racks to cool.

3. For filling, in a small bowl, cream the shortening, sugar and marshmallow creme. Add enough milk to achieve spreading consistency. Spread filling on the bottom of half of the cookies; top with remaining cookies.

★ ★ ★ ★ ★ **5 STAR TIP**

Don't have shortening? Butter can be substituted for shortening in equal amounts; however, the cookies will differ. Cookies made with butter will spread out more and have a darker color, but they'll also be loaded with buttery flavor.

ROOT BEER FLOAT COOKIES

A hint of good old-fashioned root beer flavors these chewy-soft sandwich cookies. They're great with ice cream!

—**JIM GORDON** BEECHER, IL

PREP: 45 MIN.
BAKE: 10 MIN./BATCH + COOLING
MAKES: 2½ DOZEN

- ½ cup butter, softened
- 1 cup packed brown sugar
- 1 large egg
- 1 teaspoon root beer concentrate
- 1¾ cups all-purpose flour
- ½ teaspoon salt
- ½ teaspoon baking soda

FILLING

- ¼ cup butter, softened
- 1⅓ cups confectioners' sugar
- 1 teaspoon water
- 1 teaspoon root beer concentrate

1. In a large bowl, cream butter and brown sugar until light and fluffy. Beat in egg and root beer concentrate. Combine the flour, salt and baking soda; gradually add to creamed mixture and mix well.

2. Shape dough into ¾-in. balls. Place 2 in. apart on ungreased baking sheets. Bake at 375° for 6-8 minutes or until lightly browned. Remove to wire racks to cool completely.

3. In a small bowl, beat the filling ingredients until smooth. Spread on the bottoms of half of the cookies; top with remaining cookies.

OREGON'S HAZELNUT CHOCOLATE CHIP COOKIE

These nutty cookies are popular with the ladies at my craft club. I grew up during the Depression, and my mother taught me to use what was available—like the plentiful nuts here in Oregon.

—**SELMER LOONEY** EUGENE, OR

START TO FINISH: 25 MIN.
MAKES: 3 DOZEN

- 1 cup butter, softened
- ½ cup sugar
- 1 cup packed brown sugar
- 2 large eggs
- 1 teaspoon vanilla extract
- 2⅓ cups all-purpose flour
- 1 teaspoon baking soda
- ½ teaspoon salt
- 1 cup (6 ounces) semisweet chocolate chips
- ¾ cup chopped hazelnuts

1. In a large bowl, cream butter and sugars on medium speed for 3 minutes. Add eggs, one at a time, beating well after each addition. Add vanilla. Combine flour, baking soda and salt; gradually add to batter. Fold in chocolate chips and nuts.

2. Drop by heaping tablespoonfuls 3 in. apart onto lightly greased baking sheets. Flatten lightly with a fork. Bake at 350° for 10-12 minutes or until light brown. Remove to a wire rack to cool.

AUGUST 6
NATIONAL
ROOT BEER
FLOAT
DAY

SUGAR CONE CHOCOLATE CHIP COOKIES

I made these for my boys when they were growing up, and now I treat my grandkids to them! If I could make a batch of cookies a day, I'd be in baking heaven and I'd turn to this recipe regularly.

—PAULA MARCHESI LENHARTSVILLE, PA

PREP: 25 MIN. • **BAKE:** 10 MIN./BATCH
MAKES: 6 DOZEN

- 1 cup butter, softened
- ¾ cup sugar
- ¾ cup packed brown sugar
- 2 large eggs
- 3 teaspoons vanilla extract
- 2¼ cups all-purpose flour
- 1 teaspoon baking soda
- ½ teaspoon salt
- 2 cups milk chocolate chips
- 2 cups coarsely crushed ice cream sugar cones (about 16)
- 1 cup sprinkles

1. Preheat oven to 375°. In a large bowl, cream butter and sugars until light and fluffy. Beat in the eggs and vanilla. In another bowl, whisk flour, baking soda and salt; gradually beat into creamed mixture. Stir in chocolate chips, sugar cones and sprinkles.

2. Drop by tablespoonfuls 2 in. apart onto ungreased baking sheets. Bake 8-10 minutes or until golden brown. Remove from pans to wire racks to cool.

2. Bake 10-12 minutes or until set. Cool on pans 1 minute. Remove from pans to wire racks to cool completely.

3. Drizzle cookies with melted baking chips. Top with coffee beans, attaching with melted chips if necessary.

POPCORN COOKIES

It's so much fun to surprise people with the crushed popcorn in these yummy cookies. They're definitely a distinctive confection.

—**LEIGH ANNE PRESTON** PALMYRA, IN

START TO FINISH: 30 MIN. • **MAKES:** 2½ DOZEN

- ½ cup butter, softened
- 1 cup sugar
- 1 large egg
- 1 teaspoon vanilla extract
- 1¼ cups all-purpose flour
- ½ teaspoon baking soda
  Pinch salt
- 2 cups popped popcorn, lightly crushed
- 1 cup (6 ounces) semisweet chocolate chips
- ½ cup chopped pecans

1. In a large bowl, cream butter and sugar until light and fluffy. Beat in egg and vanilla. Combine the flour, baking soda and salt; gradually add to the creamed mixture. Stir in the popcorn, chocolate chips and pecans.

2. Drop by tablespoonfuls 2 in. apart onto greased baking sheets. Bake at 350° for 13-14 minutes or until golden brown. Remove to wire racks to cool.

FROM THE COOKIE JAR

Drop cookies generally spread while baking. If your treats are spreading too much, however, it may be because the baking pan is too warm from the previous batch. A good rule of thumb is to always drop cookie dough onto cool or room-temperature pans.

MOCHA MACAROON COOKIES

Here's an updated version of the classic macaroon. With chocolate, coffee and cinnamon, it tastes like a specialty from a high-end cafe. Your friends will love it!

—**JEANNE HOLT** MENDOTA HEIGHTS, MN

PREP: 20 MIN. • **BAKE:** 10 MIN./BATCH + COOLING
MAKES: 4 DOZEN

- 2 teaspoons instant coffee granules
- 2 teaspoons hot water
- 1 can (14 ounces) sweetened condensed milk
- 2 ounces unsweetened chocolate, melted
- 1 teaspoon vanilla extract
- ¼ teaspoon ground cinnamon
- ⅛ teaspoon salt
- 1 package (14 ounces) flaked coconut
- ⅔ cup white baking chips, melted
  Plain or chocolate-covered coffee beans

1. Preheat oven to 350°. In a large bowl, dissolve coffee granules in hot water. Stir in condensed milk, melted chocolate, vanilla, cinnamon and salt until blended. Stir in coconut. Drop mixture by rounded teaspoonfuls 2 in. apart onto parchment paper-lined baking sheets.

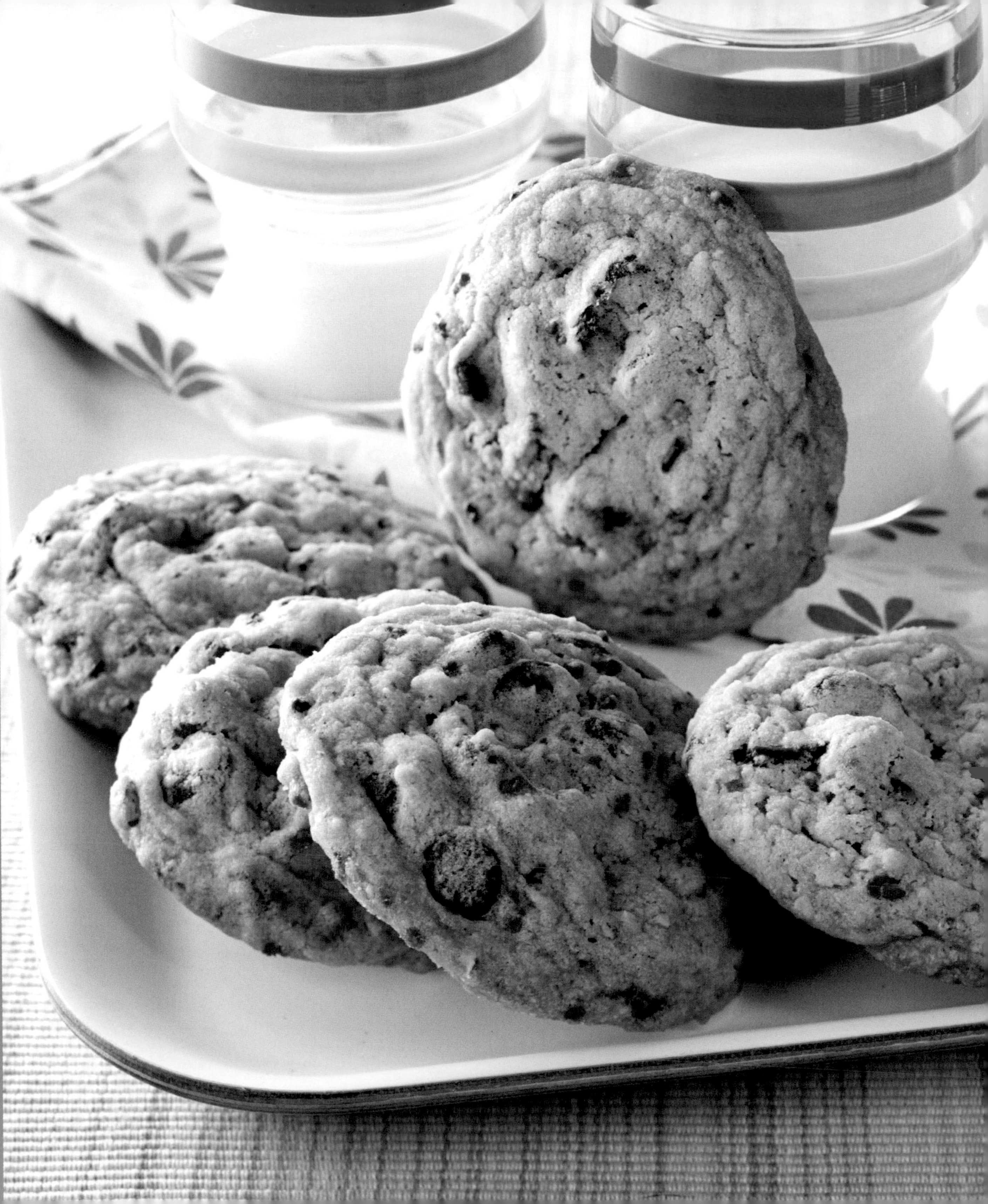

CHOCOLATE CHIP SPRINKLE COOKIES

Whenever I used to make cookies, my three boys would always find something they didn't like about them. After some trial and error, I came up with a cookie they all enjoyed.

—HEIDI CRETENS MILWAUKEE, WI

PREP: 15 MIN. • **BAKE:** 10 MIN./BATCH
MAKES: ABOUT 7½ DOZEN

- 2 **cups butter, softened**
- 1 **cup sugar**
- 1 **cup packed brown sugar**
- 2 **large eggs**
- 1½ **teaspoons vanilla extract**
- 4 **cups all-purpose flour**
- 1 **teaspoon baking soda**
- ½ **teaspoon salt**
- 2 **cups (12 ounces) semisweet chocolate chips**
- ½ **cup quick-cooking oats**
- ½ **cup crisp rice cereal**
- ½ **cup colored sprinkles**
- ½ **cup chopped pecans**

1. In a large bowl, cream butter and sugars until light and fluffy. Add the eggs, one at a time, beating well after each addition. Beat in vanilla. Combine the flour, baking soda and salt; gradually add to creamed mixture and mix well. Stir in remaining ingredients.

2. Drop by rounded tablespoonfuls 2 in. apart onto greased baking sheets. Bake at 375° for 8-10 minutes or until lightly browned. Remove to wire racks to cool.

COCONUT SLICE & BAKE COOKIES

Baking big batches of cookies is easy when you have a great recipe like this one. These are a favorite gift to give friends.

—BETTY MATTHEWS SOUTH HAVEN, MI

PREP: 30 MIN. + CHILLING
BAKE: 20 MIN./BATCH • **MAKES:** 4½ DOZEN

- 1 **cup butter, softened**
- 1 **cup sugar**
- 1 **large egg**
- 2¼ **cups all-purpose flour**
- ½ **teaspoon baking soda**
- ½ **teaspoon salt**
- 3 **cups flaked coconut, divided**
  Pecan halves

1. In a large bowl, cream the butter and sugar until light and fluffy. Beat in egg. Combine the flour, baking soda and salt; add to creamed mixture and mix well. Stir in 2 cups coconut.

2. Divide dough in half; shape each into a 7-in. long roll. Roll in remaining coconut.

Wrap in plastic; refrigerate for 1 hour or until firm.

3. Unwrap dough; cut into ¼-in. slices. Place 3 in. apart on ungreased baking sheets. Place a pecan half in the center of each. Bake at 325° for 20-25 minutes or until lightly browned. Cool 2-3 minutes before removing cookies to wire racks to cool completely.

LEMON CURD

- 4 large eggs
- 1⅓ cups sugar
- ⅓ cup lemon juice
- 4 teaspoons grated lemon peel
- 3 tablespoons butter

1. Place egg whites in a large bowl; let stand at room temperature for 30 minutes. Add vanilla and cream of tartar; beat on medium speed until soft peaks form. Gradually beat in sugar, 1 tablespoon at a time, on high until stiff peaks form.
2. Cut a small hole in the corner of a pastry or plastic bag; insert a #24 star tip. Fill bag with meringue. Pipe 1-in. circles 2 in. apart onto parchment paper-lined baking sheets. Pipe one or two circles over the edge of the base, forming sides.
3. Bake at 300° for 25 minutes or until set and dry. Turn the oven off; leave the meringues in oven for 1 hour.
4. Meanwhile, in a small heavy saucepan over medium heat, whisk the eggs, sugar, lemon juice and peel until blended. Add butter; cook, whisking constantly, until mixture is thickened and coats the back of a metal spoon. Transfer to a small bowl; cool for 10 minutes. Cover and refrigerate until chilled.
5. Just before serving, spoon lemon curd into the center of cookies. Refrigerate leftovers.

★ ★ ★ ★ ★ **READER REVIEW**

"This was definitely worth the effort. I am gluten free and always looking for dessert recipes, and this is a new favorite. My husband couldn't stop eating them!"

GREATWITHOUTGLUTEN
TASTEOFHOME.COM

PEANUT BUTTER S'MORES

I turn to this recipe when I need something fun and easy for dessert. It's a decadent take on classic campfire s'mores.
—**LILY JULOW**
LAWRENCEVILLE, GA

Short & Sweet

START TO FINISH: 10 MIN.
MAKES: 4 SERVINGS

- 8 large chocolate chip cookies
- 4 teaspoons hot fudge ice cream topping
- 4 large marshmallows
- 4 peanut butter cups

1. Spread the bottoms of four cookies with fudge topping.
2. Using a long-handled fork, grill marshmallows about 6 in. from medium-hot heat until golden brown, turning occasionally. Carefully place a peanut butter cup and a marshmallow on each fudge-topped cookie; top with remaining cookies. Serve immediately.

LEMON MERINGUE PIE COOKIES

Here's a way to have the refreshing flavor of lemon meringue pie in a cute hand-held treat. You'll love the homemade lemon curd.
—**TASTE OF HOME** TEST KITCHEN

PREP: 25 MIN. + CHILLING
BAKE: 25 MIN. + STANDING • **MAKES:** 5 DOZEN

- 3 large egg whites
- ½ teaspoon vanilla extract
- ¼ teaspoon cream of tartar
- ¾ cup sugar

BANANA CREAM SANDWICH COOKIES

People go bananas for these! The rich little sandwiches are a nice change, and they ship well, too.

—ELAINE OWENS DUBUQUE, IA

PREP: 40 MIN. + CHILLING
BAKE: 10 MIN./BATCH + COOLING
MAKES: ABOUT 2½ DOZEN

- 1 **cup butter, softened**
- 1 **cup sugar**
- 1 **medium banana, cut into ¼-inch slices**
- 1 **teaspoon vanilla extract**
- 2⅓ **cups all-purpose flour**
- ¼ **teaspoon salt**
- ½ **cup chopped salted peanuts**

FROSTING

- 3 **cups confectioners' sugar**
- 3 **tablespoons creamy peanut butter**
- 2 **tablespoons butter, softened**
- 1 **teaspoon vanilla extract**
- 3 **to 4 tablespoons 2% milk**

1. In a large bowl, cream butter and sugar until light and fluffy. Beat in banana and vanilla. In another bowl, whisk flour and salt; gradually beat into creamed mixture. Stir in salted peanuts. Divide dough in half. Shape each into a disk; wrap in plastic. Refrigerate for 30 minutes or until firm enough to roll.

2. Preheat oven to 350°. On a lightly floured surface, roll each portion of dough to ¼-in. thickness. Cut with a floured 2-in. round cookie cutter. Place 1 in. apart on ungreased baking sheets. Bake 10-12 minutes or until edges are light brown. Remove from pans to wire racks to cool completely.

3. In a small bowl, beat confectioners' sugar, peanut butter, butter, vanilla and enough milk to reach a good spreading consistency. Drop a heaping teaspoon in the center of half of the cookies; press remaining cookies on top to spread the frosting.

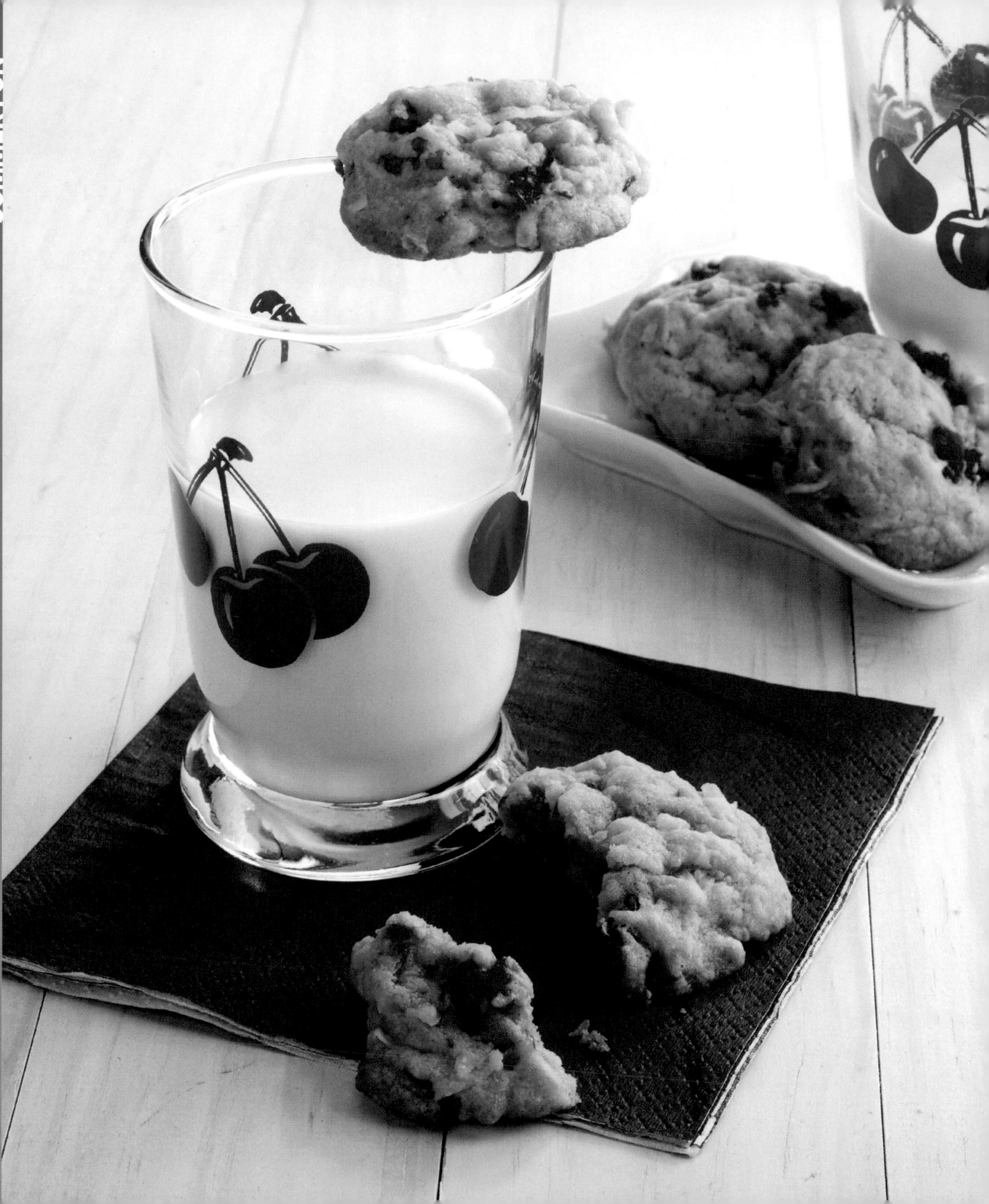

CHEERY CHERRY COOKIES

Coupled with a tall glass of ice-cold milk, a few of my cherry cookies make a great snack or dessert. I love the fun combination of coconut and bits of cherries.

—JUDY CLARK ELKHART, IN

PREP: 10 MIN. • **BAKE:** 10 MIN./BATCH
MAKES: 4 DOZEN

- 1 **cup packed brown sugar**
- ¾ **cup butter, softened**
- 1 **large egg**
- 2 **tablespoons 2% milk**
- 1 **teaspoon vanilla extract**
- 2 **cups all-purpose flour**
- ½ **teaspoon salt**
- ½ **teaspoon baking soda**
- ½ **cup maraschino cherries, well drained and chopped**
- ½ **cup flaked coconut**
- ½ **cup chopped pecans**

1. In a large bowl, cream brown sugar and butter until light and fluffy. Beat in the egg, milk and vanilla. In another bowl, mix the flour, salt and baking soda; gradually beat into creamed mixture. Stir in the cherries, coconut and pecans.

2. Drop dough by teaspoonfuls onto ungreased baking sheets. Bake at 375° for 10-12 minutes or until golden brown. Remove from pans to wire racks to cool.

GLITTERING CUTOUT COOKIES

The dessert table really sparkles when we make these crispy cookies for family weddings. Hearts, lips, doves, bells and other love-themed cutters work well.

—GRACE VAN TIMMEREN
GRAND RAPIDS, MI

PREP: 50 MIN. + CHILLING
BAKE: 10 MIN./BATCH + COOLING
MAKES: ABOUT 4 DOZEN

- ¾ **cup butter, softened**
- 1 **cup sugar**
- 2 **large eggs**
- 1 **teaspoon almond extract**
- 2½ **cups all-purpose flour**
- 1 **teaspoon baking powder**
- 1 **teaspoon salt**

FROSTING
- ½ **cup butter, softened**
- 4½ **cups confectioners' sugar**
- 1½ **teaspoons vanilla extract**
- 5 **to 6 tablespoons 2% milk**
  Paste food coloring of your choice
  Edible glitter and colored sugar
  Sprinkles, optional

1. In a bowl, cream butter and sugar until light and fluffy. Beat in eggs and extract. Combine the flour, baking powder and salt; gradually add to creamed mixture and mix well. Cover and refrigerate 1 hour or until easy to handle.

2. On a well-floured surface, roll dough to ¼-in. thickness. Cut with floured 2½-4-in. love-themed cookie cutters. Place 2 in. apart on greased baking sheets. Bake at 400° for 6-8 minutes or until set. Remove to wire racks to cool completely.

3. For frosting, in a large bowl, beat butter until light and fluffy. Beat in the confectioners' sugar, vanilla and enough milk to achieve desired consistency. Tint the frosting as desired; frost cookies.

4. Combine equal amounts of edible glitter and colored sugar; sprinkle over cookies. Decorate some cookies with sprinkles if desired.

AUGUST 26
NATIONAL
DOG DAY

PUPPY DOG COOKIE POPS

While these treats aren't safe for doggies, they're sure to steal the show at bake sales, birthday parties and other events! Best of all, the cute critters start with packaged cookies, leaving you plenty of time to turn them into adorable puppy pops.

—*TASTE OF HOME* TEST KITCHEN

PREP: 1 HOUR + STANDING
MAKES: 20 COOKIE POPS

- 1   package (14 ounces) light cocoa candy melts
- 20 Oreo cookies
- 20 lollipop sticks
- ⅓ cup white baking chips, melted
- 40 miniature semisweet chocolate chips (about 1 teaspoon)
     Chocolate jimmies
- ⅓ cup semisweet chocolate chips, melted
- 20 large marshmallows, halved
     Sweetened shredded coconut, toasted
     Finely chopped pecans, toasted
- 20 semisweet chocolate chips (about 1 tablespoon)
     Pink paste food coloring

1. In a microwave, melt candy melts; stir until smooth. Twist apart cookies. Dip the end of a lollipop stick into melted coating and place on a cookie half; replace cookie top. Repeat. Place pops on a waxed paper-lined baking sheet; refrigerate for 10 minutes or until set.

2. Reheat candy melts if necessary; dip a cookie pop in coating and allow excess to drip off. Insert stick into a foam block to stand. Repeat.

3. Using melted white chips, attach miniature chocolate chips to faces for eyes; add jimmies for eyebrows. Roll marshmallow halves in coconut and pecans. Using melted chocolate, attach the marshmallow halves for ears and chocolate chips for noses. Using the remaining melted chocolate, pipe mouths. Tint remaining melted white chips pink; pipe tongues. Let stand until set.

ORANGE SLICE COOKIES

Soft candy orange slices are a summery addition to these crispy vanilla chip cookies. To quickly cut the orange candy, use kitchen scissors, rinsing the blades with cold water occasionally to reduce sticking.

—BRITT STRAIN IDAHO FALLS, ID

PREP: 20 MIN. • **BAKE:** 10 MIN./BATCH
MAKES: ABOUT 10 DOZEN

- 1 **cup orange candy slices**
- 1½ **cups sugar, divided**
- 1 **cup butter, softened**
- 1 **cup shortening**
- 1½ **cups packed brown sugar**
- 2 **large eggs**
- 2 **teaspoons vanilla extract**
- 4 **cups all-purpose flour**
- 2 **teaspoons baking soda**
- 1 **teaspoon salt**
- 1 **package (10 to 12 ounces) white baking chips**
- 1 **cup chopped pecans**

1. Cut each orange slice into eight pieces. Roll in ¼ cup sugar; set aside. In a bowl, cream the butter, shortening, brown sugar and remaining sugar. Add eggs, one at a time, beating well after each addition. Beat in vanilla. Combine the flour, baking soda and salt; gradually add to creamed mixture. Stir in chips, pecans and orange slice pieces.

2. Roll into 1-in. balls. Place 2 in. apart on ungreased baking sheets. Bake at 375° for 10-12 minutes or until golden brown. Remove to wire racks to cool.

FROSTY ORANGE CREAM CHEESE CUPS

These bite-sized frozen treats will cool you down during the dog days of summer.

—ROXANNE CHAN ALBANY, CA

PREP: 35 MIN. + FREEZING
MAKES: 2 DOZEN

- 1¼ cups crushed gingersnap cookies (about 25 cookies)
- 5 tablespoons butter, melted
- 4 ounces cream cheese, softened
- 2 tablespoons confectioners' sugar
- 2 tablespoons plus ½ cup heavy whipping cream, divided
- ½ cup orange marmalade
- 4 ounces white baking chocolate, chopped
- ⅓ cup salted pistachios, chopped

1. In a small bowl, mix cookie crumbs and butter; press onto bottoms and up sides of ungreased mini muffin cups. Freeze 20 minutes.

2. In a small bowl, beat cream cheese, confectioners' sugar and 2 tablespoons cream until smooth. Stir in marmalade; drop by scant tablespoonfuls into cups. Freeze 2 hours or until set.

3. In a double boiler or metal bowl over hot water, melt white chocolate with remaining cream; stir until smooth. Cool slightly. Spoon or drizzle over the cups. Sprinkle with pistachios. Freeze, covered, overnight or until firm. Serve cups frozen.

CRISP SUGAR COOKIES

My grandmother always had sugar cookies in her pantry. We grandchildren would empty that big jar quickly; those cookies were the absolute best!
—**EVELYN POTEET** HANCOCK, MD

PREP: 15 MIN. + CHILLING • **BAKE:** 10 MIN.
MAKES: 8 DOZEN

- 1 cup butter, softened
- 2 cups sugar
- 2 large eggs
- 1 teaspoon vanilla extract
- 5 cups all-purpose flour
- 1½ teaspoons baking powder
- 1 teaspoon baking soda
- ½ teaspoon salt
- ¼ cup 2% milk

1. In a large bowl, cream butter and sugar until light and fluffy. Add eggs and vanilla. Combine flour, baking powder, baking soda and salt; add to creamed mixture alternately with milk. Cover dough and refrigerate 15-30 minutes or until easy to handle.

2. Preheat oven to 350°. On a floured surface, roll out dough to ⅛-in. thickness. Cut out cookies into desired shapes, and place 2 in. apart on greased baking sheets.

3. Bake 10 minutes or until edges are lightly browned. Remove from pans to wire racks to cool completely.

★ ★ ★ ★ ★ **5 STAR TIP**

Crisp Sugar Cookies are a light, buttery treat just perfect for summer snacking. Want to include them on a holiday cookie platter? Simply add pinches of ground cinnamon, nutmeg and cloves to the dough for a cozy spice cookie.

FALL
FLAVORS

There's no baking like fall baking! From spice cookies and brown sugar bites to peanutty classics and cinnamon treats, the flavors of autumn are easily captured with the 83 cookie recipes found in this section. Chase the chill away with a cup of coffee and a comforting nibble, give after-school snacks a homegrown touch and brighten up Halloween and Thanksgiving with adorable confections—you'll find nothing but delectable bites here. Turn the page for fall favorites you'll bake up all year long!

LOOK FOR THE SPECIAL DAYS IN THIS CHAPTER:

Beat the cool-weather doldrums with a little cookie fun! There's always an excuse for a party. From back-to-school season through Thanksgiving, sweet autumn treats are worth celebrating.

OCTOBER 31
NATIONAL CARAMEL APPLE DAY

BIG SOFT GINGER COOKIES

These nicely spiced cookies are perfect for anyone who likes the flavor of ginger but doesn't care for extra-crunchy gingersnaps.

—BARBARA GRAY BOISE, ID

START TO FINISH: 25 MIN.
MAKES: 2⅓ DOZEN

- ¾ **cup butter, softened**
- 1 **cup sugar**
- 1 **large egg**
- ¼ **cup molasses**
- 2¼ **cups all-purpose flour**
- 2 **teaspoons ground ginger**
- 1 **teaspoon baking soda**
- ¾ **teaspoon ground cinnamon**
- ½ **teaspoon ground cloves**
- ¼ **teaspoon salt**
-   **Additional sugar**

1. In a large bowl, cream butter and sugar until light and fluffy. Beat in egg and molasses. Combine the flour, ginger, baking soda, cinnamon, cloves and salt; gradually add to the creamed mixture and mix well.

2. Roll into 1½-in. balls, then roll in sugar. Place 2 in. apart on ungreased baking sheets. Bake at 350° until puffy and lightly browned, 10-12 minutes. Remove to wire racks to cool.

GIANT MONSTER COOKIES

Who can resist a gigantic cookie full of chocolate chips, M&M's and peanut butter? If your appetite isn't quite monster-size, scoop the dough by tablespoonfuls instead.
—JUDY FREDENBERG MISSOULA, MT

PREP: 20 MIN. + CHILLING
BAKE: 15 MIN./BATCH
MAKES: ABOUT 2½ DOZEN

- 2 cups creamy peanut butter
- ⅔ cup butter, softened
- 1⅓ cups sugar
- 1⅓ cups packed brown sugar
- 4 large eggs
- 2½ teaspoons baking soda
- 1 teaspoon vanilla extract
- 1 teaspoon light corn syrup
- 6 cups old-fashioned oats
- 1 cup semisweet chocolate chips
- 1 cup milk chocolate M&M's

1. In a large bowl, cream peanut butter, butter, sugar and brown sugar until light and fluffy, about 4 minutes. Beat in eggs, baking soda, vanilla and corn syrup. Add oats and mix well. Stir in chocolate chips and M&M's. Cover and refrigerate for 1 hour.

2. Preheat oven to 350°. Drop by ¼ cupfuls 3 in. apart onto ungreased baking sheets. Bake 14-18 minutes or until edges are lightly browned. Cool 5 minutes before removing from pans to wire racks to cool completely. Store in an airtight container.

Giant Monster Cookies

SWEET & SALTY PEANUT BUTTER BITES

My son Micah and I love peanut butter cups, so we made them into a fun new treat. We entered them in a creative baking contest and won first place!

—AUTUMN EMIGH GAHANNA, OH

PREP: 20 MIN. • **COOK:** 5 MIN. + STANDING
MAKES: ABOUT 5 DOZEN

- ½ cup semisweet chocolate chips
- 4 peanut butter cups (¾ ounce each), chopped
- 1⅓ cups creamy peanut butter
- 1 cup sugar
- 1 cup light corn syrup
- ⅛ teaspoon salt
- 4 cups Rice Krispies
- 1 cup broken pretzels

1. Freeze chocolate chips and chopped peanut butter cups until partially frozen, about 15 minutes. Meanwhile, in a 6-qt. stockpot, combine peanut butter, sugar, corn syrup and salt. Cook and stir over low heat until blended.

2. Remove from heat; stir in Rice Krispies and pretzels until coated. Let stand 5 minutes; gently fold in chocolate chips and peanut butter cups until just combined. Drop by tablespoonfuls onto waxed paper; let stand until set.

TRAIL MIX COOKIE CUPS

My granddaughter helped invent these loaded cookie cups. Take the trail-mix superstars to a back-to-school party or after-school event.

—PAMELA SHANK PARKERSBURG, WV

Short & Sweet

PREP: 20 MIN.
BAKE: 15 MIN. + COOLING
MAKES: 2 DOZEN

- 1 tube (16½ ounces) refrigerated peanut butter cookie dough
- ½ cup Nutella
- ½ cup creamy peanut butter
- 1½ cups trail mix

1. Preheat oven to 350°. Shape dough into 24 balls (about 1¼ in.). Press evenly onto bottom and up sides of greased mini muffin cups.

2. Bake 12-14 minutes or until golden brown. Using the end of a wooden spoon handle, reshape cups as necessary. Cool in pans 15 minutes. Remove to wire racks to cool completely.

3. Fill cups with 1 teaspoon each Nutella and peanut butter. Top with trail mix.

★ ★ ★ ★ ★ **READER REVIEW**

"These little treats are super yummy, easy and versatile. I changed it up a little bit using items I had on hand."

CORWIN44 TASTEOFHOME.COM

BACK-TO-SCHOOL COOKIES

These have become a favorite for almost anyone who tries them, and they make a delicious after-school treat. Especially with an ice cold glass of milk.

—FRANCES PIERCE WADDINGTON, NY

PREP: 30 MIN. • **BAKE:** 10 MIN./BATCH
MAKES: 6½ DOZEN

- 1 **cup butter-flavored shortening**
- 1 **cup creamy peanut butter**
- 2 **cups packed brown sugar**
- 4 **large egg whites**
- 1 **teaspoon vanilla extract**
- 2 **cups all-purpose flour**
- 1 **teaspoon baking soda**
- ½ **teaspoon baking powder**
- 2 **cups crisp rice cereal**
- 1½ **cups chopped nuts**
- 1 **cup flaked coconut**
- 1 **cup quick-cooking oats**

1. In a large bowl, cream the shortening, peanut butter and brown sugar until light and fluffy. Beat in egg whites and vanilla. Combine the flour, baking soda and baking powder; gradually add to creamed mixture and mix well. Stir in the cereal, nuts, coconut and oats.

2. Drop by rounded tablespoonfuls 2 in. apart onto ungreased baking sheets. Flatten with a fork, forming a crisscross pattern. Bake at 375° for 7-8 minutes. Remove to wire racks.

NOTE *Reduced-fat peanut butter is not recommended for this recipe.*

SPICED MOLASSES DOUGHNUT COOKIES

I'm originally from upstate New York, and I have yet to meet anyone who has heard of doughnut cookies outside that area. When folks try these treats, they love them!

—**BRENNA PHILLIPS** LAWRENCEVILLE, GA

PREP: 45 MIN. • **BAKE:** 10 MIN. + COOLING
MAKES: 2 DOZEN DOUGHNUT COOKIES + DOUGHNUT HOLE CUTOUTS

- ½ **cup baking cocoa**
- ½ **cup canola oil**
- 1 **cup packed brown sugar**
- ½ **cup molasses**
- ¼ **to ⅓ cup water**
- 1 **large egg**
- 3½ **cups all-purpose flour**
- ¾ **teaspoon baking soda**
- ½ **teaspoon ground cinnamon**
- ¼ **teaspoon ground cloves**
  Pinch ground nutmeg
  Pinch salt

FROSTING
- 6 **tablespoons butter, softened**
- 3 **cups confectioners' sugar**
- 3 **to 4 tablespoons 2% milk**
- ¾ **teaspoon vanilla extract**
  Pinch salt
  Assorted jimmies

1. Preheat oven to 350°. In a large bowl, mix cocoa and oil until smooth. Beat in brown sugar, molasses, ¼ cup water and egg. In a small bowl, whisk flour, baking soda, spices and salt; gradually beat into cocoa mixture.
If necessary, add additional water to form a stiff dough.
2. Transfer dough to a lightly floured surface; knead a few times, forming a smooth dough. Divide dough in half; roll each portion to ¼-in. thickness. Cut with a floured 3-in. doughnut cutter. Place doughnut and doughnut-hole cutouts 1 in. apart on ungreased baking sheets.
3. Bake for 7-9 minutes or until set. Remove cookies from pans to wire racks to cool completely.
4. In a bowl, beat butter, confectioners' sugar, 3 tablespoons milk, vanilla and salt until smooth. If necessary, beat in additional milk to reach spreading consistency. Spread over cookies. Sprinkle with jimmies. Let stand until set. Store in an airtight container.

HAPPY GRAND-PARENTS DAY!

GRANDMA'S STAR COOKIES

Surprise loved ones with these buttery treats! My husband's grandmother only used a star cutter for the cookies, but I've make them in many shapes for events throughout the year.
—**JENNY BROWN** WEST LAFAYETTE, IN

PREP: 1 HOUR + CHILLING
BAKE: 10 MIN./BATCH + COOLING
MAKES: ABOUT 7 DOZEN

- 1½ cups butter, softened
- ½ cup shortening
- 1 cup sugar
- 1 cup packed brown sugar
- 2 large eggs
- ¼ cup thawed orange juice concentrate
- 1 teaspoon vanilla extract
- 5 cups all-purpose flour
- 1 teaspoon baking soda
- 1 teaspoon salt

FROSTING

- 3 cups confectioners' sugar
- ¼ cup butter, melted
- 1½ teaspoons orange juice concentrate
- 1 teaspoon vanilla extract
- 3 to 4 tablespoons milk
  Food coloring and colored sugar, optional

1. In a large bowl, cream the butter, shortening and sugars until light and fluffy. Add eggs, one at a time, beating well after each addition. Beat in orange juice concentrate and vanilla. Combine the flour, baking soda and salt; gradually add to creamed mixture and mix well. Cover and refrigerate for 2 hours or until easy to handle.

2. On a lightly floured surface, roll out dough to ¼-in. thickness. Cut with a 3-in. star-shaped cookie cutter dipped in flour. Place 1 in. apart on ungreased baking sheets. Bake cookies at 350° for 7-8 minutes or until edges are firm. Remove to wire racks to cool.

3. For frosting, combine confectioners' sugar, butter, orange juice concentrate, vanilla and enough milk to achieve spreading consistency. Tint with food coloring if desired. Frost cookies; sprinkle with colored sugar if desired.

GRANDPA'S COOKIES

My grandpa, a widower, raised his three sons on his own and did all the cooking. He became quite the family baker! I can still picture him making these tasty snacks. The recipe makes a lot of cookies, so it's perfect for charity bake sales, potlucks, family reunions and the like.
—**KAREN BAKER** DOVER, OH

PREP: 20 MIN. + CHILLING
BAKE: 10 MIN./BATCH
MAKES: ABOUT 5 DOZEN

- 1 cup butter, softened
- 2 cups packed brown sugar
- 2 large eggs
- ¼ cup water
- ½ teaspoon vanilla extract
- 3½ cups all-purpose flour
- 1½ teaspoons cream of tartar
- 1½ teaspoons baking soda

1. Cream butter and brown sugar until light and fluffy. Beat in eggs, water and vanilla. In a separate bowl, whisk together remaining ingredients; gradually add to creamed mixture; mix well.

2. Shape into two rolls; wrap in plastic. Chill 4 hours or overnight.

3. Preheat oven to 375°. Cut rolls into ¼-in. slices; place 2 in. apart on greased baking sheets. Bake cookies until lightly browned, 8-10 minutes. Remove to wire racks to cool.

BUTTERSCOTCH-RUM RAISIN TREATS

I love making rum raisin rice pudding around the holidays, so I created these treats to enjoy those flavors all year.

—CRYSTAL SCHLUETER
NORTHGLENN, CO

START TO FINISH: 20 MIN.
MAKES: ABOUT 4½ DOZEN

- 1 package (10 to 11 ounces) butterscotch chips
- 1 package (10 to 12 ounces) white baking chips
- ½ teaspoon rum extract
- 3 cups Rice Krispies
- 1 cup raisins

1. Line 56 mini-muffin cups with paper liners. In a large bowl, combine the butterscotch and white chips. Microwave mixture, uncovered, on high for 30 seconds; stir. Microwave in additional 30-second intervals, stirring until smooth.

2. Stir in extract, Rice Krispies and raisins. Drop by rounded tablespoonfuls into prepared mini muffin cups. Chill until set.

FREEZE OPTION *Freeze in freezer containers, separating layers with waxed paper. Thaw before serving.*

CINDY'S CHOCOLATE CHIP COOKIES

Chocolate chip cookies are a mainstay in every cookie jar. They have mass appeal, making them perfect for hostess gifts, lunchbox treats or everyday snacking.

—CINDY UTTER JACKSONVILLE, IL

PREP: 10 MIN. + CHILLING
BAKE: 10 MIN./BATCH
MAKES: ABOUT 11 DOZEN

- 1 cup butter, softened
- 1 cup shortening
- 2 cups packed light brown sugar
- 1 cup sugar
- 4 large eggs
- 2 teaspoons vanilla extract
- 4½ cups all-purpose flour
- 2 teaspoons baking soda
- 2 teaspoons salt
- 2 cups (12 ounces) semisweet chocolate chips
- 1 cup chopped pecans

1. In a large bowl, cream the butter, shortening and sugars until light and fluffy. Beat in eggs and vanilla. Combine the flour, baking soda and salt; add to creamed mixture and mix well. Stir in chocolate chips and nuts (dough will be sticky). Cover and chill dough for 1 hour.

2. Drop by tablespoonfuls 2 in. apart onto greased baking sheets. Bake at 350° for 10-12 minutes or until lightly browned. Remove to wire racks to cool.

CRANBERRY CHIP COOKIES *Reduce semisweet chocolate chips to 1 cup. Along with the chips and pecans, stir in 1 cup vanilla or white chips and 1 cup dried cranberries. Bake as directed.*

WHITE CHOCOLATE CHIP COOKIES *Omit semisweet chocolate chips and pecans. Stir 2 cups vanilla or white chips and 1 cup toasted chopped hazelnuts into dough. Bake as directed.*

GLAZED CANDIED FRUIT COOKIES

Can't wait for the holidays? Get a jump start with these cookies. Candied fruit and pecans take center stage in these fun snacks that are topped with a caramel glaze.

—SUSAN HEIN BURLINGTON, WI

PREP: 30 MIN. + CHILLING
BAKE: 10 MIN./BATCH + COOLING
MAKES: 6 DOZEN

- 1 cup butter, softened
- 1 cup confectioners' sugar
- ½ cup sugar
- 1 large egg
- 2 teaspoons vanilla extract
- 2¼ cups all-purpose flour
- ½ teaspoon baking soda
- ⅔ cup chopped candied pineapple
- ½ cup chopped pecans
- ⅓ cup red candied cherries, chopped

CARAMEL GLAZE
- ½ cup packed brown sugar
- ¼ cup butter, cubed
- ⅔ cup confectioners' sugar
- 2 tablespoons 2% milk

1. In a large bowl, cream butter and sugars until light and fluffy. Beat in egg and vanilla. In another bowl, whisk flour and baking soda; gradually beat into creamed mixture. Stir in pineapple, pecans and cherries. Divide dough in half; shape each into a 9-in.-long roll; wrap each in plastic. Refrigerate 2 hours or until firm.

2. Preheat oven to 350°. Unwrap rolls and cut into ¼-in. slices. Place 2 in. apart on ungreased baking sheets. Bake 7-9 minutes or until lightly browned. Remove to wire racks to cool completely.

3. In a small saucepan, combine brown sugar and butter. Bring to a boil over medium heat. Cook and stir 30 seconds. Remove from heat; cool 5 minutes.

4. Beat in the confectioners' sugar and milk. Immediately drizzle over cookies. Let stand until glaze is set.

TO MAKE AHEAD *Dough can be made 2 days in advance. Wrap in plastic and place in a resealable plastic bag. Store in the refrigerator.*

FREEZE OPTION *Place wrapped dough rolls in a resealable plastic freezer bag. To use, unwrap frozen rolls and cut into slices. If necessary, let dough stand a few minutes at room temperature before cutting. Bake and decorate as directed, increasing bake time by 1-2 minutes.*

TRIPLE CHOCOLATE COOKIE MIX

Everyone likes a good old-fashioned cookie mix—and this one is especially popular with chocoholics! Just tie the baking directions to the jar with a ribbon.

—PATRICIA SWART GALLOWAY, NJ

PREP: 30 MIN. • **BAKE:** 15 MIN./BATCH
MAKES: 5 DOZEN

- 2¼ cups all-purpose flour, divided
- 1 teaspoon baking powder
- ½ teaspoon salt
- ½ teaspoon baking soda
- ½ cup baking cocoa
- 1 cup packed brown sugar
- ½ cup sugar
- ¾ cup semisweet chocolate chips
- ¾ cup white baking chips

ADDITIONAL INGREDIENTS
- ¾ cup butter, melted and cooled
- 3 large eggs
- 3 teaspoons vanilla extract

In a small bowl, whisk 1¼ cups flour, baking powder, salt and baking soda. In another bowl, whisk cocoa and the remaining flour. In an airtight container, layer half of flour mixture and half of cocoa mixture; repeat. Layer sugars and chips in the order listed. Cover and store in a cool dry place up to 3 months. Yield: 1 batch (about 5 cups).

TO PREPARE COOKIES Preheat oven to 350°. In a large bowl, beat butter, eggs and vanilla until well blended. Add cookie mix; mix well.

Drop by tablespoonfuls 2 in. apart on ungreased baking sheets. Bake for 12-14 minutes or until firm. Remove from pans to wire racks to cool. Store in an airtight container.

SEPTEMBER 13
INTL. CHOCOLATE DAY

OATMEAL SURPRISE COOKIES

Chocolate-covered raisins and the fall-like flavor of pumpkin pie spice turn these oatmeal cookies into prizewinning gourmet treats! Tuck one into your child's lunch for a special surprise.

—REBECCA CLARK WARRIOR, AL

PREP: 20 MIN. • **BAKE:** 15 MIN./BATCH
MAKES: 3 DOZEN

- 1 cup butter, softened
- ¾ cup packed brown sugar
- ½ cup sugar
- 2 large eggs
- 1½ cups all-purpose flour
- 1 teaspoon baking soda
- 1 teaspoon pumpkin pie spice
- 2¾ cups quick-cooking oats
- 1½ cups chocolate-covered raisins

1. Preheat oven to 350°. In a large bowl, cream butter and sugars until light and fluffy. Beat in eggs. Combine flour, baking soda and pie spice; gradually add to the creamed mixture and mix well. Stir in oats and raisins.

2. Drop by tablespoonfuls 2 in. apart onto greased baking sheets. Flatten slightly. Bake 13-15 minutes or until golden brown. Cool 5 minutes before removing to wire racks. Store in an airtight container.

★ ★ ★ ★ ★ **READER REVIEW**

"I like oatmeal cookies, raisins and chocolate. Pumpkin pie spice is also a favorite, so these cookies rate 5 stars! Flavor is even better the next day."

MONARCHSMOMMA TASTEOFHOME.COM

PUMPKIN SPICE COOKIES

These big and soft spice cookies have a rich frosting that makes them extra special for autumn. Enjoy!

—TASTE OF HOME **TEST KITCHEN**

PREP: 15 MIN. • **BAKE:** 20 MIN.
MAKES: 32 COOKIES

- 1 **package yellow cake mix (regular size)**
- ½ **cup quick-cooking oats**
- 2 **to 2½ teaspoons pumpkin pie spice**
- 1 **can (15 ounces) solid-pack pumpkin**
- 1 **large egg**
- 2 **tablespoons canola oil**
- 3 **cups confectioners' sugar**
- 1 **teaspoon grated orange peel**
- 3 **to 4 tablespoons orange juice**

1. In a large bowl, combine the cake mix, oats and pumpkin pie spice. In another bowl, beat the pumpkin, egg and oil; stir into the dry ingredients just until moistened.

2. Drop by 2 tablespoonfuls onto baking sheets coated with cooking spray; flatten with the back of a spoon. Bake at 350° for 18-20 minutes or until edges are golden brown. Remove to wire racks to cool.

3. In a bowl, combine confectioners' sugar, orange peel and enough orange juice to achieve desired spreading consistency. Frost cooled cookies.

SEPTEMBER 18
NATIONAL RICE KRISPIES TREATS DAY

NO-BAKE CEREAL COOKIE BARS

For these chewy bars, we pull out all the goodies, like raisins and coconut. For more color, sprinkle the M&M's on top once the bars are in the pan, then press them in.
—**CONNIE CRAIG** LAKEWOOD, WA

PREP: 10 MIN. • **COOK:** 15 MIN. + COOLING
MAKES: 3 DOZEN

- 4½ cups Rice Krispies
- 3¼ cups quick-cooking oats
- ½ cup cornflakes
- ½ cup flaked coconut
- ½ cup butter, cubed
- 1 package (16 ounces) miniature marshmallows
- ¼ cup honey
- ½ cup M&M's minis
- ¼ cup raisins

1. Grease a 15x10x1-in. pan. Place Rice Krispies, oats, cornflakes and coconut in a large bowl; toss to combine.
2. In a large saucepan, melt butter over low heat. Add marshmallows; stir until completely melted. Stir in honey until blended. Pour over cereal mixture; stir until evenly coated. Cool 5 minutes.
3. Stir in M&M's and raisins. Using a greased spatula, press evenly into prepared pan. Let stand 30 minutes before cutting. Store between layers of waxed paper in an airtight container.

CHOCOLATE-DIPPED ANISE BISCOTTI

Classic biscotti cookies take on a whole new level of deliciousness with help from licorice-like aniseed. Wrap up these sweet treats for your friends and family to enjoy with a steaming cup of coffee or tea.
—**LESLIE KELLEY** DORRIS, CA

PREP: 35 MIN. • **BAKE:** 40 MIN. + COOLING
MAKES: 3 DOZEN

- ½ cup butter, softened
- 1 cup sugar
- 2 large eggs
- 2 teaspoons anise extract
- 2½ cups all-purpose flour
- 1½ teaspoons baking powder
- ½ teaspoon salt
- 1½ cups sliced almonds, toasted
- 2 tablespoons aniseed
- 10 ounces milk chocolate candy coating, melted

1. Preheat oven to 325°. In a large bowl, cream butter and sugar until light and fluffy. Beat in eggs and extract. Combine flour, baking powder and salt; gradually add to creamed mixture and mix well. Stir in almonds and aniseed.
2. Divide dough in half. On a parchment paper-lined baking sheet, shape each portion into a 12x2-in. rectangle. Bake 25-30 minutes or until firm to the touch and the edges are golden brown.
3. Cool on pans on wire racks. When cool enough to handle, transfer to a cutting board; cut diagonally with a serrated knife into ¾-in. slices. Return to baking sheets cut side down.
4. Bake 6-7 minutes on each side or until golden brown. Remove to wire racks to cool completely. Dip each cookie halfway into melted candy coating, allowing excess to drip off. Place on waxed paper until set. Store in an airtight container.

EYES-WIDE-OPEN ESPRESSO COOKIES

If you're a fan of chocolate, espresso or just change-of-pace treats, these coffee-laced bites can't be beat!
—TASTE OF HOME **TEST KITCHEN**

PREP: 25 MIN. • **BAKE:** 10 MIN./BATCH
MAKES: 45 COOKIES

- ½ cup butter, softened
- ½ cup sugar
- ¼ cup packed brown sugar
- 1 large egg
- 1¼ cups all-purpose flour
- 6 tablespoons baking cocoa
- 2 teaspoons finely ground espresso beans
- ½ teaspoon baking soda
- ¼ teaspoon salt
- 1 cup (6 ounces) semisweet chocolate chips
- 45 chocolate-covered coffee beans

1. In a large bowl, cream the butter and sugars until light and fluffy. Beat in egg. Combine the flour, cocoa, espresso beans, baking soda and salt; gradually add to creamed mixture and mix well. Stir in chocolate chips.

2. Drop by rounded teaspoonfuls 2 in. apart onto parchment paper-lined baking sheets. Bake at 350° for 8-10 minutes or until the surface cracks. Immediately press a coffee bean into the center of each cookie. Cool for about 2 minutes before removing from pans to wire racks. Store cookies in an airtight container.

FROM THE COOKIE JAR

Make sure cookies are completely cool before storing. Setting warm cookies in an airtight container can affect their texture, resulting in crumbled and broken treats.

PEANUT BUTTER OATMEAL-CHIP COOKIES

This is my husband's favorite, my students' favorite, my colleagues' favorite and frankly it's my favorite, too. It's just plain yummy! It also makes about 11 dozen. (Bake sale, here we come!)

—DANA CHEW OKEMAH, OK

PREP: 35 MIN. • **BAKE:** 10 MIN./BATCH
MAKES: 11 DOZEN

- 2½ cups butter, softened
- 2 cups sugar
- 2 cups packed brown sugar
- ½ cup creamy peanut butter
- 4 large eggs
- 2 teaspoons vanilla extract
- 6 cups all-purpose flour
- 2 teaspoons salt
- 2 teaspoons baking soda
- ½ teaspoon baking powder
- 1 package (12 ounces) semisweet chocolate chips
- 1 package (11 ounces) peanut butter and milk chocolate chips
- 1 cup quick-cooking oats

1. Preheat oven to 375°. In a large bowl, cream butter, sugars and peanut butter until light and fluffy. Beat in eggs and vanilla. Combine flour, salt, baking soda and baking powder; gradually add to creamed mixture and mix well.

2. Stir in chips and oats. Drop by rounded tablespoonfuls 2 in. apart onto ungreased baking sheets. Bake 9-12 minutes or until golden brown.

3. Cool for 2 minutes before removing cookies from pans to wire racks. Store in an airtight container.

★ ★ ★ ★ ★ **5 STAR TIP**

To freeze cookies for up to 3 months, wrap them in plastic, stack and seal them in an airtight container and freeze. Thaw wrapped cookies at room temperature before serving.

PECAN TASSIES

These tiny tarts are a fun ending to any meal or a pretty addition to a dessert buffet. If you don't have miniature tart pans, use miniature muffin pans instead.

—JOY CORIE RUSTON, LA

PREP: 25 MIN. + CHILLING • **BAKE:** 20 MIN.
MAKES: 2 DOZEN

- ½ **cup butter, softened**
- 3 **ounces cream cheese, softened**
- 1 **cup all-purpose flour**

FILLING

- 1 **large egg**
- ¾ **cup packed brown sugar**
- 1 **tablespoon butter, softened**
- 1 **teaspoon vanilla extract**
  Dash salt
- ⅔ **cup finely chopped pecans, divided**

1. In a small bowl, beat butter and cream cheese until smooth; gradually beat in flour. Refrigerate, covered, for 1 hour or until firm enough to roll.

2. Preheat oven to 375°. Shape dough into 1-in. balls; press evenly onto the bottoms and up the sides of greased mini muffin cups.

3. For filling, in a small bowl, mix egg, brown sugar, butter, vanilla and salt until blended. Stir in ⅓ cup pecans; spoon into pastries. Sprinkle with remaining pecans.

4. Bake 20-25 minutes or until edges are golden and filling is puffed. Cool in pans 2 minutes. Remove to wire racks to cool completely.

FREEZE OPTION *Freeze cooled cookies, layered between waxed paper, in freezer containers. To use, thaw in covered containers.*

SEPTEMBER 21
NATIONAL
PECAN
COOKIE
DAY

PEANUT BUTTER OATMEAL COOKIES

My husband loves homemade cookies, and these are probably his favorites. The whole wheat flour and oats give these hearty cookies a distinctive flavor.

—**LINDA FOX** SOLDOTNA, AK

PREP: 15 MIN. • **BAKE:** 15 MIN./BATCH
MAKES: 6 DOZEN

- 1½ **cups shortening**
- 1½ **cups peanut butter**
- 2 **cups packed brown sugar**
- 3 **large eggs**
- 2 **teaspoons vanilla extract**
- 3 **cups quick-cooking oats**
- 2 **cups whole wheat flour**
- 2 **teaspoons baking soda**
- 1 **teaspoon salt**

In a bowl, cream shortening and peanut butter. Add brown sugar, eggs and vanilla; mix well. Combine oats, flour, baking soda and salt; add to the creamed mixture and mix well. Drop by rounded teaspoonfuls onto ungreased baking sheets. Flatten with a fork. Bake at 350° for 12 minutes or until done.

LARA'S TENDER GINGERSNAPS

Soft gingersnaps might embody the flavors of Christmas, but they are perfect for a fall gathering, too. I enjoy the flavors of cloves, cinnamon and ginger blended into this one delicious cookie.

—LARA PENNELL MAULDIN, SC

PREP: 15 MIN. + CHILLING
BAKE: 10 MIN./BATCH • **MAKES:** 3 DOZEN

- 1 **cup packed brown sugar**
- ¾ **cup butter, melted**
- 1 **egg**
- ¼ **cup molasses**
- 2¼ **cups all-purpose flour**
- 1½ **teaspoons ground ginger**
- 1 **teaspoon baking soda**
- 1 **teaspoon ground cinnamon**
- ½ **teaspoon ground cloves**
- ¼ **cup sugar**

1. In a large bowl, beat brown sugar and butter until blended. Beat in the egg and molasses. Combine the flour, ginger, baking soda, cinnamon and cloves; gradually add to brown sugar mixture and mix well (dough will be stiff). Cover and refrigerate for at least 2 hours.

2. Shape dough into 1 in. balls. Roll in sugar. Place about 2 in. apart on greased baking sheets.

3. Bake at 350° for 9-11 minutes or until set. Cool for 1 minute before removing from pans to wire racks.

CRANBERRY CHOCOLATE COOKIES WITH A KICK

This cookies will make you stop in your tracks to figure out what that delicious flavor is on the back of your palate.

—SHALANA PATOUT LAYFAYETTE, LA

PREP: 20 MIN. • **BAKE:** 10 MIN./BATCH
MAKES: 2 DOZEN

- 1 cup dried cranberries
- ¼ cup coffee liqueur or strong brewed coffee
- 1¼ cups semisweet chocolate chunks
- ¼ cup unsalted butter, cubed
- 2 large eggs
- ¾ cup packed brown sugar
- 3 teaspoons vanilla extract
- 1 cup all-purpose flour
- ½ teaspoon baking powder
- ½ teaspoon salt
- ½ teaspoon ground cinnamon
- ½ teaspoon freshly ground pepper
- ⅛ to ¼ teaspoon cayenne pepper

1. Preheat oven to 350°. In a small saucepan, combine cranberries and liqueur. Bring just to a simmer; remove from heat. In a microwave-safe bowl, microwave chocolate and butter on high in 30-second intervals until melted; stir until smooth (mixture will be thick). Cool mixture slightly.

2. In a large bowl, beat eggs, brown sugar and vanilla on high speed until thickened, about 3 minutes; beat in the chocolate mixture. In another bowl, whisk flour, baking powder, salt and seasonings; fold into sugar mixture just until combined. Fold in cranberry mixture.

3. Drop by rounded tablespoonfuls 2-in. apart onto parchment paper-lined baking sheets. Bake 10-12 minutes or until cookies are shiny and tops are crackly. Cool on pans 2 minutes. Remove to wire racks to cool completely.

MACAROON KISSES

These tempting cookies are sure to delight fans of coconut and chocolate. The sweet combination is simply irresistible.

—LEE ROBERTS RACINE, WI

PREP: 45 MIN. + CHILLING
BAKE: 10 MIN./BATCH + COOLING
MAKES: 4 DOZEN

- ⅓ cup butter, softened
- 3 ounces cream cheese, softened
- ¾ cup sugar
- 1 large egg yolk
- 2 teaspoons almond extract
- 1½ cups all-purpose flour
- 2 teaspoons baking powder
- ½ teaspoon salt
- 5 cups flaked coconut, divided
- 48 milk chocolate kisses
  Coarse sugar

1. In a large bowl, cream the butter, cream cheese and sugar until light and fluffy. Beat in egg yolk and extract. Combine the flour, baking powder and salt; gradually add to creamed mixture and mix well. Stir in 3 cups coconut. Cover and refrigerate for 1 hour or until dough is easy to handle.

2. Preheat oven to 350°. Shape into 1-in. balls and roll in the remaining coconut. Place 2 in. apart on ungreased baking sheets.

3. Bake 10-12 minutes or until lightly browned. Immediately press a chocolate kiss into the center of each cookie; sprinkle with coarse sugar. Cool on pan 2-3 minutes or until chocolate is softened. Remove to wire racks to cool completely.

SEPTEMBER 29
NATIONAL
COFFEE
DAY

COFFEE SHORTBREAD

The easy coffee drizzle on these flavored shortbreads really steals the show at bake sales and brunches.

—DIXIE TERRY GOREVILLE, IL

PREP: 15 MIN.
BAKE: 20 MIN./BATCH + COOLING
MAKES: ABOUT 2½ DOZEN

- 1 cup butter, softened
- ½ cup packed brown sugar
- ¼ cup sugar
- 2 tablespoons instant coffee granules
- ¼ teaspoon salt
- 2 cups all-purpose flour
- ½ cup semisweet chocolate chips
- 2 teaspoons shortening, divided
- ½ cup white baking chips

1. Preheat oven to 300°. In a large bowl, cream butter, sugars, coffee granules and salt until light and fluffy; gradually beat flour into creamed mixture.

2. On a lightly floured surface, roll dough to ¼-in. thickness. Cut with floured 2-in. cookie cutters. Place 2 in. apart on ungreased baking sheets.

3. Bake 20-22 minutes or until set. Remove to wire racks to cool completely. In a microwave, melt chocolate chips and 1 teaspoon shortening; stir until smooth. Repeat with baking chips and remaining shortening. Drizzle over cooled cookies; refrigerate until set. Store cookies between pieces of waxed paper in an airtight container.

HONEY MAPLE COOKIES

Honey and maple syrup make these chocolate chip cookies a little different. The maple flavor is light and subtle.

—BARBARA KUDER TRIBUNE, KS

PREP: 20 MIN. • **BAKE:** 10 MIN./BATCH
MAKES: 5 DOZEN

- 1 cup shortening
- ¾ cup honey
- ¾ cup maple syrup
- 2 large eggs
- 1 teaspoon vanilla extract
- 2½ cups all-purpose flour
- 1 teaspoon baking soda
- 1 teaspoon salt
- 2 cups (12 ounces) semisweet chocolate chips
- 1 cup chopped pecans

1. In a large bowl, beat shortening until light and fluffy. Add honey and syrup, a little at a time, beating well after each addition. Add eggs, one at a time, beating well after each addition (mixture will appear curdled). Beat in vanilla. Combine the flour, baking soda and salt. Gradually add to honey mixture and mix just until moistened. Stir in the chocolate chips and pecans.

2. Drop by rounded tablespoonfuls onto greased baking sheets. Bake at 350° for 8-10 minutes or until golden brown. Remove to wire racks to cool.

PUMPKIN SUGAR COOKIES

I've been making these quick and easy cookies for over 20 years. They're the first to go at our annual church bake sale.
—**PAULA MARCHESI** LENHARTSVILLE, PA

PREP: 20 MIN. + CHILLING
BAKE: 15 MIN./BATCH • **MAKES:** 4 DOZEN

- 1 **cup butter, softened**
- 2 **cups sugar**
- 2 **large eggs**
- 2¾ **cups all-purpose flour**
- 2 **tablespoons pumpkin pie spice**
  Cinnamon sugar, optional

1. In a large bowl, cream butter and sugar until light and fluffy. Beat in eggs. In another bowl, whisk flour and pie spice; gradually beat into creamed mixture. Divide dough in half. Shape each half into a disk; wrap in plastic. Refrigerate 1 hour or until firm enough to roll.

2. Preheat oven to 350°. On a lightly floured surface, roll each portion of dough to ¼-in. thickness. Cut with a floured 2½-in. round cookie cutter. Place 1 in. apart on ungreased baking sheets. If desired, sprinkle with cinnamon sugar.

3. Bake 12-14 minutes or until edges are light brown. Cool on pans 1 minute. Remove to wire racks to cool.

FREEZE OPTION *Transfer wrapped disks to a resealable plastic freezer bag; freeze. To use, thaw dough in refrigerator overnight or until soft enough to roll. Prepare and bake cookies as directed.*

SOFT GINGER PUFFS

These spice cookies are loaded with raisins and walnuts, and they really do appeal to all generations. I found the recipe in a 1901 South Dakota cookbook. Sour cream adds a wonderful flair.

—MARION LOWERY MEDFORD, OR

PREP: 15 MIN. • **BAKE:** 10 MIN./BATCH
MAKES: 8 DOZEN

- ½ cup butter, softened
- ¾ cup sugar
- 3 large eggs
- 1 cup molasses
- 1 cup (8 ounces) sour cream
- 3½ cups all-purpose flour
- 2 teaspoons ground ginger
- 1 teaspoon baking soda
- ½ teaspoon each ground allspice, cinnamon and nutmeg
- 1½ cups raisins
- 1½ cups chopped walnuts

1. In a large bowl, cream butter and sugar until light and fluffy. Add eggs, one at a time, beating well after each addition. Beat in the molasses and sour cream. Combine the flour, ginger, baking soda, allspice, cinnamon and nutmeg; gradually add to the creamed mixture and mix well. Stir in raisins and walnuts.
2. Drop by tablespoonfuls 1 in. apart onto greased baking sheets. Bake at 375° for 10-12 minutes or until the edges begin to brown. Remove to wire racks to cool.

AUTUMN LEAF CUTOUTS

Classic cookies become autumn leaves in this delectable recipe. Make them in solid colors or combine pieces of tinted dough for a multicolored effect.

—DARLENE BRENDEN SALEM, OR

PREP: 25 MIN. + CHILLING
BAKE: 15 MIN./BATCH + COOLING
MAKES: 4 DOZEN

- 2 cups butter, softened
- 1½ cups sugar
- 2 large eggs
- 2 teaspoons vanilla extract
- 5½ cups all-purpose flour

- ½ teaspoon baking soda
- ½ teaspoon salt
    Red, green, orange and yellow paste food coloring
- 1⅓ cups confectioners' sugar
- 5 to 7 teaspoons warm water
- 1 tablespoon meringue powder
- ¼ teaspoon almond extract
- 2 tablespoons coarse sugar

1. In a large bowl, cream butter and sugar until light and fluffy. Beat in eggs and vanilla. In another bowl, whisk flour, baking soda and salt; gradually beat into creamed mixture.
2. Divide dough into four portions; tint one red, one green, one orange and one yellow. Shape each into a disk; wrap in plastic. Refrigerate 30 minutes or until firm enough to roll.
3. Preheat oven to 350°. On a lightly floured surface, roll each portion of dough to ¼-in. thickness. Cut with a floured 3-in. leaf-shaped cookie cutter. Place cookies 2 in. apart on greased baking sheets.
4. Bake 14-17 minutes or until edges are golden brown. Remove from pans to wire racks to cool completely.
5. Meanwhile, in a large bowl, combine confectioners' sugar, water, meringue powder and almond extract; beat on low speed just until blended. Pipe or drizzle on cookies as desired. Sprinkle with coarse sugar. Let stand until set. Store in an airtight container.

CHEWY MAPLE COOKIES

My husband, Bob, and I have a small sugaring operation with Bob's father. I love to put some of our syrup to use in these quick, golden cookies.
—REBA LEGRAND JERICHO, VT

START TO FINISH: 30 MIN. • **MAKES:** 3 DOZEN

- ½ cup shortening
- 1 cup packed brown sugar
- 1 large egg
- ½ cup maple syrup
- ½ teaspoon vanilla extract or maple flavoring
- 1½ cups all-purpose flour
- 2 teaspoons baking powder
- ½ teaspoon salt
- 1 cup flaked coconut

1. In a bowl, cream shortening and brown sugar until fluffy. Beat in the egg, syrup and vanilla until well mixed. Combine flour, baking powder and salt; add to the creamed mixture. Stir in coconut.

2. Drop by tablespoonfuls 2 in. apart onto greased baking sheets. Bake cookies at 375° for 12-15 minutes or until lightly browned.

FLUFFERNUTTER TREATS

My family adores these snacks. No matter how many cookies I make, they never seem to last long!
—D. WEAVER EPHRATA, PA

Short & Sweet

PREP: 1 HOUR + CHILLING
MAKES: 4 DOZEN

- 96 Ritz crackers
- 1 cup creamy peanut butter
- 1 cup marshmallow creme
- 2 pounds milk chocolate candy coating, melted

1. Spread half of the crackers with the peanut butter. Spread remaining crackers with the marshmallow creme; place creme side down over peanut butter crackers, forming a sandwich.

2. Dip sandwiches in melted candy coating, allowing excess to drip off. Place on waxed paper-lined pans; refrigerate for 15 minutes or until set. Store in an airtight container.

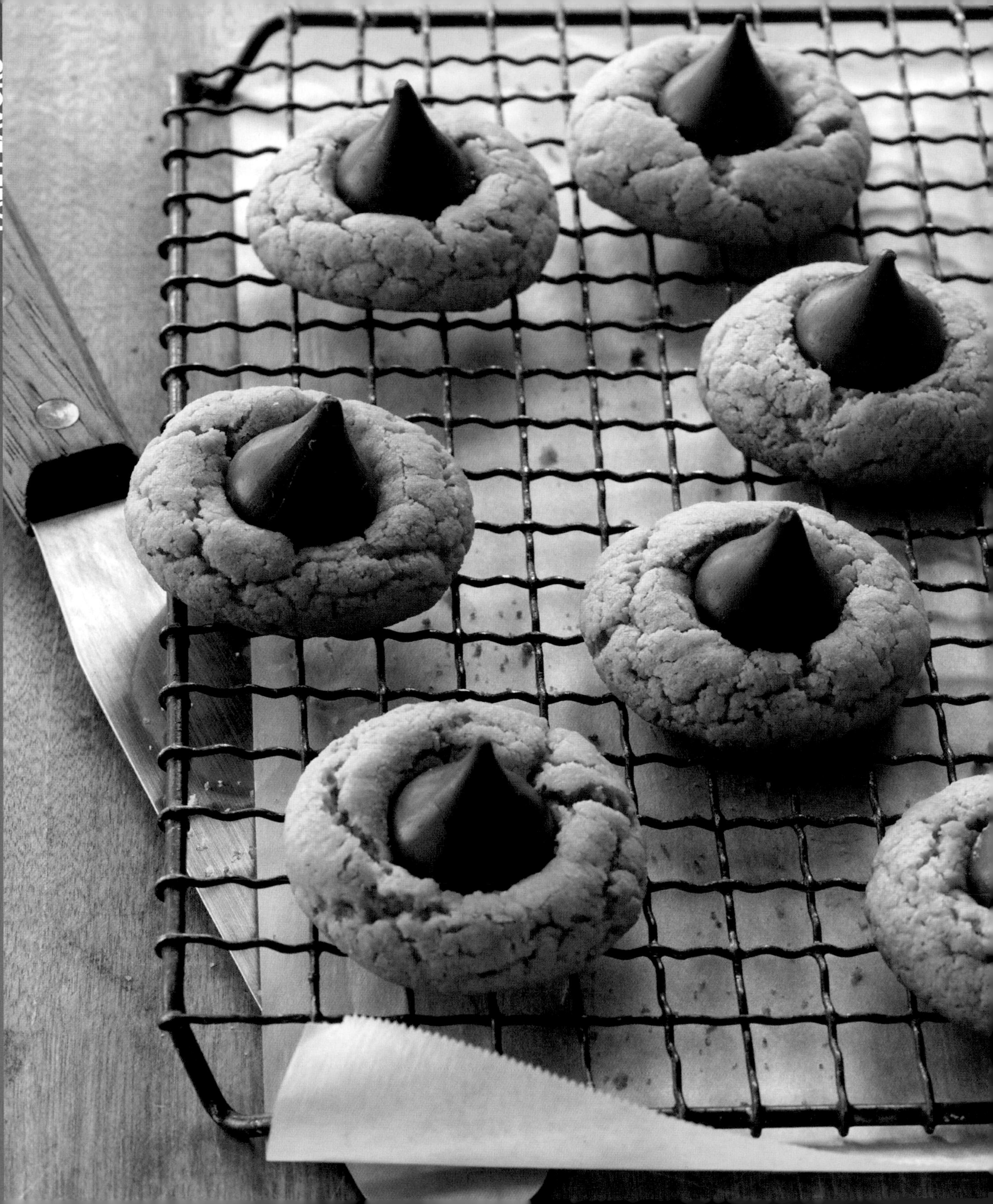

GLUTEN-FREE PEANUT BUTTER KISS COOKIES

Serve these chocolate-topped cookies, and everyone will want to kiss the cook! For a change of pace, try them with chunky peanut butter instead.

—CANADA60, *TASTE OF HOME* ONLINE COMMUNITY

PREP: 20 MIN. + CHILLING
BAKE: 10 MIN./BATCH • **MAKES:** 4 DOZEN

- ¼ **cup butter-flavored shortening**
- 1¼ **cups packed brown sugar**
- ¾ **cup creamy peanut butter**
- 1 **large egg**
- ¼ **cup unsweetened applesauce**
- 3 **teaspoons vanilla extract**
- 1 **cup white rice flour**
- ½ **cup potato starch**
- ¼ **cup tapioca flour**
- 1 **teaspoon baking powder**
- ¾ **teaspoon baking soda**
- ¼ **teaspoon salt**
- 48 **milk chocolate kisses, unwrapped**

1. In a large bowl, beat shortening, brown sugar and peanut butter until blended. Beat in egg, applesauce and vanilla (mixture will appear curdled). In another bowl, whisk rice flour, potato starch, tapioca flour, baking powder, baking soda and salt; gradually beat into creamed mixture. Refrigerate, covered, for 1 hour.
2. Preheat oven to 375°. Shape dough into forty-eight 1-in. balls; place 2 in. apart on ungreased baking sheets. Bake for 9-11 minutes or until slightly cracked. Immediately press a chocolate kiss into center of each cookie. Cool on pans for 2 minutes. Remove to wire racks to cool.
NOTE *Read all ingredient labels for possible gluten content prior to use. Ingredient formulas can change, and production facilities vary among brands. If you're concerned that your brand may contain gluten, contact the company.*

CHOCOLATE & VANILLA SPRITZ

If you're looking for a gorgeous cookie, try my spritz. These tender treats are so cute and have a great buttery flavor. The dough is easy to work with and the cookies bake up beautifully every time.

—MARY BETH JUNG HENDERSONVILLE, NC

PREP: 40 MIN.
BAKE: 10 MIN./BATCH + COOLING
MAKES: 9 DOZEN

- 1½ **cups butter, softened**
- 1 **cup sugar**
- 1 **large egg**
- 2 **tablespoons 2% milk**
- 1 **teaspoon vanilla extract**
- ½ **teaspoon almond extract**
- 3½ **cups all-purpose flour**
- 1 **teaspoon baking powder**
- 3 **tablespoons baking cocoa**
  Melted chocolate and chocolate jimmies, optional

1. Preheat oven to 375°. In a large bowl, cream butter and sugar until light and fluffy. Beat in the egg, milk and extracts. Combine the flour and baking powder; gradually add to the creamed mixture and mix well.
2. Divide dough in half; add cocoa to one portion and mix well. Divide each portion into six pieces; shape each into a 5-in. log. Place a chocolate log and vanilla log together, pressing to form another log.
3. Using a cookie press fitted with the disk of your choice, press dough 2 in. apart onto ungreased baking sheets. Bake 9-11 minutes or until edges are lightly browned. Remove to wire racks to cool.
4. If desired, dip each cookie halfway into melted chocolate, allowing excess to drip off. Place on waxed paper; sprinkle with jimmies. Let stand until set.

HAZELNUT CHOCOLATE CHIP PIZZELLE

I've experimented with different varieties of pizzelle recipes, but this is definitely a favorite. My dad likes to help make them so that we don't run out!

—AIMEE MCCULLEN YOUNGWOOD, PA

PREP: 15 MIN. • **COOK:** 5 MIN./BATCH
MAKES: 3 DOZEN

- 4 large eggs
- 1 cup sugar
- ¾ cup butter, melted
- 2 cups all-purpose flour
- ½ cup finely chopped hazelnuts, toasted
- ½ cup miniature semisweet chocolate chips

1. In a large bowl, beat the eggs, sugar and butter until smooth. Gradually add flour and mix well. Fold in hazelnuts and chocolate chips.

2. Bake in a preheated pizzelle iron according to manufacturer's directions until golden brown. Remove to wire racks to cool. Store in an airtight container.

BOSTON CREAM PIE COOKIES

Here, vanilla custard is sandwiched between tender, cake-like cookies. With their shiny chocolate glaze, these bite-sized snacks remind everyone of Boston cream pie.

—EVANGELINE BRADFORD ERLANGER, KY

PREP: 70 MIN. + CHILLING
BAKE: 5 MIN./BATCH + COOLING
MAKES: 4 DOZEN

- 6 tablespoons sugar
- 3 tablespoons cornstarch
- ¼ teaspoon salt
- 1 cup 2% milk
- 6 tablespoons heavy whipping cream
- 1 large egg yolk, beaten
- 2 teaspoons vanilla extract

COOKIES

- 9 tablespoons butter, softened
- 1 cup sugar
- 2 large egg yolks
- 1 large egg
- 2 teaspoons vanilla extract
- ½ teaspoon grated lemon peel
- 1 cup plus 2 tablespoons cake flour

- 1 cup all-purpose flour
- ¾ teaspoon baking soda
- ½ teaspoon salt
- ½ cup plus 2 tablespoons buttermilk

GLAZE

- 2 ounces unsweetened chocolate, chopped
- 4 teaspoons butter
- ½ cup whipping cream
- 1 cup confectioners' sugar

1. In a small heavy saucepan, combine the sugar, cornstarch and salt. Stir in milk and cream until smooth. Cook and stir over medium-high heat until thickened and bubbly. Reduce heat to low; cook and stir 2 minutes longer.

2. Remove from the heat. Stir a small amount of hot mixture into egg yolk; return all to the pan, stirring constantly. Bring to a gentle boil; cook and stir for 2 minutes longer. Remove from heat. Stir in vanilla. Cool for 15 minutes, stirring occasionally. Transfer to a small bowl. Press waxed paper onto surface of custard. Refrigerate for 2-3 hours.

3. In a large bowl, cream butter and sugar until light and fluffy. Beat in the egg yolks, egg, vanilla and lemon peel. Combine the cake flour, all-purpose flour, baking soda and salt; gradually add to the creamed mixture alternately with buttermilk and mix well.

4. Drop by rounded teaspoonfuls 2 in. apart onto greased baking sheets. Bake at 400° for 5-7 minutes or until firm to the touch. Remove to wire racks to cool completely.

5. Spread custard over the bottoms of half of the cookies; top with remaining cookies.

6. For glaze, place chocolate and butter in a small bowl. In a small saucepan, bring cream just to a boil. Pour over chocolate and butter; whisk until smooth. Stir in confectioners' sugar. Spread over cookies; let dry completely. Store in refrigerator.

TO MAKE AHEAD *Package cookies in an airtight container, separating the layers with waxed paper. Cookeis can be frozen for up to a month. Thaw in a single layer before assembling.*

GERMAN CHOCOLATE TASSIES

My son and I love chocolate, and this is a recipe I came up with that is guaranteed to satisfy any chocolate lover.
—**JOHN WILLIAMS** BEAUMONT, TX

PREP: 30 MIN. + CHILLING • **BAKE:** 20 MIN.
MAKES: 2½ DOZEN

- ⅔ **cup butter, softened**
- 4 **ounces cream cheese, softened**
- ½ **cup granulated sugar**
- 2 **teaspoons vanilla extract**
- 1 **cup all-purpose flour**
- ½ **cup baking cocoa**
  Dash salt

FILLING

- ½ **cup pecan halves, toasted**
- ¼ **cup sweetened shredded coconut, toasted**
- ½ **cup packed brown sugar**
- 1 **large egg**
- 1 **tablespoon butter, melted**
- 1 **teaspoon vanilla extract**
- ⅛ **teaspoon salt**
- 2 **ounces semisweet chocolate, melted**

1. Cream butter, cream cheese and sugar until light and fluffy. Beat in vanilla. In another bowl, whisk flour, cocoa and salt; gradually beat into creamed mixture. Refrigerate, covered, for 30 minutes.

2. Preheat oven to 350°. Shape dough into 1-in. balls; press evenly onto bottom and up sides of ungreased mini-muffin cups.

3. Pulse pecans and coconut in a food processor until finely chopped. In a small bowl, whisk the brown sugar, egg, butter, vanilla and salt. Whisk in melted chocolate. Stir in pecan mixture. Place a rounded teaspoon of filling in each cup. Bake until filling is set, 17-20 minutes. Cool in pans 5 minutes. Remove to wire racks to cool completely.

NOTE *To toast nuts and coconut, bake in separate shallow pans in a 350° oven for 5-10 minutes or until golden brown, stirring occasionally.*

BLACK CAT COOKIES

Our children look forward to helping me bake these cute cat cookies each fall. They've become experts at making the faces with candy corn and red-hot candies.

—**KATHY STOCK** LEVAY, MO

PREP: 25 MIN. • **BAKE:** 10 MIN.
MAKES: 2 DOZEN

- 1 **cup butter, softened**
- 2 **cups sugar**
- 2 **large eggs**
- 3 **teaspoons vanilla extract**
- 3 **cups all-purpose flour**
- 1 **cup baking cocoa**
- ½ **teaspoon baking powder**
- ½ **teaspoon baking soda**
- ½ **teaspoon salt**
- 24 **wooden craft or Popsicle sticks**
- 48 **candy corn candies**
- 24 **Red Hot candies**

1. In a bowl, cream butter and sugar. Beat in eggs and vanilla. Combine the flour, cocoa, baking powder, baking soda and salt; gradually add to the creamed mixture. Roll dough into 1½-in. balls. Place about 3 in. apart on lightly greased baking sheets.

2. Insert a wooden stick into each cookie. Flatten with a glass dipped in sugar. Pinch top of cookie to form ears. For whiskers, press a fork twice into each cookie.

3. Bake at 350° for 10-12 minutes or until cookies are set. Remove from the oven; immediately press on candy corn for eyes and Red Hots for noses. Remove to wire racks to cool.

ACORN TREATS

You only need three ingredients to make these super simple sweets!

—**JANE STASIK** GREENDALE, WI

Short & Sweet

PREP: 35 MIN. + CHILLING
MAKES: 4 DOZEN

- ½ **cup semisweet chocolate chips**
- 48 **milk chocolate kisses**
- 48 **Nutter Butter Bites**

1. In a microwave, melt chocolate chips; stir until smooth. Spread the flat side of each kiss with a small amount of melted chocolate; immediately attach each kiss to a cookie.

2. Cut a small hole in the corner of a pastry or plastic bag; insert a small round tip. Fill with remaining melted chocolate. Pipe a stem onto each acorn. Place on waxed paper-lined baking sheets; refrigerate until set. Store in an airtight container.

CHAI-CHOCOLATE CHIP BISCOTTI

This crunchy cookie was made to be dunked! Enjoy it with a hot cup of coffee or cold glass of milk.

—PAT RUNTZ HUNTLEY, IL

PREP: 30 MIN. + CHILLING
BAKE: 30 MIN. + COOLING
MAKES: 2½ DOZEN

- 2⅓ cups all-purpose flour
- 1 cup sugar
- ¾ teaspoon ground cinnamon
- ½ teaspoon baking powder
- ½ teaspoon baking soda
- ¼ teaspoon salt
- ¼ teaspoon ground allspice
- ¼ teaspoon ground cardamom
- ¼ cup strong brewed chai tea, room temperature
- 1 large egg
- 1 large egg white
- 1 tablespoon fat-free milk
- 1 teaspoon vanilla extract
- ½ cup chopped walnuts
- ½ cup miniature semisweet chocolate chips

1. In a large bowl, combine the first eight ingredients. In a small bowl, whisk the tea, egg, egg white, milk and vanilla. Stir into dry ingredients just until combined. Stir in walnuts and chocolate chips. Divide dough in half. Wrap each portion in plastic and refrigerate for 1 hour.

2. On a baking sheet coated with cooking spray, shape each half into a 10x2-in. rectangle. Bake at 350° for 20-25 minutes or until golden brown. Place pans on wire racks. When cool enough to handle, transfer to a cutting board; cut diagonally with a serrated knife into ¾-in. slices. Place cut side down on baking sheets coated with cooking spray.

3. Bake for 6-9 minutes on each side or until firm. Remove to wire racks. Store in an airtight container.

CHOCOLATE-COVERED MARSHMALLOW COOKIES

I've always liked to bake, and this cookie recipe was a favorite of my eight children. Now it's a favorite of my 11 grandchildren!

—MARY MARGARET LAKE
INDEPENDENCE, IA

PREP: 20 MIN. • **BAKE:** 10 MIN. + COOLING
MAKES: 3 DOZEN

- 1¾ cups sifted cake flour
- ½ cup baking cocoa
- ½ teaspoon salt
- ½ teaspoon baking soda
- ½ cup shortening
- 1 cup sugar
- 1 large egg
- 1 teaspoon vanilla extract
- ¼ cup milk
- 18 large marshmallows, halved
- 36 pecan halves

FROSTING

- 2 cups confectioners' sugar
- 5 tablespoons baking cocoa
- ⅛ teaspoon salt
- 3 tablespoons butter, softened
- 4 to 5 tablespoons half-and-half cream

1. Sift together flour, cocoa, salt and soda; set aside. In a bowl, cream shortening and sugar until light and fluffy; add the egg, vanilla and milk. Gradually add dry ingredients and mix well.

2. Drop by heaping teaspoonfuls about 2 in. apart on greased baking sheets. Bake at 350° for 8 minutes. Do not overbake. Remove cookies from the oven and top each with a marshmallow half. Return to oven for 2 minutes. Remove cookies to wire racks to cool.

3. Meanwhile, beat all of the frosting ingredients together. Spread frosting on each cookie and top with a pecan half.

★ ★ ★ ★ ★ 5 STAR TIP

No cake flour? No problem. For each cup of cake flour needed, substitute 1 cup minus 2 tablespoons all-purpose flour. Replace the missing flour with 2 tablespoons cornstarch. Sift mixture to distribute cornstarch evenly.

CARAMEL APPLE COOKIES

Children find these cute treats especially appealing. They can help out by inserting the toothpicks and dipping the baked cookies in the caramel and nuts. These always disappear at my house.

—DARLENE BRENDEN SALEM, OR

PREP: 25 MIN. + STANDING
BAKE: 15 MIN. + COOLING
MAKES: ABOUT 3 DOZEN

FILLING
- ⅓ **cup finely chopped unpeeled apple**
- ⅓ **cup evaporated milk**
- ⅓ **cup sugar**
- ⅓ **cup chopped walnuts**

DOUGH
- ½ **cup butter, softened**
- ¼ **cup confectioners' sugar**
- ¼ **cup packed brown sugar**
- 1 **large egg**
- 1 **teaspoon vanilla extract**
- 2 **cups all-purpose flour**
- ¼ **teaspoon salt**

TOPPING
- 1 **package (14 ounces) caramels**
- ⅔ **cup evaporated milk**
  Green toothpicks
- 1 **cup chopped walnuts**

1. In a small saucepan, combine filling ingredients. Cook and stir over medium heat until thickened; set aside to cool.
2. In a large bowl, cream butter and sugars until light and fluffy. Beat in egg. Beat in vanilla. Combine flour and salt. Gradually add to creamed mixture and mix well.
3. Shape dough into 1-in. balls. Flatten and place ¼ teaspoon filling in center of each. Fold dough over filling and reshape into balls. Place 1 in. apart on greased baking sheets.
4. Bake at 350° for 12-15 minutes or until lightly browned. Remove to wire racks to cool.
5. In a small saucepan over low heat, heat caramels and evaporated milk until caramels are melted; stir until smooth. Insert a toothpick into each cookie and dip into caramel until completely coated; allow excess to drip off. Dip bottoms into nuts. Place on wire racks to set.

CARAMEL APPLE SHORTBREAD COOKIES

There is nothing like seeing my friends melt to the floor when they bite into a treat I baked. These cookies never fail to elicit all sorts of oohs and aahs.

—AMBER TAYLOR LENOIR CITY, TN

PREP: 35 MIN. + CHILLING
BAKE: 10 MIN./BATCH + COOLING
MAKES: 3 DOZEN

- 1 **cup butter, softened**
- ⅔ **cup confectioners' sugar**
- 2¼ **teaspoons ground cinnamon, divided**
- 2 **cups all-purpose flour**
- ⅓ **cup finely chopped dried apple chips**
- 15 **caramels**
- 2 **tablespoons heavy whipping cream**
  Additional finely chopped dried apple chips, optional

1. In a large bowl, beat the butter, confectioners' sugar and 2 teaspoons cinnamon until blended. Gradually beat in flour. Stir in ⅓ cup apple chips.
2. Divide dough in half. Shape each into a disk; wrap in plastic. Refrigerate 1 hour or until firm enough to roll.
3. Preheat oven to 350°. On a lightly floured surface, roll each portion of dough to ¼-in. thickness. Cut with a floured 2-in. apple-shaped cookie cutter. Place 1 in. apart on greased baking sheets.
4. Bake 9-11 minutes or until light brown. Remove from pans to wire racks to cool completely.
5. In a small saucepan, melt caramels with cream and remaining cinnamon over medium heat, stirring frequently. Drizzle over cookies. If desired, sprinkle with additional apple chips. Let stand until set.

OCTOBER 31
NATIONAL
CARAMEL
APPLE
DAY

CHERRY CHOCOLATE CHUNK COOKIES

These rich, fudgy cookies are chewy and studded with tangy dried cherries. It's a good thing the recipe makes only a small batch, because we eat them all in one night!

—TRISHA KRUSE EAGLE, ID

START TO FINISH: 30 MIN.
MAKES: 10 COOKIES

- ¼ **cup butter, softened**
- 6 **tablespoons sugar**
- 2 **tablespoons beaten egg**
- 4 **teaspoons 2% milk**
- ¼ **teaspoon vanilla extract**
- ½ **cup all-purpose flour**
- 3 **tablespoons baking cocoa**
- ⅛ **teaspoon baking soda**
- ⅛ **teaspoon salt**
- ½ **cup semisweet chocolate chunks**
- ¼ **cup dried cherries**

1. In a small bowl, cream butter and sugar. Beat in the egg, milk and vanilla. Combine the flour, cocoa, baking soda and salt; add to creamed mixture and mix well. Stir in chocolate and cherries.

2. Drop by rounded tablespoonfuls 2 in. apart onto baking sheets lightly coated with cooking spray. Bake at 350° for 12-14 minutes or until firm. Cool for 1 minute before removing to a wire rack.

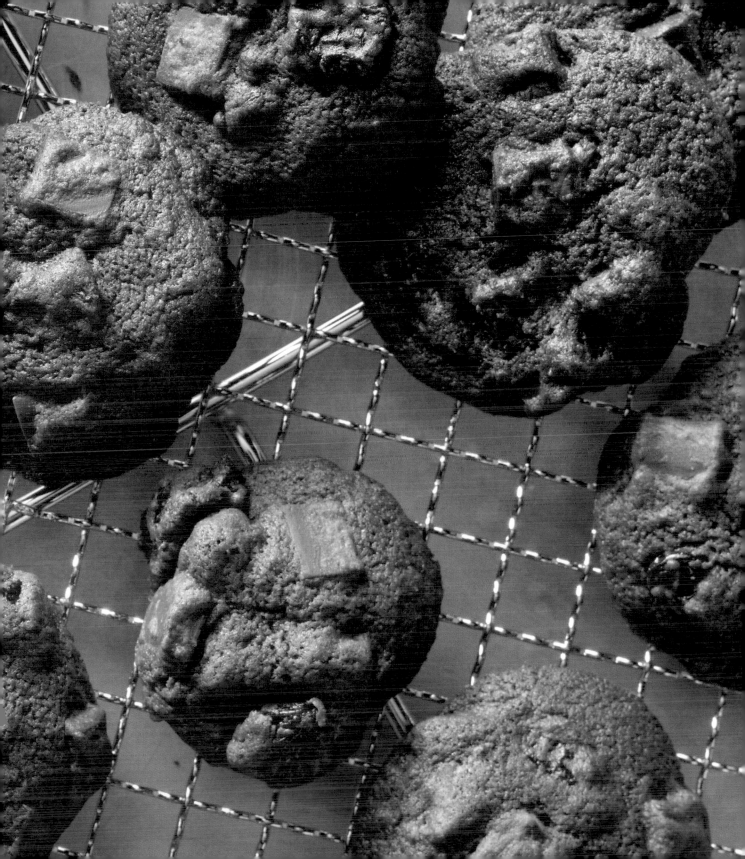

DRACULA COOKIES

Come late October, our friends and family can "count" on me to re-introduce them to my darling Dracula Cookies!

—CHRISTY HINRICHS PARKVILLE, MO

START TO FINISH: 30 MIN.
MAKES: 6 COOKIES

Short & Sweet

- 6 **hazelnut truffles**
- 5 **ounces white candy coating, chopped**
- 1 **green or red Fruit Roll-Up**
- 6 **Oreo cookies**
- 1 **can (6.4 ounces) black decorating icing**
- 6 **slivered almonds, cut in half**

1. Place truffles on a waxed paper-lined pan. Freeze 10 minutes or until chilled. Meanwhile, in a microwave, melt candy coating; stir until smooth. Dip truffles in coating to cover completely; allow excess to drip off. Return to prepared pan. Refrigerate until hardened.
2. Cut Fruit Roll-Up into 2½x1½-in. strips. Reheat candy coating if necessary. Dip truffles in candy coating again; allow excess to drip off. Place one on each cookie. Wrap a fruit strip around base of truffle for cape. Let stand until set.
3. Using decorating icing and a round tip, gently pipe hair, eyes and mouth on each. Insert almonds for fangs. Store in an airtight container.
NOTE *This recipe was tested with Ferrero Rocher hazelnut truffles.*

GOBLIN CHEWIES

These light, crispy cookies are packed with fun ingredients that are absolutely perfect for Halloween.

—BERNICE MORRIS MARSHFIELD, MO

PREP: 30 MIN. • **BAKE:** 10 MIN.
MAKES: ABOUT 6 DOZEN

- 1 **cup shortening**
- 1 **cup packed brown sugar**
- 1 **cup sugar**
- 2 **large eggs**
- 1 **teaspoon vanilla extract**
- 2 **cups all-purpose flour**
- 1 **teaspoon baking soda**
- ½ **teaspoon baking powder**
- ½ **teaspoon salt**
- 1½ **cups old-fashioned oats**
- 1 **cup crisp rice cereal**
- 1 **cup diced candy orange slices**
- 1 **cup (6 ounces) semisweet chocolate chips or raisins**
  Additional raisins or chocolate chips and candy orange slices

1. In a bowl, cream shortening and sugars. Add eggs and vanilla; mix well. Combine the flour, baking soda, baking powder and salt; add to creamed mixture. Stir in oats, cereal, orange slices and chips or raisins.
2. Drop by tablespoonfuls 2 in. apart onto greased baking sheets. Flatten slightly with a fork. Decorate with raisin or chocolate chip eyes and orange slice mouths. Bake at 350° for 10-14 minutes. Cool on wire racks.
NOTE *Orange slices cut more easily if microwaved first for 5 seconds on high. Cut with a sharp knife or kitchen scissors.*

MAGIC MACAROONS

Candy corn, peanut butter and macaroons are three of my favorite things, so I combine them all to make one magical sweet that's perfect for Halloween.

—JEANETTE NELSON BRIDGEPORT, WV

PREP: 10 MIN. • **COOK:** 20 MIN.
MAKES: 2 DOZEN

- 2 **large egg whites**
- ½ **cup sugar**
- 1 **teaspoon vanilla extract**
- ¼ **teaspoon cream of tartar**
- ⅛ **teaspoon salt**
- 2¾ **cups flaked coconut**
- ⅓ **cup candy corn, chopped**
- ¼ **cup dark chocolate chips**
- ¼ **cup peanut butter chips**
- ¼ **cup finely chopped macadamia nuts**
- ⅔ **cup white baking chips, melted**

1. Preheat oven to 300°. In a small bowl, whisk the first five ingredients until blended. In a large bowl, mix coconut, candy corn, dark chocolate chips, peanut butter chips and nuts; gently stir in egg white mixture.

2. Drop by tablespoonfuls 1 in. apart onto parchment paper-lined baking sheets. Bake 20-22 minutes or until light brown. Remove from pans to wire racks to cool completely.

3. Drizzle cookies with melted baking chips; let stand until set. Store in an airtight container.

BONEYARD COOKIES

These bone-chilling treats promise to sweeten up any scary soiree this Halloween. A hint of raspberry makes them extra special.

—CELENA CANTRELL-RICHARDSON
EAU CLAIRE, MI

PREP: 1 HOUR + CHILLING
BAKE: 10 MIN./BATCH + COOLING
MAKES: 34 SANDWICH COOKIES

- 1 cup confectioners' sugar
- ½ cup cornstarch
- ½ cup cold butter, cubed
- 2 large eggs
- 1 teaspoon almond extract
- 2 cups all-purpose flour
- ⅛ teaspoon salt
- 2 to 3 tablespoons seedless raspberry jam
- 16 to 18 ounces white baking chocolate, chopped

1. In a small bowl, combine the confectioners' sugar and cornstarch. Cut in butter until mixture resembles coarse crumbs. Add eggs, one at a time, beating well after each addition. Beat in extract. Combine flour and salt; gradually add to sugar mixture and mix well.

2. Shape dough into a ball; flatten into a disk. Wrap in plastic; refrigerate for 30 minutes or until easy to handle.

3. On a lightly floured surface, roll dough to ⅛-in. thickness. Cut with a floured 3½-in. bone-shaped cookie cutter. Place cookies 1 in. apart on parchment paper-lined baking sheets. Bake at 350° for 8-10 minutes or until edges begin to brown. Remove to wire racks to cool.

4. On the bottoms of half the cookies, spread ⅛ to ¼ teaspoon jam down the center; top with remaining cookies.

5. In a microwave, melt white baking chocolate at 70% power for 1 minute; stir. Microwave at additional 10- to 20-second intervals, stirring until smooth.

6. Dip each cookie in chocolate, allowing excess to drip off. Place on waxed paper; let stand until set.

HALLOWEEN PEANUT BUTTER COOKIE POPS

A miniature candy bar is hidden inside these fun pops. Colored frosting and candy faces make these addicting cookies the perfect trick-or-treat handout.

—**MARTHA HOOVER** COATESVILLE, PA

PREP: 20 MIN.
BAKE: 15 MIN./BATCH + COOLING
MAKES: 1 DOZEN

- ½ **cup butter, softened**
- ½ **cup creamy peanut butter**
- ½ **cup packed brown sugar**
- ½ **cup sugar**
- 1 **large egg**
- 1 **teaspoon vanilla extract**
- 1½ **cups all-purpose flour**
- ½ **teaspoon baking powder**
- ½ **teaspoon baking soda**
- ¼ **teaspoon salt**
- 12 **lollipop sticks**
- 12 **fun-size Snickers or Milky Way candy bars**
- **Prepared vanilla frosting**
- **Food coloring**
- **Black decorating gel**
- **Optional decorations: Reese's mini peanut butter cups, M&M's minis, mini Chiclets gum, candy corn and candy eyeballs**

1. Preheat oven to 375°. In a small bowl, cream butter, peanut butter and sugars until blended. Beat in egg and vanilla. In a small bowl, whisk flour, baking powder, baking soda and salt; gradually beat into creamed mixture.

2. Insert a lollipop stick into a small end of each candy bar. Divide dough into 12 pieces; wrap one piece around each candy bar. Place 4 in. apart on ungreased baking sheets.

3. Bake 14-16 minutes or until golden brown. Cool on pans 10 minutes; remove to wire racks to cool completely. Tint frosting; frost cookies. Decorate with gel and optional decorations as desired.

MELTED WITCH PUDDLES

In honor of the doomed wicked witch in *The Wizard of Oz,* we had fun fashioning these simply delicious snacks using a variety of convenience foods.

—TASTE OF HOME **TEST KITCHEN**

PREP: 1 HOUR + CHILLING
MAKES: 3 DOZEN

- 1 **teaspoon water**
- 4 **drops yellow food coloring**
- 1½ **cups sweetened shredded coconut**
- 2 **cups (12 ounces) semisweet chocolate chips**
- 6 **tablespoons shortening, divided**
- 36 **chocolate cream-filled chocolate sandwich cookies**
- 36 **Bugles**
- 4 **cups vanilla or white chips**
- 36 **pretzel sticks**

1. In a large resealable plastic bag, combine water and food coloring; add coconut. Seal bag and shake to tint the coconut; set aside. In a microwave, melt chocolate chips and 2 tablespoons of shortening; stir until smooth.

2. For witches' hats, place about ⅓ cup chocolate mixture in a resealable plastic bag; cut a small hole in a corner of bag. Pipe a small amount of chocolate on a cookie. Dip a Bugle in the remaining chocolate; allow the excess to drip off. Position Bugle over chocolate on cookie, forming a witch's hat. Set on waxed paper to dry. Repeat with remaining chocolate, Bugles and cookies.

3. For puddles, melt vanilla chips and the remaining shortening; stir until smooth. Place the mixture in a large heavy-duty resealable plastic bag; cut a small hole in a corner of bag. Pipe mixture into the shape of a puddle onto waxed paper-lined baking sheets.

4. Immediately place a witch's hat on the puddle. Place a pretzel stick alongside the hat; sprinkle reserved tinted coconut at the end of the pretzel stick. Repeat with remaining puddles, hats and brooms. Chill for 15 minutes or until set. Store in an airtight container.

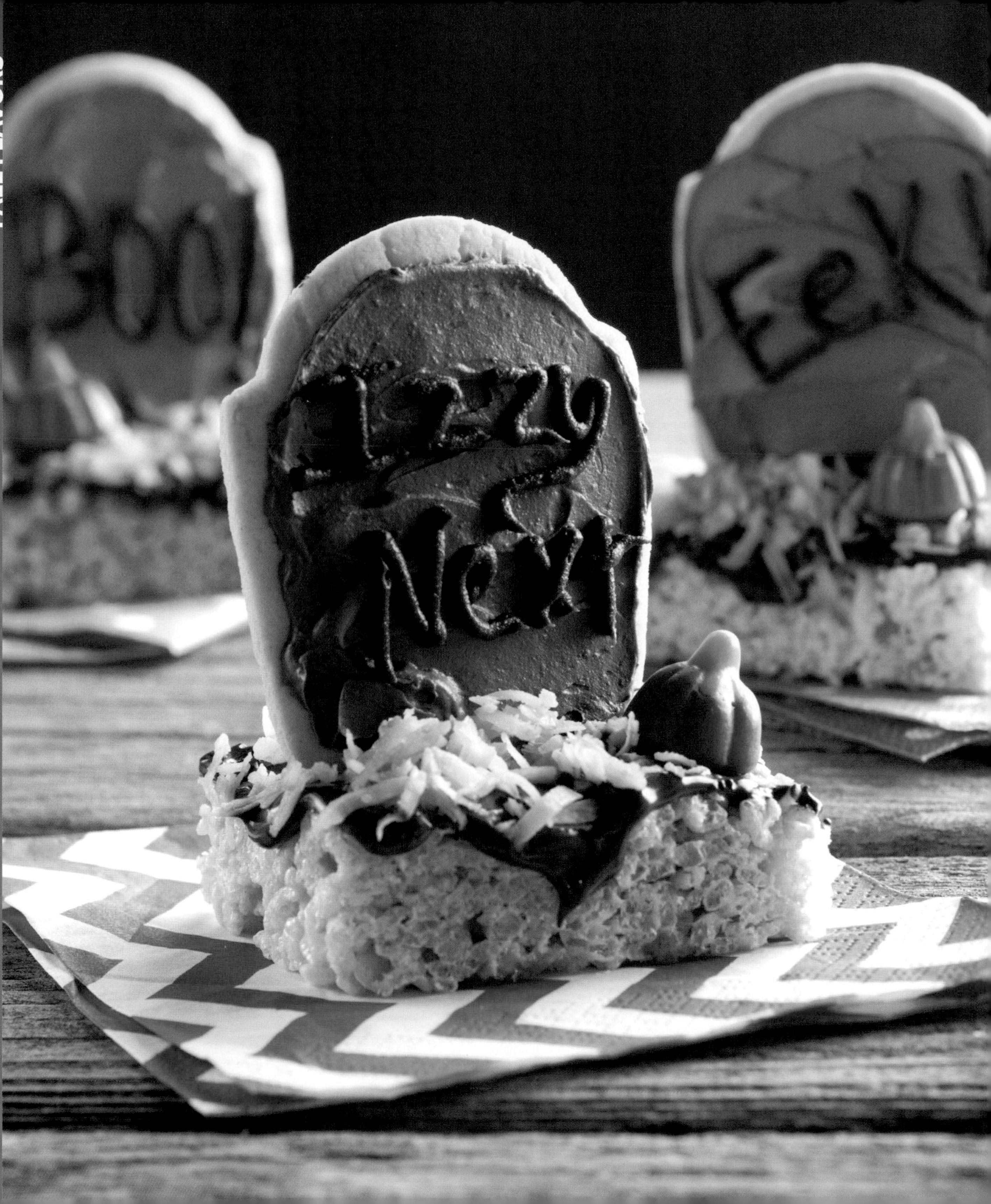
BOO

TOMBSTONE TREATS

My brother loves Rice Krispies squares, and my mom loves sugar cookies. To please both of them, I came up with a cute treat they can agree on!

—**JILL WRIGHT** DIXON, IL

PREP: 45 MIN. • **BAKE:** 10 MIN. + COOLING
MAKES: 16 SERVINGS

- 3 tablespoons butter
- 4 cups miniature marshmallows
- 7½ cups crisp rice cereal
- 1 tube (16½ ounces) refrigerated sugar cookie dough
- ⅔ cup all-purpose flour
- 1 teaspoon water
- 4 drops green food coloring
- 1½ cups flaked coconut
  Black paste food coloring
  Vanilla frosting
  Brown decorating icing
- 1 cup (6 ounces) semisweet chocolate chips, melted
  Candy pumpkins

1. In a large saucepan over low heat, melt the butter. Stir in marshmallows until melted. Remove from heat. Stir in cereal until well coated. With a buttered spatula, press into a greased 13x9-in. pan. Cool.

2. Beat cookie dough and flour until combined. On a lightly floured surface, roll out dough to ¼-in. thickness. Trace tombstone pattern onto waxed paper; cut out 16 tombstones from dough. Place 2 in. apart on ungreased baking sheets.

3. Along bottom edge of each cookie, insert two toothpicks halfway into dough. Bake at 350° until edges are golden brown, 8-10 minutes. Remove to wire racks to cool.

4. In a large resealable plastic bag, combine water and green food coloring. Add coconut; seal bag and shake to coat. Toast coconut; set aside. Using black paste food coloring, tint frosting gray. Frost sugar cookies; decorate with brown decorating icing.

5. Cut cereal bars into 3x2-in. rectangles; spread with melted chocolate chips. Using toothpicks, insert cookies into cereal bars. Decorate cookies and bars with coconut and candies as desired.

COLORFUL PEANUT BUTTER CRACKERS

Ghosts have you up at night? If you aren't too afraid to head to the kitchen, you'll want to indulge in this sweet-n-salty midnight snack.

—**RUTH CASSIS** UNIVERSITY PLACE, WA

PREP: 35 MIN. + CHILLING
MAKES: 2 DOZEN

Short & Sweet

- 4 ounces cream cheese, cubed
- ½ cup creamy peanut butter
- ¼ cup honey
- 48 butter-flavored crackers
- 2 cups (12 ounces) semisweet chocolate chips
- 4 teaspoons shortening
- ¼ cup 2% milk
  Cake decorator holiday shapes

1. In a microwave-safe bowl, heat cream cheese on high for 15 seconds or until very soft. Add peanut butter and honey; stir until smooth. Spread over half of the crackers; top with remaining crackers.

2. In a microwave, melt chocolate chips and shortening; stir until smooth. Heat milk; stir into chocolate mixture.

3. Dip each cracker sandwich into the chocolate mixture, allowing excess to drip off. Place on waxed paper-lined baking sheets; decorate as desired. Refrigerate for 45 minutes or until set.

NOTE *This recipe was tested in a 1,100-watt microwave.*

BUTTER PECAN ICEBOX COOKIES

My grandmother used to bake a very similar cookie. I always loved them because of their butterscotch flavor. As a little girl, I was fascinated by the way Grandmother prepared these cookies (from logs that she took out of the icebox!). These are simple but delicious old-fashioned cookies. The dough logs can be formed and stored in the freezer, then pulled out to defrost a day or two before baking time.

—LISA VARNER EL PASO, TX

PREP: 15 MIN. + CHILLING
BAKE: 10 MIN./BATCH
MAKES: ABOUT 6½ DOZEN

- ½ **cup butter, softened**
- ½ **cup shortening**
- 1 **cup granulated sugar**
- 1 **cup packed brown sugar**
- 2 **large eggs**
- 1 **teaspoon vanilla extract**
- 3 **cups all-purpose flour**
- 1 **teaspoon baking soda**
- ½ **teaspoon salt**
- 1 **cup finely chopped pecans**

1. Cream butter, shortening and sugars until light and fluffy. Beat in eggs and vanilla. In another bowl, whisk flour, baking soda and salt; gradually beat into creamed mixture. Stir in pecans.
2. Divide dough in half; shape each into a 10-in. long roll. Wrap in plastic; refrigerate 8 hours or overnight.
3. Preheat oven to 350°. Unwrap and cut dough crosswise into ¼-in. slices. Place 2 in. apart on ungreased baking sheets. Bake until edges begin to brown, 7-9 minutes. Remove from pans to wire racks to cool.

HAPPY SWEETEST DAY!

ULTIMATE CANDY BAR COOKIES

I created these after Halloween, when I had way too much candy left over. You can make them with any kind of little candy bars or chocolate candies you have on hand.
—**TARA JOHN** PLYMOUTH, MN

PREP: 30 MIN. • **BAKE:** 10 MIN./BATCH
MAKES: 4½ DOZEN

- 7 Butterfinger candy bars (2.1 ounces each), coarsely chopped
- 1 cup butter, softened
- 2 large eggs
- 3 cups all-purpose flour
- 1 teaspoon baking powder
- ½ teaspoon salt
- 27 Reese's mini peanut butter cups
- 27 miniature Snickers candy bars

1. Preheat oven to 375°. Place Butterfinger candy bars in a food processor; process until ground. In a large bowl, cream butter and 2 cups ground candy bars until blended. Beat in eggs. In another bowl, whisk flour, baking powder and salt; gradually beat into creamed mixture.

2. Shape into 1-in. balls; roll in remaining ground candy bars. Place 2 in. apart on parchment paper-lined baking sheets. Bake 8-10 minutes or until the tops are cracked.

3. Immediately press a piece of candy into the center of each cookie. Cool on pans 2 minutes. Remove to wire racks to cool completely.

FREEZE OPTION *Freeze cookies, layered between waxed paper, in freezer containers. To use, thaw before serving.*

FROM THE COOKIE JAR

Always use a dry measuring cup when measuring out chips, nuts or candy bits for cookies. Dry measuring cups are usually plastic or stainless steel, while liquid measuring cups tend to be glass.

CHOCOLATE PEANUT COOKIES

When I want chocolate chip cookies, I bake this variation, which is full of other goodies such as candy and peanuts. The cookies are crisp on the outside and moist and tender in the middle.
—**CLARA COULSON MINNEY** WASHINGTON COURT HOUSE, OH

PREP: 20 MIN. • **BAKE:** 10 MIN./BATCH
MAKES: ABOUT 2 DOZEN

- ¼ cup butter, softened
- ¼ cup peanut butter
- ¼ cup packed brown sugar
- 2 tablespoons sugar
- 2 tablespoons beaten egg
- 2 tablespoons 2% milk
- ½ teaspoon vanilla extract
- 1 cup all-purpose flour
- ½ teaspoon baking soda
- ⅛ teaspoon salt
- ⅓ cup honey-roasted peanuts
- ⅓ cup semisweet chocolate chips
- ⅓ cup coarsely chopped miniature peanut butter cups

1. In a large bowl, cream the butter, peanut butter and sugars until light and fluffy. Beat in the egg, milk and vanilla. Combine the flour, baking soda and salt; gradually add to creamed mixture and mix well. Stir in the peanuts, chocolate chips and peanut butter cups.

2. Drop by tablespoonfuls 2 in. apart onto ungreased baking sheets. Bake at 350° for 10-12 minutes or until golden brown. Remove to wire racks to cool. Store in an airtight container.

CRANBERRY OATMEAL COOKIES

Featuring cranberries, raisins, orange peel and vanilla chips, these cookies are always a fun, colorful option for fall snacking. They look lovely on a dessert tray and make a great addition to winter baking lineups as well.
—**PAT HABIGER** SPEARVILLE, KS

PREP: 15 MIN. • **BAKE:** 10 MIN./BATCH
MAKES: 6 DOZEN

- 1 **cup butter, softened**
- 1½ **cups sugar**
- 2 **large eggs**
- 1 **teaspoon vanilla extract**
- 2 **cups all-purpose flour**
- 1 **teaspoon baking powder**
- ½ **teaspoon salt**
- ¼ **teaspoon baking soda**
- 2 **cups quick-cooking oats**
- 1 **cup raisins**
- 1 **cup coarsely chopped fresh or frozen cranberries**
- 1 **tablespoon grated orange peel**
- 1 **package (10 to 12 ounces) white baking chips**

1. In a large bowl, cream butter and sugar until light and fluffy. Add eggs, one at a time, beating well after each addition. Beat in vanilla. Combine the flour, baking powder, salt and baking soda; add to the creamed mixture. Stir in the oats, raisins, cranberries and orange peel. Stir in the baking chips.
2. Drop by rounded teaspoonfuls 2 in. apart onto greased baking sheets. Bake at 375° for 10-12 minutes or until the edges are lightly browned. Cool on wire racks.

★ ★ ★ ★ ★ **5 STAR TIP**
A quick and easy way to switch up cookie recipes is to replace vanilla extract with almond extract or imitation maple or caramel extract.

SNICKERDOODLES

The history of these whimsically named treats is widely disputed, but their popularity is undeniable! Help yourself to one of our soft, cinnamon-sugared cookies and see for yourself.

—TASTE OF HOME **TEST KITCHEN**

PREP: 20 MIN. • **BAKE:** 10 MIN./BATCH
MAKES: 2½ DOZEN

- ½ **cup butter, softened**
- 1 **cup plus 2 tablespoons sugar, divided**
- 1 **large egg**
- ½ **teaspoon vanilla extract**
- 1½ **cups all-purpose flour**
- ¼ **teaspoon baking soda**
- ¼ **teaspoon cream of tartar**
- 1 **teaspoon ground cinnamon**

1. Preheat oven to 375°. Cream butter and 1 cup sugar until light and fluffy; beat in egg and vanilla. In another bowl, whisk together the flour, baking soda and cream of tartar; gradually beat dry ingredients into the creamed mixture.

2. In a small bowl, mix cinnamon and remaining sugar. Shape dough into 1-in. balls; roll in cinnamon sugar. Place 2 in. apart on ungreased baking sheets.

3. Bake until light brown, 10-12 minutes. Remove from pans to wire racks to cool.

OAT-RAGEOUS CHOCOLATE CHIP COOKIES

My aunt gave me this recipe, and my family thinks these cookies are delicious. We enjoy all different kinds of cookies, and with this recipe, we combine three of our favorite kinds—oatmeal, peanut butter and chocolate chip—in one!

—JAYMIE NOBLE KALAMAZOO, MI

PREP: 25 MIN. • **BAKE:** 10 MIN./BATCH
MAKES: ABOUT 3 DOZEN

- ½ cup butter, softened
- ½ cup creamy peanut butter
- ½ cup sugar
- ⅓ cup packed brown sugar
- 1 large egg
- ½ teaspoon vanilla extract
- 1 cup all-purpose flour
- ½ cup quick-cooking oats
- 1 teaspoon baking soda
- ¼ teaspoon salt
- 1 cup (6 ounces) semisweet chocolate chips

In a large bowl, cream butter, peanut butter and sugars; beat in egg and vanilla. Combine flour, oats, baking soda and salt. Add to the creamed mixture and mix well. Stir in the chocolate chips. Drop by rounded tablespoonfuls onto ungreased baking sheets. Bake at 350° for 10-12 minutes or until lightly browned.

VEGAN CHOCOLATE CHIP COOKIES

As a competitive figure skater, I came up with this high-energy recipe. When I bring these cookies to the rink, coaches are always snitching two or three. I also like them with macadamia nuts.

—**CASSANDRA BRZYCKI** WAUWATOSA, WI

PREP: 15 MIN. + CHILLING
BAKE: 10 MIN./BATCH • **MAKES:** 3½ DOZEN

- 1¼ cups packed dark brown sugar
- ½ cup canola oil
- 6 tablespoons vanilla soy milk
- ¼ cup sugar
- ¼ cup unsweetened applesauce
- 2 teaspoons vanilla extract
- 2¼ cups all-purpose flour
- 1 teaspoon baking soda
- ¾ teaspoon salt
- 1 cup dairy-free semisweet chocolate chips
- ½ cup finely chopped walnuts

1. In a large bowl, beat the first six ingredients until well blended. Combine the flour, baking soda and salt; gradually add to sugar mixture and mix well. Stir in chocolate chips and nuts. Cover and refrigerate 1 hour.

2. Drop by rounded tablespoonfuls 2 in. apart onto parchment paper-lined baking sheets. Bake at 375° for 10-12 minutes or until edges are lightly browned. Cool for 1 minute before removing from pans to wire racks.

MINI MERINGUE PUMPKINS

Using a basic meringue recipe spiced with pumpkin flavor, you can prepare these festive, fun-to-eat cookies, perfect for fall.
—TASTE OF HOME **TEST KITCHEN**

PREP: 1 HOUR • **BAKE:** 40 MIN. + STANDING
MAKES: 2 DOZEN

- 2 large egg whites
- ¼ teaspoon cream of tartar
- ⅛ teaspoon salt
- ½ cup sugar
- ½ teaspoon pumpkin pie spice
- ½ teaspoon vanilla extract
- 2 teaspoons orange colored sugar
- 2 teaspoons orange edible glitter
- 3 pieces green Fruit by the Foot fruit roll
- 2 teaspoons vanilla frosting

1. In a small bowl, beat egg whites, cream of tartar and salt on medium speed until soft peaks form. Gradually add sugar, 1 tablespoon at a time, beating on high until stiff peaks form. Add pumpkin pie spice and vanilla.

2. Place egg white mixture in a pastry bag fitted with a large star tip. Pipe 1½-in.-diameter pumpkins onto parchment paper-lined baking sheets.

3. In a small resealable plastic bag, combine the orange sugar and glitter. Seal bag; crush mixture to break glitter into small pieces. Sprinkle over pumpkins.

4. Bake at 250° for 40-45 minutes or until set and dry. Turn oven off; leave meringues in oven for 1½ hours.

5. Carefully remove meringues from parchment paper. Cut leaf and vine shapes from fruit roll; attach to pumpkins with a dab of frosting. Store meringues in an airtight container.

DAY OF THE DEAD COOKIES

I make these almond butter cookies for all occasions. Using candies, food coloring and a wild imagination, try your hand at this Halloween-inspired version. In the spring, cut them into flower shapes and insert lollipop sticks in them to make a bouquet.

—KRISSY FOSSMEYER HUNTLEY, IL

PREP: 2 HOURS + CHILLING
BAKE: 10 MIN./BATCH + COOLING
MAKES: 1 DOZEN

- 1¼ **cups butter, softened**
- 1¾ **cups confectioners' sugar**
- 2 **ounces almond paste**
- 1 **large egg**
- ¼ **cup 2% milk**
- 1 **teaspoon vanilla extract**
- 4 **cups all-purpose flour**
- ½ **teaspoon salt**
- 2 **packages (12 ounces each) white candy coating melts**
  Decorations of your choice: jumbo sprinkles, peppermint candies, candy-coated sunflower kernels, Skittles, Twizzlers Rainbow Twists and Good & Plenty candies
  Black paste food coloring

1. In a large bowl, cream butter and confectioners' sugar until light and fluffy; add almond paste. Beat in the egg, milk and vanilla. Combine flour and salt; gradually add to creamed mixture and mix well. Cover and refrigerate for 1 hour.

2. On a lightly floured surface, roll out dough to ¼-in. thickness. Cut out with a floured 5-in. skull-shaped cookie cutter. Place 1 in. apart on ungreased baking sheets.

3. Bake at 375° for 7-9 minutes or until firm. Let stand for 2 minutes before removing to wire racks to cool completely.

4. In a large shallow microwave-safe dish, melt white candy melts according to package directions. Dip top side of each cookie into coating, allowing excess to drip off; place on waxed paper.

5. Add decorations as desired. Tint remaining white coating black; pipe on mouth. Let stand until set.

MAPLE WALNUT BISCOTTI

Biscotti is the perfect complement to coffee or tea. For even more maple flavor, replace the melted chocolate with an icing of ½ cup confectioners' sugar mixed with 2 tablespoons maple syrup. Lightly drizzle over the cookies and allow to set.

—SUSAN ROGERS BRATTLEBORO, VT

PREP: 30 MIN. • **BAKE:** 35 MIN. + COOLING
MAKES: 28 BISCOTTI

- 2 large eggs
- 1 large egg white
- ⅓ cup maple syrup
- ¼ cup sugar
- 1 teaspoon vanilla extract
- 1¾ cups all-purpose flour
- ½ cup oat flour
- 1 teaspoon baking soda
- ½ cup chopped walnuts
- ½ cup dried cranberries
- ⅓ cup dark chocolate chips or white baking chips

1. In a small bowl, beat eggs, egg white, syrup, sugar and vanilla until blended. Combine the flours and baking soda; gradually add to egg mixture and mix well (dough will be sticky). Stir in walnuts and cranberries.

2. With floured hands, shape into two 10x2½-in. rectangles on a parchment paper-lined baking sheet. Bake at 350° for 22-26 minutes or until set.

3. Reduce heat to 325°. Place pan on a wire rack. When cool enough to handle, transfer to a cutting board; cut diagonally with a serrated knife into ½-in. slices. Place cut side down on ungreased baking sheets. Bake for 9-11 minutes on each side or until golden brown. Remove to wire racks to cool.

4. In a microwave, melt chocolate chips; stir until smooth. Place biscotti on a waxed paper-lined baking sheet. Drizzle with chocolate; chill until set. Store in an airtight container.

NOTE *As a substitute for ½ cup oat flour, process ½ cup plus 2 tablespoons quick-cooking or old-fashioned oats until finely ground.*

ELECTION DAY COOKIES

For one presidential election, I made these for my co-workers as a reminder to head to the polls.

—COLLEEN STURMA MILWAUKEE, WI

PREP: 30 MIN. + CHILLING
BAKE: 10 MIN./BATCH + COOLING
MAKES: ABOUT 5 DOZEN

- 1 **cup butter, softened**
- 1 **cup confectioners' sugar**
- 1 **large egg**
- 1½ **teaspoons almond extract**
- 1 **teaspoon vanilla extract**
- 2½ **cups all-purpose flour**
- 1 **teaspoon salt**

FROSTING
- 6 **tablespoons butter, softened**
- 2⅔ **cups confectioners' sugar**
- 1 **teaspoon vanilla extract**
- 1 **to 2 tablespoons milk**
  Red and blue food coloring
  Assorted patriotic decorations

1. In a small bowl, cream butter and confectioners' sugar until light and fluffy. Beat in egg and extracts. Gradually add flour and salt; mix well. Divide in half, flatten and wrap each portion in plastic. Refrigerate for at least 30 minutes or until easy to handle.

2. On a floured surface, roll dough to ⅛-in. thickness. Cut with floured 2½-in. donkey and elephant cookie cutters. Place 2 in. apart on baking sheets coated with cooking spray.

3. Bake at 375° for 10 minutes or until lightly browned. Remove to wire racks to cool.

4. For frosting, in a small bowl, beat the butter, confectioners' sugar, vanilla and enough milk to achieve spreading consistency. Tint some frosting red and some blue; leave some white. Frost cookies; decorate as desired.

HAPPY ELECTION DAY!

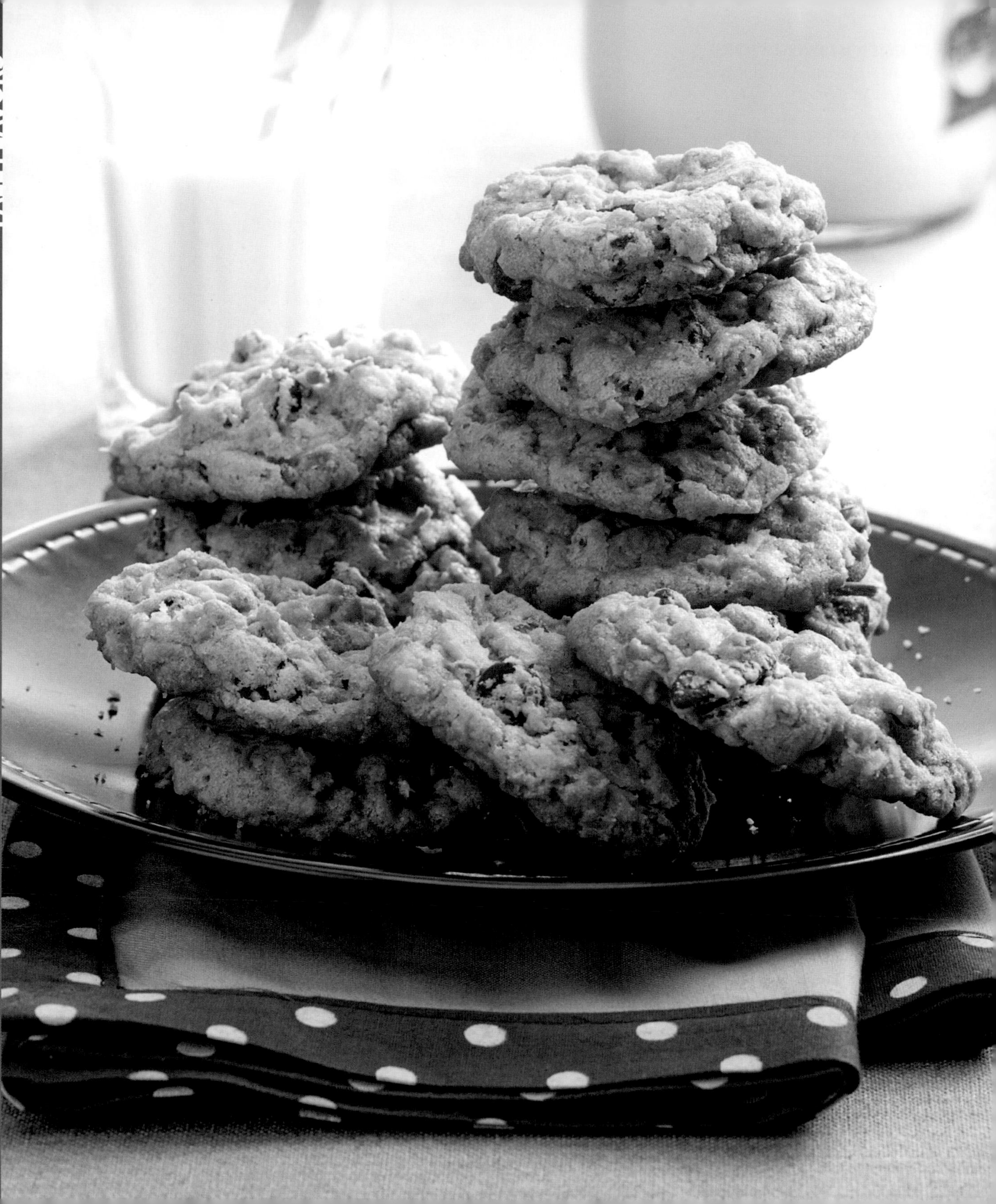

WYOMING COWBOY COOKIES

These cookies are very popular in Wyoming. They're great for munching anytime.

—PATSY STEENBOCK SHOSHONI, WY

PREP: 25 MIN. • **BAKE:** 15 MIN.
MAKES: 6 DOZEN

- 1 cup flaked coconut
- ¾ cup chopped pecans
- 1 cup butter, softened
- 1½ cups packed brown sugar
- ½ cup sugar
- 2 large eggs
- 1½ teaspoons vanilla extract
- 2 cups all-purpose flour
- 1 teaspoon baking soda
- ½ teaspoon salt
- 2 cups old-fashioned oats
- 2 cups (12 ounces) chocolate chips

1. Place coconut and pecans on a 15x10x1-in. baking pan. Bake at 350° for 6-8 minutes or until toasted, stirring every 2 minutes. Set aside to cool.

2. In a large bowl, cream butter and sugars until light and fluffy. Add eggs vanilla; beat well. Combine the flour, baking soda and salt. Add to creamed mixture; beat well. Stir in the oats, chocolate chips and toasted coconut and pecans.

3. Drop by rounded teaspoonfuls onto greased baking sheets. Bake at 350° for about 12 minutes or until browned. Remove to wire racks to cool.

FROM THE COOKIE JAR

When a cookie recipe calls for brown sugar, it's likely referring to light brown sugar, which has a delicate flavor. Dark brown sugar, which offers a strong molasses flavor, can be used if that's what you have on hand.

FIVE-CHIP COOKIES

With peanut butter, oats and five kinds of chips, these cookies make a hearty snack that appeals to kids of all ages. I sometimes double the recipe to share with my friends and neighbors.

—SHARON HEDSTROM MINNETONKA, MN

START TO FINISH: 25 MIN. • **MAKES:** 4½ DOZEN

- 1 cup butter, softened
- 1 cup peanut butter
- 1 cup sugar
- ⅔ cup packed brown sugar
- 2 large eggs
- 1 teaspoon vanilla extract
- 2 cups all-purpose flour
- 1 cup old-fashioned oats
- 2 teaspoons baking soda
- ½ teaspoon salt
- ⅔ cup each milk chocolate chips, semisweet chocolate chips, peanut butter chips, white baking chips and butterscotch chips

1. Preheat oven to 350°. In a large bowl, cream butter, peanut butter and sugars until light and fluffy. Add eggs, one at a time, beating well after each addition. Beat in vanilla. Combine flour, oats, baking soda and salt; gradually add to creamed mixture and mix well. Stir in the chips.

2. Drop by rounded tablespoonfuls 2 in. apart onto ungreased baking sheets. Bake 10-12 minutes or until lightly browned. Cool about 1 minute before removing to wire racks.

NOTE *Reduced-fat peanut butter is not recommended for this recipe.*

FROSTED PUMPKIN COOKIES

These soft cookies are almost like little pieces of cake. With chopped pecans sprinkled over a confectioners' sugar frosting, they're a pretty addition to a dessert buffet.
—**BEV MARTIN** HARDIN, MT

PREP: 20 MIN.
BAKE: 10 MIN./BATCH + COOLING
MAKES: 7 DOZEN

- 1 package (8 ounces) cream cheese, softened
- 1½ cups packed brown sugar
- ½ cup sugar
- 2 large eggs
- 1 cup canned pumpkin
- 1 teaspoon vanilla extract
- 3½ cups all-purpose flour
- 1 to 1½ teaspoons pumpkin pie spice
- 1 teaspoon baking soda
- 1 teaspoon salt
- ½ teaspoon baking powder

FROSTING

- 2 cups confectioners' sugar
- ¼ cup butter, melted
- 1 teaspoon vanilla extract
- 2 to 3 tablespoons boiling water
- 2 cups chopped pecans

1. In a large bowl, beat cream cheese and sugars until smooth. Add eggs, one at a time, beating well after each addition. Beat in pumpkin and vanilla. Combine the dry ingredients; gradually add to pumpkin mixture and mix well.

2. Drop by rounded teaspoonfuls 2 in. apart onto ungreased baking sheets. Bake at 350° for 10-12 minutes or until golden brown. Remove to wire racks to cool.

3. For frosting, in a small bowl, combine the confectioners' sugar, butter, vanilla and enough water to achieve frosting consistency. Frost cookies; sprinkle with pecans.

BAKLAVA ROUNDS

I wanted to make mini baklava for an elegant tea I catered several years ago. I came up with these rounds, and they completely disappeared at the party.
—**META WEST** ABILENE, KS

PREP: 40 MIN. • **BAKE:** 20 MIN. + STANDING
MAKES: 32 COOKIES

- 1 cup sugar
- ¾ cup water
- 10 orange peel strips (1 to 3 inches)

FILLING

- 1½ cups chopped walnuts
- ½ cup slivered almonds
- ¼ cup sugar
- 1 teaspoon almond extract
- ½ teaspoon ground cinnamon
- ½ teaspoon ground cloves
- 18 sheets phyllo dough (14x9-inch sheet size)
- ¾ cup butter, melted

1. In a large saucepan, bring the sugar, water and orange peel to a boil. Reduce heat; simmer, uncovered, 30-35 minutes or until thickened. Strain and discard peel; set aside.

2. In a food processor, combine the walnuts, almonds, sugar, almond extract, cinnamon and cloves. Cover and process until finely chopped.

3. Place one sheet of phyllo dough on a work surface; brush with butter. Repeat with two more sheets of phyllo, brushing each with butter. (Keep remaining phyllo covered with plastic wrap and a damp towel to prevent it from drying out.) Sprinkle with ⅓ cup nut mixture. Repeat layers twice.

4. Roll up jelly-roll style, starting with a long side. Brush roll with butter. Trim edges. Cut into 16 slices, about ¾ in. each. Place cut side down on a greased 15x10x1-in. baking pan. Repeat with remaining phyllo, butter and filling.

5. Bake at 350° for 10 minutes. Gently turn cookies over; bake 10-15 minutes longer or until golden brown. Cool for 5 minutes before removing from pans to wire racks over waxed paper.

6. Spoon half of the syrup over cookies. Let stand for 15 minutes. Drizzle with remaining syrup. Cool completely.
TO MAKE AHEAD *Prepare as directed. Freeze in a single layer on a waxed paper-lined baking sheet. Once frozen, package in freezer bags, separating layers with waxed paper. Thaw in a single layer before serving.*

NOVEMBER 17
NATIONAL
BAKLAVA
DAY

NOVEMBER 21
NATIONAL GINGERBREAD DAY

GINGERBREAD BABIES

It's that time of year again...time for gingerbread! These mini treats are sturdy enough to pack and ship to friends and family.
—*TASTE OF HOME* TEST KITCHEN

PREP: 2 HOURS + CHILLING
BAKE: 10 MIN./BATCH + STANDING
MAKES: ABOUT 2½ DOZEN

- ¾ cup butter, softened
- 1 cup packed brown sugar
- 1 large egg
- ¾ cup molasses
- 4 cups all-purpose flour
- 2 tablespoons baking cocoa
- 2 teaspoons ground ginger
- 1½ teaspoons baking soda
- 1½ teaspoons ground cinnamon
- ¾ teaspoon ground cloves
- ½ teaspoon ground cardamom
- ½ teaspoon ground nutmeg
- ¼ teaspoon salt

ICING

- 2 cups confectioners' sugar
- 2 tablespoons plus 2 teaspoons water
- 4½ teaspoons meringue powder
- ¼ teaspoon cream of tartar
  Red paste food coloring

1. In a large bowl, cream butter and brown sugar until light and fluffy. Beat in egg and molasses. Combine flour, cocoa, ginger, baking soda, cinnamon, cloves, cardamom, nutmeg and salt; gradually add to creamed mixture and mix well. Cover and refrigerate 2 hours or until easy to handle.

2. Preheat oven to 350°. On a lightly floured surface, roll dough to ⅜-in. thickness. Cut with a floured 4-in. gingerbread man cookie cutter. Place 2 in. apart on ungreased baking sheets; reroll scraps.

3. Bake 8-10 minutes or until edges are firm. Remove to wire racks to cool.

4. For icing, in a large bowl, combine the confectioners' sugar, water, meringue powder and cream of tartar; beat on low speed just until combined. Beat on high 4-5 minutes or until stiff peaks form. Tint desired amount of icing red. (Keep unused icing covered at all times with a damp cloth.)

5. Using pastry bags and small round tips, decorate cookies as desired. Let dry at room temperature for several hours or until firm. Store in an airtight container.

FREEZE OPTION *Freeze undecorated cookies, layered between waxed paper, in freezer containers. To use, thaw and decorate as desired.*

PEPPERY SNAPS

I love to bake, and I spend most of my time at it. I have a job as a baker and keep my family supplied with sweet treats. My father-in-law said he'd love a cookie that was "snappy," so I combined a few recipes into this one.
—JOANIE ELBOURN GARDNER, MA

PREP: 15 MIN. + CHILLING
BAKE: 10 MIN./BATCH • **MAKES:** 6-7 DOZEN

- 1¼ cups all-purpose flour
- 1 cup whole wheat flour
- 1½ teaspoons baking soda
- 1 teaspoon ground aniseed
- ½ teaspoon salt
- ½ teaspoon ground ginger
- ¼ teaspoon pepper
- 1 cup packed light brown sugar
- 3 tablespoons light molasses
- ¾ cup butter, softened
- 1 large egg
  Sugar

1. Combine first seven ingredients; set aside. In a bowl, beat the brown sugar, molasses, butter and egg. Stir in dry ingredients; mix well. Chill for 1 hour.

2. Shape into 1-in. balls. Roll in sugar and place on ungreased baking sheets. Bake at 350° for 10-13 minutes. Cool cookies about 1 minute before removing to wire racks.

MACADAMIA-COFFEE BEAN COOKIES

Nearly anyone who loves coffee will perk up for this java-infused cookie. What hot beverage would you pair these treats with? For me, there's only one answer!

—KATHY SPECHT CLINTON, MT

PREP: 20 MIN. • **BAKE:** 10 MIN./BATCH
MAKES: ABOUT 2½ DOZEN

- 1 package (17½ ounces) double chocolate chunk cookie mix
- 1 large egg
- ¼ cup canola oil
- 2 tablespoons water
- 1½ cups chocolate-covered coffee beans, finely chopped
- 1 cup macadamia nuts, chopped

1. In a large bowl, beat the cookie mix, egg, oil and water until blended. Stir in coffee beans and nuts.

2. Drop by tablespoonfuls 2 in. apart onto greased baking sheets. Bake at 375° for 8-10 minutes or until set. Remove to wire racks to cool. Store in an airtight container.

HAPPY THANKS-GIVING!

TURKEY PILGRIM COOKIES

These darling little gobblers are fun to make and will bring smiles to all of your Turkey Day guests.

—TASTE OF HOME **TEST KITCHEN**

START TO FINISH: 30 MIN.
MAKES: 1 DOZEN

Short & Sweet

- 84 **pieces candy corn**
- 24 **Oreo Double Stuf cookies**
- ¾ **cup canned chocolate frosting**
- 12 **miniature peanut butter cups**
- 12 **Hershey Kisses of your choice**
- ¾ **cup canned vanilla frosting**
  Orange food coloring
- 6 **miniature marshmallows, halved**
- 6 **mini Oreo cookies**
- 12 **Rolo candies**

1. Insert seven pieces of candy corn in a fan shape into half of the Double Stuf cookies. Position each of the cookies perpendicular to a remaining Double Stuf cookie; attach cookies with chocolate frosting.

2. Using chocolate frosting, attach a peanut butter cup and a kiss to the front of each cookie. Tint vanilla frosting with orange food coloring. For eyes, attach two marshmallow halves to each kiss with a small amount of orange frosting.

3. Twist mini cookies apart; remove and discard cream filling. Attach a Rolo to each mini cookie half with chocolate frosting and attach to tops of turkeys.

4. Using remaining frosting, pipe pupils, mouths and legs on turkeys. Let stand until set.

PILGRIM HAT COOKIES

We dreamed up this combination for a yummy treat to take to school before our Thanksgiving break. Everyone loved them!

—**MEGAN AND MITCHELL VOGEL**
JEFFERSON, WI

Short & Sweet

PREP: 1 HOUR
MAKES: 32 COOKIES

- 1 **cup vanilla frosting**
- 7 **drops yellow food coloring**
- 32 **miniature peanut butter cups**
- 1 **package (11½ ounces) fudge-striped cookies**
- 32 **pieces orange mini Chiclets gum**

1. In a small shallow bowl, combine frosting and food coloring. Remove paper liners from peanut butter cups.

2. Holding the bottom of a peanut butter cup, dip top of cup in the yellow frosting. Position over center hole on the bottom of cookie, forming the hatband and crown. Add a buckle of Chiclets gum. Repeat with remaining cups and cookies.

★ ★ ★ ★ ★ **READER REVIEW**

"Super easy and very cute. Had 2 dozen Pilgrim Hat Cookies done in minutes. Could not find the Chiclets, but was able to find Tic Tacs in a color that worked perfectly."

WINTERMOM9597 TASTEOFHOME.COM

HANDPRINT TURKEY COOKIES

Creating these tom treats is just as much fun as gobbling them up! When preparing this delicious cookie recipe years ago, I used to help our children cut out their own hand shapes from the rolled dough. Today they're all grown, but they still remember how much they enjoyed baking their hands!

—PAT THOMPSON SUN PRAIRIE, WI

PREP: 30 MIN. + CHILLING
BAKE: 10 MIN./BATCH
MAKES: ABOUT 3 DOZEN

- ¼ cup shortening
- ¼ cup butter, softened
- 1 cup sugar
- 1 large egg
- 1 teaspoon vanilla extract
- 2⅔ cups all-purpose flour
- 1 teaspoon baking powder
- ½ teaspoon baking soda
- ½ teaspoon salt
- ¼ teaspoon ground nutmeg
- ½ cup sour cream

GLAZE
- 5 cups confectioners' sugar
- 3 to 4 tablespoons water
- 2¼ teaspoons light corn syrup
- ¾ teaspoon vanilla extract
  Red, yellow, orange, green and brown gel food coloring

1. In a large bowl, cream the shortening, butter and sugar until light and fluffy. Beat in egg and vanilla. Combine the flour, baking powder, baking soda, salt and nutmeg; add to the creamed mixture alternately with sour cream. Cover and refrigerate for 2 hours or until dough is easy to handle.

2. Use a floured 3¾-in. hand-shaped cookie cutter or trace a child's hand onto a piece of cardboard with pencil and cut out for a pattern.

3. On a well-floured surface, roll out dough to a ½-in. thickness. Either use cookie cutter to cut dough into hand shapes or use a sharp knife to cut around the cardboard hand pattern in the dough. Place 2 in. apart on ungreased baking sheets. Bake at 425° for 7-9 minutes or until lightly browned. Remove to wire racks to cool.

4. In a small bowl, combine the glaze ingredients and beat until smooth. If desired, set aside 1 teaspoon of white glaze for eyes. Place ¼ cup of glaze into each of four bowls. Tint one red, one yellow, one orange and one green. Place 1 tablespoon of glaze in another bowl and tint dark brown. Tint remaining glaze light brown.

5. Frost the palm and thumb of each cookie light brown. Frost each finger a different color, using red, yellow, orange and green.

6. Place the remaining yellow glaze in a pastry or plastic bag. Cut a small hole in the corner of bag. Pipe a beak onto each thumb.

7. Repeat with dark brown glaze to pipe wings in the center of each cookie and eyes on each thumb (or, if desired, pipe white glaze for eyeballs and dark brown glaze for pupils).

8. Use remaining red glaze to pipe wattles on each thumb. Let cookies dry completely.

FINISHED SIZE *Cookies shown measure about 2¾ inches across.*

CRANBERRY PUMPKIN COOKIES

Brightly colored dried cranberries add a pleasant tang to these moist gems. You'll want to have these handy for snacking after Thanksgiving dinner!

—**KRISTEN FITZGERALD** STRATFORD, CT

PREP: 15 MIN. • **BAKE:** 20 MIN.
MAKES: ABOUT ½ DOZEN

- 6 tablespoons butter, softened
- ½ cup packed brown sugar
- ¼ cup sugar
- ½ cup canned pumpkin
- 2 tablespoons beaten egg
- ¼ teaspoon vanilla extract
- ¾ cup all-purpose flour
- ½ cup quick-cooking oats
- ¼ cup whole wheat flour
- ½ teaspoon baking soda
- ¼ teaspoon ground ginger
- ¼ teaspoon ground cinnamon
- ⅛ teaspoon salt
- ⅛ teaspoon ground nutmeg
- ⅛ teaspoon ground allspice
- ¼ cup dried cranberries

1. In a large bowl, cream butter and sugars until light and fluffy. Beat in the pumpkin, egg and vanilla. Combine the all-purpose flour, oats, whole wheat flour, baking soda, ginger, cinnamon, salt, nutmeg and allspice; gradually add to creamed mixture. Fold in cranberries.
2. Drop by ¼ cupfuls 2 in. apart onto a baking sheet coated with cooking spray. Bake at 350° for 20-22 minutes or until lightly browned. Remove to wire racks to cool.

TOM TURKEYS

With a little prep work by Mom or Dad, these make a great before- or after-dinner craft project for kids.

—TASTE OF HOME **TEST KITCHEN**

PREP: 30 MIN. • **COOK:** 5 MIN. + COOLING
MAKES: 26 TURKEYS

- 1 **package (12 ounces) semisweet chocolate chips**
- 1 **package (11 ounces) candy corn**
- 52 **fudge-striped cookies**
- ¼ **cup butter, cubed**
- 4 **cups miniature marshmallows**
- 6 **cups crisp rice cereal**
- 52 **white confetti sprinkles**

1. In a microwave, melt chocolate chips; stir until smooth. For tails, use a dab of chocolate to attach five candy corns to the chocolate side of half of the cookies in a fan shape; refrigerate until set.

2. In a large saucepan, melt butter. Add marshmallows; stir over low heat until melted. Stir in cereal. Cool for 10 minutes. With buttered hands, form cereal mixture into 1½-in. balls.

3. Remelt chocolate if necessary. Using chocolate, attach the cereal balls to the chocolate side of the remaining cookies. Position tails perpendicular to the base cookies; attach with chocolate. Refrigerate until set.

4. For turkey feet, cut off white tips from 52 candy corns; discard tips. Attach feet to base cookies with chocolate. Attach one candy corn to each cereal ball for heads.

5. With a toothpick dipped in chocolate, attach two confetti sprinkles to each head. Using chocolate, dot each sprinkle to make pupils. Let stand until set. Store in an airtight container.

OWL COOKIES

I came up with these cookies as a treat for my kids' class parties. They're a hit!
—**STARRLETTE HOWARD** OGDEN, UT

PREP: 35 MIN. + CHILLING • **BAKE:** 15 MIN.
MAKES: 1 DOZEN

- ⅔ **cup butter, softened**
- 1 **cup creamy peanut butter**
- 1 **cup packed brown sugar**
- 1 **large egg**
- 1 **teaspoon vanilla extract**
- 1⅓ **cups all-purpose flour**
- 1 **cup quick-cooking oats**
- 1 **teaspoon baking powder**
- ½ **teaspoon salt**
- 1 **ounce unsweetened chocolate, melted**
- 12 **whole cashews**
- 24 **striped chocolate kisses, unwrapped**
- 24 **semisweet chocolate chips**

1. In a large bowl, beat butter, peanut butter and brown sugar until blended. Beat in egg and vanilla. In another bowl, mix flour, oats, baking powder and salt; gradually beat into creamed mixture.

2. If necessary, cover and refrigerate dough 1 hour or until firm enough to shape. Divide dough in half; shape one portion into an 8-in.-long roll. Mix melted chocolate into remaining dough. Roll chocolate dough between two sheets of waxed paper into an 8-in. square. Place plain roll on chocolate dough. Wrap chocolate dough around plain dough, pinching together at the seam to seal. Wrap in plastic; refrigerate 3 hours or until firm.

3. Preheat oven to 350°. Unwrap and cut dough crosswise into 24 slices ⅜ in. thick. To make owls, place two slices side by side on an ungreased baking sheet; pinch the top of each slice for ears. Place a cashew between slices for a beak. Repeat with remaining dough.

4. Bake 12-15 minutes or until set. Cool on pans 5 minutes before removing to wire racks. While cookies are warm, place two kisses on each cookie, pointed side down, for eyes. (Kisses will melt slightly.) Top each kiss with a chocolate chip.

APPLE OATMEAL COOKIES

I took these yummy cookies to work and they were gone in seconds. They're a welcome snack that's low in calories!

—NICKI WOODS SPRINGFIELD, MO

PREP: 10 MIN.
BAKE: 15 MIN./BATCH
MAKES: ABOUT 5 DOZEN

Short & Sweet

- 1 package yellow cake mix (regular size)
- 1½ cups quick-cooking oats
- ½ cup packed brown sugar
- 2 teaspoons ground cinnamon
- 1 large egg
- ¾ cup unsweetened applesauce
- 1 cup finely chopped peeled apple
- ½ cup raisins

1. In a large bowl, combine the cake mix, oats, brown sugar and cinnamon. In a small bowl, combine the egg, applesauce, apple and raisins. Stir into oat mixture and mix well.

2. Drop by heaping teaspoonfuls 2 in. apart onto baking sheets coated with cooking spray. Bake cookies at 350° for 12-14 minutes or until golden brown. Let stand for 2 minutes before removing to wire racks to cool.

★ ★ ★ ★ ★ **READER REVIEW**

"My picky 3-year-old came back begging for more cookies! These cookies make me feel less guilty for eating them and giving them to my son since they have apples, oatmeal and raisins in them."

AMANDA TASTEOFHOME.COM

VANILLA-GLAZED APPLE COOKIES

My mother gave me the recipe for this fruit and nut cookie. It has been a favorite in our family for many years.

—**SHARON CRIDER** JUNCTION CITY, KS

PREP: 25 MIN. • **BAKE:** 10 MIN./BATCH
MAKES: ABOUT 4 DOZEN

- ½ **cup shortening**
- 1⅓ **cups packed brown sugar**
- 1 **large egg**
- ¼ **cup 2% milk**
- 2 **cups all-purpose flour**
- 1 **teaspoon baking soda**
- 1 **teaspoon ground nutmeg**
- 1 **teaspoon ground cinnamon**
- ½ **teaspoon ground cloves**
- 1 **cup chopped walnuts**
- 1 **cup finely diced peeled apple**
- 1 **cup raisins**

VANILLA GLAZE

- 1½ **cups confectioners' sugar**
- 1 **tablespoon butter, melted**
- ½ **teaspoon vanilla extract**
- ⅛ **teaspoon salt**
- 2 **to 4 teaspoons 2% milk**

1. Preheat oven to 400°. In a large bowl, cream shortening and brown sugar until light and fluffy. Beat in egg and milk. Combine the flour, baking soda, nutmeg, cinnamon and cloves; gradually add to the creamed mixture and mix well. Stir in walnuts, apple and raisins.

2. Drop by rounded tablespoonfuls 2 in. apart onto ungreased baking sheets. Bake 8-10 minutes or until edges begin to brown. Remove to wire racks to cool.

3. In a small bowl, combine the confectioners' sugar, butter, vanilla, salt and enough milk to achieve drizzling consistency. Drizzle over warm cookies.

CINNAMON STARS

These cookies are such a hit with my family. A few always disappear before I can finish decorating them! They're nice for any time.
—**FLO BURTNETT** GAGE, OK

PREP: 25 MIN. + CHILLING • **BAKE:** 10 MIN.
MAKES: 2½ DOZEN SANDWICH COOKIES

- 2 **cups all-purpose flour**
- 1 **cup sugar**
- 1 **teaspoon ground cinnamon**
- ¾ **teaspoon baking powder**
- ¼ **teaspoon salt**
- ½ **cup cold butter, cubed**
- 1 **large egg, lightly beaten**
- ¼ **cup milk**

GLAZE/FILLING

- 2 **cups confectioners' sugar**
- ½ **teaspoon vanilla extract**
- 2 **to 3 tablespoons milk**
  Colored sugar, optional
- ⅔ **cup raspberry, strawberry or apricot jam**

1. In a medium bowl, combine flour, sugar, cinnamon, baking powder and salt. Cut in butter until crumbly. Combine egg and milk; add to flour mixture and stir just until moistened. Cover and chill at least 1 hour.

2. On a lightly floured surface, roll dough to ⅛-in. thickness. Cut with a 3-in. cookie cutter dipped in flour. Place on ungreased baking sheets. Bake at 375° for 7-9 minutes or until edges are lightly brown. Remove to a wire rack; cool completely.

3. For glaze, combine sugar, vanilla and enough milk to achieve a spreading consistency. Spread on half of the cookies; sprinkle with colored sugar if desired. Let stand until sugar is set. Place 1 teaspoon of jam on each of the unglazed cookies and top each with a glazed cookie.

NOVEMBER 28
NATIONAL FRENCH TOAST DAY

FRENCH TOAST COOKIES

I created these soft, sparkly cookies because my sister loves cinnamon French toast covered in maple syrup. In the case of these cookies, bigger is definitely better! I like to use white whole wheat flour, but any whole wheat flour will work.

—MARY SHENK DEKALB, IL

PREP: 25 MIN. + CHILLING • **BAKE:** 15 MIN.
MAKES: 1½ DOZEN

- ¾ cup butter, softened
- ¾ cup sugar, divided
- ½ cup packed brown sugar
- 1 large egg
- ⅓ cup corn syrup
- 2 teaspoons vanilla extract
- 2 teaspoons maple flavoring
- 1¼ cups all-purpose flour
- 1 cup whole wheat flour
- 2 teaspoons ground cinnamon
- 1 teaspoon baking soda
- ½ teaspoon salt

1. In a large bowl, cream butter, ½ cup sugar and brown sugar until light and fluffy. Beat in egg, corn syrup, vanilla and flavoring. In another bowl, whisk the remaining ingredients; gradually beat into creamed mixture. Refrigerate, covered, 1 hour or until firm enough to shape.

2. Preheat oven to 375°. Place remaining sugar in a shallow bowl. Shape dough into 1¾-in. balls; roll in sugar. Place 2 in. apart on parchment paper-lined baking sheets.

3. Bake 11-13 minutes or until edges are golden brown. Remove from pans to wire racks to cool.

MAYAN CHOCOLATE BISCOTTI

Those who enjoy Mexican hot chocolate will also like the subtle sweetness and slight heat found in every bite of this perked-up biscotti.

—CHRIS MICHALOWSKI DALLAS, TX

PREP: 35 MIN. • **BAKE:** 40 MIN. + COOLING
MAKES: 2 DOZEN

- ½ cup butter, softened
- ¾ cup sugar
- 2 large eggs

- 1½ teaspoons coffee liqueur
- 1½ teaspoons vanilla extract
- 2 cups all-purpose flour
- 1½ teaspoons ground ancho chili pepper
- ½ teaspoon baking soda
- ½ teaspoon baking powder
- ½ teaspoon ground cinnamon
- ⅛ teaspoon salt
- 1½ cups chopped pecans
- 1 cup (6 ounces) semisweet chocolate chips
- 1 ounce 53% cacao dark baking chocolate, grated

1. In a large bowl, cream the butter and sugar until light and fluffy. Add eggs, one at a time, beating well after each addition. Stir in coffee liqueur and vanilla. Combine the flour, chili pepper, baking soda, baking powder, cinnamon and salt; gradually add to creamed mixture and mix well. Stir in the chopped pecans, chocolate chips and grated chocolate.

2. Divide dough in half. On an ungreased baking sheet, shape each half into a 10x2-in. rectangle. Bake at 350° for 20-25 minutes or until set and lightly browned.

3. Place pans on wire racks. When cool enough to handle, transfer to a cutting board; cut diagonally with a serrated knife into ¾-in. slices. Place cut side down on ungreased baking sheets.

4. Bake for 8-10 minutes on each side or until both sides are golden brown. Remove to wire racks to cool completely. Store in an airtight container.

TAKE-ALONG BREAKFAST COOKIES

These cookies are perfect for an energizing breakfast when you're on the go. Although they're called breakfast cookies, they're delicious any time of the day any season of the year.

—PAM CROCKETT HUNTSVILLE, UT

PREP: 25 MIN. • **BAKE:** 10 MIN.
MAKES: 1 DOZEN

½ cup butter, softened
½ cup peanut butter
1 cup packed brown sugar
1 large egg
3 tablespoons milk
1 teaspoon vanilla extract
1 cup old-fashioned oats
¾ cup whole wheat flour
½ cup nonfat dry milk powder
¼ cup toasted wheat germ
½ teaspoon salt
¼ teaspoon baking soda
¼ teaspoon baking powder
1 cup golden raisins
3 tablespoons sesame seeds

1. In a large bowl, cream the butter, peanut butter and brown sugar until light and fluffy. Beat in the egg, milk and vanilla. Combine the oats, flour, milk powder, wheat germ, salt, baking soda and baking powder; gradually add to creamed mixture and mix well. Stir in raisins.

2. Drop by ¼ cupfuls 4 in. apart onto a greased baking sheet. Flatten into 3-in. circles. Sprinkle with sesame seeds.

3. Bake at 375° for 10-12 minutes or until edges are lightly browned. Cool for 5 minutes before removing to a wire rack.

SOUTHERN TEA CAKES

There were nine children in our family, and Mother had to stretch the budget, so she made these often for dessert. I loved them when I was a child, and they're still a special treat today. I've never met anyone who doesn't like the cookies. They're so simple, quick to make and delightful.

—MARY SINGLETARY CONVERSE, LA

START TO FINISH: 30 MIN.
MAKES: ABOUT 3 DOZEN

- 1 **cup shortening**
- 1¾ **cups sugar**
- 2 **large eggs**
- ½ **cup milk**
- ½ **teaspoon vanilla extract**
- 3 **cups self-rising flour**

1. In a bowl, cream together shortening and sugar. Beat in eggs. Add milk and vanilla; beat well. Stir in flour; mix well.
2. Drop by tablespoonfuls 2½ in. apart onto greased baking sheets. Bake at 350° for 15-20 minutes.

MINIATURE PEANUT BUTTER TREATS

I have three children and eight grandchildren, and every one of them loves these "peanut butter thingies," as the grandchildren like to call them.

—JODIE MCCOY TULSA, OK

PREP: 20 MIN. + CHILLING
BAKE: 10 MIN./BATCH + COOLING
MAKES: ABOUT 3½ DOZEN

COOKIE
- ½ **cup butter, softened**
- ½ **cup sugar**
- ½ **cup packed brown sugar**
- 1 **large egg**
- ½ **cup creamy peanut butter**
- ½ **teaspoon vanilla extract**
- 1¼ **cups all-purpose flour**
- ¾ **teaspoon baking soda**
- ½ **teaspoon salt**

FILLING
About 42 miniature peanut butter-chocolate cups

1. In a bowl, combine the butter, sugars, egg, peanut butter and vanilla; beat until smooth. Combine the flour, baking soda and salt; gradually add to creamed mixture. Cover and chill for 1 hour or until easy to handle.

2. Roll into walnut-sized balls; place in greased miniature muffin cups. Bake at 375° for 8-9 minutes.

3. Remove from oven; gently press one peanut butter cup into each cookie, forming a depression. Cool for 10 minutes before removing to wire racks to cool completely.

★ ★ ★ ★ ★ **READER REVIEW**

"A peanut-butter-cup lover's dream—and so easy! Family and friends loved these, and it's something I'll fix when I need a quick dessert."

LUIGIMON TASTEOFHOME.COM

CHOCOLATE CHIP OATMEAL COOKIES

I am crazy about chocolate chips, and this chewy cookie has enough to satisfy me. My husband nibbles on the dough, and my kids love the cookies. This big batch is perfect, even for our small family.

—DIANE NETH MENNO, SD

PREP: 20 MIN. • **BAKE:** 10 MIN./BATCH
MAKES: ABOUT 7 DOZEN

- 1 cup butter, softened
- ¾ cup sugar
- ¾ cup packed brown sugar
- 2 large eggs
- 1 teaspoon vanilla extract
- 3 cups quick-cooking oats
- 1½ cups all-purpose flour
- 1 package (3.4 ounces) instant vanilla pudding mix
- 1 teaspoon baking soda
- 1 teaspoon salt
- 2 cups (12 ounces) semisweet chocolate chips
- 1 cup chopped nuts

1. In a large bowl, cream butter and sugars until light and fluffy. Beat in eggs and vanilla. Combine the oats, flour, dry pudding mix, baking soda and salt; gradually add to creamed mixture and mix well. Stir in chocolate chips and nuts.
2. Drop by level tablespoonfuls 2 in. apart onto ungreased baking sheets. Bake at 375° for 10-12 minutes or until lightly browned. Remove to wire racks.

DECEMBER 4
NATIONAL COOKIE DAY

THE MOST WONDERFUL TIME OF YEAR

Everyone is a cookie lover this time of year! After all, cute cutouts, spritz cookies, peppermint bites and other holiday classics hit everyone's sweet spot. Turn to this bonus chapter for all your Christmas cookie needs. Whether baking treats with the kids, planning homemade gifts, hosting a cookie exchange or simply celebrating the season with friends, you can't go wrong with the Christmas cookies found here. Happy holidays!

LOOK FOR THE SPECIAL DAYS IN THIS CHAPTER:

Make this Christmas your merriest yet with five tasty nods to seasonal classics. The perfect excuse for a sweet snacking, these holidays promise to make spirits bright!

DECEMBER 27
NATIONAL FRUITCAKE DAY

WHIPPED SHORTBREAD

I love this version of shortbread because it's tender, not too sweet and melts in your mouth. Mostly I make it for the holidays, but I'll also prepare it year-round for wedding showers and afternoon tea parties.
—**JANE FICIUR** BOW ISLAND, AB

PREP: 50 MIN. • **BAKE:** 20 MIN./BATCH
MAKES: 16-18 DOZEN

   3   **cups butter, softened**
   1½ **cups confectioners' sugar, sifted**
   4½ **cups all-purpose flour**
   1½ **cups cornstarch**
       **Nonpareils and/or halved
       candied cherries**

1. In a large bowl, cream butter and confectioners' sugar until light and fluffy. Gradually add flour and cornstarch, beating until well blended.

2. With hands lightly dusted with additional cornstarch, roll dough into 1-in. balls. Place 1 in. apart on ungreased baking sheets. Press lightly with a floured fork. Top with nonpareils or candied cherry halves.

3. Bake at 300° for 20-22 minutes or until bottoms are lightly browned. Cool for 5 minutes before removing from pans to wire racks.

BUTTERY LEMON SANDWICH COOKIES

My grandson approves of these lemony sandwich cookies made with crackers and prepared frosting. Decorate with whatever sprinkles you like.

—NANCY FOUST STONEBORO, PA

PREP: 20 MIN. + STANDING
MAKES: 2½ DOZEN

- ¾ cup lemon frosting
- 60 Ritz crackers
- 24 ounces white candy coating, melted
  Nonpareils, jimmies or sprinkles, optional

Spread frosting on bottoms of half of the crackers; cover with remaining crackers. Dip sandwiches in melted candy coating; allow excess to drip off. Place on waxed paper; decorate as desired. Let stand until set. Store in an airtight container in the refrigerator.

STACKED SNOWMAN COOKIES

Though they hold their cute snowman shape well, these cookies are still nice and soft. Kids love the design and everyone loves the chocolate flavor packed into every bite.

—EVANGELINE BRADFORD ERLANGER, KY

PREP: 1 HOUR + CHILLING
BAKE: 10 MIN. + STANDING • **MAKES:** 3 DOZEN

- 1 cup unsalted butter, softened
- 1¾ cups sugar
- 2 large eggs
- 2 teaspoons vanilla extract
- 2¾ cups all-purpose flour
- ¾ cup Dutch-processed cocoa
- 1 teaspoon baking powder
- ½ teaspoon salt

ICING

- 2 cups confectioners' sugar
- 4½ teaspoons meringue powder
- ⅓ to ½ cup water
- ¼ teaspoon almond extract, optional
  Black, orange and brown paste food coloring

1. In a large bowl, cream butter and sugar until light and fluffy. Beat in eggs and vanilla. In another bowl, whisk flour, cocoa, baking powder and salt; gradually beat into creamed mixture. Divide dough in half. Shape each into a disk; wrap in plastic. Refrigerate for 30 minutes or until firm enough to roll.

2. Preheat oven to 350°. On a lightly floured surface, roll one portion of dough to ¼-in. thickness. With a 2-in. round cookie cutter, cut out 18 circles. Repeat with 1½-in. and 1-in. round cookie cutters. Place 1 in. apart on parchment paper-lined baking sheets. Repeat with remaining dough. Bake for 7-10 minutes or until edges are set. Cool completely on wire racks.

3. Meanwhile, in a small bowl, combine confectioner's sugar, meringue powder, ⅓ cup water and, if desired, extract; beat on low speed just until combined. Beat on high 4-5 minutes or until stiff peaks form. Add enough remaining water until icing no longer holds a peak. Keep unused icing covered at all times with a damp cloth. Using a pastry bag and #2 round tip, pipe icing over cookies. Let stand at least 5 minutes before gently stacking cookies to create snowmen. Let stand at room temperature several hours or until frosting is dry and firm. Using a new paintbrush, decorate snowmen as desired with food coloring.

BRANDY SNAP CANNOLI

This recipe combines two classics...brandy snaps and cannoli. You can assemble and chill them up to an hour before serving.
—TASTE OF HOME **TEST KITCHEN**

PREP: 1½ HOURS
BAKE: 5 MIN./BATCH + COOLING
MAKES: ABOUT 2 DOZEN

- ½ **cup butter, cubed**
- ½ **cup sugar**
- 3 **tablespoons molasses**
- 1 **teaspoon ground ginger**
- ¼ **teaspoon salt**
- 1 **cup all-purpose flour**
- 2 **tablespoons brandy**

FILLING
- 1½ **cups ricotta cheese**
- 3 **tablespoons grated orange peel**
- 3 **tablespoons sugar, divided**
- 1½ **cups miniature semisweet chocolate chips, divided**
- 1½ **cups heavy whipping cream**

1. In a small saucepan, combine the first five ingredients. Cook and stir over medium heat until butter is melted. Remove from the heat. Stir in flour and brandy; keep warm.

2. Drop tablespoonfuls of batter onto a well-greased or parchment paper-lined baking sheet; spread each into a 4-in. circle. Bake at 350° for 5-6 minutes or until edges begin to brown. Cool for about 1 minute or just until cookie starts to firm.

3. Working quickly, loosen each cookie and curl around a metal cannoli tube to shape. Remove cookies from tubes; cool on wire racks.

4. For filling, in a large bowl, combine the ricotta, orange peel and 1 tablespoon sugar; stir in ½ cup chocolate chips. In a small bowl, beat cream on medium speed until soft peaks form. Gradually add remaining sugar, beating on high until stiff peaks form. Fold into ricotta mixture. Chill until serving.

5. Just before serving, pipe filling into cannoli shells. Dip ends in remaining chocolate chips.

MERINGUE STOCKINGS

Stocking-shaped meringues hold tangy cranberry and sweet cream cheese fillings. They're a festive addition to any Christmas cookie tray.

—CYNTHIA HAGEN GREENFIELD, WI

PREP: 30 MIN. • **BAKE:** 35 MIN. + COOLING
MAKES: 16 COOKIES

- 3 **large egg whites**
- ¼ **teaspoon cream of tartar**
- ¼ **teaspoon vanilla extract**
- ¾ **cup sugar**

CRANBERRY FILLING
- 1 **cup sugar**
- 2 **tablespoons cornstarch**
- 1 **cup cranberry juice**
- 1½ **cups fresh or frozen cranberries**

CREAM CHEESE FILLING
- 6 **ounces cream cheese, softened**
- 1 **cup confectioners' sugar**
- 1 **teaspoon vanilla extract**
- 1 **cup heavy whipping cream, whipped**
- 32 **to 48 small mint leaves**
- 24 **dried cranberries, halved**

1. Place egg whites in a large bowl; let stand at room temperature for 30 minutes. Add cream of tartar and vanilla; beat on medium speed until soft peaks form. Gradually beat in sugar, a tablespoon at a time, on high speed until stiff peaks form.

2. Line a baking sheet with parchment paper. Spoon meringue into 16 mounds on the paper. Using icing spatula, shape each into a 4½-in. stocking. Bake at 300° for 35 minutes. Turn oven off and do not open door; let meringues dry in oven for 1 hour.

3. Remove from oven and cool on baking sheet. When meringues are completely cooled, remove from parchment paper and store in an airtight container at room temperature.

4. For cranberry filling, combine the sugar, cornstarch and cranberry juice in a saucepan until smooth. Stir in the cranberries. Bring to a boil; cook and stir for 2 minutes. Reduce heat; cook until berries pop, about 5 minutes. Mash and cool.

5. For cream cheese filling, in a small bowl, beat the cream cheese, confectioners' sugar and vanilla. Fold in whipped cream. Spoon into a pastry or plastic bag. Cut a small hole in the corner of bag; insert a #18 star tip. Pipe cream cheese mixture in a 1-in. band at the top of each stocking; pipe mixture to form heel and toe of stocking.

6. Spread 4½ teaspoons cranberry filling in the center of each stocking. For the holly decoration on the stocking cuff, garnish with mint leaves and dried cranberries.

FROSTED ANISE SUGAR COOKIES

The anise flavor in these cookies is distinct but not overpowering. I add red and green sprinkles for Christmas, but you could decorate them to suit any occasion.

—JANICE EANNI WILLOWICK, OH

PREP: 30 MIN.
BAKE: 10 MIN./BATCH + COOLING
MAKES: 7 DOZEN

- 1 cup butter, softened
- 1½ cups sugar
- 6 large eggs
- 1 teaspoon vanilla extract
- ¾ teaspoon anise extract
- 3½ cups all-purpose flour
- 4 teaspoons baking powder

GLAZE

- 3 cups confectioners' sugar
- 4 teaspoons butter, softened
- ¾ teaspoon vanilla extract
- ¼ to ⅓ cup whole milk
  Colored sprinkles, optional

1. Preheat oven to 350°. In a large bowl, cream butter and sugar until light and fluffy. Beat in eggs and extracts. In another bowl, whisk flour and baking powder; gradually beat into creamed mixture.

2. Drop by tablespoonfuls 2 in. apart onto greased baking sheets. Bake for 8-10 minutes or until light brown. Remove from pans to wire racks to cool completely.

3. For glaze, in a large bowl, mix confectioners' sugar, butter, vanilla and enough milk to achieve spreading consistency. Dip tops of cookies into glaze. If desired, decorate with sprinkles. Let stand until set.

S'MORE SANDWICH COOKIES

Capture the taste of campfire s'mores in your kitchen. Graham cracker crumbs added to chocolate chip cookie dough bring out the flavor of the fireside favorite. Melting the marshmallow centers in the microwave helps make these cookies simple to assemble.

—ABBY METZGER LARCHWOOD, IA

PREP: 25 MIN. • **BAKE:** 10 MIN. + COOLING
MAKES: ABOUT 2 DOZEN

- ¾ cup butter, softened
- ½ cup sugar
- ½ cup packed brown sugar
- 1 large egg
- 2 tablespoons milk
- 1 teaspoon vanilla extract
- 1¼ cups all-purpose flour
- 1¼ cups graham cracker crumbs (about 20 squares)
- ½ teaspoon baking soda
- ¼ teaspoon salt
- ⅛ teaspoon ground cinnamon
- 2 cups (12 ounces) semisweet chocolate chips
- 24 to 28 large marshmallows

1. In a large bowl, cream butter and sugars until light and fluffy. Beat in the egg, milk and vanilla. Combine the flour, graham cracker crumbs, baking soda, salt and cinnamon; gradually add to creamed mixture and mix well. Stir in chocolate chips.

2. Drop by tablespoonfuls 2 in. apart onto ungreased baking sheets. Bake at 375° for 8-10 minutes or until golden brown. Remove to wire racks to cool.

3. Place four cookies bottom side up on a microwave-safe plate; top each with a marshmallow. Microwave, uncovered, on high for 10-15 seconds or until the marshmallows begin to puff (do not overcook). Top each with another cookie. Repeat.

NOTE *This recipe was tested in a 1,100-watt microwave.*

PEANUT BUTTER BEARS

My granddaughter wants to make cookies with me every year around the holidays. This is one of her favorite recipes.
—**ROSE REISER** GREENFIELD, IL

PREP: 30 MIN. + CHILLING • **BAKE:** 10 MIN.
MAKES: ABOUT 3 DOZEN

- 1 **cup butter, softened**
- 1 **cup creamy peanut butter**
- 1 **cup packed brown sugar**
- ⅔ **cup light corn syrup**
- 2 **large eggs**
- 4 **cups all-purpose flour**
- 3 **teaspoons baking powder**
- ¼ **teaspoon salt**

ICING
- 3¾ **to 4 cups confectioners' sugar**
- 5 **to 6 tablespoons warm water**
- 3 **tablespoons meringue powder**
  Food coloring, optional

1. In a large bowl, cream the butter, peanut butter and brown sugar. Beat in the corn syrup and eggs. Combine the flour, baking powder and salt; gradually add to the creamed mixture. Cover and refrigerate for 2 hours or until dough is easy to handle.

2. On a lightly floured surface, roll out dough to ⅛-in. thickness. Cut with a floured 4-in. bear-shaped cookie cutter. Place 2 in. apart on ungreased baking sheets. Roll leftover dough. Cut circles with a floured ¾-in. pastry tip; press gently into each cookie, forming the bear's muzzle.

3. Bake at 350° for 10-12 minutes or until set. Remove to wire racks to cool.

4. In a large bowl, combine the confectioners' sugar, water and meringue powder; beat on low speed just until blended. Beat on high for 4-5 minutes or until stiff peaks form. Tint as desired with food coloring. Keep unused icing covered at all times with a damp cloth. If necessary, beat again on high speed to restore texture.

5. Using pastry bags and small round tips, decorate as desired. Let stand at room temperature until frosting is dry and firm. Store in an airtight container.

STAINED GLASS CHERRY MACAROONS

Macaroons have been around for ages. I wanted to keep true to the original family-favorite cookie but add a neat twist. Make sure the eggs are at room temperature before beating them.
—**JAMIE JONES** MADISON, GA

PREP: 45 MIN. • **BAKE:** 15 MIN./BATCH
MAKES: ABOUT 7 DOZEN

- 6 **large egg whites**
- ¾ **teaspoon vanilla extract**
- ½ **teaspoon salt**
- ¾ **cup sugar**
- 8 **cups flaked coconut (22 ounces)**
- ¾ **cup finely chopped green candied cherries**
- ¾ **cup finely chopped red candied cherries**
- ⅓ **cup all-purpose flour**

1. Place egg whites in a large bowl; let stand at room temperature for 30 minutes. Preheat oven to 325°. Add vanilla and salt to egg whites; beat on medium speed until foamy. Gradually add sugar, 1 tablespoon at a time, beating on high after each addition until sugar is dissolved. Continue beating until stiff glossy peaks form. In another bowl, combine coconut, cherries and flour; stir into egg white mixture.

2. Drop by tablespoonfuls 1 in. apart onto parchment paper-lined baking sheets. Bake for 14-16 minutes or until edges are golden. Cool on pans for 2 minutes. Remove to wire racks to cool. Store in an airtight container.

FREEZE OPTION *Freeze cookies, layered between waxed paper, in freezer containers. To use, thaw in covered containers.*

DECEMBER 8
NATIONAL
BROWNIE
DAY

JUMBO BROWNIE COOKIES

Bring these deeply fudgy cookies to a party, and you're sure to make a friend. A little espresso powder in the dough makes them over-the-top good.

—REBECCA CABABA LAS VEGAS, NV

PREP: 20 MIN. • **BAKE:** 15 MIN./BATCH
MAKES: ABOUT 1½ DOZEN

- 2⅔ cups (16 ounces) 60% cacao bittersweet chocolate baking chips
- ½ cup unsalted butter, cubed
- 4 large eggs
- 1½ cups sugar
- 4 teaspoons vanilla extract
- 2 teaspoons instant espresso powder, optional
- ⅔ cup all-purpose flour
- ½ teaspoon baking powder
- ¼ teaspoon salt
- 1 package (11½ ounces) semisweet chocolate chunks

1. Preheat oven to 350°. In a large saucepan, melt chocolate chips and butter over low heat, stirring until smooth. Remove from the heat; cool until mixture is warm.

2. In a small bowl, whisk the eggs, sugar, vanilla and, if desired, espresso powder until blended. Whisk into chocolate mixture. In another bowl, mix the flour, baking powder and salt; add to chocolate mixture, mixing well. Fold in the chocolate chunks; let stand for 10 minutes or until the mixture thickens slightly.

3. Drop by ¼ cupfuls 3 in. apart onto parchment paper-lined baking sheets. Bake for 12-14 minutes or until set. Cool on pans for 1-2 minutes. Remove to wire racks to cool.

NOTE *This recipe was tested with Ghirardelli 60% Cacao Bittersweet Chocolate Baking Chips; results may vary when using a different product.*

PIZZELLE

This recipe was adapted from one used by my Italian-born mother and grandmother. They used old irons on a gas stove, but now we have the convenience of electric pizzelle irons. The cookies are so delectable and beautiful...they're always worth making!

—ELIZABETH SCHWARTZ TREVORTON, PA

PREP: 10 MIN. • **COOK:** 5 MIN./BATCH
MAKES: 7 DOZEN

- 18 large eggs
- 3½ cups sugar
- 1¼ cups canola oil
- 1 tablespoon anise oil
- 6½ cups all-purpose flour

1. In a large bowl, beat the eggs, sugar and oils until smooth. Gradually add flour and mix well.

2. Bake in a preheated pizzelle iron according to manufacturer's directions until golden brown. Remove to wire racks to cool. Store in an airtight container.

FROM THE COOKIE JAR

I keep a chopstick in my flour and sugar canisters and use it to quickly level off the measuring cup without making a mess.

—TINA H. HICKORY, PA

MOLASSES CUTOUTS

Make these spicy cutouts as cute as can be, and you'll have the most popular treat at your next cookie swap.
—**DEB ANDERSON** JOPLIN, MO

PREP: 30 MIN. + CHILLING
BAKE: 10 MIN./BATCH
MAKES: ABOUT 3 DOZEN

- ⅔ **cup shortening**
- 1¼ **cups sugar**
- 2 **large eggs**
- 2 **tablespoons buttermilk**
- 2 **tablespoons molasses**
- 3½ **cups all-purpose flour**
- 1 **teaspoon salt**
- 1 **teaspoon baking soda**
- 1 **teaspoon baking powder**
- 1 **teaspoon ground ginger**
- ½ **teaspoon ground cloves**
  Optional decorations: confectioners' sugar icing, colored sugar, sprinkles and nonpareils

1. In a large bowl, cream shortening and sugar until light and fluffy. Beat in eggs, buttermilk and molasses. In another bowl, whisk flour, salt, baking soda, baking powder, ginger and cloves; gradually beat into creamed mixture.
2. Divide dough in half. Shape each into a disk; wrap in plastic. Refrigerate for 2 hours or until firm enough to roll.
3. Preheat oven to 375°. On a lightly floured surface, roll each portion of dough to ⅛-in. thickness. Cut with a floured 3-in. cookie cutter. Place 2 in. apart on greased baking sheets.
4. Bake for 8-10 minutes or until edges begin to brown. Remove from pans to wire racks to cool completely. Decorate as desired.
FREEZE OPTION *Freeze undecorated cookies in freezer containers. To use, thaw in covered containers and decorate as desired.*

PECAN PINWHEELS

Chewy centers, a fancy shape and candied cherries make these cookies fun and festive. They're a favorite in my house at Christmastime.

—LORRAINE ROTHERMICH
PORTAGE DES SIOUX, MO

PREP: 1 HOUR + CHILLING
BAKE: 10 MIN./BATCH • **MAKES:** 5 DOZEN

- 1 **cup heavy whipping cream**
- 1 **teaspoon white vinegar**
- 1 **package (¼ ounce) active dry yeast**
- 2 **large egg yolks**
- 2 **cups all-purpose flour**
- ½ **teaspoon salt**
- ½ **cup cold butter**

FILLING

- ½ **cup finely chopped pecans**
- ¼ **cup plus 2 tablespoons sugar, divided**
- ¼ **cup packed brown sugar**
- 2 **tablespoons 2% milk**
- 30 **candied cherries, halved**

1. Place cream in large bowl; let stand out at room temperature for 1 hour. Add vinegar; stir until thickened. Stir in yeast until dissolved; add the egg yolks. In a small bowl, combine flour and salt. Cut in butter. Gradually add to creamed mixture and mix well. Divide dough in half; wrap in plastic. Cover and refrigerate dough overnight.

2. In a small saucepan, combine the pecans, ¼ cup sugar, brown sugar and milk. Cook and stir over medium heat for 3 minutes; set aside.

3. On a floured surface, roll each portion of dough into a 12x10-in. rectangle. With a sharp knife or pastry wheel, cut dough into 2-in. squares. Place 3 in. apart on lightly greased baking sheets.

4. Cut through the dough from each corner of the square to within ½ in. of the center. Spoon ½ teaspoon of filling into the center of each square. Fold alternating points of the square to the center to form a pinwheel. Press a cherry half into the center of each. Sprinkle with remaining sugar.

5. Bake at 350° for 10-12 minutes or until edges begin to brown. Remove to wire racks. Store in an airtight container.

ELF COOKIES

A sweet frosting glaze, colorful candies and well-placed almond slices turn these sugar cookie diamonds into a big batch of Santa's helpers. Bake a batch of the adorable elves as a classroom treat or use a few to brighten each of your cookie trays.

—TASTE OF HOME TEST KITCHEN

PREP: 45 MIN. • **BAKE:** 10 MIN.
MAKES: 28 COOKIES

- ½ **tube refrigerated sugar cookie dough, softened**
- ⅓ **cup all-purpose flour**
- 2½ **cups confectioners' sugar**
- 10 **teaspoons water**
- 4 **teaspoons meringue powder**
  Assorted food coloring
  Assorted sprinkles, candies and almond slices

1. Preheat the oven to 350°. In a small bowl, beat cookie dough and flour until combined. Roll out on a lightly floured surface to ⅛-in. thickness. Cut with a floured 1¾x3¼-in. diamond cookie cutter. Place 2 in. apart on ungreased baking sheets. Bake for 7-9 minutes or until edges are golden brown. Remove to wire racks to cool.

2. In a large bowl, combine the confectioners' sugar, water and meringue powder; beat on low speed just until blended. Beat on high for 4-5 minutes or until stiff peaks form. Divide icing into portions and tint as desired. Keep unused icing covered at all times with a damp cloth. If necessary, beat again on high speed to restore texture.

3. Frost and decorate cookies as desired with assorted sprinkles and candies; add almonds for ears.

MINI CINNAMON ROLL COOKIES

Intense cinnamon flavor fills this yummy cross between a snickerdoodle and a cinnamon roll. They taste best with a cup of freshly brewed coffee.

—MARY GAUNTT DENTON, TX

PREP: 1 HOUR
BAKE: 10 MIN./BATCH + COOLING
MAKES: ABOUT 2½ DOZEN

- 1 **cup butter, softened**
- 1¾ **cups sugar, divided**
- 3 **large egg yolks**
- 1 **tablespoon plus 1 teaspoon honey, divided**
- 1 **teaspoon vanilla extract**
- 2½ **cups all-purpose flour**
- 1 **teaspoon baking powder**
- ½ **teaspoon salt**
- ½ **teaspoon cream of tartar**
- 1 **tablespoon ground cinnamon**
- 8 **ounces white baking chocolate, chopped**

1. In a large bowl, cream butter and 1¼ cups sugar until light and fluffy. Beat in egg yolks, 1 tablespoon honey and vanilla. Combine the flour, baking powder, salt and cream of tartar; gradually add to creamed mixture and mix well.

2. Shape a heaping tablespoonful of dough into a 6-in. log. In a shallow bowl, combine cinnamon and remaining sugar; roll log in cinnamon sugar. Loosely coil log into a spiral shape; place on a greased baking sheet. Repeat, placing cookies 1 in. apart. Sprinkle with remaining cinnamon sugar.

3. Bake at 350° for 8-10 minutes or until set. Remove to wire racks to cool completely. In a small bowl, melt the baking chocolate with remaining honey; stir until smooth. Drizzle over cookies. Let stand until set. Store in an airtight container.

ALMOND CREAM SPRITZ

Love spritz cookies at Christmas? Try this almond-flavored version. Decorate them with colorful sprinkles for the holidays or with chopped almonds anytime.

—JO-ANNE COOPER BONNYVILLE, AB

PREP: 30 MIN. + CHILLING
BAKE: 10 MIN./BATCH • **MAKES:** 3 DOZEN

- 1 **cup butter, softened**
- 1 **package (3 ounces) cream cheese, softened**
- ½ **cup sugar**
- ½ **teaspoon almond extract**
- ¼ **teaspoon vanilla extract**
- 2 **cups all-purpose flour**
  Colored sugar or ½ cup finely chopped almonds

1. In a large bowl, cream the butter, cream cheese and sugar until light and fluffy. Beat in extracts. Gradually add flour. Cover and refrigerate for 30 minutes.

2. Using a cookie press fitted with the disk of your choice, press dough 2 in. apart onto ungreased baking sheets. Decorate with colored sugar or chopped almonds. Bake at 375° for 8-10 minutes or until set. Cool for 1 minute before removing from pans to wire racks. Store in an airtight container.

HOW TO MAKE SPRITZ

Beat the butter, cream cheese and sugar very well, then beat in extracts and flour. Fit the cookie press with the disk of your choice.

Use cookie press on an ungreased pan so the dough will stick to the pan, separating from the press. Apply even pressure for uniform cookies. If you make a mistake, lift the dough with a spatula and try again.

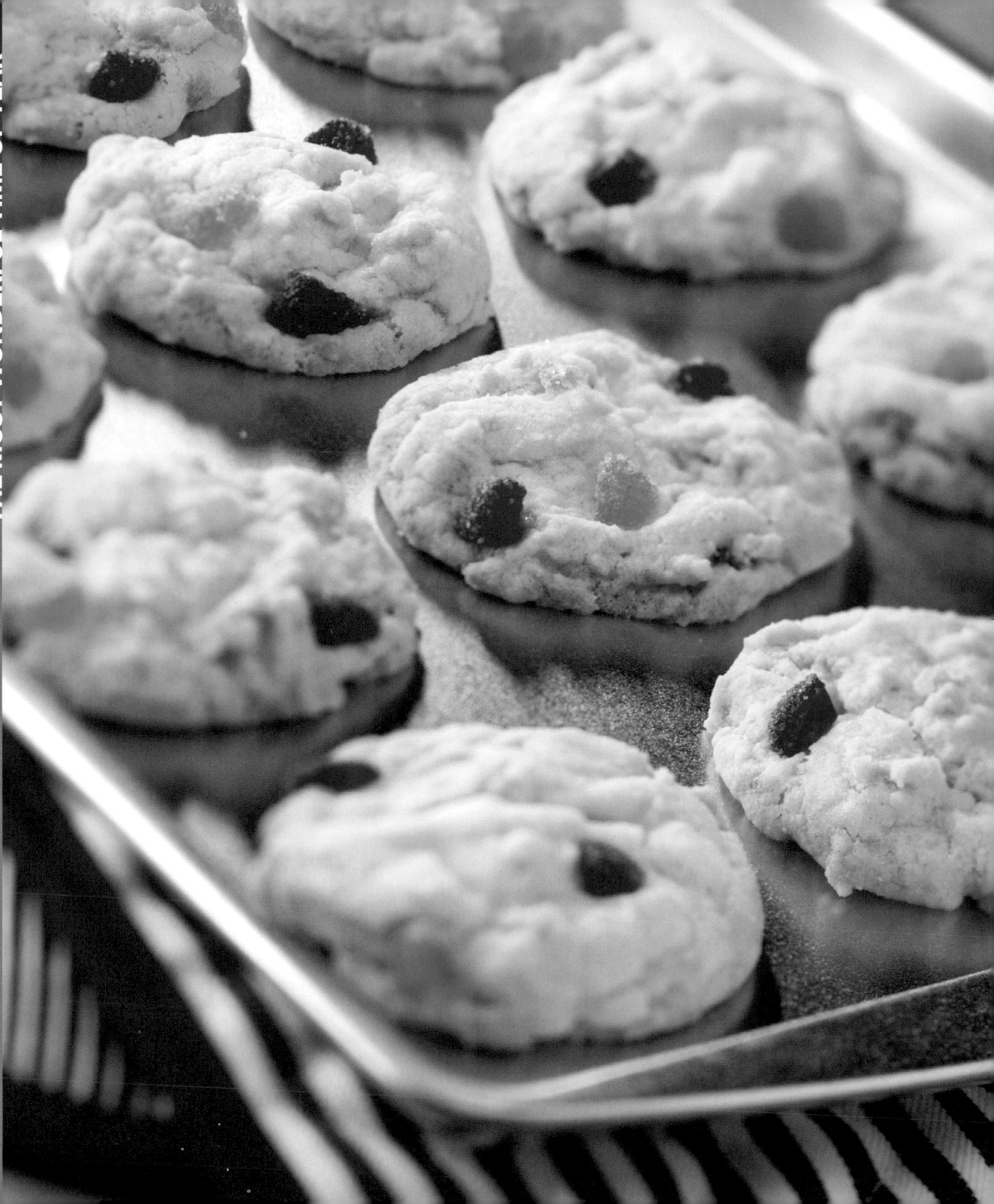

HOLIDAY GUMDROP COOKIES

Children really get a kick out of these candy cookies dotted with chewy gumdrops. I use different colors to make these treats for a variety of holidays.
—CAROLYN STROMBERG WEVER, IA

PREP: 20 MIN. • **BAKE:** 15 MIN. + COOLING
MAKES: 3½ DOZEN

- ¾ cup shortening
- 1 cup sugar, divided
- ½ teaspoon almond extract
- 1¾ cups all-purpose flour
- ½ teaspoon baking soda
- ¼ teaspoon salt
- 1 cup chopped fruit-flavored or spiced gumdrops
- 2 large egg whites

1. In a large bowl, cream shortening and ¾ cup sugar until light and fluffy. Beat in extract. Combine the flour, baking soda and salt; gradually add to creamed mixture and mix well. Stir in gumdrops.
2. In a small bowl, beat egg whites until soft peaks form. Gradually add remaining sugar, beating until stiff peaks form. Fold into dough.
3. Drop by heaping teaspoonfuls 2 in. apart onto ungreased baking sheets. Bake at 350° for 12-15 minutes or until golden brown. Cool for 1 minute before removing from pans to wire racks to cool completely.

SCOTTIE COOKIES

These decked-out doggies are all bundled up in colorful sweaters for the holidays. The frosted sugar cookies are almost too adorable to eat!
—TASTE OF HOME TEST KITCHEN

PREP: 2½ HOURS + CHILLING
BAKE: 10 MIN./BATCH + STANDING
MAKES: 7 DOZEN

- ½ cup butter, softened
- ½ cup butter-flavored shortening
- 2 tablespoons cream cheese, softened
- 1 cup sugar
- 2 large eggs
- 1 teaspoon vanilla extract

- 1 teaspoon light corn syrup
- 4 cups cake flour
- 1 teaspoon baking powder
- ½ teaspoon salt

FROSTING
- 3 cups confectioners' sugar
- 3 tablespoons cream cheese, softened
- 4½ teaspoons light corn syrup
- 3 to 4 tablespoons 2% milk
  Black liquid food coloring

ROYAL ICING
- 4 cups confectioners' sugar
- 6 tablespoons warm water (110° to 115°)
- 3 tablespoons meringue powder
  Red and green paste food coloring
  Assorted sprinkles

1. In a large bowl, cream the butter, shortening, cream cheese and sugar until light and fluffy. Beat in the eggs, vanilla and corn syrup. Combine the flour, baking powder and salt; gradually add to creamed mixture and mix well.
2. Divide dough in thirds. Shape each into a ball, then flatten into a disk. Wrap in plastic and refrigerate for 2 hours or until easy to handle.

3. On a lightly floured surface, roll one portion of dough to ¼-in. thickness. Cut with a floured 3-in. dog-shaped cookie cutter. Place 1 in. apart on parchment paper-lined baking sheets. Repeat with remaining dough.
4. Bake at 375° for 7-9 minutes or until edges are lightly browned. Remove to wire racks to cool completely.
5. For frosting, in a large bowl, combine the confectioners' sugar, cream cheese and corn syrup. Add enough milk to make a thin spreading consistency. Divide in half; tint one half with black food coloring and leave remaining half plain.
6. For the royal icing, in a large bowl, combine confectioners' sugar, water and meringue powder; beat on low speed just until combined. Beat on high for 4-5 minutes or until stiff peaks form. Divide in half; tint one portion red and the other green. (Keep unused icing covered at all times with a damp cloth.)
7. Decorate cookies as desired with frosting, icing and sprinkles. Let dry at room temperature for several hours or until firm. Store in an airtight container in the refrigerator.

roll up jelly-roll style, starting with a short side.

4. Place the rolls 4 in. apart on a lightly greased baking sheet, seam side down. Bake for 25-30 minutes or until lightly browned.

5. Carefully transfer rolls to a cutting board; cool for 5 minutes. Using a serrated knife, cut crosswise into 1/2-in. slices. Place slices upright on lightly greased baking sheets.

6. Bake 15-20 minutes longer or until centers are firm and dry. Remove from pans to wire racks.

7. In a small bowl, mix the glaze ingredients. Drizzle over the warm cookies; cool completely. Store in an airtight container.

WAFFLE IRON COOKIES

This recipe is the easiest to find in my recipe book because it's the dirtiest page, covered with fingerprints, flour smudges and memories of 30-plus Christmases! I made these with my daughters, and now I make them with my granddaughters.

—JUDY TAYLOR QUARRYVILLE, PA

PREP: 10 MIN. • **BAKE:** 5 MIN./BATCH + COOLING
MAKES: 32 COOKIES (8 BATCHES)

- 1/2 **cup butter, softened**
- 1 **cup sugar**
- 2 **large eggs**
- 1 **teaspoon vanilla extract**
- 1 1/2 **cups all-purpose flour**
- 1 **teaspoon baking powder**
- 1/2 **teaspoon salt**
  Confectioners' sugar

1. In a large bowl, cream butter and sugar until light and fluffy. Beat in eggs and vanilla. In another bowl, whisk flour, baking powder and salt; gradually beat into creamed mixture (mixture will be thick).

2. Drop dough in batches by tablespoonfuls 3-4 in. apart onto a greased preheated waffle iron. Bake for 2-3 minutes or until dark brown.

3. Remove cookies to wire racks to cool completely. Sprinkle with confectioners' sugar.

CRANBERRY SWIRL BISCOTTI

Crunchy glazed biscotti is ideal for dunking into a hot cup of coffee, cocoa or tea.
—LISA KILCUP GIG HARBOR, WA

PREP: 20 MIN. • **BAKE:** 40 MIN. + COOLING
MAKES: ABOUT 2 1/2 DOZEN

- 2/3 **cup dried cranberries**
- 1/2 **cup cherry preserves**
- 1/2 **teaspoon ground cinnamon**
- 1/2 **cup butter, softened**
- 2/3 **cup sugar**
- 2 **large eggs**
- 1 **teaspoon vanilla extract**
- 2 1/4 **cups all-purpose flour**
- 3/4 **teaspoon baking powder**
- 1/4 **teaspoon salt**

GLAZE
- 3/4 **cup confectioners' sugar**
- 1 **tablespoon 2% milk**
- 2 **teaspoons butter, melted**
- 1 **teaspoon almond extract**

1. Preheat oven to 325°. Place cranberries, preserves and cinnamon in a food processor; process until smooth.

2. In a large bowl, cream butter and sugar until light and fluffy. Beat in eggs and vanilla. In another bowl, whisk flour, baking powder and salt; gradually beat into creamed mixture.

3. Divide dough in half. On a lightly floured surface, roll each portion of dough into a 12x8-in. rectangle. Spread each with half of the cranberry mixture;

PFEFFERNUSSE COOKIES

A German holiday tradition, these fragrant cookies deliver a warm rush of spices with every bite. Also called pepper nuts, they go wonderfully with coffee or tea.

—JOANNE NELSON
EAST STROUDSBURG, PA

PREP: 35 MIN. + CHILLING
BAKE: 15 MIN./BATCH • **MAKES:** 10 DOZEN

- ½ cup molasses
- ¼ cup honey
- ¼ cup butter, cubed
- ¼ cup shortening
- 2 large eggs
- 1½ teaspoons anise extract
- 4 cups all-purpose flour
- ¾ cup sugar
- ½ cup packed brown sugar
- 2 teaspoons ground cinnamon
- 1½ teaspoons baking soda
- 1 teaspoon ground ginger
- 1 teaspoon ground cardamom
- 1 teaspoon ground nutmeg
- 1 teaspoon ground cloves
- ¾ teaspoon coarsely ground pepper
- ½ teaspoon salt
- 1 cup confectioners' sugar

1. In a small saucepan, combine molasses, honey, butter and shortening. Cook and stir over medium heat until melted. Remove from heat; cool to room temperature. Stir in eggs and extract.

2. Combine flour, sugar, brown sugar, cinnamon, baking soda, ginger, cardamom, nutmeg, cloves, pepper and salt. Gradually add molasses mixture and mix well. Cover and refrigerate at least 2 hours or overnight.

3. Preheat oven to 325°. Roll dough into 1-in. balls. Place 1 in. apart on greased baking sheets. Bake for 12-15 minutes or until golden brown.

4. Remove cookies to wire racks. Roll warm cookies in confectioners' sugar. Cool completely. Store in an airtight container.

DECEMBER 23
NATIONAL PFEFFER-NUSSE DAY

GINGERBREAD HAZELNUT BISCOTTI

My biscotti won a blue ribbon at the county fair. They have a great gingerbread flavor and are crunchy on the outside and chewy in the center.

—**KAREN PAVLOV** CANFIELD, OH

PREP: 30 MIN. + STANDING
COOK: 35 MIN. + COOLING
MAKES: ABOUT 2½ DOZEN

- 1¾ cups all-purpose flour
- ¾ cup packed dark brown sugar
- 1 teaspoon baking powder
- ¾ teaspoon ground cinnamon
- ½ teaspoon ground ginger
- ½ teaspoon baking soda
- ½ teaspoon kosher salt
- ⅛ teaspoon ground cloves
- 1 cup old-fashioned oats, divided
- 2 large eggs
- ¼ cup molasses
- 2 tablespoons canola oil
- ½ teaspoon vanilla extract
- ¾ cup coarsely chopped hazelnuts, toasted
- ¾ cup raisins

DRIZZLE

- ¼ cup white baking chips
- ½ teaspoon shortening

1. Preheat oven to 350°. In a large bowl, whisk the first eight ingredients. Place ½ cup oats in a small food processor; cover and process until ground. Stir remaining oats and ground oats into flour mixture. In a small bowl, whisk eggs, molasses, oil and vanilla; gradually beat into flour mixture. Stir in hazelnuts and raisins (dough will be thick).

2. Divide dough in half. Using lightly floured hands, shape each into a 12x2-in. rectangle on parchment paper-lined baking sheets. Bake for 25-30 minutes or until a toothpick inserted in center comes out clean. Cool on pans on wire racks for 8-10 minutes or until firm.

3. Transfer baked rectangles to a cutting board. Using a serrated knife, cut diagonally into ¾-in. slices. Return to baking sheets, cut side down.

4. Bake for 5-6 minutes on each side or until firm. Remove from pans to wire racks to cool completely.

5. In a microwave, melt baking chips and shortening; stir until smooth. Drizzle over biscotti; let stand until set. Store between pieces of waxed paper in airtight containers.

NOTE *To toast nuts, bake in a shallow pan in a 350° oven for 5-10 minutes or cook in a skillet over low heat until lightly browned, stirring occasionally.*

FROM THE COOKIE JAR

The word biscotti is derived from *bis* (twice) and *cotto* (cooked). This crunchy confection has its roots in the Tuscan region of Italy, in a city called Prato. Because it could be stored for a long time, biscotti was ideal for sailors, soldiers and fishermen; it's said Columbus carried some on his most famous voyage. Many European countries have adopted their own versions. For example, England has rusks and Germany has zwieback.

mixture and mix well. Stir in walnuts and raisins.

3. Drop by rounded tablespoonfuls 2 in. apart onto greased baking sheets. Flatten with a glass. Bake at 325° for 8-10 minutes or until bottoms are browned. Remove to wire racks.

DELUXE SUGAR COOKIES

Christmas cutouts signal the holiday season. For variety, sprinkle half of the cookies with colored sugar before baking and frost the remaining ones after they're cooled.
—DAWN FAGERSTROM WARREN, MN

PREP: 20 MIN. + CHILLING
BAKE: 10 MIN./BATCH
MAKES: 5 DOZEN 2-INCH COOKIES

- 1 **cup butter, softened**
- 1½ **cups confectioners' sugar**
- 1 **large egg, beaten**
- 1 **teaspoon vanilla extract**
- ½ **teaspoon almond extract**
- 2½ **cups all-purpose flour**
- 1 **teaspoon baking soda**
- 1 **teaspoon cream of tartar**

1. In a large bowl, cream butter and sugar until light and fluffy. Beat in egg and extracts. Combine flour, baking soda and cream of tartar; gradually add to the creamed mixture and mix well. Chill dough for at least 1 hour or until easy to handle.
2. Divide dough into four portions. On a surface lightly sprinkled with confectioners' sugar, roll out one portion of dough to ⅛-in. thickness. Cut into desired shapes. Place on ungreased baking sheets. Repeat with the remaining dough. Bake at 350° for 7-8 minutes, or until the edges begin to brown. Remove to wire racks to cool.

GRANDMA'S OATMEAL RAISIN COOKIES

I look forward to cooking, baking and entertaining during the holidays. These cookies are a mainstay at my gatherings.
—SUSANNE SPICKER NORTH OGDEN, UT

PREP: 25 MIN. • **BAKE:** 10 MIN./BATCH
MAKES: 4 DOZEN

- 2 **cups raisins, chopped**
- 2 **cups boiling water**
- ¾ **cup butter-flavored shortening**
- 1 **cup sugar**
- 3 **large eggs**
- 2½ **cups all-purpose flour**
- 2 **cups old-fashioned oats**
- 1¼ **teaspoons baking soda**
- ½ **teaspoon salt**
- 2 **cups chopped walnuts**

1. Place raisins in a small bowl. Cover with boiling water; let stand for 5 minutes. Drain and set aside.
2. In a large bowl, cream shortening and sugar until light and fluffy. Beat in eggs. Combine the flour, oats, baking soda and salt; gradually add to creamed

DECEMBER 25
MERRY
CHRISTMAS!

APPLE CRISP CRESCENTS

Cinnamony apples are wrapped in a tender pastry to create this crispy delicacy. The flavor reminds me of apple crisp.

—BETTY LAWTON PENNINGTON, NJ

PREP: 30 MIN. + CHILLING
BAKE: 20 MIN./BATCH • **MAKES:** 3 DOZEN

- 2 cups all-purpose flour
- 1/8 teaspoon salt
- 1 cup cold butter
- 1 large egg, separated
- 2/3 cup sour cream
- 1/2 teaspoon vanilla extract
- 1 cup finely chopped peeled tart apple
- 1/3 cup finely chopped walnuts
- 1/4 cup raisins, chopped
- 2/3 cup sugar
- 1 teaspoon ground cinnamon

1. In a large bowl, combine flour and salt; cut in butter until mixture resembles coarse crumbs. In a small bowl, whisk the egg yolk, sour cream and vanilla; add to crumb mixture and mix well. Cover and refrigerate for 4 hours or overnight.
2. Divide dough into thirds. On a lightly floured surface, roll each portion into a 10-in. circle. Combine the apple, walnuts, raisins, sugar and cinnamon; sprinkle 1/2 cup over each circle. Cut each circle into 12 wedges.
3. Roll up each wedge from the wide end and place point side down 1 in. apart on greased baking sheets. Curve ends to form crescents. Whisk egg white until foamy; brush over crescents.
4. Bake at 350° for 18-20 minutes or until lightly browned. Remove to wire racks to cool. Store in an airtight container.

★ ★ ★ ★ ★ **READER REVIEW**

"I used cranberry raisins to make these crescents festive for Christmas. They were a hit."

WWMEH TASTEOFHOME.COM

COLORFUL CANDY BAR COOKIES

No one will guess these sweet treats with the candy bar centers begin with store-bought dough. Roll them or dip the tops in colored sugar. Instead of using miniature candy bars, you could slice regular-size Snickers candy bars into 1-inch pieces for the centers.

—TASTE OF HOME **TEST KITCHEN**

PREP: 35 MIN.
BAKE: 10 MIN./BATCH
MAKES: ABOUT 3 DOZEN

Short & Sweet

- 1 tube (16½ ounces) refrigerated sugar cookie dough, softened
- 2/3 cup all-purpose flour
- 40 miniature Snickers candy bars
  Red and green colored sugar

1. Preheat oven to 350°. Beat cookie dough and flour until combined. Shape 2 teaspoonfuls of dough around each candy bar. Roll in colored sugar.
2. Place 2 in. apart on parchment paper-lined baking sheets. Bake until set, 9-11 minutes. Cool on pans 1 minute. Remove to wire racks to cool.

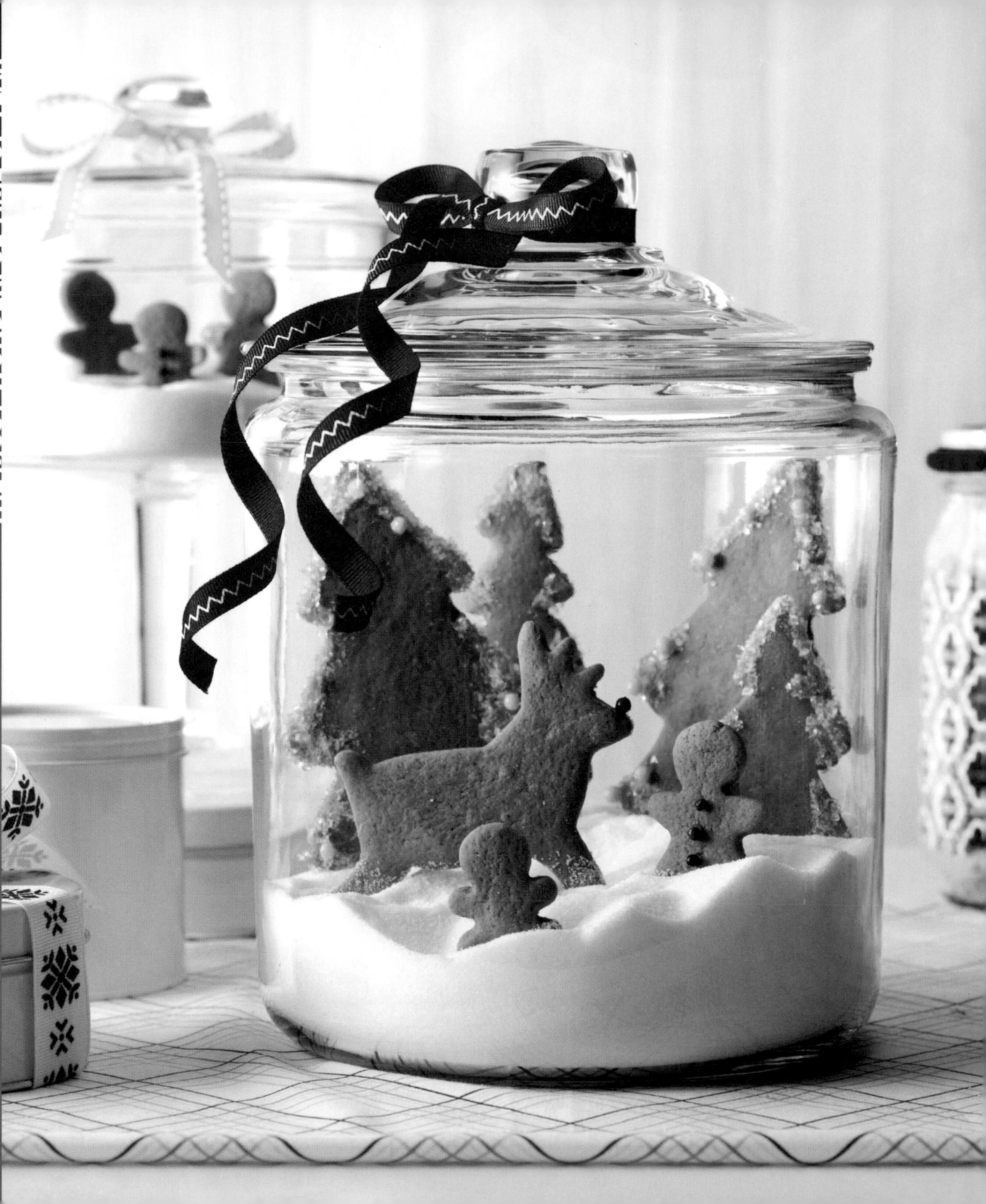

GINGERBREAD SNOW GLOBE

I make a big batch of these gingerbreads every Christmas to give to co-workers and family. For a festive decoration, arrange cookies in a large clear jar to look like a snow globe.
—**KELLY KIRBY** WESTVILLE, NS

PREP: 1¼ HOURS + CHILLING
BAKE: 10 MIN./BATCH + COOLING
MAKES: ABOUT 6 DOZEN 4-IN. COOKIES

- ½ cup warm water
- 2 tablespoons white vinegar
- 1 cup shortening
- 1 cup sugar
- 1 cup molasses
- 6 cups all-purpose flour
- 3 teaspoons ground cinnamon
- 3 teaspoons ground ginger
- 2 teaspoons baking soda
- 1 teaspoon salt
- ½ teaspoon ground cloves
   Light corn syrup
   Coarse sugar
   Assorted sprinkles

1. Mix water and vinegar. In a large bowl, cream shortening and sugar until light and fluffy. Beat in molasses. In another bowl, whisk flour, cinnamon, ginger, baking soda, salt and cloves; add to creamed mixture alternately with water mixture, beating well after each addition.
2. Divide dough into six portions. Shape each into a disk; wrap in plastic. Refrigerate for 2 hours or until firm enough to roll.
3. Preheat oven to 350°. On a lightly floured surface, roll each portion of dough to ¼-in. thickness. Cut dough with assorted holiday cookie cutters. Place 2 in. apart on ungreased baking sheets. Bake for 10-12 minutes or until set. Cool on pans for 1 minute. Remove to wire racks to cool completely.
4. Using a new paintbrush, brush corn syrup onto edges of cookies; dip into coarse sugar. Decorate with sprinkles. Let stand until set.
NOTE *You can also frost or pipe cookies with plain or tinted frosting and decorate with sprinkles. Let stand until set. For*

DECEMBER 26
NATIONAL CANDY CANE DAY

snow globe, place coarse sugar in a decorative glass jar. Arrange cookies in jar. Decorate jar with ribbon.

MERINGUE CANDY CANES

These red-and-white striped treats get lots of compliments for their cute looks and minty taste. The seasonal confections are easy to make and so light that they melt in your mouth!
—**ANNE LINDWAY** INDIANAPOLIS, IN

PREP: 20 MIN. • **BAKE:** 50 MIN. + STANDING
MAKES: 4 DOZEN

- 3 large egg whites
- ½ teaspoon cream of tartar
- ¾ cup sugar
- ¼ teaspoon peppermint extract
   Red paste food coloring

1. In a large bowl, beat egg whites until foamy. Add cream of tartar; beat on medium speed until soft peaks form. Gradually add sugar, 1 tablespoon at a time, beating on high until stiff peaks form and sugar is dissolved, about 6 minutes. Beat in peppermint extract.
2. Cut a small hole in the corner of a pastry bag; insert a #21 star tip. With a new paintbrush, brush three evenly spaced ¼-in. strips of red food coloring on the inside of the bag from the tip to three-fourths of the way to the top of the bag. Carefully fill bag with meringue.
3. Pipe 3-in. candy canes onto parchment-lined baking sheets. Bake at 225° for 25 minutes; rotate baking sheets to a different oven rack. Bake 25 minutes longer or until firm to the touch. Turn oven off; leave cookies in oven with door ajar for at least 1 hour or until cool.

NO-BAKE MINTY OREO BLOSSOMS

My blossoms take the Oreo truffle just a little further—and fancier. They're dressed up with a candy coating and a kiss of mint.
—CONNIE KRUPP RACINE, WI

PREP: 25 MIN. + FREEZING
MAKES: ABOUT 1 DOZEN

- 3 **cups Oreo cookie crumbs (about 12 ounces)**
- 6 **ounces cream cheese, softened**
- 12 **ounces chocolate mint candy coating**
- 4 **teaspoons shortening**
- 15 **striped peppermint kisses**
  Red and white nonpareils, optional

1. In a large bowl, beat cookie crumbs and cream cheese until blended. Shape dough into 1½-in. balls; place 2 in. apart on a waxed paper-lined baking sheet. Flatten to ½-in. thickness with bottom of a glass. Freeze for 30 minutes or until firm.

2. In a microwave, melt candy coating and shortening; stir until smooth. Working with one at a time, dip cookies in chocolate coating mixture; allow excess to drip off. Place on a waxed paper-lined baking sheet. Immediately press a kiss in center. If desired, immediately sprinkle with nonpareils. Store between layers of waxed paper in an airtight container in the refrigerator.

CHOCOLATE GINGERSNAPS

When my daughter Jennifer was 15 years old, she created this recipe as a way to combine two of her favorite flavors. These cookies are great with a glass of milk.

—PAULA ZSIRAY LOGAN, UT

PREP: 45 MIN. + CHILLING
BAKE: 10 MIN./BATCH • **MAKES:** 3 DOZEN

- ½ cup butter, softened
- ½ cup packed dark brown sugar
- ¼ cup molasses
- 1 tablespoon water
- 2 teaspoons minced fresh gingerroot
- 1½ cups all-purpose flour
- 1 tablespoon baking cocoa
- 1¼ teaspoons ground ginger
- 1 teaspoon baking soda
- 1 teaspoon ground cinnamon
- ¼ teaspoon ground nutmeg
- ¼ teaspoon ground cloves
- 7 ounces semisweet chocolate, finely chopped
- ¼ cup sugar

1. In a large bowl, cream butter and brown sugar until light and fluffy. Beat in the molasses, water and gingerroot. Combine the flour, cocoa, ginger, baking soda, cinnamon, nutmeg and cloves; gradually add to creamed mixture and mix well. Stir in chocolate. Cover and refrigerate for 2 hours or until easy to handle.

2. Shape dough into 1-in. balls; roll in sugar. Place 2 in. apart on greased baking sheets.

3. Bake at 350° for 10-12 minutes or until tops begin to crack. Cool for 2 minutes before removing to wire racks.

SNOWCAPPED GINGERBREAD BISCOTTI

These cookies are one of my favorites to add to the holiday cookie trays I make. They have the traditional flavor of gingerbread cookies, the refinement of Italian biscotti and a playful snow-dipped decoration.

—TRISHA KRUSE EAGLE, ID

PREP: 45 MIN. + CHILLING
BAKE: 35 MIN. + COOLING • **MAKES:** 2½ DOZEN

- ⅓ **cup butter, softened**
- 1 **cup packed brown sugar**
- ¼ **cup molasses**
- 3 **large eggs**
- 3¾ **cups all-purpose flour**
- 3 **teaspoons ground cinnamon**
- 1 **teaspoon ground nutmeg**
- ½ **teaspoon baking powder**
- ½ **teaspoon salt**
- ½ **teaspoon ground allspice**
- ½ **teaspoon ground cloves**
- 1 **cup hazelnuts, toasted and chopped**
- ¼ **cup finely chopped crystallized ginger**
- 1 **cup butterscotch chips, melted**
- 1 **cup vanilla or white chips, melted**

1. In a large bowl, cream butter and brown sugar until light and fluffy. Beat in molasses. Add eggs, one at a time, beating well after each addition. Combine the flour, cinnamon, nutmeg, baking powder, salt, allspice and cloves; gradually add to creamed mixture and mix well. Stir in hazelnuts and ginger.

2. Divide the dough in half. Cover and refrigerate for 30 minutes.

3. On a lightly floured surface, shape dough into two 10x3-in. logs. Transfer to greased baking sheets. Bake at 350° for 20-25 minutes or until lightly browned and firm to the touch.

4. Transfer to a cutting board; cut diagonally with a sharp knife into ½-in. slices. Place cut side down on greased baking sheets. Bake for 7-9 minutes on each side or until lightly browned. Remove to wire racks to cool.

5. Dip biscotti halfway into melted butterscotch chips; shake off excess. Place on waxed paper until set. Dip butterscotch-coated ends partially into melted vanilla chips; shake off excess. Place on waxed paper until set. Store in an airtight container.

MERRY GRINCHMAS COOKIES

Baking cookies around the holidays is a big deal in our house. Some are a must every year, and we also come up with new recipes. This one is simple, delicious and fun to make with the kids!

—ANGELA LEMOINE HOWELL, NJ

PREP: 20 MIN. + CHILLING
BAKE: 15 MIN. + COOLING
MAKES: ABOUT 4 DOZEN

- ½ cup butter, softened
- 1 package (8 ounces) cream cheese, softened
- 1¼ cups sugar
- 2 teaspoons vanilla extract
- 1 teaspoon green food coloring
- 2 large eggs
- 3 cups all-purpose flour
- 2 teaspoons baking powder
- ¼ teaspoon salt
- 1 cup confectioners' sugar
- 48 heart-shaped gumdrops

1. In a large bowl, beat butter, cream cheese and sugar until smooth. Beat in vanilla, food coloring and eggs, one at a time, beating well after each addition. In another bowl, whisk together flour, baking powder and salt; gradually beat into creamed mixture. Refrigerate, covered, 1 hour or until firm enough to shape.

2. Preheat oven to 350°. Shape dough into 1½-in. balls; roll in confectioners' sugar. Place 2 in. apart on ungreased baking sheets.

3. Bake cookies until tops are cracked and edges are set, 12-15 minutes. Immediately press a gumdrop into each. Cool cookies on pans 5 minutes before removing to wire racks to cool.

SNOWMAN COOKIES

I wrap these chocolate-capped snowmen in colored tissue and place them in holiday containers. Like real snowmen, they don't last long.

—BETTY TABB MIFFLINTOWN, PA

PREP: 20 MIN. + CHILLING
BAKE: 20 MIN./BATCH + COOLING
MAKES: 4 DOZEN

- 1 cup butter, softened
- 1 package (8 ounces) cream cheese, softened
- 2 cups sugar
- 1 large egg
- 1 teaspoon vanilla extract
- ¼ teaspoon almond extract
- ¼ teaspoon coconut extract
- 3½ cups all-purpose flour
- 1 teaspoon baking powder
  Miniature semisweet chocolate chips and green and red M&M's minis

FROSTING

- 1 cup confectioners' sugar
- ⅛ teaspoon coconut extract
- 2 to 4 teaspoons 2% milk
  Red and/or green food coloring
  Miniature milk chocolate kisses, unwrapped

1. In a large bowl, cream butter, cream cheese and sugar until light and fluffy. Beat in egg and extracts. In another bowl, whisk flour and baking powder; gradually beat into creamed mixture. Refrigerate, covered, overnight.

2. Preheat the oven to 325°. Shape dough into forty-eight 1-in. balls, forty-eight ¾-in. balls and forty-eight ½-in. balls. On ungreased baking sheets, place one ball of each size side by side for each snowman.

3. Bake for 18-20 minutes or until light brown. Remove from oven; cool on pans for 2 minutes. Press on chocolate chips for eyes and M&M's for buttons. Carefully remove from pans to wire racks to cool completely.

4. For frosting, in a small bowl, beat the confectioners' sugar, extract and enough milk to reach a piping

consistency. If two colors of frosting are desired, transfer half of the frosting to another bowl and tint each with a different food coloring.

5. Cut a small hole in a corner of a food-safe plastic bag; fill with frosting. Pipe scarves on snowmen. Use frosting to attach chocolate kisses for hats.

ALMOND OATMEAL CUTOUTS

Almond gives these cutout oatmeal cookies added flavor. The dough is slightly sticky, so I suggest rolling it out between pieces of waxed paper.

—MARTHA DAHLMAN REGINA, SK

START TO FINISH: 30 MIN.
MAKES: 2½ DOZEN

- ½ cup butter, softened
- ½ cup shortening
- ¾ cup sugar
- 2 teaspoons almond extract
- 1¼ cups all-purpose flour
- 1¼ cups old-fashioned oats

1. In a large bowl, cream the butter, shortening and sugar until light and fluffy. Beat in extract. Combine flour and oats; gradually add to creamed mixture and mix well.

2. Roll between pieces of waxed paper to ¼-in. thickness. Remove paper and cut with floured 2½-in. cookie cutters.

3. Place 1 in. apart on ungreased baking sheets. Bake at 350° for 12-15 minutes or until lightly browned. Remove to wire racks to cool.

FRUITCAKE-INSPIRED COOKIES

Once after making a fruitcake, I had some fruit and nuts left over. I mixed them into a basic cookie dough along with pineapple and coconut. These soft, colorful cookies are a nice addition to a Christmas dessert tray.
—**JENNIE LOFTUS** GASPORT, NY

PREP: 15 MIN. + CHILLING
BAKE: 10 MIN./BATCH • **MAKES:** 7 DOZEN

- ¾ cup butter, softened
- ¾ cup shortening
- 1¼ cups packed brown sugar
- 2 large eggs
- 1 teaspoon vanilla extract
- 4 cups all-purpose flour
- 2 teaspoons baking powder
- ½ teaspoon salt
- 1 can (8 ounces) crushed pineapple, drained
- ½ cup chopped dates
- ½ cup chopped red candied cherries
- ½ cup chopped green candied cherries
- ½ cup flaked coconut
- ½ cup chopped pecans or walnuts

1. Cream butter, shortening and brown sugar until light and fluffy. Add eggs, one at a time, beating well after each addition. Beat in vanilla. In another bowl, combine flour, baking powder and salt; gradually add to creamed mixture. Stir in remaining ingredients. Shape into three 10-in. rolls; wrap each in plastic. Refrigerate until firm, about 2 hours.
2. Preheat oven to 375°. Unwrap dough and cut into ¼-in. slices. Place 2 in. apart on ungreased baking sheets. Bake until golden brown, 8-10 minutes. Remove to wire racks to cool.

★ ★ ★ ★ ★ **READER REVIEW**

"These raspberry jam cookies are so quick and easy. We all love them. They can be made with so many variations."
SHAYBE TASTEOFHOME.COM

SPLIT-SECOND COOKIES

I love baking cookies, and this is a recipe I've used for many Christmases over the years. Raspberry jam makes these cookies flavorful and colorful.
—**NANCY FOUST** STONEBORO, PA

PREP: 20 MIN. • **BAKE:** 15 MIN. + COOLING
MAKES: ABOUT 5 DOZEN

- ¾ cup butter, softened
- ⅔ cup sugar
- 1 large egg
- 1 teaspoon vanilla extract
- 2 cups all-purpose flour
- ½ teaspoon baking powder
- ½ teaspoon salt
- ⅓ cup raspberry jam

1. In a large bowl, cream butter and sugar until light and fluffy. Beat in egg and vanilla. Combine the flour, baking powder and salt; gradually add to creamed mixture and mix well.
2. Divide dough into four equal portions; shape each into a 12x¾-in. log. Place 4 in. apart on two greased baking sheets. Make a ½-in. depression down the center of logs; fill with jam. Bake at 350° for 15-20 minutes or until lightly browned. Cool for 2 minutes; cut diagonally into ¾-in. slices. Remove to wire racks to cool completely.

DECEMBER 27
NATIONAL FRUITCAKE DAY

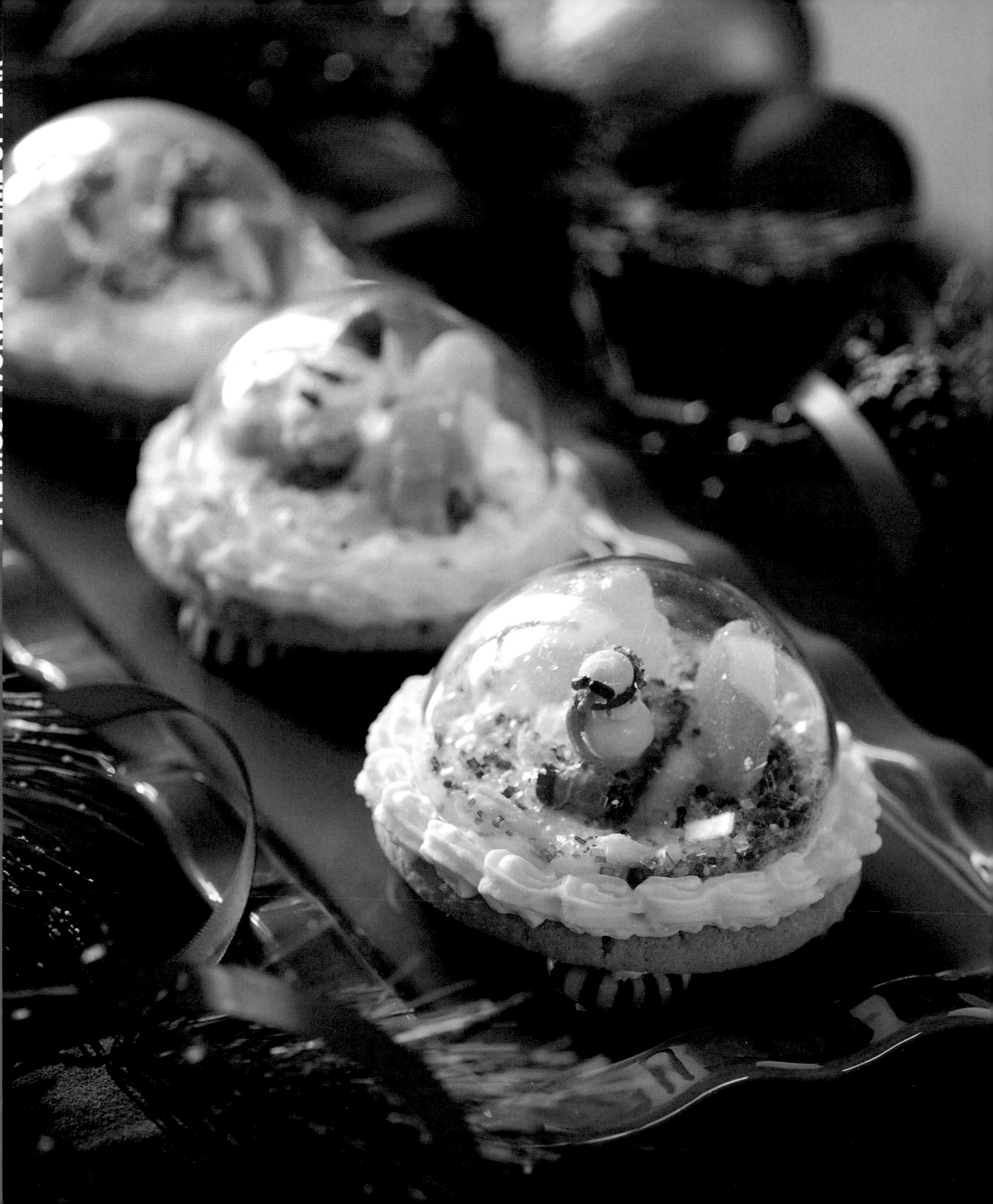

HOMEMADE SNOW GLOBES

Kids will be jumping to help assemble these cute snow globes. Just make sure they don't nibble up all the ingredients before they're decorated! Group the globes together for a fun centerpiece, or use them individually as creative place cards.

—**GEORGIA KOHART** OAKWOOD, OH

PREP: 1 HOUR + STANDING
MAKES: 6 SNOW GLOBES

- 2 **cups confectioners' sugar**
- 2 **tablespoons plus 2 teaspoons water**
- 4½ **teaspoons meringue powder**
- ¼ **teaspoon cream of tartar**
- 6 **sugar cookies (about 3½ inches)**
   Assorted decorations: miniature marshmallows, orange and brown jimmies, Fruit Roll-Ups, candy spearmint leaves, peppermint candies, edible glitter and holiday sprinkles
- 3 **clear plastic ornaments (3 inches)**

1. In a small bowl, combine the confectioners' sugar, water, meringue powder and cream of tartar; beat on low speed just until combined. Beat on high for 4-5 minutes or until stiff peaks form. Cover frosting with a damp cloth between uses. If necessary, beat again on high speed to restore texture.
2. Working with one cookie at a time, spread 2 tablespoons frosting over the top of each cookie.
3. For snowman, cut two miniature marshmallows in half. Attach three halves with a small amount of frosting. Decorate face with jimmies. For scarf, trim a thin 1½-in. strip from a Fruit Roll-Up. Shape a toboggan from a strip of Fruit Roll-Up. Attach toboggan to frosted cookie; attach snowman to toboggan. Add the candy spearmint leaves for trees.
4. With dabs of frosting, attach four peppermint candies to the bottom of each cookie. Let stand overnight to dry completely.
5. To assemble, separate ornaments into halves. Working with one cookie at a time, spread edge of ornament half with frosting. Place 1 teaspoon edible glitter and 1 teaspoon holiday sprinkles inside ornament; carefully place decorated cookie onto ornament half, sealing edges. Stand upright; use frosting and a star tip to pipe a decorative edge around globe. Let stand until set. Store snow globes in an airtight container.
NOTE *This recipe was tested with 80mm clear plastic fillable ball ornaments, which are available at many craft stores and online.*

SANTA CLAUS COOKIES

Store-bought peanut butter sandwich cookies become jolly Santas in a snap! These are simple, tasty and so much fun.

—**MARY KAUFENBERG**
SHAKOPEE, MN

Short & Sweet

PREP: 40 MIN. + STANDING
COOK: 5 MIN.
MAKES: 32 COOKIES

- 12 **ounces white baking chocolate, chopped**
- 1 **package (1 pound) Nutter Butter sandwich cookies**
   Red colored sugar
- 32 **vanilla or white chips**
- 64 **miniature semisweet chocolate chips**
- 32 **Red Hots**

1. In a microwave, melt the white chocolate at 70% power for 1 minute; stir. Microwave at additional 10- to 20-second intervals, stirring until chocolate is smooth.
2. Dip one end of each cookie into melted white chocolate, allowing the excess to drip off. Place on wire racks. For Santa's hat, sprinkle red sugar on top part of chocolate. Press one vanilla chip off-center on hat for pompom; let stand until set.
3. Dip other end of each cookie into melted chocolate for beard, leaving center of cookie uncovered. Place on wire racks.
4. With a dab of melted chocolate, attach semisweet chips for eyes and a Red Hot for a nose. Place on waxed paper until set.

ANGEL MACAROONS

These chewy coconut cookies start with
an angel food cake mix. A fresh-baked
batch always disappears in a flash.

—RENEE SCHWEBACH DUMONT, MN

Short & Sweet

PREP: 5 MIN.
BAKE: 10 MIN./BATCH + COOLING
MAKES: 5 DOZEN

- 1 **package (16 ounces)
     angel food cake mix**
- ½ **cup water**
- 1½ **teaspoons almond extract**
- 2 **cups flaked coconut**

1. In a large bowl, beat the cake mix,
water and almond extract on low speed
for 30 seconds. Scrape bowl; beat on
medium for 1 minute. Fold in coconut.
2. Drop by rounded teaspoonfuls
2 in. apart onto a parchment paper-
lined baking sheet. Bake at 350° for
10-12 minutes or until lightly browned.
Remove paper with cookies to wire
racks to cool.

ANISE SUGAR COOKIES

As much as I love sharing my baked goods,
sometimes I want to keep these cookies
just for me. The light anise flavor and
melt-in-your-mouth texture make them
a perfect Christmas treat.

—P MARCHESI
ROCKY POINT, NY

PREP: 40 MIN. • **BAKE:** 10 MIN./BATCH
MAKES: 9 DOZEN

- 1 **cup butter, softened**
- 1½ **cups sugar**
- 2 **large eggs**
- ¼ **to ½ teaspoon anise extract**
- 3 **cups all-purpose flour**
- 1 **to 1½ teaspoons aniseed**
- 1 **teaspoon salt**
- 1 **teaspoon baking powder**
- 1 **teaspoon baking soda**
     Frosting and coarse sugar, optional

1. In a large bowl, cream butter and
sugar until light and fluffy. Beat in eggs
and extract. Combine the flour, aniseed,
salt, baking powder and baking soda;
gradually add to creamed mixture and
mix well.
2. Shape into 1-in. balls; place on greased
baking sheets. Flatten with a glass dipped
in sugar.
3. Bake at 375° for 6-7 minutes or until
set. Cool on wire racks. If desired, frost
cookies and sprinkle with coarse sugar.

GINGERBREAD YULE LOGS

I was never fond of gingerbread until I rolled it up with Nutella. These logs make a fabulous addition to any cookie platter.

—TERRI GILSON CALGARY, AB

....

PREP: 20 MIN. + CHILLING
BAKE: 20 MIN. + COOLING
MAKES: 1 DOZEN

- 3⅓ cups all-purpose flour
- 1½ teaspoons ground cinnamon
- ¾ teaspoon ground ginger
- ½ teaspoon baking powder
- ¼ teaspoon salt
- ¾ cup light corn syrup
- ⅔ cup packed light brown sugar
- ½ cup butter, cubed
- 4 ounces cream cheese, softened
- ¾ cup Nutella
- 1½ teaspoons grated lime peel, optional

DRIZZLE

- ¾ cup confectioners' sugar
- 2 tablespoons water or lime juice
  Holiday sprinkles, optional

1. In a small bowl, whisk the first five ingredients. In a large saucepan, combine corn syrup, brown sugar and butter; cook and stir over medium heat until butter is melted. Transfer to a large bowl; gradually beat flour mixture into corn syrup mixture. Beat in cream cheese. Shape dough into a disk; wrap in plastic. Refrigerate for 30 minutes or until firm enough to roll.

2. Preheat oven to 350°. On parchment paper, roll dough into an 18x12-in. rectangle. Cut into three 12x6-in. rectangles.

3. In a small bowl, mix Nutella and, if desired, grated lime peel; spread over rectangles. Roll up jelly-roll style, starting with a long side; pinch seams to seal. Cut each roll crosswise into four logs; place on greased baking sheets, seam side down. With the tines of a fork, make strokes in dough to resemble bark if desired.

4. Bake for 20-25 minutes or until bottom and edges are light brown. Remove from pans to wire racks to cool completely.

5. In a small bowl, mix confectioners' sugar and water until smooth; drizzle over cookies. If desired, decorate with sprinkles. Let stand until set.

GENERAL COOKIE INDEX

This handy index lists every cookie in the book by type and major ingredient.

SOFT BLUEBERRY BUTTON COOKIES, 227

CHOCOLATE PUDDLES, 42

MINTY CHOCOLATE HEARTS, 63

MACADAMIA-COFFEE BEAN COOKIES, 370

CHERRY KISSES, 23

GINGERSNAP CREAM COOKIE CUPS, 32

WINTER FRUIT MACAROONS, 42

Italian Honey Ball Cookies, 45
Soft Honey Cookies, 258

ICE CREAM
Ice Cream Kolachkes, 115
Oatmeal Cookie Ice Cream Sandwiches, 238
Snickerdoodle Ice Cream Sandwich
  Minis, 255
Sugar Cone Chocolate Chip Cookies, 274

LAVENDER
Lavender Cookies, 222

LEMON
Buttery Lemon Sandwich Cookies, 393
Citrus Cookies, 122
Crisp Lemon Shortbread, 111
Iced Cookies, 184
Lemon & Rosemary Butter Cookies, 34
Lemon Crisp Cookies, 224
Lemon Meringue Pie Cookies, 280
Lemon Oatmeal Sugar Cookies, 120
Lemon Poppy Seed Slices, 107
Lemon Slice Sugar Cookies, 93
Lemon Star Cookies, 240
Lemon Tea Cookies, 24
Lemon Zucchini Drops, 219
Lemony Gingerbread Whoopie Pies, 81
Lemony Macaroons, 182
Melt-In-Your-Mouth Lemon Cutouts, 95
Rosemary-Lemon Slice & Bake
  Cookies, 148

LIME
Cornmeal Lime Cookies, 116
Honey-Lime Almond Cookies, 152
Lime & Gin Coconut Macaroons, 151
Lime Coconut Biscotti, 249
Monogrammed Cookies, 221

LIQUOR
Brandy Snap Cannoli, 394
Butterscotch-Rum Raisin Treats, 302
Lime & Gin Coconut Macaroons, 151

MACADAMIA NUTS
Macadamia-Coffee Bean Cookies, 370

MACADAMIA NUT COOKIES, 261

Macadamia Nut Cookies, 261
White Chocolate-Macadamia Nut
  Cookies, 130
White Chocolate Nut Crackles, 202

MACARONS
Hazelnut Espresso Macarons, 243
Pistachio Macarons, 168

MACAROONS
Angel Macaroons, 430
Chewy Coconut Macaroons, 41
Chocolate-Dipped Almond Macaroons, 77
Lemony Macaroons, 182
Lime & Gin Coconut Macaroons, 151
Macaroon Kisses, 318
Magic Macaroons, 344
Mocha Macaroon Cookies, 276
Stained Glass Cherry Macaroons, 398
Winter Fruit Macaroons, 42

MALT
Chocolate Malted Cookies, 107
Malted Milk Cookies, 190

MAPLE
Chewy Maple Cookies, 326
French Toast Cookies, 383
Honey Maple Cookies, 321
Maple Walnut Biscotti, 362
Peanut Butter Maple Cookies, 71

MARSHMALLOWS & MARSHMALLOW CREME
Cathedral Cookies, 108
Chocolate-Covered Marshmallow
  Cookies, 337
Cute Pig Cookies, 234
Fluffernutter Treats, 326
Oatmeal Sandwich Cookies, 271
Peanut Butter S'mores, 280
Puppy Dog Cookie Pops, 286
Rainbow S'moreo Cookies, 256
Rocky Road Cookie Cups, 195
S'mookies, 216
S'more Sandwich Cookies, 397
Whoopie Pies, 192

MINT
Chocolate-Mint Cookie Cups, 76
Mint Creme Cookies, 196
Minty Chocolate Hearts, 63
Monogrammed Cookies, 221
No-Bake Chocolate Mint
  Treats, 100
No-Bake Minty Oreo Blossoms, 420

MOLASSES
Molasses Cookies with a Kick, 38
Molasses Cutouts, 402
Peppery Snaps, 369
Spiced Molasses Doughnut
  Cookies, 298

OREO COOKIE BITES, 98

COLORFUL PEANUT BUTTER CRACKERS, 349

Short & Sweet

AMISH SUGAR COOKIES, 262

ALPHABETICAL COOKIE INDEX

This convenient index lists every cookie in alphabetical order, so you can easily find your favorites.

CHOCOLATE-PEANUT BUTTER CUP COOKIES, 266

FROSTED CRANBERRY DROP COOKIES, 13

MERINGUE CANDY CANES, 419

PEANUT BUTTER PENGUINS, 66